MANHATTAN FOR RENT,

1785–1850

Elizabeth Blackmar

Manhattan for Rent, 1785–1850

MANHATTAN FOR RENT, 1785–1850

Elizabeth Blackmar

Cornell University Press

Ithaca and London

First published 1989 by Cornell University Press.
First printing, Cornell Paperbacks, 1991.

International Standard Book Number 0-8014-2024-5 (cloth)
International Standard Book Number 0-8014-9973-9 (paper)
Library of Congress Catalog Card Number 88-47926
Printed in the United States of America

Librarians: Library of Congress cataloging information
appears on the last page of the book.

To my father, Charles B. Blackmar, and the memory of my mother, Ellen Day Blackmar, and for my nieces and nephews

Contents

Acknowledgments   xi

Introduction   1

1. The Formation of Manhattan's Rentier and Landlord Classes   14

2. The Formation of the Urban Tenancy   44

3. "Unlike Republican Simplicity": The Shaping of a New Social Landscape   72

4. The Social Meanings of Housing, 1800–1840   109

5. Public, Private, and Common: The Regulation of Streets and Neighborhoods   149

6. Building a Housing Crisis   183

7. "The Quality of Pay": Landlord–Tenant Relations   213

Conclusion: The Housing Question   250

Appendix: Tables
1. Number and percentage of freeholders, renters, and others who voted in New York City elections, 1790–1821   271
2. Number and percentage of freeholders and renters who voted in New York City elections, 1807, by ward   272

3. Assessed values of real estate in Manhattan, 1817–1850   273
4. Assessed values of lots and population density, Manhattan, 1825 and 1830, by ward   274
5. Number of new buildings constructed in Manhattan, 1834–1842, by ward   275
6. Number of new buildings and dwellings constructed in Manhattan, 1834–1850   276
7. Number of families and of landowners and density per house, Manhattan, 1855, by ward   277

Abbreviations   279

Notes   281

Index   343

Maps

Plan of New York Surveyed in 1766 and 1767 by Bernard Ratzer   22
A Plan of the City and Environs of New York, c. 1780   29
Plan of the City of New York, c. 1798   90
City of New York, 1839   198

Illustrations

Hudson River and Dey Street, 1810   46
Corner of Greenwich Street, 1810   74
Broadway from the Bowling Green, c. 1826   111
Junction of Broadway and the Bowery, 1831   163
Leroy Place, c. 1830   165
Five Points, 1827   174
Broadway, New York, 1836   215

Acknowledgments

THE LIST OF PEOPLE who have helped me through the researching and writing of this book is longer than John Jacob Astor's rent rolls. I have accumulated the wealth of their ideas, encouragement, and practical support, and although it pains me to relegate so many of these colleagues, friends, and family members to the position of unnamed "sundry tenants," I hope that they recognize themselves in these acknowledgments.

I thank my teachers, particularly R. Jackson Wilson, Stephan Thernstrom, and Morton Horwitz, for opening my mind to new questions and offering strategies to pursue answers. I am saddened that Steve Botein is not here to thank in person. I am grateful to John Brinckerhoff Jackson for opening my eyes to the built environment as a field of historical inquiry. I do not use the phrase lightly when I say that his thinking, writing, and teaching have been an ongoing source of inspiration.

I thank the staffs of the New York Public Library, the New York County Clerk's Office, the Columbia University Library, the Library of Congress, and the New-York Historical Society (particularly the curator of manuscripts, Thomas Dunning) for their assistance. The collections of the Historical Society and the Public Library are among the great benefits of working on New York City history.

I thank the Harvard—MIT Joint Center for Urban Studies, the Columbia University Social Science Council, and the National Endowment for the Humanities for financial assistance during the writing and revision of this book. And although my Smithsonian fellowship was awarded for another project, I must confess that I owe the National Museum of American History a debt for time that was stolen from that project to return to housing questions.

To contemplate the number of people who have read, commented on, and discussed this book's various drafts, fragments, and arguments is to realize how long I have been working on it. At various points in the manuscript's evolution, my thinking has benefited from the observations and help of Christine Rosen, Carol Lasser, Gary Kornblith, Warren Leon, David Rosner, Kathlynn Conway, Thomas Bender, Michael Wallace, Conrad Wright, and Paul Groth. I also appreciate the support of Peter Dimock, Robert Westbrook, Barbara Melosh, Gary Kulick, Colleen Dunleavy, Eric Foner, William Taylor, and Ann Withington. The insights of other New York City historians are reflected in these pages, and I particularly thank Joshua Brown, Peter Buckley, Iver Bernstein, Sean Wilentz, Paul Gilje, and Howard Rock for sharing their understandings of the city's complex history. Discussions of the history of housework with Jeanne Boydston have greatly influenced my own thinking about housing as a workplace. I thank members of the *Radical History Review* collective, the American Studies Department of Yale University, Columbia University's Seminar on the City, the New York University Institute for the Humanities Seminar on Commercial Culture, the New-York Historical Society conferences on antebellum New York City, the Columbia Institute for Research on Women and Gender, and the 1985–1986 Smithsonian fellows for stimulating my historical thinking. And I owe a great debt to my students, whose questions have repeatedly prompted me to rethink my own historical and political interpretations.

Over the years, other friends have provided indispensable support beyond the walls of academe. I thank Catharine Kautsky, Claudia Jaker, Rita Rack, Dennis Peterson, Michele and Frederick Schwarzbach, Leslie Agnew, Elinor Daily, Thomas Abram, and Marc Augustin.

Then there are the people who have spent hours talking history, reading my work, and arguing with me. I especially thank Jean-Christophe Agnew for his graceful and reliable wit, as well as for his insights into the meanings of market relations. Discussions with Deborah Kaplan have helped me immeasurably in thinking about the problems of language and cultural interpretation. Elizabeth Cromley's forthcoming book on the history of New York City apartments offers a sequel to my own, and one of the greatest pleasures of working on this topic has been the opportunity to exchange ideas with her. I only wish that I had gained the power of her visual and spatial imagination. The book that I am now writing with Roy Rosenzweig on the social history of Central Park is the latest stage in a long and rich intellectual collaboration and friendship. This book's analysis in Chapter 5 and the Conclusion reflects our discussions on the meanings of public space, and the book has gained throughout from his always energetic and thought-ful readings and comments. As these friends and colleagues will readily testify, this book's interpretations are stubbornly my own, but that is not because they didn't try to help me see more clearly.

I thank Peter Agree for his enthusiastic confidence in this book and his unfailing patience as I struggled to let go of the manuscript. Julie Abraham was the first editor to push me to clarify the book's structure and arguments; and Miranda Pollard's, Kristen Miller's, and Kelly-Anne Jenkins' last-minute labors helped get the final manuscript to the publisher. In between, another group of scholars came to my aid. I thank Christine Stansell for making many helpful suggestions on the first manuscript; her own book on laboring women in antebellum New York City has further influenced my thinking. I benefited from Michael Frisch's critical and sympathetic reading of two drafts; if I didn't worry that it would keep him from his own writing, I would urge all historians to turn to him as a reader. Jeanie Attie lent her sharp eye and intellect to improving the last draft, especially Chapter 4; and Richard Joffe's comments on the style and substance of the Introduc-tion prompted me to rethink arguments throughout. Peter Marcuse's work on the history of New York City housing offers a model of clear analysis, and his queries on the last three chapters were valuable in the last revision.

I am especially grateful to Barbara Salazar for the care, skill, and intelligence with which she edited the final manuscript. And I thank James O'Brien for preparing the index.

Throughout the final throes of rethinking and rewriting, William Leach lent a generous hand to editing, a friendly ear to listening, and an engaged imagination to sharing my efforts to interpret the past; without his support, this would have been a very uncertain book.

My greatest debt is to my family. Words are inadequate to thank my father, my brothers and sisters, and Jeanne Lee Blackmar for their faith and encouragement. They share with me knowledge of the satisfaction that Bessie Bonnifield, Jessie Madden, Margaret Blakey, Lucy Mazur, and especially Ellen Day Blackmar would have taken in knowing that "Betsy's project" is finally done.

ELIZABETH BLACKMAR

Carmel, New York

Manhattan for Rent, 1785–1850

Introduction

ALL CULTURES have their creation myths, and according to cherished New York legend, the Manhattan real estate market was born when the Dutch paid $24 in shells to the Indians for an island that is today worth billions of dollars. The persistence of this story tells us more about the justifying strategies of our own times than about the past. The Manhattan real estate market, the myth implies, is as natural as its bedrock and harbor, and real estate magnates who today pursue the "art of the deal" are only fulfilling their forefathers' vision of the profits embedded in Manhattan land.

The conditions of Manhattan's land and housing markets, far from being part of the natural order of things, are rooted in a social history. It is, after all, people who organize, use, and allocate the benefits of natural and social resources, and the value they assign to land depends on the larger set of social relations that organize property rights and labor. When European settlers established a port at the island's tip, they regarded Manhattan land not primarily as a salable commodity but as a resource necessary for subsistence—a site for housing that sheltered trade and domestic work. Land was abundant, and settlers acquired a town lot, built their own houses, and organized labor through household property relations that ranged from slavery to family obligation. These social relations did not differ greatly from those on rural lands, and seventeenth-century colonists did not regard housing as a special kind of institution separated from the productive economy. How, then, did land become "scarce"? How did Manhattan's landlord and tenant classes first form? How did housing become a commodity separated from land? Who profited, who lost, and what difference did the flow of rents make to New Yorkers' understanding of their social responsibilities within a shared landscape?

In a country that affirms the sanctity of private property rights as one foundation of democratic freedom, the social history of real property relations has been curiously neglected. Historians who have examined dramatic changes in nineteenth-century American society—from the struggles to end slavery and to secure women's economic rights to the growth of industrial cities and suburbs and westward expansion—have of course addressed the organization of landownership and changing definitions of property rights. Yet the formation, operation, and negotiations of city land and housing markets have largely been taken for granted, and unequal distribution of real property has been analyzed more as a measure than as a source of social inequality.

This neglect is surprising if only because the displacement of people from land and houses as resources for living—the "means of production"—has been so clearly recognized as a critical part of the industrial transformation of American society. Yet often this story is told with reference only to rural land or craft workshops. One consequence of this neglect is that we have little insight into the dimension of everyday life in which new class relations first became widely visible in antebellum northern cities. And we understand even less about the way changing land and household labor relations in cities supported and then subverted the republican ideal of independent proprietorship, which remains a critical part of American political and cultural discourse today.

Three hundred years ago, on farms and in towns, the institutions of landed property organized housing as a labor institution. The very designation of land and housing as "*real* property" (that is, rights in permanent or fixed resources as opposed to movable "personal property") suggested their centrality to economic, political, social, and family relations. In England from the late Middle Ages, recognition of *private* property rights to *exclusive* uses and benefits of land had evolved through restrictions on the exercise of royal powers and prerogatives. The concept of private property had also emerged in distinction to common property rights, the customary rights of members of a community not to be excluded from the uses and benefits of natural resources. Furthermore, proprietorship in the resources of land and houses incorporated rights over the persons and labor of household "dependents." The legal fiction of marital unity (coverture, which assigned married women's property rights to their husbands), the rights of paternal authority, and the custom of housing apprentices and servants (and, in the colonies, slaves)—all permitted a household head to appropriate the value produced through the interdependent activities of farm, trade, and domestic work.[1]

English landed property relations, inscribed by centuries of custom, conferred privileges of class and sex that maintained a social hierarchy and determined individual expectations. Yet the prescriptive hierarchies of landed society were far from static. From the sixteenth and seventeenth centuries, the political scientist C. B. Macpherson has argued, customary property rights, "often not freely disposable" and carrying with them prescribed social obligations, were "becoming private property and private property was becoming an individual right, unlimited in amount, unconditional on the performance of social functions, and freely transferrable."[2]

The social dislocations that accompanied this changing concept of property reached from the empire's core to its colonies. Even as the commercial revolution and rural enclosures transformed landholding in England, merchants, government officials, and the younger sons of landed families turned their attention to organizing the commodities of land and labor in Ireland, the West Indies, and North America. In contrast to the Old World, where conditions of social monopoly created a scarcity of land, in North America colonists confronted a vast expanse of land that they claimed was a "vacant," unappropriated, and unorganized wilderness. Indeed, in the eyes of John Locke, America represented a state of nature in which land awaited the hand of the "Civiliz'd part of Mankind" to fulfill God's mandate "to improve [the earth] for the Benefit of Life, and therein lay out something upon it that was [man's] own, his labour," an act that in turn established private property rights. Europeans' first labor was securing land from indigenous peoples. Acting on behalf of joint stock companies, royal patrons, and corporate communities, colonial agents fought, treated, and bargained with Native Americans to secure European claims on tribal territories.[3]

To imperial officials, the abundant land of North America, once claimed as colonies, represented more than Locke's state of nature. In their eyes, the goal of colonization was to organize land and labor in such a way as to deliver wealth to the crown and to the European investors who financed and promoted colonial adventures. The systems of land appropriation and distribution varied widely in England's thirteen North American colonies, but in each of them, the "egalitarian" potential of abundant land threatened to undermine a social hierarchy that organized and controlled labor to serve investors' interests as well as settlers' needs. Thus in 1768, New York's colonial governor, Henry Moore, had expressed his particular frustration to the English Board of Trade that skilled artisans imported to run a glass manufactory had deserted to establish their own farms. "The satisfaction of being

Landholders," Moore reported, "smooths every difficulty and makes [artisans] prefer this manner of living to that comfortable subsistence which they could procure for themselves and their families by working at the Trades in which they were brought up." One "solution" to colonial investors' problems of controlling labor consisted of African slavery and laws that forbade free blacks to own land. Another was to attract English settlers to North America by promising access to land. European settlers could secure English territorial claims and organize labor through their households, as well as through the management and maintenance of slave labor.[4]

On one level it seems remarkable that colonial administrators succeeded in drawing boundaries, establishing exclusive rights of ownership, and creating social monopolies of resources within a "wilderness." Yet, despite officials' worries that abundant land would dissolve the traditional structures of social authority, few European settlers rejected the principle of private property rights, which protected their own proprietary ambitions. Fears of hostile Indians, the need for community cooperation in the process of settlement, the expense of migration, the enforced privileges of race and sex, and entrenched habits of social deference—all constrained settlers from moving outside the boundaries of policies and laws that regulated access to land and transplanted landed inequality alongside new opportunities to acquire real property.

This book begins by looking at how colonial land distribution on Manhattan initially organized housing and labor relations in the port. The first two chapters analyze the social composition and relations of eighteenth-century propertied and propertyless New Yorkers: elite landowning merchants who controlled vast stretches of the Manhattan countryside as well as the waterfront; independent traders, artisans, and laborers who owned houses, stores, and shops on town lots within one mile of the Battery; and household "dependents"—slaves, freed Africans, married women, children, and bound servants, excluded from property ownership by law, custom, or economic circumstance.

Chapter 1 explores the formation of the town's rentier and landlord classes by examining the negotiations between New Yorkers who managed real property as a form of wealth and those who used land and houses as resources for work and family life. Looking closely at two farms on the periphery of the colonial port, the chapter explains how the town's large landowners developed strategies first to attract tenants to their estates and then to promote land circulation, regulate tenants' use of leased lots, and encourage improvements that increased property values. Rising land prices and the growing concentration of landownership after the Revolution marked both the rise of real estate as a major investment sector—a resource managed to expand as well as to store wealth—and the decline of conditions that supported the proprietary independence of Manhattan's "productive classes"—the families of the port's artisans and laborers.

Chapter 2 examines the formation of a wage-earning tenant class at the end of the eighteenth century. Colonial New Yorkers' houses had incorporated craft workshops, stores, kitchens, and yards; and family members, servants, and slaves worked and lived in these spaces under the authority of the household head. Colonists called workers who were paid largely "in kind," with shelter, meals, and domestic services, "found labor": workers received a small amount in cash "and found." But as the cost of establishing an independent house and shop increased and as slavery and indentured servitude declined in New York, the wage labor market offered an alternative labor system that freed employers from responsibility for their workers' maintenance and workers from paternalism and outright slavery. Far from removing economic activity from housing, as some historians have suggested, the rise of the wage labor market prompted the selling of domestic space and services as a commodity. Taking in boarders or renting out rooms offered a new source of income for proprietary artisan households and expanded the principal field of women's employment. And seeing a new source of revenues, prosperous merchants and artisans who in earlier generations had invested in land began to buy and sell houses as rental properties.

In the eyes and language of many republican New Yorkers, the distribution of land and housing through the market represented the best means of overcoming the prescriptive hierarchies of a landed society. Republicans reasoned that white men's individual rights in landed property derived from individual rights in the property of their own labor (and that of their household "dependents"). An essential corollary to this conception of property as the "fruit of labor" was an open land market that preserved white men's access to proprietary independence, which was in turn understood to be the foundation of national independence. These republican precepts, of course, most readily applied to agrarian land. Yet they also had meaning for those city residents who aspired to control their own houses and shops as the means of independent living.

Chapter 3 looks at how, against the backdrop of this republican faith in access to property as the fruit of labor, the emerging labor and housing markets intersected to reshape Manhattan's social geography in the first quarter of the nineteenth century. Artisan and wage-earning tenants paid rents to the city's propertied merchants and artisan entrepreneurs, who in turn directed a portion of that wealth into a new institution of domestic property, the "modern-style dwelling." The rising land costs and rents that accompanied the development of a specialized housing market—as well as investment in commercial property and speculation—pushed craft and laboring households into new domestic quarters and new territories of the city. Even as city leaders embraced the rectilinear and "egalitarian" grid street system as a republican landscape that would preserve access to proprietorship by facilitating the subdivision and circulation of land, the formation of the housing market transformed the city's old trade neighborhoods and rural estates. Concentrated tenant and boardinghouse districts appeared alongside blocks of spacious single-family dwellings.

In the "age of egalitarianism," when New Yorkers abolished the political privileges of landowning and embraced the market as the agent of opportunity, how did they interpret the increasingly visible inequalities of city housing? In order to address this question, Chapters 4 and 5 move into the cultural and political arenas. Chapter 4 explores how the republican aspiration to independent proprietorship gave way to new cultural goals of independent housekeeping. It examines the tensions between women and men, domestic employers and workers, and "respectable" and "unrespectable" citizens which underlay the presumed rise in the standard of living, most readily apparent in new housing standards. These "domestic" tensions as to the social meaning and value of housing framed perceptions of the relations between classes.

Historians who have adopted nineteenth-century categories to oppose "private" and "public" spheres all too often overlook the intersection of class values of respectable home life and new government policies. Chapter 5 shows how, at the very moment when the abolition of property qualifications opened the polity to white propertyless men, elected officials applied the domestic equation of prosperity and morality to an expanded program of city improvements. Policies for street openings and new public squares promoted the rising land values that displaced older institutions of proprietary independence, and they endorsed and even subsidized residential development for the elite. When propertyless New Yorkers' customary uses of the streets as "common" property threatened to contradict this program for city improvement, moral reformers and real estate investors joined in campaigns to clear the city's poorest, racially mixed tenant neighborhoods for redevelopment. Yet in drawing on domestic moral prescriptions to sanction entrepreneurial goals, public officials encountered divided investment interests within a bifurcated housing market. For as respectable householders and developers sought to enhance home life, land values, and social order with new public utilities and amenities, some landlords and employers sought to enhance profits by mixing brothels, saloons, sweatshops, and domestic quarters in the subdivided tenant houses of the city's old mechanic neighborhoods.

Chapter 6 looks more closely at the structure and operation of this divided housing market and at the relation between new construction and the deteriorating housing conditions of the city's working people. The class judgments evident in public improvement policies also shaped private investment practices that determined what kinds of housing got built where in antebellum New York City. Although Manhattan experienced a remarkable building boom, especially following the opening of the Erie Canal in 1825, builders concentrated on producing dwellings at the town's periphery for what they perceived to be the most reliable and therefore most profitable market—the city's wealthy and middling households. Defined as an "unproductive" market for new housing, New York's working people in the 1820s and 1830s had no choice but to crowd into subdivided older housing stock, paying more and more rent for less and less space.

In the first three decades of the century, the real estate market had spurred and profited from the city's economic expansion. When the economy collapsed in the panic of 1837, so did the housing market. Exposing landed capital's own dependence on those sectors of the economy that paid out wages and salaries, the depression of the 1840s revealed landowners' declining power within the urban industrial economy. Even as builders consolidated and aligned themselves more closely to financial institutions to reduce risk, they embraced the investment logic that had emerged over the previous two decades. Thus in the late 1840s and 1850s, developers pursued the advantages of scale in building middle-class housing at the periphery, and smaller builders rationalized ad hoc tenant crowding—the principle of more rent for less space—into the systematic production of multifamily dwellings, the tenements that formed the core of working-class neighborhoods for the rest of the century.

New York's working families, caught between employers and landlords, lost power and went on the defensive in the first half of the nineteenth century as they confronted a declining standard of living. Through trade unions, journeymen and laborers organized resistance to low wages, longer hours, and the degradation of craft skills, but it was the pressures of rents that most dramatically eroded real wages and devalued the working conditions and labor of women and children.

Nonetheless, there were limits to the power of the city's landlord classes, and Chapter 7 and the Conclusion explore how these limits arose out of the competing interests of private property organized as different forms of capital, out of wage earners' practical strategies of resistance to paying rents they could not afford, and out of the social contradictions—ranging from rising mortality rates to labor militancy— that a housing crisis produces for all city residents, even those insulated from its worst effects.

This book examines the emergence of a particular set of housing and property relations in a particular time and place. Antebellum New York City was exceptional: it was the nation's largest, wealthiest, and poorest city; and Walt Whitman called it the nation's most radical city.[5] The investment relation of landed and merchant property is part of the story of the antebellum port's remarkable expansion of wealth; the pressure of rents is part of the story of the remarkable depths of poverty; and the experience of social displacement that betrayed republican expectations for proprietary independence surely fueled the militancy of New York's artisans and laborers. In the mid–nineteenth century, new immigration exacerbated the deteriorating living and working conditions of thousands of Manhattan families, but the systematic building of social inequality into the housing market did not result from numbers alone. The specific contours of New York City's inequality derived from the historical evolution of social monopolies of land and investment strategies for its management, from the changing structure of employment, and from cultural and entrepreneurial redefinitions of housing's value and people's needs. And, as Henry George was to observe in the 1880s, the specific structure of real estate profit derived not from the land at all but from the paid and unpaid labors of New York City's working people. New York's housing market underwent further changes after 1850, yet many of its basic operating assumptions and its justifying language, first forged in this period, have persisted to our own time.

The transformation of property and housing relations in other cities, though perhaps showing structural resemblances, involved a different balance of class powers and different processes of negotiation. I hope, therefore, that this book will stimulate more attention to housing relations as one of the key variables that determine the material conditions of everyday life.

I must add here a word about definitions. The language of real property, deriving from the vocabularies of seventeenth-century English law, is occasionally arcane and often unstable. The language of housing, overlaid by gender prescriptions, class perceptions, and our own contemporary experiences, is even more slippery. Thus, for example, the legal term "tenement" in the eighteenth century referred to any building, and as late as the 1820s, John Pintard used the word to describe a private dwelling; but by the mid–nineteenth century most New Yorkers used the word "tenement" to refer to purpose-built (as opposed to subdivided) multifamily working-class housing. I use it in this last sense, but have not altered the quotations that carry an early meaning. To help orient the reader to my own descriptive and analytic vocabularies, it is necessary to review some of the other concepts and terms that run throughout this book.

Property itself signifies not things but various kinds of rights in things. Landownership—"freeholds" or rights to land or other resources held "in fee"—implies exclusive rights to use, possess, devise, transfer, and sell land. Other property rights are conditional. Thus, for example, a widow's "dower estate," her right to the use and benefit of one-third of her husband's land during her lifetime, did not include the right to sell that property. Leases transferred rights in real property for a specific term of years in exchange for rent and could include other conditions that restricted tenants' use of land or imposed particular obligations. A "building lease," for example, generally required a tenant to construct improvements according to specifications recorded in the lease. Leases also established landlords' obligations—for example, a guarantee that the land or house was not tenanted by someone else.

When discussing the distribution of *land* through leases, I generally use the term "rentiers" to describe New York landowners who collected "ground rent" in exchange for rights to use their land. Unless a ground lease specified otherwise, the tenants—or "leaseholders"—could use the land as they chose during the term of the lease and retained ownership of any improvements they added to the land. New York's large landowners and rentiers adopted the English system of agricultural tenures and leased land for terms that ranged from twenty-one to ninety-nine years. A tenant who held a long-term ground lease (a "leasehold") retained a proprietary interest in the land for the specified term of years; that is, leaseholders could transfer, bequeath, sell, or sublet their leases (unless the lease explicitly proscribed such actions or specified a fine if they were taken). Thus, for example, a leaseholder who held a twenty-one-year lease on a piece of land might, after five years, sell that lease (the right to use the land for the remainder of the lease's term subject to the ground rent), having first fenced the land or added a new barn or house. The price of such a lease or leasehold depended both on the nature of the improvements and the number of years left in the term; and in areas of the city that were becoming more desirable as a result of settlement or speculation, that price would generally be more than the total remaining ground rent even if no improvements had been added. Thus Manhattan's land market circulated ground leases alongside titles to land in fee. Because long-term leasehold included some of the rights of freeholding, however conditional, eighteenth-century leaseholders could and did view themselves as having a "propertied" status, that is, they held a negotiable interest in land and improvements they added to it.

In general I have tried to use the term "landlords" to designate people who owned and rented out *buildings* on land they either owned themselves or leased from rentiers. Because the owners of buildings on leased land could also sublet their interests in the buildings, a tiered system of tenures emerged in New York which transferred conditional rights for a term of years from rentiers to "chief landlords" to sublandlords to tenants. And rents flowed upward through this chain from the tenants or subtenants who paid house rents for the space they occupied to landlords, who paid building rents to a leaseholder, who paid ground rent to a rentier.

The nature of the lease as a contractual agreement between parties was the subject of debate in the early nineteenth century. Seventeenth- and eighteenth-century common law favored landlords, who retained certain implicit legal privileges as part of their landowning status. For example, landlords could seize tenants' personal property for payment of rent, a procedure aptly called "distress." In the mid–nineteenth century, American judges tried to move away from enforcing landlords' and tenants' customary legal rights and obligations by invoking the principles of commercial contracts—for example, *caveat emptor* (buyer beware)—and enforcing terms expressly stipulated within the lease.

One of this book's principal arguments is that we must recognize that today as well as historically, housing is a site of work, and that the labor that goes on within households is essential to personal subsistence and to the larger economy. This view, although something of a commonplace, runs counter to both liberal and Marxist economic theories, which see money payment as necessary to establish labor's economic value (or the appropriation of "surplus value") and which generally regard housing as part of the "consumption fund," that is, part of the "nonproductive" circulation of revenues that do not propel the economy. It is beyond the scope of this book to engage in theoretical argument over the ways in which political economy has prevented investigation of the social relations of unpaid labor and its working conditions. But it is essential to understand that private property rights historically incorporated claims to the economic value of unpaid household labor, a term I use to refer to the domestic work of housing maintenance (including the provision of heat, water, waste disposal, and lighting), food preparation and service, cleaning, sewing, child care, entertaining, and, before the rise of the wage market, many forms of trade labor. That today we pay cash for so much of this household labor or take it for granted as part of housing utilities should only remind us that we are looking at a very different set of housing and labor relations in the late eighteenth and early nineteenth centuries (which nonetheless helped shape the ways we think about housing today). I have tried to avoid referring to housing as simply "residence" or "living space," terms that reinforce notions that the site of domestic work and family relations is somehow set apart or sheltered from the working economy.

This book also argues that changes in domestic labor relations transformed the uses and meanings of housing as a workplace in different ways for different classes of New Yorkers. I generally use the term "domestic property," the "modern dwelling," or "home" to distinguish single-family or two-family houses from older "integrated houses," which included workshops and stores on the premises, and from subdivided "tenant houses," which often sheltered people who engaged in the paid labor of taking in boarders or of outwork. This is not to argue either that modern dwellings did not continue to shelter paid as well as unpaid work or that wage-earning tenants did not regard the site of their domestic labor as "home" or associate it primarily with family relations. Rather it is to stress the extent to which a uniform and prescriptive language of housing—and particularly "home"—has interfered with our thinking about what actually goes on in houses.

"Neighborhood" is yet another concept that requires a sense of a different past. In the early nineteenth century, New Yorkers used the term to describe spatial proximity—the "vicinity"—as much as a socially homogeneous district or community within the city. The formation of class neighborhoods took place by degrees; even in the colonial port, poor tenant households dominated certain waterfront (and sunken) streets while wealthier New Yorkers concentrated on blocks leading inland from the wharves. And through the 1830s, particular blocks or neighborhoods assumed their social character less by their geographic extent than by the uniformity of housing types and uses. Thus I refer to blocks of single-family dwellings as "respectable neighborhoods," blocks with artisans' integrated houses and shops as "trade neighborhoods," and blocks that mixed trade workshops, artisan houses, and boarding and tenant houses as "tenant neighborhoods." I use these terms to suggest the perceptions of the period rather than to claim that these territories of the city spatially and socially enclosed the everyday lives of their residents in the ways that we associate with suburban or inner-city neighborhoods today. The latter aspect of neighborhood formation, of course, becomes more evident in the later period covered by this book with the elaboration of localized networks and institutions that reinforced a spatial sense of collective identity and with the stablilization of land-use patterns that linked an extensive neighborhood geography with social identity.

The hardest concept to define is power—the ability to enforce one's will on others—and particularly class power, the collective exercise of that ability. In order to animate concepts of class or gender relations beyond static sociological categories that identify people primarily by occupational statuses or "roles"—or, indeed, by sources or levels of income, wealth, and authority—I have tried to think about power as a matter of conflict and negotiation which rested both on social means—the material, human, and legal resources that supported claims—and on social definitions of legitimate ends. We need also to think about how collective consciousness or a subjective sense of shared identities, motives, and goals shaped the process of social negotiation. It seems to me that part of propertied New Yorkers' exercise of class power in this period rested on denial of the relation between their motives and means of private accumulation (whether for wealth or for security) and the social conditions of propertyless New Yorkers. As part of the process of denying social accountability, nineteenth-century propertied New Yorkers pointed to socially "neutral" rules of supply and demand to explain why their city had the worst housing conditions in the country. It is a strategy that persists today.

The myth that celebrates a real estate deal as New York's primal historical act lends an aura of inevitability to the real estate market's power to shape the city landscape and determine the physical conditions of everyday life. New Yorkers today live in the shadows of deals that have produced the glitter of Trump Tower, the polished facades of renovated brownstones, and the shells of abandoned buildings. These shadows especially darken the paths of those who are getting a bad deal: the more than 50,000 people who have been displaced onto the city's streets and sleep in doorways, subway stations, railroad terminals, or temporary shelters. Contemporary politicians, like nineteenth-century New Yorkers, invoke this landscape of light and shadows to point to the contradictions of our time: a city that can indulge extravagent displays of wealth cannot afford to house its people.

These contradictions have become increasingly visible. The conditions of the Manhattan housing market—its social geography, institutional forms, credit structures, political supports, construction processes, and the people and buildings themselves—have all changed dramatically over the course of the twentieth century; little of the intricacy of contemporary property relations was to be seen in the nineteenth-century port. Yet, against myths of progress as the sum of free and shrewd market dealings, the experience of the last decade suggests that when people who claim social resources as private property grow more powerful, the condition of those without property grows worse. Let us look back over a century and a half to the formation of the Manhattan housing market and see how the contradiction between private profit and social need created New York City's first housing crisis.

CHAPTER 1

The Formation of Manhattan's Rentier and Landlord Classes

ONCE UPON A TIME, owning, renting out, or trading in Manhattan real estate was not particularly profitable. Through the mid–eighteenth century other enterprises—exporting fur and flour, importing tools and tea, transporting slaves and rum, privateering, brokering loans, brewing—brought steadier and higher returns to colonial officials, merchants, and artisan entrepreneurs. With the port of New York's wealth coming primarily through international trade rather than from the local production and exchange of goods, the greatest value of Manhattan land lay in its broad distribution as a site of houses that sheltered the shipping, craftwork, and domestic maintenance necessary for survival. Proprietorship in land organized the household labor that operated the port and secured individual livelihoods. In order to understand how city real estate—and particularly housing—became a profitable commodity, we must begin by looking at the colonial system of land tenure.

This story of landed property relations begins as a history of how one class of colonial Manhattan proprietors transformed a geographic abundance of land into a limited supply and thus established claims on their neighbors for rent. The process of creating land scarcities—the formation of social monopolies of landownership—predated the pressures of rapid population growth and competition for particular locations. That process began with European colonial officials' policies for distributing land unequally to settlers.

Dutch and, after the 1664 conquest, English colonial administrators endowed Manhattan's mercantile elite with large land grants in order to secure political support and to reward investment in colonial enterprise. By 1700, prosperous merchants and artisans were also assembling large landed estates through the market and transferring them through marriage and bequests. Nonetheless, through the first half of the eighteenth century, the majority of the port's households were able to preserve their own proprietary independence—control over houses, shops, and a dependent household labor force—by acquiring town lots in a fluid and inexpensive land market. In New York's Hudson Valley powerful rentiers, who established monopolies on prime agricultural land, imported or attracted agrarian tenants and collected ground rents, milling fees, and profits from selling tenants' wheat. Accumulation of land in Manhattan, in contrast, produced the curious social anomaly of a rentier class that formed itself in the absence of a dependent tenant class.

Even after 1760, when Manhattan rentiers immediately adjacent to the port settlement succeeded in attracting artisan tenants to their land, market conditions allowed those leaseholders to negotiate terms that satisfied their own requirements for control of real property, and particularly control of the houses and shops they built on leased land. Whereas rentiers and leaseholders (with support from migrating freeholders) in New York's northern countryside were beginning to confront each other as representatives of antagonistic social and political systems—landed mercantilism versus agrarian republicanism—tenure relations in the city did not establish such clear polarities. Rather, with poor laboring families subsisting at the margins of the town's dominant property relations, freeholds and long-term ground leases structured gradations of interests in real property which limited the powers and benefits of monopoly.

Only in the last quarter of the century, and especially after the Revolution, did demand from a growing population, intensified competition for strategic locations, and changes in the household labor system intersect with established social monopolies on land supply. And only then did rentiers gain the upper hand in Manhattan's tiered system of tenures and begin to realize profits in landholding at the expense of artisans' and laborers' control of land and housing as the means to personal independence.

The Distribution of Land in Colonial Manhattan

The interdependent strategies of seventeenth-century colonial administrators, investors, and settlers set the initial terms of Manhattan property relations. It is difficult to isolate and assess the social and economic impact of forty years of Dutch colonization on New York's subsequent development. In many respects the colony's early history seems of a piece with foundering contemporary English adventures in Virginia. Despite the intense rivalry and trade wars of the seventeenth century, Dutch and English administrators shared common assumptions regarding the goals of empire, and they chartered joint-stock companies to secure territory, hunt for precious medals or other valuable resources, and open new trade routes. Even as the Virginia Company finally discovered its lucre in tobacco, the Dutch West Indies Company pursued the fur trade. Thus New York's first colonists regarded land primarily as an extractive resource.[1]

When the Dutch initiated European settlement of New York in the 1620s, the first colonists brought with them a language and system of governance; national ties within an international trade and credit economy; a dissenting Protestant tradition; and farming, craft, and building techniques that remained part of the fabric of New York's culture for the next century. When company servants deserted their assigned agricultural tasks to pursue the fur trade themselves, the Dutch West Indies Company introduced slave labor to the colony. And though Dutch settlers' commercial orientation and customs of partible inheritance structured a fluid land market, Dutch colonial officials also initiated mercantilist land policies—government-sponsored monopolies—that English administrators extended forty-three years later.[2]

The Dutch West Indies Company, chartered in 1621 by the States-General, retained the exclusive power to appropriate and grant land in New Netherlands, including the port of New Amsterdam, until 1653. Company directors initially secured land rights from Native Americans and established settlements to guard their monopoly on the Hudson Valley fur trade and to facilitate export. On Manhattan the company sought to create an interdependent port and farm landscape that satisfied the commercial expectations of shareholders and met the survival needs of the colony itself; it thus laid the foundation for the coexistence of large landed estates and small independent freeholds which characterized Manhattan property relations a century later.[3]

The West Indies Company established New Amsterdam by building a fort and trading post, and by distributing town lots to settlers and absentee investors. In keeping with conventions of social hierarchy and political influence, company officials granted larger and multiple town lots (as well as farm tracts) to themselves, to military and church officials, and to influential merchant stockholders or their agents. The original grantees and immediately succeeding proprietors of the port, however, also included artisans whose trades were essential to the port's operation—brewers, masons, tailors, coopers, carters, and tavernkeepers. With fewer than two thousand residents before 1650—

many of them transients—town landowners developed a local real estate market by subdividing larger tracts and transferring land and buildings through sales, mortgages, direct trades, short-term leases, and bequests. The company policy of confiscating town lots left unimproved by grantees further prompted the subdivision and distribution of land to artisan settlers. In 1657 the port's residents negotiated through the States-General to free themselves of the company's rule and claimed their independent corporate rights as town "burghers."[4]

From the beginning of settlement, the West Indies Company had tried to organize the Manhattan countryside to feed and to shield company employees and port households. In the 1630s, company directors established six Manhattan farms, but they failed to find long-term tenants for these "boweries." Poor soil, Indian raids, and competition with Long Island farmers for imported livestock subverted the company's plan for a yeoman's countryside enclosing and succoring the port. When in the 1640s the company granted "half-freedom" to eleven slaves (that is, freedom contingent upon payment of an annual fee and not extended to children), it endowed them with "Negro lots" (from one to twenty acres) in the vicinity of the Fresh Pond, a mile and a half from the fort. The policy served to create another buffer around the New Amsterdam trading post as well as to spare the company the expense of maintaining its slaves. Though some absentee Dutch merchants also acquired substantial "farm" grants within four miles of the fort, in the unstable years between 1630 and 1650 the property proved worthless even as a paper speculation.[5]

Despite this uncertain beginning, interest in owning Manhattan land increased as Dutch policies shifted from securing a trade outpost to establishing a settler colony. The pace of land appropriation accelerated in the second half of the century, when unhappy investors persuaded the States-General to loosen the joint-stock company's monopoly and encourage private or syndicated adventures. Increasingly confident of permanent settlement, both resident and absentee traders began to accumulate multiple tracts of land at the port, in the adjacent countryside, and in the Hudson Valley. Needing labor to work this land and finding Dutch yeomen and artisans reluctant to emigrate, proprietors continued to purchase slaves.[6]

Amsterdam merchants' disappointment in the Dutch West Indies Company's management of New Netherlands strengthened the position of private investors. In a move that pointed in the direction of subsequent British policy, the stockholder Kiliaen Van Rensselaer successfully lobbied officials to grant him more than 500,000 acres of land in the Albany region, a "manor" to which he promised to import settlers.

In the face of such initiatives, even the company's own loyal leaders could see a new handwriting on the wall. Thus, in an analogous Manhattan appropriation, the company's director, Peter Stuyvesant—who owned forty slaves—claimed three of the Dutch West Indies boweries as his own between 1645 and 1651. Besides Van Rensselaer and Stuyvesant, a select group of New York's wealthiest eighteenth-century merchant families dated their substantial Manhattan landholdings from the late Dutch period—Kips, Webbers, Beekmans, Bayards—but most "Knickerbocker" elites acquired their real property after the British conquest of 1664.[7]

In the face of a depressed fur trade, the British agenda for New York colony centered on the organization of land as an agricultural resource and the port as an entrepôt in the trade triangle. Agents of the Duke of York (later James II, who was granted the "proprietary colony" by his brother Charles II) promoted political stability, settlement, and agricultural development with generous land grants that also generated revenues for royal patrons. Between 1666 and 1720, patriarchs of New York's most powerful landed families—Livingston, Morris, Philipse, Schuyler, Van Cortlandt—imitated the seignorial aspiration of the Dutch "patroon" Kiliaen Van Rensselaer and acquired thousands of acres of land along the Hudson River. Arranged through political connections and strategic marriages and lubricated by fees, bribes, and the promise of quitrents (annual payments to the governor), this wholesale land grab north of the port established a new provincial colonial elite.[8]

English governors expected large proprietors to import tenants, livestock, and equipment in exchange for their right to collect ground rents and milling fees and to control the export of colonial commodities. Officials also encouraged the use of slave labor to support England's expanding slave trade. As New York's cash crops shifted from furs to wheat and timber, the Hudson Valley estates established the landed basis of political power throughout the colony. Despite repeated controversies with merchant factions over import duties and the expense of intercolonial wars, rentier families aggressively pursued their own interests in policies governing Indian relations, colonial boundaries, commerce, land speculation, landlord–tenant law, and slavery.[9]

The policies that governed British officials' distribution of land in late-seventeenth-century Manhattan mirrored developments in the Hudson Valley. Thus Governors Richard Nicolls and Edmund Andros sought to bolster local political support and to reward absentee friends by making expansive grants of previously undistributed Manhattan land and defunct Dutch West Indies Company patents. They had few illusions that proprietors would organize these Manhattan "farms" to attract settlers; rather, they distributed land titles as speculative interests. Between 1666 and 1686, rugged bluffs, tablelands, and swamps situated from four to eight miles from the port settlement (from the present-day 34th Street to 125th Street on the west side of the island and to 82nd Street on the east) moved into private hands, generally in tracts that ranged from one to two hundred acres. One syndicate of five proprietors received and quickly subdivided 1,300 acres on the island's west side, more than an hour's walk from the Battery. Later governors, and then the Common Council, granted smaller patents closer to the wharf district, such as a Wall Street tract secured by the meat merchant (and Stuyvesant son-in-law) Nicholas Bayard and the shipper Abraham De Peyster in 1695.[10]

As important for the organization of Manhattan property as the distribution of private patents was the English governors' endowment of New York City's closed municipal corporation, "the Mayor, Common Council and Commonalty." Governor Thomas Dongan's 1686 charter granted the corporation nearly 1,500 acres of "waste and common" lands, including a 900-acre central column punctuated by rocky outcroppings (between the present-day Sixth and Third avenues north of 34th Street). In 1730 the Montgomerie Charter extended the corporation's control of property to shoreline water lots between high and low tide. These charters and common lands shifted the political administration of Manhattan real estate from royal governors and their councils to the city's mayor and aldermen, a shift to "local control" that testified to the growing power of city proprietors, who also became municipal officials. Although artisans who purchased the "freedom of the city" (that is, the legal right to work in the city) could vote in municipal elections, only freeholders worth £40 could hold office. Corporation officers managed common lands to generate revenues that paid for the regulation and promotion of commerce.[11]

The late-seventeenth-century Manhattan land grants, which generally enriched people who had already gained the privileges of wealth or office, spurred the local land market, as some absentee grantees resold their tracts within five to ten years. But real estate speculation on the island did not take off. By the end of the century, local "gentlemen" and officials had begun to acquire and hold land as reserve wealth or as a long-term investment. Prospering shippers, brewers, butchers, and sugar refiners also began to assemble landed estates (consolidating, for example, old Dutch West Indies boweries or the scattered "Negro lots," which had been bought up by land traders) at prices that were, by European standards, quite low.[12]

In the eyes of colonial officials and Hudson Valley magnates, New York City existed primarily as an entrepôt, the exchange point for exporting flour and naval stores and importing slaves and English manufactured goods. Although a ten-year wheat-bolting monopoly stimulated the port's economy in the last quarter of the seventeenth century, relatively slow population growth before 1730 undercut the Manhattan real estate market. So did the predominance of slave labor.[13]

Even more readily than Long Island and Westchester farmers or Hudson Valley rentiers, Manhattan proprietors adopted slave labor to operate the port. Between 1665 and 1712, while the town's white population was doubling, the number of slaves increased eightfold, from 120 to 960.[14] By 1730, slaves made up nearly one-fifth of the port's population, and New York City contained one-fifth of the entire provincial slave population. As labor was scarce throughout the colony, slaves were trained and employed in skilled crafts that supported shipping— from ship carpentry to printing—as well as in domestic labor and heavy transport and construction work. The majority of the port's merchant and artisan masters owned fewer than three slaves. Eighteenth-century observers explained the port's labor shortage and reliance on slave labor as a consequence of free immigrants' preference for subsistence farming, "land being easily come at, or vacant, which induces the people to scatter . . . [and] content themselves with a scanty living."[15]

Unlike indentured servants or free laborers, who might eventually (and in the eyes of employers often prematurely) become landholders, slaves remained permanently outside the land market. Indeed, in contrast to the ambiguities of the Dutch policy of granting "half-freedom" and land to slaves in order to save maintenance costs, the British in 1702 passed stringent provincial slave codes that sharply distinguished the condition of slavery from that of indentured servitude. Local laws, recognizing bound workers' own customs of socializing and cooperation, threatened free blacks with reenslavement to keep them from "entertaining sundry of the [white] servants and negroes belonging to the Burghers and inhabitants to the great damage of their owners." In 1712 a bloody slave insurrection at the port fanned fears that the presence and autonomy of free blacks undermined the discipline of slaves; a law passed by the Assembly that year further discouraged manumission and extended the color line into free society by declaring that "no Negro, Indian or mulatto, that shall hereafter be made free, shall enjoy, hold or possess any houses, lands, tenements or Hereditaments."

The 1712 law further required that any property that was already owned by free blacks be forfeited to the British crown.[16]

By excluding Africans and Indians from the free landed economy, New York lawmakers conferred a new racial privilege on Dutch and English artisans, who, fearing the competition of slave labor, had agitated for its restriction. Following the 1712 uprising, Governor Robert Hunter joined in urging the Assembly to restrict the slave trade, to "take away the root of Evil [and] Encourage the Importation of white Servants."[17] Worried that widespread use of slave labor prompted immigrants to settle in New England, administrators regarded the promise of exclusive access to land to Europeans as one means of attracting free settlers to New York in greater numbers. Nonetheless, slave labor remained a mainstay of the Manhattan economy and an integral part of the port's system of independent proprietorship for another forty years.

Officials, merchants, and artisans who purchased and inherited large tracts of Manhattan land operated in the shadow of Hudson Valley rentier families, who dominated the province's agricultural and commercial economies, and no doubt they shared those rentiers' ambition for economic and political power. Many large Manhattan proprietors were members of the same elite families. But despite colonial administrators' endorsement and endowment of landed inequality on the island and despite merchants' acquisition of large farm estates, eighteenth-century Manhattan property relations assumed a dynamic that differed from that of the long-term agricultural tenures of the northern countryside. The income-producing value of Manhattan land depended not on its cultivation but on the expansion of the port, and one way the port economy expanded was through the encouragement of free craft labor, which in turn stimulated the circulation of land.

Port and Countryside

Through the first half of the eighteenth century, people who owned land at the port and in the Manhattan countryside—sometimes the same people—did so for different reasons. Land at the port, of course, did not offer a subsistence agrarian livelihood or produce a cash crop for export. Town residents acquired town lots—generally 20 to 25 by 100 feet—in the first instance to build the houses, shops, and warehouses necessary for their trades and domestic maintenance.

Before 1730, New York City's traders and artisans rejected the long-term tenures of landed society in favor of a system of petty

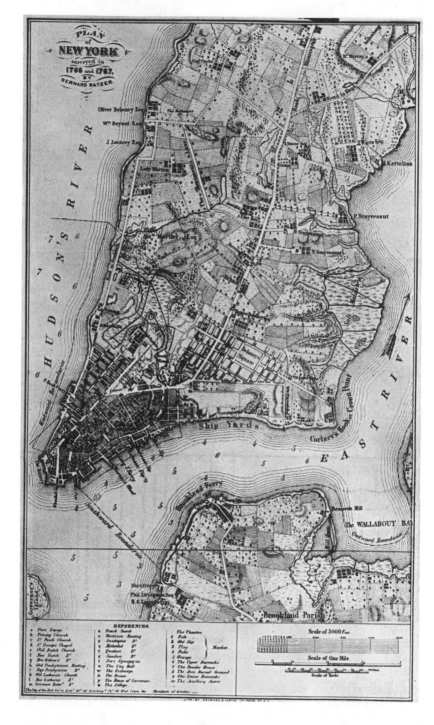

Plan of New York Surveyed in 1766 and 1767 by Bernard Ratzer. Courtesy of The New-York Historical Society, New York City.

proprietorship that relied on the labor of slaves, indentured servants, and family members. From 1701 to 1730 (when the population reached 8,000), over two-thirds of New York City's taxpayers were freeholding proprietors, and roughly one-third of its households owned an average of two slaves. The high proportion of freeholding taxpayers, of course, discounts people who did not control enough property to be taxed in the first place, a group whose ranks began to swell with white settlement after 1730. Then, too, the top 10 percent of assessed citizens controlled 46 percent of assessed wealth. Nonetheless, the initial distribution of town patents, the early subdivision of larger tracts along the shoreline, and a century-old real estate market had combined to disperse landholdings socially and geographically within the built town. And many New Yorkers who could afford to purchase a well-situated town lot for £50 to £100 could also afford to buy a slave who cost the same amount.[18]

The port land market was fluid and prices advanced relatively slowly in the early eighteenth century. Instead of holding large contiguous tracts of land, wealthier proprietors often owned multiple town lots scattered throughout the port. This geographic dispersal of landholdings opened market competition and limited the advantages of locational monopoly. The exception was the lower East River wharf district, where merchants who held shoreline property could also petition the Common Council for adjacent water lots. On Pearl and Water streets, merchants owned two or three houses on a block. But for the most part, before 1730, gains from selling or renting out town lots or houses paled against the profits of shipping, smuggling, slave trading, brewing, or sugar refining and limited heavy investment in lower Manhattan real estate.[19]

The freeholding port's broad land distribution contrasted dramatically with concentrated landownership in the adjacent Manhattan countryside. The late-seventeenth-century land grants had launched the formation of large landed estates—ranging from fifty to three hundred acres—which proliferated in tandem with booms in colonial trade. Periods of economic expansion (from 1674 to 1684, the early 1690s, from 1713 to the early 1720s, the 1740s, during the Seven Years' War, and again in the mid-1760s) prompted merchants, gentlemen, artisan entrepreneurs, and lawyers to place their shipping profits in country estates. Conversely, during troubled years (following the end of New York City's wheat-bolting monopoly in 1684, in the late 1720s, the 1730s, the postwar recession of 1762, and the late 1760s), the assembling and transfer of major Manhattan tracts appears to have slowed down. In general, before 1760, rural Manhattan land values did not advance rapidly enough to sustain speculation—quick sale for profit. Indeed, land prices occasionally declined in an economy plagued by wars, money and credit shortages, and a relatively slow population growth beyond the port. But as a general trend, the countryside was moving into the hands of fewer and fewer New Yorkers.[20]

The transfer of large Manhattan landed estates through familial structures further concentrated control of property in the hands of a local rentier class even as it dispersed land among male heirs. Marriages, which made in-laws of such prominent families as the Rutgerses, Beekmans, Bayards, and Livingstons and of the Van Cortlandts, De Lanceys, Wattses, and Warrens, merged those families' landholdings or (when wives retained their property in trusts) established alliances of landed interests. The consolidation and transfer of wealth through marriage was all the more important to those elite New York families that adopted the Dutch custom of devising equal shares to all children. Still, although New York's wealthy English colonists frequently distributed equal shares of personal wealth to daughters, they were more inclined to reserve land for sons. Whereas the proportion of women property holders in Manhattan—primarily widows and unmarried inheriting daughters—declined only slightly over the course of the eighteenth century, from 14 percent in 1701 to 12 percent in 1789, among the economic elite the proportion dropped from 10 percent in 1701 to 3 percent in 1789.[21]

For Hudson Valley rentiers the value of landownership stemmed directly from tenants' cultivation of cash crops and payment of ground rents and milling fees. For Manhattan's large proprietors, land served initially as a different kind of asset, as a means of storing, transferring, and displaying wealth rather than generating it. An uneven terrain of swamps and bedrock limited the agricultural potential of much rural Manhattan land. Some tracts were cultivated as orchards or as pastures to support livestock, and the slaves of Harlem proprietors produced wheat and vegetables on the island's best farmland. But the very abundance of more fertile soil in New Jersey, on Long Island, and in Westchester offset the advantage of Manhattan farms' proximity to a town market.[22]

Despite the land's uncertain value for cultivation and despite the difficulty of attracting tenants whose agricultural labor and rents could realize that value, leading port citizens as well as members of Hudson Valley patroon families formed their own class market for rural Manhattan estates by buying and selling farms to one another. In the 1770s, the island's countryside was divided into approximately 137 "farms" owned or leased by fewer than one hundred families, at least one-third of whom were related to other landowning families. These large proprietors initially managed their land investments with an eye less to ground rents than to other forms of wealth.[23]

Land's greatest advantage to Manhattan merchants was its permanence. Between 1700 and 1770, New York's erratic shipping economy periodically contracted in response to European wars, tight credit, navigation acts, and competition from other American ports. Merchants and other investors who placed all of their capital in ships and merchandise risked unpredictable turns in the market as well as the hazards of privateers, storms, and damaged cargoes. Merchants perceived Manhattan land, in contrast, as a reliable capital investment; though short-term returns might be low or nonexistent, the commodity could not be lost or destroyed.

Mortgages translated this figurative security of land into literal security for credit. Though such wealthy proprietors as Admiral Peter Warren relied primarily on reputation and penal bonds to secure loans, such families as the Bayards and the Livingstons also mortgaged their property to raise capital. By borrowing against their land, merchants offset the disadvantage of nonliquid assets. When currency was in short supply, the use of land as collateral also encouraged local creditors to circulate rather than hoard their wealth.[24]

Then, too, the security of landownership could be transferred over generations to ensure a family's financial support and status. In 1722 Robert Livingston expressed this expectation when he gave his daughters a double house and lot in the South Ward. In the deed, Livingston specified that the dower right of his wife, Alida, was to be protected so that if she "by war, fire or other inevitable accident be reduced to want a convenient and suitable support and aliment according to her quality . . . she may freely demand and receive her third of rents and proffitts and income of the said house and lotts above conveyed." For wives and children who were not likely to carry on the family business or trade, real property stored wealth that, properly managed, might in turn generate annuities. Frequently family agents exercised the powers of landownership for female heirs as well as for absentee owners.[25]

In pursuing the interlocking financial and familial advantages of landholding even in the absence of tenants, Manhattan's wealthy merchant landowners adapted strategies developed by England's gentry elite. By the mid–eighteenth century, large proprietors who admired English gentry culture were building country houses on farm tracts along the Boston Post Road (Bowery and Bloomingdale roads, the latter now Broadway) and in the environs of Greenwich Village. These houses served as summer retreats, retirement homes, and entertainment centers for their owners, who often maintained town or manor houses as well. The estate names—many recalling London pleasure gardens—reflected the social pretensions of their owners: Roxborough, the Hermitage, Spring Valley, Louvre, Rose Hill, Bellevue.[26]

The gentrification of the Manhattan countryside in the mid–eighteenth century can be read as part of a larger process of Anglicization in New York, a move to reassert through law and custom a social hierarchy reminiscent of the landed English social order. Though country estates represented a secure family investment, they also rendered the wealth of Manhattan merchants, lawyers, and artisan entrepreneurs visible throughout provincial society. And even as eighteenth-century travelers commented on the provincial display of gentility and luxury, these residences served as clearinghouses for the intricate business and political negotiations of a provincial ruling class. The ideological message of proprietary authority and status was not lost on New York City's artisan ranks. From the late seventeenth century, such successful artisans as the butcher Nicholas Bayard and the brewer Hendrick Rutgers had purchased large estates. By the mid–eighteenth century their heirs were joined by such artisan entrepreneurs as the blacksmith Matthew Buys, the cordwainer John Sickles, and the baker John Orchard, whose farms exceeded 150 acres. Smaller "country seats" and pleasure gardens, from 25 to 50 acres, were owned by lawyers, butchers, innkeepers, sugar boilers, and merchants who had transformed themselves into gentlemen.[27]

Yet it would be a mistake to interpret the creation of Manhattan country estates and houses simply as a cultural imitation of the English gentry's consumption habits. Manhattan's predominantly merchant landowners were far from indifferent to the economic potential of their property. In the absence of tenants, Manhattan's wealthiest landowners initially found that the investment value of their land rested on demand from members of their own class. By the eve of the Revolution, however, changes in the port's land market brought tenants within reach of the island's rentiers. The subdivision and distribution of the adjacent countryside through ground leases opened a new channel for the circulation and accumulation of local wealth and established a new relation between the port's merchant landholding families and its craft and laboring households.

It is difficult to pinpoint the time when New Yorkers started to view town lots as an attractive investment. Before 1730, the port's most active real estate agent was probably the municipal corporation itself, which secured its annual £300 budget by selling water lots, leasing out common lands, and collecting ferry fees. Between 1730 and 1760, however, as the volume of shipping doubled and the town's population grew to 20,000, widening price and rent differentials signaled heightened competition for strategic trade locations, particularly in the Dock and East wards. Land prices also rose as part of a general inflation of New York's currency. Population growth stemmed primarily from the accelerated immigration of English artisans and laborers, but both the attraction of the port to these free immigrants and the rising demand for town lots reveal changes in the structure of New York's craft economy.[28]

English officials sought by mercantilist regulations to restrict the local production of goods that threatened to satisfy the colonial market for English imports. In 1732, for example, Parliament had passed an act limiting New York's master hatters to two apprentices to prevent competition with England's own extensive workshops. Yet the need to provision British troops during the Seven Years' War (1755–1762) stimulated the local production of hats, shoes, and houses as well as of processed foods and shipping supplies. High colonial wage rates during the war offered free artisan immigrants opportunities to save the means to proprietary independence.[29]

Furthermore, a decline in the proportion of New York City's enslaved population and a shift in its composition after 1746 suggest that even as local craft production gained strength, master artisans were moving away from their reliance on slave labor. From the late seventeenth century, free laborers had repeatedly protested competition from hired slaves in their trades; and in 1737, Governor George Clarke endorsed the complaint of city coopers when he attacked "the pernicious custom of breeding slaves to trades whereby the honest and industrious tradesmen are reduced to poverty for want of employ, and many of them forced to leave us to seek their living in other countries." New York City's 1741 slave conspiracy and revolt, which resulted in the execution of thirty slaves and four whites, further increased anxieties about the control of slave labor within a fluid commercial economy. As a result of these fears of insurrection as well as of craft competition, in the mid–eighteenth century the composition of the city's slave labor force shifted from adult men to women and children. Thus whereas in 1746 the city had 126 male to every 100 female slaves, by 1771 there were only 85 males to every 100 females. Even as the proportion of the enslaved population declined, New Yorkers used slaves for domestic work, from household maintenance to cloth production. In artisan households, the use of female slaves for domestic work freed wives and children to assist in craftwork or shopkeeping.[30]

Despite their dependence on importing goods, New York City's merchant proprietors benefited from local craft expansion, for, unlike slaves, free artisans reinforced the local real estate market. The expectations of growing numbers of free male workers were tied to a structure of local craft succession, from apprentice to journeyman to independent proprietor. Shippers, who from the seventeenth century had controlled waterfront property for their own use, began to acquire and manage wharf district lots, stores, and houses, as well as docks, as rental properties. Although there remained a *geographic abundance* of town lots in lower Manhattan, landownership among town taxpayers declined from 70.5 percent at the beginning of the eighteenth century to 58 percent by 1789. This decline marked the emergence of a new set of tenure relations that first organized the city's rental housing market as part of its land market.[31]

The economic satisfactions of large proprietors, who began to see a steady and profitable return from land held as an investment, contrasted with those of New York's artisans and laborers, who needed land for immediate use as the sites of their houses and shops. Despite governors' worries that the abundance of rural land drew skilled workers away from their trades, many New York artisans were less inclined to transform themselves into agrarian freeholders than to negotiate the conditions imposed by the mercantile elite's organization of port property. When land prices and rents in the wharf district began to rise, artisans moved to less expensive land farther inland. There they encountered the town's leading gentlemen and merchants as rentiers.

Rentiers and Leaseholders: The Formation of Manhattan's Tiered Tenure System

From the mid–seventeenth century, Manhattan port proprietors who held multiple lots had leased out land and occasionally buildings. Yet early-eighteenth-century accounts suggest that the pursuit of rental income was little more than a subsidiary enterprise for most wealthy landholders. As conditions of the port land market gradually changed in the mid–eighteenth century, however, large proprietors began to cash in on their monopolies and to organize nearby rural tracts for town use. Working with legal instruments and privileges derived from a rural landed social order, rentiers paved the way for new commercial relations between city landowners and tenants.

The emergence of the tiered system of tenures that characterized Manhattan property relations for the next fifty years can be seen in the

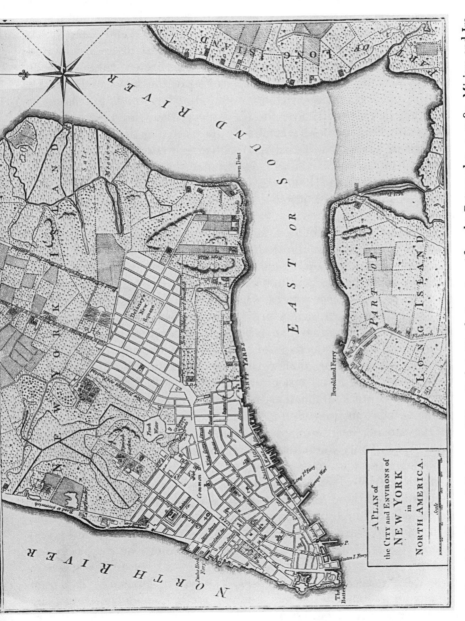

A Plan of the City and Environs of New York in North America. After the Ratzer plan, c. 1780. Miriam and Ira D. Wallach Division of Art, Prints, and Photographs; The New York Public Library; Astor, Lenox, and Tilden Foundations.

history of lands at the northern and western peripheries of the colonial port. At the time of the Revolution, six large farms dominated the meadows and wooded bluffs that absorbed most of the city's expansion between 1760 and 1810. To the west of Broadway, Trinity Church held over 100 acres of land between Cortlandt Street and Christopher Street. To the northeast of the port, along the East River, Henry Rutgers owned a 108-acre farm assembled by his brewer father between 1728 and 1732. North of Rutgers' farm were the lands of James De Lancey, 300 acres between Division and Houston streets purchased by his father in 1747; and above the De Lancey farm, three heirs of Peter Stuyvesant held a 300-acre estate. To the east, the three daughters of the British admiral Sir Peter Warren had inherited over 200 acres of farmland in Greenwich Village. In the middle of the island, north of Chambers Street and below Houston, the butcher Nicholas Bayard controlled 200 acres acquired by his grandfather in the seventeenth century.[32]

As fiduciary responsibilities pushed family agents as well as landowners to measure their administrative skills according to rates of return from land—annuities that could be compared with alternative investments—they began to consider new strategies for the profitable management of these farm estates. Only Bayard sold off a large tract of land to a syndicate of buyers in 1771, a number of whom in turn became rentiers. The other five proprietors devised strategies to bring surplus land into "productive use" without surrendering the benefits of ownership. Subdividing their estates into blocks and lots and adapting the English long-term agricultural lease to still semirural settings, eighteenth-century Manhattan proprietors leased out land for terms that generally ran from fifteen to ninety-nine years. The strategy and effects of using long-term ground leases can be seen in the management of the Trinity Church farm, the first large rural Manhattan estate to be organized for a town rental market.[33]

In 1705 Trinity Church, under its official corporate title of the "Rector and all those Inhabitants of our City of New York in Communion with the Church of England," secured a patent from Queen Anne for thirty-two acres of land west of Broadway between Fulton and Duane streets. The church augmented its holdings by claims on and purchases of farmland (extending from Duane to Christopher streets in Greenwich Village) totaling over 100 acres, and by gifts and grants from the city for shoreline water lots, building ground, and a churchyard. By the end of the eighteenth century, Trinity Church controlled land containing nearly a thousand city lots. The importance of Trinity Church's real estate holdings to the development of the city landscape lay not merely in the size and location of its estate but specifically in the construction of a distribution policy that promoted settlement without the sale of land. The wealthy laymen of the vestry board managed the church's land as they would their own.[34]

Although Trinity Church's very status as a nonprofit institution belied a simple profit motive in its acquisition of land, it used real property to guarantee its financial independence and to generate revenue for building, for yearly operational expenses (including housing for the rector), and for an outreach program of parish chapels. The terms of Trinity's initial grant and a law passed by a coalition of Dutch and Presbyterian assemblymen limited the Anglican church's annual income. This revenue ceiling indirectly encouraged policies that produced a yearly income stream rather than lump profits from land sales.[35] Further, the capital produced by sales would have required reinvestment in a period when land seemed to offer the most stable outlet for accumulated wealth. Many private landowners followed a comparable logic in seeking to lease out rather than sell their subdivided estates.

In 1734 a vestry resolution authorized the church "to lease out lotts of ground for any number of years not exceeding forty." The systematic distribution of church lands, however, did not get under way until the 1750s, when the city's 12,000 inhabitants began to seek space beyond the concentrated settlement below Cortlandt Street and east of Broadway. Even in 1752, the church continued to advertise for lease its thirty-two-acre King's Farm as well as "good pasture for cattle and horses." In 1762, having had its property surveyed and mapped into rectilinear "city" blocks, Trinity advertised two hundred lots on the church farm, most of them 20 by 100 feet, for terms of twenty-one, forty-two, and sixty-three years.[36]

Before 1770, the church leased lots at a single rate: £2 annual ground rent for the first seven years, £3 a year for the second seven years, and £4 annually for the remainder of the twenty-one-year term. The vestrymen calculated graduated increases to cover the doubling of land values which they expected after twenty-one years. But they did not initially differentiate location by price, as by charging more for a corner lot; leaseholders determined the values of particular locations by their own investments in improvements. Most leases provided that at the end of the term, tenants should remove within ten days any buildings they had added to the land. Well into the nineteenth century, aldermen complained of the nuisance caused by New Yorkers who moved houses to new locations at the expiration of their long-term ground leases.[37]

By the mid-1760s, the opening of new streets, wharves, and markets west of Broadway and north of Cortlandt Street had begun to attract settlers to the west side of the island. Not only was the church farm within one mile of the center of business and trade, the town had already pushed its northeastern boundary to the then-perceived limits of convenience. The relatively low ground rents on church lots attracted artisans and shopkeepers who could no longer compete with the purchasing power of merchants or craftsmen for lots near the wharves. There, annual ground rent for a lot ranged between £10 and £20, with the supply of vacant lots rapidly diminishing, and house rents cost tenants from £50 to £200 a year. For the same amount of money, artisans and laborers could build wooden houses to shelter domestic and trade activities on land leased from the church, and after that initial building cost pay from £1 to £4 annual ground rent.[38]

Advertisements for leases to Trinity lots stressed the "convenience of the situation" for carters, butchers, and shopkeepers. Surviving leases suggest that such appeals to artisan households were successful: laborers, carters, stonecutters, grocers, butchers, ropemakers, house carpenters, masons, cabinetmakers, and shoemakers all took up ground leases for terms of either twenty-one or sixty-three years and built their own houses and shops. Tax records show that by 1789, half or more of the city's carters and masons, roughly two-fifths of taxpaying carpenters and laborers, and one-third of the city's shoemakers lived on church farm lots, which constituted the West Ward of the port. The church farm had become artisan territory.[39]

If Trinity's long-term leases gave artisans access to land essential to their independent livelihood, ground leases also introduced a new marketable instrument into the local real estate market. Tenants could sell a ground lease—that is, their interest in land for the remaining term of years—just as they could sell a title to land in fee. With this market value of leases in mind, the church vestry adjusted its land policy several times to spur distribution.[40]

Trinity's most common leases, like those of most Manhattan rentiers, ran twenty-one years and anticipated occupancy. Such a term was long enough to give tenants the benefit of any buildings they added to the lot. In contrast, longer leases, especially those running sixty-three or ninety-nine years (with rent increases at intervals of twenty-one or thirty-three years), projected a proprietary interest that extended beyond the lifetime of the leaseholder. Under these longer leases the leaseholder, who paid a fixed ground rent to the rentier, retained any intermediary increases in the rent-generating value of property. Thus sixty-three- and ninety-nine-year leases offered land investors a cheap and profitable alternative to outright purchase. Other large landowners noted that the church's longer-term leases found a ready market. In 1774, for example, Oliver De Lancey, Peter Warren's brother-in-law and family agent, "complained to the [Warren] heirs that by granting leases at only twenty-one years they were competing unfavorably with their neighbors, Bayard, Rutgers, Herring and the Church, who were all busily subdividing their adjoining estates on longer leases and at higher rates."[41]

Trinity's longer leases and better-situated lots often went to wealthy proprietors and particularly to members of the church vestry. In 1767, for example, the church granted a ninety-nine-year lease for approximately 220 lots between Spring and Christopher streets to Abraham Mortier, who served as one of the church's major creditors. This lease to the Richmond Hill estate, just south of Greenwich Village, changed hands several times before John Jacob Astor purchased it from Aaron Burr thirty-seven years later and laid the foundation for his real estate fortune. The church extended other favors to vestrymen, granting an eighty-three-year lease for eighty-one lots north of Chambers Street to Anthony Lispenard, and ninety-nine-year leases for prime property on Broadway to the merchants Walter Rutherford, William Antell, and Alexander de la Montagne. Many such investors, managing leased property as they would land that they owned in fee, in turn leased out single lots in exchange for a second ground rent.[42]

Artisans, shopkeepers, and laborers also took leases for multiple church farm lots on sixty-three-year terms. The joiner Samuel Ellis, the tavernkeeper Francis Child, the distiller Emanuel Myers, and the laborers Peter Utenberg and James Freeman, for example, probably intended to occupy one or two of their leased lots and either sell or sublet the leases to the others. Artisans in the construction trades used Trinity's long-term leases to obtain land to build one or two houses on speculation in the 1770s and 1780s. Thus the leasehold system encouraged small-scale speculative ventures among artisans and shopkeepers, who could use long-term leases as an exchangeable commodity to secure credit or generate revenues that helped maintain their economic independence.[43]

Before the Revolution, landowners to the northeast of the wharf district had greater difficulty attracting artisan settlers but successfully appealed to New Yorkers interested in land investments. The James De Lancey farm offers a second case study of a transitional Manhattan landscape and of the evolving expectations and strategies of both rentiers and leaseholders at the time of the Revolution.

In 1741, Lieutenant Governor James De Lancey had purchased the impressive Dominie Farm, more than three hundred acres on the lower east side of Manhattan (west of the Bowery, between Division and Houston streets). Before the Revolution his son James De Lancey had the land surveyed and mapped into blocks with potential building lots. A 1766 city plan shows the farm laid out with "De Lancey Square," reminiscent of London's Georgian residential squares, at its center. The Revolution interrupted De Lancey's plans, however, and in 1784 the State Commission of Forfeiture confiscated and auctioned the lands of one of New York's staunchest loyalists. De Lancey's subsequent claims to the English Commission of Enquiry into Loyalist Losses reveal both his own management strategies and larger trends in real estate investment emerging at the end of the eighteenth century.[44]

Though parts of the estate were organized as a farm, De Lancey explained to the commissioners that his property "was extremely valuable for its contiguity to the Town of New York, there being no other way of extending the Town but by building upon this Land."[45] In making a claim for reparations, De Lancey stressed (and in all likelihood exaggerated) the revenue-generating and speculative value of his Bowery farm. Whatever lordly status other large proprietors may have attached to their country seats, as far as De Lancey was concerned, Manhattan's gentry had disappeared with British rule; his confiscated land represented nothing more and nothing less than lost opportunity for profit.

"There were three houses upon the whole of the 343 acres" of the Bowery farm when his father purchased it in 1747, and in 1760, eighty leased acres had brought a total ground rent of £148. In 1761 the younger De Lancey had issued new twenty-one-year leases for blocks and lots on this eighty-acre tract, and he claimed that at the time of confiscation in 1785, he collected annual rents of £994 (in New York currency), an increase of £846 in rental revenues. Furthermore, land prices and ground rents were continuing to rise as settlement increased along with inflation. "Most of his leases fell in in 1782, most of the front lots were relet at double Rents," De Lancey noted. "He thinks if the Troubles h[a]d not happened the Rents would have doubled at the expiration of the terms."[46]

Like Trinity Church, De Lancey leased most lots unimproved. "Every tenant has permission by the Terms of his Lease to remove his House at the expiration of his Lease, leaving the Lands under fence. They were wooded houses in the Suburbs of the City." De Lancey listed 112 leaseholders on lots that ranged from 25 by 100 feet to the equivalent of a full city block. Along the Boston Post Road (the Bowery) and on the intersecting Front Street, forty-six artisan leaseholders generally occupied their "front" lots. But the thirty-five persons who leased 283 lots in the Great Square and twelve leaseholders who held 58 lots on Division Street, leading to Corlear's Hook, acquired their leases from the outset as investments rather than for occupancy. With settlement gradually extending up the Bowery Road, these leaseholders expected the rent-generating value and the price of their ground leases to increase, even as the remaining years in the term decreased.[47]

Unlike Trinity Church, De Lancey improved some of his property before he leased it out. Besides ground rent, De Lancey collected rents for five houses that he commissioned himself, according to the claims, at the substantial building cost of £400 per house. By adding the houses, De Lancey significantly increased the rent he could collect from those five properties. Indeed, if De Lancey had been successful in collecting rents (as he is unlikely to have been, given the disruption of the war), five houses would have paid back the expense of their construction within seven years and by 1785, at £310 a year, produced nearly one-third of the £994 revenue generated by eighty acres of land.[48]

At the end of his claim for lots already improved or leased, De Lancey included a claim for an additional 120 acres, which, not having been leased out, did not meet the standard criteria for valuation based on the capitalization of ground rent over a twenty-year period. De Lancey had mapped this land into 1,240 lots, "intending to let them on building lease," and valued them "on the idea of their being valuable to build upon and at a rate of rather more than 21 pounds a lot," as compared with the £8 to £12 per lot he was then collecting in Bowery ground rents. Building leases, in widespread use in Georgian London, contained a covenant requiring the leaseholder to build a house according to certain specifications and binding the rentier to purchase the improvement at the expiration of the lease. From the map of the square it would appear that De Lancey envisioned a luxury suburb, though in the 1760s leading merchants had shown little inclination to move their town houses away from their wharves and stores.[49]

De Lancey's policies for managing various portions of his estate represent the range of strategies opening to Manhattan's large proprietors in the last quarter of the eighteenth century. Having long regarded their land as valuable for storing and transferring family wealth and securing credit, elite proprietors now saw real estate as a means of accumulating more wealth. Commercial expansion, inflation, population growth, and locational competition shifted the balance of market power, and ground leases gradually replaced freeholds as city artisans' primary means of access to land and housing.

Manhattan's tenure system differed in significant ways from that of large rural proprietors and leaseholders. Hudson Valley rentiers aggressively asserted exclusive rights to the benefits of landed wealth, including political authority gained initially through imperial patronage. Yet without controlling the tenants who raised, harvested, and processed cash crops, rural rentiers could extract little value from their agricultural estates. To inhibit tenant migration to "free" lands and, when that movement couldn't be controlled, to extract market fees and penalties in addition to ground rents, rural landlords imposed fines for the selling of leases (claiming that they were protecting their interest in resources, such as firewood, that had been consumed by the leaseholder). Rural leaseholders, farming alongside freeholders, demanded access to proprietary independence. Identifying rentiers' powers and privileges with royal governors' sanction of land frauds and the abuses of "aristocratic" monopoly, they framed principles of republican freeholding in terms of the unconstrained circulation of land.[50]

In contrast to their country cousins, large city landowners used the instruments of landed society—particularly the long-term lease—to promote rapid turnover of property and encourage investment in real estate. Thus unlike the Hudson Valley rentiers, whose fines on sales of ground leases constrained the circulation of land, Manhattan rentiers welcomed lease sales, which encouraged leaseholders to develop their property and investors to speculate in land. City leaseholders could occupy the land themselves or they could lease it out for a second ground rent; they could sell their interest in the lease, or they could improve the property and then collect a building rent. Without surrendering the satisfactions of being landholders, city rentiers delegated control of the distribution, development, and use of land to leaseholders.

City rentiers' policies initially shaped the formation of Manhattan's housing market by preserving broad access to land. Ground leases, though restricted to a term of years, allowed many artisan households to establish ownership and control over their houses and shops. Emerging at the same time that the proportion of slave-owning households began to decline, long-term leaseholds extended proprietary independence to the growing ranks of nonslaveholding artisans and laborers. Still, widespread use of ground leases restructured Manhattan landed property relations by introducing a new channel through which local wealth could be accumulated, one that carried a portion of the household earnings of the city's shopkeepers, artisans, and laborers into rentiers' account books. At from £2 to £6, annual ground rents for individual leaseholders might seem relatively modest, but by 1770, the cumulative rents of Trinity's first generation of leaseholders added more than £1,000 annually to the church's coffers.[51]

Although rentiers came into their own as a class in the last quarter of the eighteenth century, Manhattan's large landowners had not become the city's housing landlords. Leaseholders as well as landowners owned city houses, which were also the sites of craft production. Yet, even as Manhattan landownership was becoming more concentrated in the late eighteenth century, so was the ownership of housing.

A British survey of property holdings of New York City patriots during the Revolution provides a sample of changing patterns of land and house ownership in the city's West, North, and Montgomery wards. Over half of the 170 proprietors (including three church congregations) held more than one property in Manhattan, ranging from standard town lots to multiacre tracts within the city's ward boundaries. Taken as a sample of the composition of *house* ownership, the inventory suggests that as many landholders owned two or more houses as owned only one house and lot, but only 18 (11 percent) of the patriot proprietors held more than three houses in one ward, and only 11 landowners out of 167 owned more than four houses altogether.[52]

Despite the evidence of limited investment in rental housing, house ownership at the edge of the port, where city artisans began to settle on leased land in the late 1760s, was the most concentrated. In Montgomery Ward, on the East River north of Pearl Street, three out of five proprietors (out of a total of forty-six) owned more than one house and lot; two-fifths held three or more houses; and one-fifth of the proprietors owned at least four houses. Henry Rutgers owned twelve houses in the Out Ward; his neighbor Evert Byvanck owned eleven. This trend, the concentrated ownership of houses as well as of land or ground leases, pointed a new direction for Manhattan real estate investment beyond the wharf district.[53]

De Lancey's strategies of land management, as well as the patriot survey, suggest that even before the Revolution, New York City rentiers—like "improving" English landholders—had begun to direct their attention to controlling the use of land in order to increase its productivity, its rent-generating value. Within the city, of course, improvements did not entail the enclosure of arable fields, introduction of cash crops, and displacement of tenants; rather, city "enclosures" required control over the construction and use of buildings in order to attract "better" tenants. Thus rentiers' strategy of leasing land on long terms began gradually to expand to include the commissioning of buildings, as with De Lancey's five houses, and the addition of covenants to ground leases which required the leaseholder to build a house according to the rentier's specifications.

The ownership of multiple houses also points to some leaseholders' pursuit of these new investment strategies. Spared the cost of purchasing land outright, merchants, shopkeepers, and artisans could raise capital to build or acquire several houses on leased lands. With the collection of rents often supplementing incomes from trade, the circulation of revenues through ground leases and subleases blurs the analytic distinction between controlling property as a means to earn a living and managing it for profit. But as the port's merchant rentiers and artisan leaseholders placed their savings in houses as well as in land, they introduced new conditions to be met by other artisans and laborers in quest of proprietary independence. New strategies to maximize profits from land worked to separate city producers from access to housing, which was as essential a resource to independent city workers as the soil had been to English farmers. The growing concentration of landownership and new tactics for managing long-term tenure relations signaled the further redefinition of the social relations between propertied and propertyless New Yorkers after the Revolution.

Landed Inequality in Republican Manhattan

Economic and demographic growth following the Revolution crystallized the changing structure of Manhattan tenure relations. The number of people in New York County increased from 23,000 in 1785 to 31,131 in 1790 and then doubled to 60,529 in 1800. As peace restored European trade routes and lines of credit, New York shipping expanded. Local craft production embraced the growing local market for tools, shoes, clothing, and processed food. New York merchants and artisans also extended trade lines into the slave South even as they abandoned slave owning in their own city.[54]

The trend toward concentrated landownership in Manhattan continued in the fifty years following the Revolution. With the confiscation and sale of loyalists' estates between 1785 and 1790, the death of a generation of gentry proprietors in the 1790s and early 1800s, and the subdivision of several farms near the built city, hundreds of acres of land came onto the market. But the availability of land for sale did not result in an equitable redistribution. Instead, the booming land market, with inflated prices floating on unstable currency, attracted new investors who perpetuated the rentier system even as they adapted it to intensified development.[55]

The transfer of the confiscated farmlands of New York loyalists provides one indication of the trends in proprietorship. Some loyalist tracts, such as those of James Watts and Thomas White, reverted back to the families of their proprietors. Others passed into other hands in one tract, as when John Somerindyck purchased the 300-acre estate of Oliver De Lancey in 1785. To avoid confiscation, Oliver De Lancey had in 1779 conveyed another 182-acre farm to his daughter, who in turn sold it to the baker John Orchard. The most important loyalist estate to be sold in the town proper was that of James De Lancey, divided into 1,920 lots. Individual artisans, builders, shopkeepers, and lesser merchants—some of them former tenants—were able to purchase one or two lots for prices ranging from £25 to £100. Seventy-five percent of the De Lancey property, however, went to a select group of seventeen buyers, virtually all of them wealthy merchants or members of mercantile landholding families. Some of these seventeen proprietors purchased the land as a speculation and resold it immediately. Isaac Roosevelt, Morgan Lewis, and Janet Montgomery, for example, conveyed portions of their De Lancey holdings to John R. Livingston in the 1790s. Livingston, on the other hand, waited nearly twenty years before subdividing the blocks and selling single lots. Many others who held large tracts subdivided and leased out town lots on long terms.[56]

After a century of uncertainty, new expectations of profit propelled the circulation of Manhattan farmland. The manipulation of real estate as an investment determined the timing of land subdivisions and sales. New Yorkers who owned large tracts of land also exercised the power to hold land back from the market when prices dropped, to sell it in blocks to people with capital to purchase larger tracts, and to set their own terms for ground leases.

Land prices rose in the 1780s, and in the mid-1790s they soared. Thus John Ousterman sold his farm to Josiah Ogden Hoffman for £2,400 ($6,000) in 1794, and Hoffman resold it in 1798 for $10,000. Trinity Church, which before the Revolution had calculated that land prices would double in twenty-one years, graduated rents in its 1780s ground leases in anticipation that land values would triple. The vestrymen might have been bolder in their expectations. The historian Edmund Willis has found that the assessed value of Manhattan real property increased by over 700 percent between 1795 and 1815; controlling for inflation, he estimates that land values appreciated four times in that twenty-year period. New York real estate investors bitterly complained when speculative land bubbles burst (as in the late 1790s) and when the economic dislocations of the 1807 embargo and the War of 1812 disappointed their expectations. In the long run, however, it was the city's artisan and laboring families that most suffered as steadily rising land prices increased the economic burden of gaining and maintaining an independent living in their own houses and shops.[57]

Despite the subdivision of some large estates, ownership of real property continued the trend toward increasing concentration at the turn of the nineteenth century. By one measure, the proportion of property-owning voters in the city declined by nearly one-fourth between 1790 and 1814, from 46.9 percent to 22.7 percent, while the proportion of renting voters increased from 51.3 percent to 77.2 percent (with artisans who could vote by virtue of having purchased the "freedom of the city" dropping to a mere 0.1 percent as Federalist mayors sought to abolish the freeman voter status; see Appendix, table 1). This overall pattern dramatically illustrates the demise of artisan freeholding. But the aggregate figures also obscure a shift within the ranks of proprietors which tells us something about who, as landlords, benefited from the expanding ranks of propertyless citizens.

When Willis analyzed the distribution of wealth among a sample of landowning voters between 1789 and 1815, he found that the lower economic half of the 1815 sample owned slightly less of the total assessed real property than that same group had owned in 1789—7.4 percent versus 6.4 percent. That is, the economic position of a core of proprietary households did not change much. Among the upper economic half of freeholding voters, property was more broadly distributed, so that the top tenth of the 1815 voter sample lost 5 percent of the total wealth that they had controlled in 1789. The seventh and eighth decimal ranks increased their share of property ownership from one-fifth to one-fourth of the total assessed wealth. These figures suggest that the breaking up of large tracts of land (such as the Roosevelt holding in the Fourth Ward, from which the 1815 sample was drawn) did redistribute property from the economic elite to a strong middle rank. The 5 percent gain of those in the seventieth and eightieth percentiles supported the rising expectations of successful traders and artisan entrepreneurs, who either were able to purchase land as an investment or saw property that they already held increase in value with development. As these wealthier artisans and traders joined the town's elite shipping families in pursuing profits out of real estate, they together formed the city's nineteenth-century bourgeoisie as a rentier/landlord class.[58]

New strategies for managing land, evident in De Lancey's claims, became more prevalent following the Revolution and further altered the conditions of proprietorship. Large landowners sought to control the quality of building on their property while still limiting their own outlay of capital. Thus more and more rentiers replaced lease clauses that allowed tenants to remove their improvements when the lease expired with covenants that required the leaseholder to build a house according to certain specifications and gave the landowner the right either to purchase the building when the lease expired or to renew the lease at 5 percent of the appraised value of the house and lot.

Typical building lease covenants required the leaseholder to build, usually within a year's time, a "substantial, workmanlike and well built" two-story brick or brick-front house (in contrast to the wooden houses of the prerevolutionary period). As the rents from improved land continued to rise, landowners further elaborated the conditions of their building leases. Thus, in the early nineteenth century, Henry Rutgers' standard lease for lots on his Lower East Side farm required that the leaseholder build a "good, substantial and workmanlike brick building not less than two stories in height and not less than thirty-six feet in depth . . . so as to cover the whole front" of the lot. Rutgers also specified that at no period during the term of the lease "shall there be more than one dwelling house on the premises," a measure aimed at countering the practice of adding houses in the rear. Though such houses might increase the leaseholder's income from the lot and provide cheap housing for subtenants, they seldom advanced the land's market value. From the perspective of the landowner, rear houses tended to depress future land values by attracting poorer tenants. In order to maintain further control over the lease and land market, Rutgers also required that a leaseholder who wished to sell the lease and improvements secure his permission and give him the first option to purchase.[59]

Rutgers had the bargaining power to set strict terms for his leases because he held geographic monopoly of the Lower East Side's Seventh Ward, an emerging center of Manhattan shipbuilding. Other rentiers competing for tenants could stipulate only the minimum value of a house that they would purchase back at the lease's expiration. In 1811 Morgan Lewis leased two lots at the corner of Leonard and Chapel streets to the carter Stephen Baxter for $270 a year. Lewis agreed that at the end of the twenty-one-year term he would pay Baxter "for any dwelling house which shall then be and remain on each of the said lots which shall be of the value of $1750, the said value to be ascertained by two sworn appraisers." For Lewis, a house worth less than $1,750—

that is, most likely a house constructed of wood—was not worth keeping as rental property. The lease held that "Baxter shall be permitted to remove the said dwelling [worth less than $1,750] from the premises within ten days" or keep it there for an additional year at a rent of $270 per lot—thus in effect giving the tenant an additional year's option to build while Lewis doubled the ground rent.[60]

Lewis and like-minded rentiers expected such building leases to encourage their leaseholders to invest in substantial construction. The effect of building covenants when they made construction mandatory (as Rutgers' did) was to limit long-term ground leases to people who had or could obtain the capital to make the specified improvements. Geared to the emerging speculative housing market, building leases constrained artisan leaseholders from building their own low-cost wooden houses in certain areas of the city. At the same time, by increasing the predictability of rising land values and development, such leases established real estate as an investment outlet that competed with government bonds, insurance company stocks, and even craft production for the savings of the city's lesser merchants and artisan entrepreneurs.

By allowing leaseholders to secure the "use value" of land for an extended period of time while reserving to owners ground rents and future capital gains, eighteenth-century leaseholds had initially resolved the conflicting interests of New York City's landowning mercantile class and its artisan and laboring classes. Long-term leases had enabled mechanics to establish proprietorship without the burden of purchasing property outright. Thus ground leases had given the city's producers a measure of control over the land and housing necessary for their livelihoods. At the same time, by rights vested in the very institution of private property, rentiers skimmed off a portion of the value produced by artisan households as a "tax" for access to land and housing. Following the Revolution, as property ownership became more concentrated and the rules of leaseholding more elaborate, the private "tax" of ground rents dramatically increased.

The profitability of Manhattan real estate at the end of the eighteenth century rested in large measure on family monopolies that restricted the supply of land in the midst of vacant territory. The system of long-term tenures made these monopolies permeable: investing leaseholders inserted themselves as middlemen into a revenue circuit that transferred wealth up the economic ladder. Where did the revenues that propelled rising rents and land values come from? In part, prospering business enterprises were paying higher rents for choice locations. In part, land values (and rent revenues) rose because new families settled in New York. But as important as either commercial expansion or population growth for the development of the Manhattan real estate market was the formation of a new housing market within the tiered system of land tenures.

Even as more and more New Yorkers found their access to land and housing governed by ground leases, the organization of housing itself, and hence the nature of demand for shelter, was changing. Colonial houses, sheltering workshops, kitchens, offices, and stores, had integrated trade and domestic labor. As the household labor system and slavery gave way to the free labor market at the end of the eighteenth century, domestic and trade quarters became two distinct arenas of economic activity, and New Yorkers who earned cash wages began to pay "domestic rents." Manhattan's eighteenth-century merchant rentiers had opened the channels for the accumulation of local wealth from *ground* rents, but it was a new entrepreneurial class of landowners that extended the real estate market's reach by capitalizing on housing. Having explored the formation of the city's rentier and leaseholding/landlord classes, we turn now to the transformation of household property and labor relations which created a new wage-earning tenant class.

CHAPTER 2

The Formation of
the Urban Tenancy

ON APRIL 13, 1794, Grant Thorburn, son of a Scottish nailmaker, emigrated with his brother from a village six miles south of Edinburgh to New York City. "With above a hundred persons," their ship was crowded, "having only four feet and a half between decks, with two tiers of berths to sleep in round both sides of steerage: three persons slept in a berth." The ship also provided twenty cabins, but passengers in steerage had little contact with those who could afford to establish themselves as a class apart. Thorburn reconstructed the experience of the voyage vividly forty years later: "Here I was in my twentieth year without having experienced or seen aught of the world, set as it were on my own feet close jammed in a crowd from whom there was no retreating, whose ends, motives and dispositions were as various as their faces." For Thorburn, who from the age of five could not "remember having slept three nights out of my father's house," it was a fitting embarkation on a new world of city living.[1]

The Thorburn brothers were two of thousands who came to New York City in the decades following the Revolution. Brigs and schooners that docked at Manhattan slips embarked from Boston, Philadelphia, Charlestown, Baltimore, London, Liverpool, Glasgow, Le Havre, and Santo Domingo. Sloops brought new arrivals down the Hudson River from upstate farms, ferries ran from Long Island, Connecticut, and New Jersey, and post-road coaches and wagons carried passsengers from the interior. Waves of new arrivals followed the rhythms of political upheavals in Ireland, Scotland, and France; the slave revolt in Haiti; New England's farming depressions; and the irregular trade cycles that registered foreign treaties, embargoes, and European wars.[2]

Between 1790 and 1800, New York City's population nearly doubled to 60,489 people, and it increased by another 36,000 in the decade that followed. "Yankee" New Englanders and Irish, Scotch, French, Caribbean, and German immigrants joined English settlers, who had outnumbered old Dutch-stock families for over half a century. Ten percent of city residents at the turn of the nineteenth century were of African descent; 5 percent were enslaved. Following a dramatic decline in the slave population during the Revolution, the number of free blacks had tripled during the 1790s. The port population grew through natural increase as well as from migration and immigration, though recurrent yellow fever epidemics kept mortality rates high. And New York was a youthful city: young men and women migrated there in search of opportunities within an expanding port economy.[3]

By 1790, New York had already passed Philadelphia in population. By 1800 both the volume of shipping and the value of goods imported and exported established New York as the trade capital of the new nation. New city residents could find ready work not only in shipping but in building, equipping, and provisioning ships; in processing food and drink; in making shoes, hats, furniture, and tools; in constructing wharves, streets, stores, and houses; in cooking, sewing, nursing, and cleaning; and in printing newspapers, brokering loans, litigating contracts, and keeping accounts.[4]

Having heard promising reports from relatives, neighbors, agents, or circulars, new arrivals probably oriented themselves and formed their own first impressions of the city's "ends, motives and dispositions" by observing the physical organization and activity of the landscape. A walk through the streets revealed a city undergoing a transformation within the shell of the eighteenth-century port.

The harbor with its forest of ship masts and sails and radiating slips and wharves formed New York City's most striking feature. Though New Yorkers had spent a decade rebuilding portions of the East and Dock wards destroyed by fires during the British occupation, Thorburn recalled that in 1794, the townscape itself still "made a very poor appearance from the water as the stores were all built of wood" and only three churches had steeples "high enough to be seen to advantage." But upon coming ashore, visitors noted with awe the bustling commotion of commerce, the congested traffic of carts transporting merchandise, dockworkers loading and unloading ships, barrels and bales obstructing paths, and hucksters selling wares. And by the late 1790s, the face of New York's wharf district was being lifted by the very height of new three- and four-story brick stores and coffeehouses. The new four-story brick store of the importer William Lupton, for example, covered two town lots and ran back sixty feet. Other substantial merchant establishments—town houses and stores—fronted the lower

Hudson River and Dey Street. Watercolor and pencil on paper by Baroness Hyde de Neuville, 1810. Courtesy of The New-York Historical Society, New York City.

wharves, and gentlemen's coffeehouses and taverns at the foot of Wall and Broad streets served as headquarters for auctions and negotiations.[5]

To rural migrants who had grown up surrounded by dispersed timber farmhouses, cottages, barns, and isolated church steeples, the solidity and scale of these new commercial blocks and the density of the wharf district's crowds and traffic offered evidence of a special order of enterprise and energy, one that they associated with the prosperity of Liverpool.[6] With the harbor and adjacent stores dominating first impressions, the narrow and often crooked streets leading up from the wharves carried new arrivals farther into the social landscape that supported and propelled the port's economic growth.

On most streets, the absence of footpaths forced pedestrians, carts, and carriages to compete for passage along cobbled pavements. Where brick sidewalks had been laid, as on Wall and Broad streets, visitors complained about the protrusion of stoops, the steps to a raised first floor characteristic of Dutch town houses. Unaligned block fronts of intermixed two- or three-story wood or brick buildings projected an irregular skyline of chimneys, peaked roofs, gables, and dormer windows. The landmark spires of Trinity Church and St. Paul's could be seen from docking ships; the town's other churches more modestly identified their sanctuaries with posted placards. Taverns spread their doorways around corners with single posts supporting overhanging roofs under which passers-by could gather to exchange greetings and news.[7]

"Some good brick houses are situated in these narrow streets," the French émigré La Rochefoucauld-Liancourt had found in 1797, "but in general the houses are mean, small and low, built of wood, and a great many of them yet bear marks of Dutch taste." Houses built after the Revolution tended to adopt the new "federal" style—considered "Georgian" in England—with lower entries, higher stories, flatter roofs, and classical detailing on windows and doors. But as many of the town's buildings could probably have been described as cottages, sturdy wooden houses that displayed minimal concern with ornamentation. Placards over doors announced craft shops on first floors and in cellars, while brass plates identified the counting rooms and offices of the city's merchants, brokers, and lawyers. There was "no appearance of shop windows as in London," one English observer noted, "only stores which make no shew till you enter the houses."[8]

The interiors of most houses probably reminded rural arrivals such as the Thorburns of the arrangement of work and living space in the village houses they left behind. Front rooms, with easy access from the street, usually accommodated the household trade, while cellars and back rooms on the first floor served as centers of domestic work. Work space ranged from equipped shops furnished with workbenches, tools, cases, and storage areas to halls and kitchens with fireplaces for cooking, worktables, spinning wheels, bins, and tubs. Second stories and attics provided sleeping quarters. A house's quality was most obviously indicated by building materials, dimensions (breadth and ceiling heights), number of fireplaces, and furnishings rather than through the arrangement of rooms. Even the most substantial merchant town houses, which featured formal parlors or drawing rooms screened by entry halls, maintained offices and counting rooms facing the street.[9]

Behind the houses of eighteen- to twenty-five-foot width, fenced-in yards stretched for from fifty to one hundred feet. Fences were important features of the yard, as they protected vegetable crops and fruit trees from the town's large and ambulatory population of hogs. For bakers, blacksmiths, stonecutters, potters, and tanners, the yard and occasionally an adjacent lot provided space for bakehouses, stables, ovens and forges, molds, kilns, millstones, and even tanning pits where they were not expressly banned by city ordinances. Wheelwrights, carpenters, coopers, carriage makers, and joiners also required large work and storage areas for their building materials and often ungainly products. Whatever the trade in the house, in every yard a new arrival would have observed the necessary accoutrements to household maintenance: privies, woodpiles, pumps, cisterns, vaults, smokehouses, and occasional kitchen sheds. Depending on the season, women could be seen working in the yards, weeding a garden, doing wash in tubs boiling over open fires, salting pork after a butcher, carrying water necessary for cooking. The yard gave a household added space to cultivate, produce, and process household necessities.[10]

It is difficult to know how accurately a new arrival in the 1790s could have apprehended the range, proportion, and organization of various city enterprises from the streetscape. Moving from block to block, a perceptive stranger might have gained some sense of the city's economy by observing trade clusterings along particular streets.[11]

The proximity of importers' houses to their waterfront stores and wharves suggested eighteenth-century New York merchants' attention to the physical processes and goods of trade. But shippers' establishments built fifty years earlier had been converted into mariners' boardinghouses or workshops. Newer and finer merchant houses were turning inward on lower Broadway and Bowling Green. Wholesale and retail establishments—hardware and dry goods stores—predominated on streets immediately above the wharves. Interspersed among these stores, handicraft shops of watchmakers and silversmiths, printers and bookbinders, tailors and hatters offered consumer goods and services to a restricted clientele. Furniture makers often located near warehouses that contained supplies of imported woods and fabrics. Blacksmiths, coachmakers, wheelwrights, and saddle and harness makers clustered their shops near the intermittent alleys leading to stables in back.[12]

The wharves that stretched almost a mile north along the shore of the East River (like the fewer docks along the Hudson River) pulled warehouses, taverns, and converted boardinghouses with them. Immediately north of the East River docks, extensive shipyards were surrounded by a mesh of coopers', ropemakers', metalworkers', and joiners' houses, which served the construction, repair, and outfitting of ships. Several blocks inland from the shipyards, the stench of tanning identified the "swamp district," surrounded by leather and shoemaking shops. Half a mile farther north, at the edge of town, other processing trades—pottery, candlemaking, brewing—relied on the Fresh Pond both for water and for dumping waste. Beyond the pond, New York's butchers, preeminent among local artisans, had claimed the Bowery (with its stockyards and slaughterhouses) as their special territory.[13]

Aside from the clusterings of prominent brick merchant houses on Wall and State streets, most of the houses and shops east of Broadway were sited unevenly along irregular streets. But La Rochefoucauld-Liancourt had also admired "the new part of the city built adjoining to Hudson's River . . . infinitely more handsome, the streets there being generally straight broad and better built." A mixture of tradespeople—carpenters, carters, grocers, stonecutters—occupied these wooden and newly constructed brick-front row houses on the rectilinear streets of the Trinity Church farm.[14]

Across the town, in dispersed sheds, shanties, and cellars along the East River, men, women, and children worked in small groups at shoemaking or needlework on materials carried in bundles from a main shop. Then there were the laborers of the streets, from peddlers to scavengers. It would have been hard to know precisely to which houses they returned for meals and sleep. Indeed, the fluidity of street life would have made it difficult for a visitor to place many of New York's residents in particular houses, for from the exterior, many houses appeared interchangeable in their occupancy and use.

To an outside observer, New York's landscape revealed varying concentrations of capital and labor within trades and houses. The territory of the waterfront and the shipyards was perhaps the most impressive consolidated workplace, with gangs of workers serving multiple employers. In the workshops of bakers, hatters, and wheel-wrights, three to five people might be found working at a trade, while other houses, such as those of druggists, jewelers, and bookbinders, might accommodate only one or two apprentices, journeymen, or clerks in addition to the proprietor's family. Domestic work—including spinning, weaving, and making clothes—was commonly done by two or three women or girls, depending on the size of the house. The slaves and servants who served mariners' boardinghouses and merchants' es-tablishments, however, formed dometic labor concentrations for house-hold maintenance analagous to that in crafts. [15]

Although from the outside they were indistinguishable from houses that mixed trade and domestic labor, some establishments were given over entirely to a craft. The saddler John Smart, for example, adver-tised a 20-by-30-foot frame house: "the cellar is occupied as a workshop for the Trunk and Harness Making, and is calculated to accommodate six workmen; the first floor is also occupied as a work and sale shop, it has convenient work benches for six men, and well-arranged glass cases . . . on the second floor is a harness case . . . a workbench for three men, and sundry other convenient features. The garret's used to contain the hair, wool, hides, trunk boxes etc necessary to business." Smart's workshop had space for fifteen workers. Other nascent manu-factories ranged from the cabinetmaker George Shipley's workshop, where "there is always employment for about ten men," to the "well-known Nail Manufactory and Smithy Works, no. 22 Cherry Street," which included "tools and implements sufficient to employ 28 workmen."[16]

A visitor might gain a clearer sense of New York's economic organi-zation by studying the city directories, the roll call of the people who had established themselves within the commercial community. The 1795 city directory showed that just over two-fifths of listed New York-ers were artisans, the people who produced goods, and just under one-fifth were cartmen and laborers, the people who transported those commodities through city streets or supplied manual labor to build the streets. One-twelfth of the city's men were merchants—importers, fac-tors, and wholesalers; another twelfth were grocers or tavern or board-inghouse keepers. Women were listed in the directory as widows, boardinghouse keepers, mantua makers, and milliners. But the city directory did not record the vast numbers of servants and appren-tices who composed a substantial portion of the city's paid work force; nor did it note that roughly 6 percent of the city's residents in 1795 were slaves. [17]

To a new arrival, the landscape of New York City revealed the centrality of shipping, the vitality of crafts, and the constancy of domestic labor as essential aspects of the town's economy. But the town's buildings and streets alone revealed little about the underlying social relations of property and labor which organized this economy. In the late eighteenth century, the social and spatial ordering of everyday lives was gradually changing within the port's existing houses. For generations, household dependencies (from family relations, servitude, and apprenticeship to slavery) had bound labor to property—the house and shop—under the authority of a household head. And in the 1790s new arrivals found that the majority of houses still sheltered trade and domestic work under one roof. Yet as economic growth brought new opportunities and pressures, customs that had integrated property and labor relations within houses gave way to the market exchange of cash wages and rents. As more and more households abandoned slavery, found labor, and traditional boarding practices, "detached" wage earners formed a new tenant class within the city. The emergence of the city's rental housing market, the market that in turn drew new investors into Manhattan real estate, gradually reshaped the town's social landscape. To understand how these changes came about, we must first look more closely at the social relations of people inside New York City's houses at the end of the eighteenth century.

"Private Economical Relations": Household Property and Labor Relations at the End of the Eighteenth Century

The tradition of English legal discourse identified a household as the primary social institution of "private economical relations." As on farms, the heads of town households controlled the resources that supported their households—land, shelter, materials, and tools—and the "natural," covenanted, contracted, or enslaved labor of dependents. The product of the household's labor became the property of its head. That proprietary and appropriative power consolidated under one roof the fluid relations of domestic and trade work and integrated the household economy.[18]

New Yorkers regarded this private order as the basis of social order, a means of situating all members of society. Town and church officials held household heads accountable for the conduct and claims of their dependents; people who were not attached to a household—"settled" within the community—could be ordered to leave town or sent to the almshouse. Under the proprietor's authority, a hierarchy arose within the household on the basis of sex, age, race, contractual or enslaved status, and future access to household property. This hierarchy, which determined who could give orders, who must be obeyed, and what claims could be made on household resources, also established prescriptive social identities that determined household members' expectations.[19]

Household heads exercised authority over four groups of dependents: wives, children, slaves, and servants. English common law, molded through centuries of social custom and extended to New York colony in the eighteenth century, governed the way household relations were to be maintained, the rights and duties they entailed, and the remedies and relief to be had in the event of violation. Slave codes governed the labor, movement, and manumission of slaves. Although New Yorkers may have deviated from and contested legal prescriptions, the rules of law throw light on the dominant social relations of New York City's houses and households, which were giving way to new relations of employment and tenancy at the end of the eighteenth century.

On the most basic level, law organized household property and labor relations by establishing the absolute legal condition of married women's dependency on their husbands. Under the doctrine of coverture—in Sir William Blackstone's classic 1788 formulation—"the very being or legal existence of the woman is suspended during the marriage or at least is consolidated into that of her husband, under whose wing, protection, and cover she performs everything." Thus a wife could not own or convey property, make contracts, or bring suit for damages—that is, participate in the market—without her husband's consent and cooperation. Husbands who controlled their wives' property also commanded their labor. At an extreme that reveals the underlying logic of coverture, Blackstone reiterated the common law remedy that enforced a husband's power over the property of his wife's person: a husband could sue a third party for damages in the event of abduction, adultery, or assault of a wife, just as he could sue if someone injured or stole his livestock.[20]

The powers of household patriarchy, like those of feudal proprietorship, carried with them prescribed obligations. As a protector, a husband remained legally liable for all of his wife's wrongful actions short of treason or murder. As provider, the husband was "bound to provide his wife with necessities," which included shelter, fuel, food, and clothing. A wife, usually through the agency of a "next friend," could seek court enforcement for the specific performance of these obligations. But common law delegated to the husband the authority to enforce (through the "right of correction," which sanctioned wife beating) a wife's "duty" to provide her husband with "necessities"—the labor that transformed raw materials into her own and the household's subsistence.[21]

On a very practical level, the concept of a "wife's duties" supported a husband's proprietary privileges—the authority over *his* household—by in effect incorporating domestic labor into the property of the house. Within poorer households wives themselves did the housework of laying and maintaining fires for heat and cooking, carrying water, cleaning, fueling lamps, and throwing out slops and trash (as well as, of course, the "family labor" of cooking, caring for young children, nursing the sick, and making clothes). Within larger and wealthier households wives supervised and worked alongside other dependent household members. Men who observed mothers, wives, sisters, and female slaves and servants interchangeably performing the tasks of household maintenance—"women's work"—came to understand the benefits of that labor as one of the entitlements of proprietorship. What good was a house without utilities?[22]

As a household member, a married woman of course shared some of the benefits of her own labor, and she retained a future interest in household property by virtue of her claim on her husband's estate—a widow's dower right to one-third of her husband's real property. But the legal definition of a wife's dependency had far-reaching implications for the status of all women. A propertied widow may have gained in social authority from her power to contract and bequeath, for example. But the economic independence of a widow who inherited only a "life estate" in land or in her husband's house remained restricted. And an eighteenth-century woman who never married generally assumed the status of dependent in the household of another family member. Still, within the frame of coverture, most wives and husbands probably negotiated their own implicit contracts as to how they would live and work together as a household unit. The relative strength of women and men in such personal negotiations turned in part on their respective access to or control of resources.

In New York City, conditions affecting women's control over their own labor and property changed over the course of the eighteenth century. In the seventeenth and early eighteenth centuries, liberal Dutch inheritance customs had favored women's bargaining position in the marriage market, and families of Dutch origin generally looked after daughters' interests. Under English rule married daughters of wealthy families retained some rights to their own property—though not necessarily to their own labor—through antenuptial agreements and equity trusts negotiated and managed by fathers or brothers. Furthermore, wives of all classes acted as their husbands' agents in managing household and trade resources, and no doubt they often did so beyond the boundaries of common law prescriptions. Practical experience as trade helpmates (more easily come by in those households that used slaves for domestic labor), as well as inheritance of a husband's house and shop, gave some widows an economic foothold. Before 1760, New York's fluid economy, plagued by a chronic shortage of skilled labor, allowed women—especially widows—to engage successfully in both shipping and craft production, as well as in managing boardinghouses.[23]

It appears, however, that New York women's access to property and to skills declined in the second half of the eighteenth century. Though the proportion of women among propertied citizens remained relatively stable (between 12 and 14 percent), they controlled a steadily decreasing proportion of the city's total taxable wealth. Excluded from trade networks by male competitors, independent female shippers and artisans became less prominent in the town economy. Women with property could still gain a comfortable subsistence as boardinghouse keepers or mantua makers, but increasing numbers of single women earned their livings by working as servants, seamstresses, milliners, and laundresses. Regarding women of the laboring classes as "public dependents," New York merchants presented their employment as an act of charity. As early as 1762, St. Andrew's Society for Improving the Arts organized a linen manufactory and paid women wages in exchange for spinning in their homes.[24]

By 1790, when women headed one of every ten New York households, their economic position as a group had become far more precarious. Lacking the traditions of craft associations, excluded from most licensed trades, surrendering patrimonies or savings upon marriage, and frequently separated from their families of origin, the city's wage-earning women embodied not simply the traditional conditions of female dependency but the emerging market dependency of a propertyless class. Still, wives of middling merchants and artisans may have gained some personal bargaining power as market demand for domestic space and labor increased at the end of the eighteenth century: household services, like houses, could be organized as commodities to be both traded and sold. In contrast to single female wage earners, wives were in a position to negotiate with husbands over the use of house space by virtue of their ability to generate cash income from its management. Although it is difficult to assess their "power" in this position, women, as we shall see, became central agents in the formation of New York's rental housing market.[25]

Children constituted the second dependent class within the "private economical relations" of eighteenth-century New York households. The common law required parents to provide their children with maintenance, protection, and education "suitable to their station in life," and it gave household heads authority over children's discipline. Child maintenance did not have to take place in the parents' household, however. Eighteenth-century New York parents frequently contracted their children out to other adults—*in loco parentis*—for purposes of education, apprenticeship, or servitude.[26]

In a colonial port where chronic shortages of skilled labor pushed up wages, the unpaid labor of children, like that of wives, made an essential contribution to a household's subsistence and even to the accumulation of property. And children's expectations of inheriting property—in effect a delayed payment for labor—distinguished their claims on household resources from those of unrelated household members. Then, too, parents who had economic resources customarily assumed the responsibility of establishing their children in society and not only provided for training and education but made gifts and loans as well. But the "exchange" of children through apprenticeship formed one foundation of a larger system of household labor exchange that tied workers to particular houses.

New York's colonial households were flexible institutions that changed to accommodate the productive and personal life cycles of family members. Relatives arrived from the countryside or from abroad and moved in. Family members grew up and moved out to establish their own households, or they aged and cut back their contributions. A household that did not include sufficient family members to do the household work secured the labor of unrelated members by purchasing slaves or by hiring servants, apprentices, and journeymen in exchange for training and maintenance and/or wages.

In the first half of the eighteenth century slaves rather than indentured servants had made up a significant portion of New York's craft and manual labor force. As chattel property, slaves stood outside the covenanted and contracted relations of the household and the community; they existed entirely under their masters' authority. Slaves, like servants, lived within their masters' houses, generally sleeping in kitchens or attics; but unlike servants, they were restricted in their movements—for example, they needed a pass to travel through city streets, and no more than three slaves were permitted to assemble beyond a master's household. New York masters who hired out their slaves' labor—generally for a year at a time—assigned the responsibility for their maintenance and discipline to the employers; but it is one of the ambiguities of slaves' status in the port that slaves claimed the customary right to choose their hirers. Then, too, slaves permitted by masters to hire out their own labor could retain—either illicitly or by agreement—some of their earnings, and some slaves were able to purchase their freedom and that of family members.[27]

The steady rise in slave prices and hiring rates between 1730 and 1760 suggests that owning slaves could be profitable in New York City, but by the mid–eighteenth century, the demographics and organization of slave labor were undergoing significant changes. Free craftworkers' opposition to slave competition, fears of insurrection, and chronic discipline problems intersected with increased European immigration to shift the composition of New York's slave labor force from a preponderance of men to increasing numbers of women and children. Even as slave labor—whether owned or hired—became associated with domestic labor, including cloth manufacturing, the proportion of slaves dropped from 20 percent of the city's population in 1730 to 7.4 percent in 1790. Still, in 1790, one of every five city households owned one or two slaves.[28]

During the Revolution, British and patriot masters emancipated slaves in exchange for army service, and many slaves took advantage of the war to run away. After the peace, the steadily growing supply of free labor encouraged New Yorkers who opposed slavery to place abolition on the legislative agenda. New York lawmakers ended slave trading in 1785, but it took them another fourteen years to arrive at a gradual abolition plan. Under the 1799 manumission law, children born to slaves after July 4, 1799, were to be indentured to their masters for twenty-five years (in the case of girls) or twenty-eight years (in the case of boys) and then emancipated. In 1817 the Legislature set July 4, 1827, as the end date of slavery in New York, except for those children born between 1799 and 1827, who under the old law still had to serve out the terms of their indentures.[29]

The history of slavery in New York, as elsewhere, cast a long shadow. Much of the debate over manumission had centered on white New Yorkers' concerns about the future economic and political position of free blacks. Eighteenth-century manumission laws had required owners to post substantial bonds for the maintenance of their freed slaves; and the 1799 law required that the almshouse certify an adult slave's capacity for self-support before permitting emancipation. White artisans' hostility to the employment of first slaves and then free blacks in

crafts or on the docks and Democratic Republicans' opposition to granting free blacks political rights set the terms of a new social dependency
within the wage economy. Only in 1809 did New York's Afro-Americans
gain legislated rights to marry and to inherit and bequeath property,
that is, the rights that organized the dominant system of property and
labor relations in free households.[30]

With black men increasingly excluded from skilled trades, black
women continued to provide the backbone of the city's heavy domestic
labor. In the early decades of emancipation, nearly one-third of the
city's Afro-Americans continued to reside as domestic workers in white
households. The end of slavery marked one dramatic break with the
property and labor relations of colonial households. But the early concentration of slaves in domestic work also helped to prepare the cultural and economic ground for devaluing wage labor in what was to
become the city's single largest field of employment, and for many
black New Yorkers the primary means of making a living.[31]

Though family and slave labor had formed the early core of colonial
New Yorkers' construction of the "private economical relations" of
household property and labor, in the second half of the eighteenth century a third group—servants—had become increasingly important to
the household labor system. In elucidating the classes of servants,
Blackstone had identified two legal categories: servants *intra moenia*
(within the walls) and laborers "hired by the day or week who do not
live *intra moenia* as part of the family." When Blackstone wrote in the
late eighteenth century, New York's proprietors—like those in England—often employed household workers under both arrangements.
"Found labor"—workers who were provided with shelter, meals, and
household services ("found") as a condition of employment—integrated
household economies through the direct exchange of dependents' labor
in trade and domestic tasks. "Free waged labor" established a cash
nexus for both labor and housing relations. In New York City, the practice of boarding bridged the social transition from integrated household
economies to the divided economies of capitalist proprietorship and
wage-earning tenancy.[32]

The colonial practice of found labor grew most clearly out of the customs of apprenticeship and indentured service. In eighteenth-century
New York City, apprenticeship or indenture (generally arranged in exchange for passage from abroad) bound a worker to an artisan or merchant household for a term of (usually) seven years, sometimes as many
as fifteen years. In exchange for teaching the "art and mystery" of a
craft, a master agreed to "find and provide unto said apprentice sufficient meat drink apparel lodging and washing." At the end of the term,

the contract generally obliged the master to supply the apprentice with a full suit of clothing and in some instances with a set of working tools. The contract for a young woman apprenticed as a domestic servant occasionally provided that the master should also continue to supply an additional year's lodging during the "time that she is learning a trade"—most commonly needlework. Customarily, an apprentice resided in the master's house, though the contract apprenticing Christopher Roberts to the silversmith John Hastier in 1723 provided that the master should "give him the liberty to go and sleep at his mother's house every night." Furthermore, New York contracts allowed the master to "find" (provide) living accommodations for servants and apprentices by paying their board in a neighbor's house if they did not have room in their own.[33]

The employment of found labor thrived in the skill- and cash-short port before the Revolution, particularly as the use of slave labor in trades declined. The system was based in part on an exchange of household labor: women's domestic work for journeymen's craftwork. The calculation of found wages required that household heads set an implicit price on their employees' living necessities, a proportion of the costs of rent, food, and fuel as well as of the value of wives', daughters', and servants' or slaves' cooking, washing, weaving, sewing, nursing, and housekeeping. The found labor system secured a household's claims on skilled labor and heightened the proprietor's powers of imposing work discipline. Within the gender prescriptions of the era, the incorporation of workers into the household spared unmarried male workers the trouble of domestic maintenance and provided unmarried female workers with paternal protection.

Found labor perpetuated a particular structure of social obligations and expectations. As employers, household heads were responsible for the training and supervision of employees; as landlords, proprietors assumed responsibility for dependents' maintenance. Household members were called upon to defer to the protective paternalism of their masters and mistresses. Most apprentices and bound servants who joined a household in their teens obtained their personal freedom between the ages of twenty-one and twenty-five. At the expiration of their contracts, women servants gained their liberty to find a new employer or to marry. Apprentices who became journeymen, "day workers," or clerks moved into a new working relation with their own or another master. Young adult workers, who often owned tools but neither a workshop nor the raw materials of their trade, exchanged their skilled labor for wages. Through most of the eighteenth century, some journeymen and laborers had continued to reside within a master's household, with domestic maintenance deducted from their earnings.[34]

Sons' and male employees' expectations rested on traditions of craft or property succession which perpetuated the household labor system. In advertising a new shop or store, journeymen often noted their own passage through the craft to establish their credentials. In 1775, Joseph Bell, "who lately served apprenticeship to the tanning business in England, worked several years in England as a journeyman and then in New York City for Mr. Griggs, a currier," noted that he had "taken a house and shop opposite [the] end of Vandewater Street, leading from Queens Street to the Swamp." In 1775, when a skilled journeyman was paid approximately £50 to £60 a year and found, such a house probably cost Bell £150 to £250 to purchase or £10 to £18 a year to lease. Before a young man could set up an independent household, he had to acquire the means of proprietorship—through savings, patrimony, advantageous marriage, or a loan. Many New York artisans striking out on their own initially leased and shared their quarters and moved into full proprietorship with age and success.[35]

While sons and male employees could aspire to personal independence through control of their own house and shop or store, daughters and female servants expected to succeed to wifehood. They were trained in skills of housewifery which were essential to their own and their future household's maintenance. When domestic labor might bring them little more than £10 to £12 a year and found, women sought to marry well—that is, to trade their domestic skills for secure access to the resources of cash and property legally controlled by their husbands.

"Private economical relations" within eighteenth-century households had not operated without strain. New York slaves ran away, saved or stole the means to purchase their freedom, and resisted masters' power over their lives and families with tactics that ranged from arson to the skillful invention and negotiation of "customary" rights. Household heads and servants alike took disputes over discipline, conduct, and remuneration to the Mayor's Court. Other dependent household members voted with their feet: in the 1760s and 1770s, New York newspapers published numerous notices of runaway apprentices and servants alongside those of runaway slaves. Following the Revolution, notices of desertion or abandonment by spouses, as well as less common divorce petitions, reveal struggles between husbands and wives over household resources and practical rejections of the legal fiction of marital unity. Masters, too, complained that their civic responsibility for their household workers imposed an unfair economic burden. In 1747, for example, a householder had objected to having to provide household members for the watch, noting that "many inhabitants of the City have 3 or 4 sons and as many servants and apprentices and all those with themselves are obliged to watch in their turn which falls out or happens about once in every four or five weeks[;] the plain consequence thereof is the loss of fifty shillings and sometimes more to every inhabitant."[36]

Such conflicts over discipline, duties, and the costs of maintenance undermined the advantages of patriarchal authority and strained the familial mode of labor and housing relations. More important, the integrated economies of some New York households could not generate the cash necessary to maintain a comfortable subsistence within the city's expanding market economy. In others, the merger of familial, enslaved, and waged labor and the requirements of maintenance limited flexibility in organizing labor to increase their property. Household labor relations changed as household property relations changed, and by the late 1790s, both were shifting to a cash nexus.

From Found Labor to Cash Tenancy

Not all colonial New Yorkers had lived and worked as members of an integrated household within the dominant system of "private economical relations." By the mid–eighteenth century, more than 1,200 mariners moved in and out of New York every year. Although accommodations on ships implicitly followed the found labor system, on shore sailors relied on their earnings to purchase temporary housing and domestic services. For over a century, New Yorkers had organized boardinghouses and taverns to accommodate this growing population of mariners between sailings as well as other transients.[37]

Carters, dockworkers, and casual laborers did not require extensive training, a craft workshop, or a resident labor force; and they contracted with multiple employers. Thus they, too, used wages to acquire housing and domestic services through the market. The same kinds of affinities that prompted certain craftworkers to share houses and shops encouraged social and residential alliances among the city's transportation workers and shopkeepers. Carters and laborers often boarded or lived with one another or with grocers or tavernkeepers who, lacking a large household work force, had extra space in their houses. The flow of young immigrants in these and other trades spurred the development of the free waged labor economy in trades.[38]

In the last quarter of the eighteenth century, inflation, rising land costs, and the expansion of commodity production for the local market all placed pressures on the integrated household labor system. Some artisans—such as masons and carpenters—found they could save cash by giving employees "full" wages and employing them irregularly according to seasonal demand. Other craft households hired more workers than they chose to accommodate. As immigration after the Revolution relieved the acute shortage of skilled labor, masters in processing, construction, and consumer finishing trades rejected the paternal obligations of training and maintaining household employees in favor of the "convenience" of the competitive labor market. Given the price differential between skilled trade and domestic labor, as well as rising rents, some artisan householders may also have calculated that they could realize more cash by selling shares of house space and domestic services than they could save by providing room and board to their employees.[39]

Some journeymen and mechanics, too, perceived an opportunity for greater personal freedom and mobility in selling their skills to the highest bidder or in working for more than one employer. As the starting-up costs of establishing an independent house and shop increased, older journeymen rejected the household dependency of found employment in favor of controlling their own domestic economies of wages, living expenses, and savings. In his *Autobiography*, Ben Franklin had proudly illustrated this path to personal independence by recalling how as a young journeyman printer he had saved money by bargaining down the cost of his room and board from a widow. A journeyman who married might also turn wages to better account within his own household by replacing a landlady's charge with his wife's labor.[40]

Structural changes in craft production created a new demand among male wage earners for the commodities of domestic space and services in the late eighteenth century. Those commodities, however, were still produced through household labor. If young men sought new measures of personal control in allocating earnings for room and board, young women found expanding employment opportunities as domestic servants in houses that took boarders. Insofar as family labor obligations remained the mainstay of household economies, partriarchal social relations continued to govern the provision of domestic services. Yet even as black and white female servants continued to receive most of their earnings as "found," their status as waged rather than enslaved or bound employees also allowed them to bargain with employers and even to change positions when they found working conditions unacceptable. The exceptions before 1827, of course, were those women who remained slaves, or whose age upon emancipation limited their access to alternative employment.[41]

The demise of the household labor system occurred gradually and unevenly in Manhattan. Looking at the 1790 census of heads of households, we can only speculate as to internal social relations. Aside from merchant houses, the households with the largest number of resident adult males belonged to trades that were among the first to expand production for a generalized market—shoemakers, cabinetmakers, hatters, metal craftsmen, and carpenters. The printers Samuel Loudon and Thomas Greenleaf, for example, listed respectively ten and six adult males over sixteen years of age in their houses, some of whom were surely journeymen printers. Aaron Pell, a prosperous coachmaker, also probably housed employees among the five adult males in his household, as did the cardmaker Rowland Howard, with nine adult males, and the shipwrights Samuel Ackly and Ebenezer Young, with, respectively, five and six men residing in their houses. The ropemaker Elias De Grush and the nailmaker Peter Ustick each had eleven adult male household members. These resident craft work forces suggest that the found labor system persisted in late-eighteenth-century New York, but the limits of the household labor force also emerge from the census. The nail manufacturer Jacob Foster had four adult males living in his household but employed twenty workers at his work establishment. It is also possible that such artisans as the shoemaker Andrew Menel, who had seven adult males in his house, accommodated them as boarders and not as employees.[42]

With a steady stream of visitors and new arrivals to the port at the end of the eighteenth century, more and more New York households took in boarders for cash payments rather than as workers. Artisans advertising products and services occasionally took the opportunity to advertise available housing space and services as well. In 1796, for example, a cabinetmaker on Fulton Street who offered "his services to the public for everything that belongs to his line" added that "he takes boarders at a reasonable price." Similarly, an engraver advertised his skills and then offered "to let to a single gentleman, a large unfurnished room on the second floor who likewise can be accommodated with board by the year or shorter period." And the widow of an organ builder on Pearl Street who continued her husband's trade supplemented her income by taking in "two or three gentlemen in a family way."[43]

In an often unstable economy, the selling of surplus housing space, and indeed the creation of that surplus through decisions about density and use, provided households with an additional source of cash. This additional revenue allowed some households to meet rising expenses, especially rent, and thus to preserve their own independent status. For others, particularly for leaseholders who owned their own houses and shops, cash from boarders flowed into accumulated savings that could be reinvested in the household trade or in additional property. And taking boarders offered women a means to make an independent living.[44]

Though most notices for boarders indicated room for one or two "gentlemen," an advertisement for board "in a private family for six gentlemen on Greenwich street" suggests the fine line that existed between taking boarders and operating a boardinghouse as a trade. Women, who headed one of every ten households in 1790, often acquired boardinghouses by lease or purchase with the intention of going into business. Thus in 1800, Mrs. Avery "respectfully inform[ed] her Friends and the public that she had removed to that large and elegant white brick house #7 State Street for a boarding and lodging house." That same year Mrs. Bradley advertised for sale a three-story brick house that, by virtue of its fourteen fireplaces, was "well calculated for a boarding house." By the end of the eighteenth century, women ran at least half of the commercial boardinghouses listed in the city directory. Of the proprietors of the 50 boardinghouses listed in 1790, 26 were women; a decade later, women ran 88 of the 150 listed boarding-houses.[45]

Late-eighteenth- and early-nineteenth-century New York boarding practices retained vestiges of earlier household relations. The custom of boarding adult relatives, for example, blurred the lines between familial and market exchanges, and, as in rural communities, rents themselves were not confined to cash payments. Unlike the British practice of renting lodgings, boarding continued to incorporate—if not integrate—tenants into the household with the sharing of meals and possibly other maintenance responsibilities. Master artisans who continued to board out their employees retained close supervision of their personal conduct. In some trades, such as shipbuilding, masters built boardinghouses for their workers and deducted rent from wages. In other trades, such as shoemaking and carpentry, journeymen formed their own "trade houses" by taking board at the same establishment. The youth of the city's general boarding population meant further that proprietors could invoke the traditions of familial deference to age.[46]

Whatever the residual practices, the conversion of household space and services into a commodity gradually established a new cash nexus for household relations. In integrated household economies, the household head had claimed the authority of proprietor and employer as one. Within a market, boarders as purchasers could claim a status equal to that of the seller. As boarding emerged as a dominant housing form, household market relations required parties to assess, calculate, and negotiate the price of a product that was not easily defined.

Like the found labor system, commercial boarding could create particular household tensions, as illustrated in the angry exchange of letters between the republican pamphleteer Tom Paine and his blacksmith landlord, William Carver. At the heart of their argument stood the question of how the commodity being sold could be defined and valued. When Carver tried to recover overdue rent and payment for board, Paine responded with an attack on the quality of the living arrangements and services for which he had implicitly contracted.

Paine started by contrasting Carver's accommodations with his earlier situation: the $4 a week he paid Carver was $1 less than he had paid his previous landlord, but he "had not the same convenience of a room" and supplied his own liquor. Paine further complained that he had received substantially less service for the money. "The things which Mrs. Palmer [a traveling companion who occasionally boarded at the same house as Paine] did for me were those which belonged to the house to do, making the bed and sweeping the room," Paine charged, and when Mrs. Palmer was not available, he "had a great deal of trouble to get it done; the black woman said she should not do anything but what Mrs. Carver told her to do, and I had sometimes to call John from his work to the servant-woman's work, and your wife knew it." Furthermore, Mrs. Carver did not defer to her boarder: "she did not send me my tea or coffee till every body else was served and many times it was not fit to drink." Paine knew his rights as a boarder. "There ought to have been a fire in the parlour," and Carver himself "ought not to have left me the night I was struck with the apoplexy."[47]

Carver indignantly responded that Paine made unreasonable demands on both the household's budget and its labor. Claiming that he had been an attentive landlord, taking responsibility for Paine's not infrequent episodes of inebriation, Carver reminded his boarder that nursing customarily carried an extra charge. Furthermore, it was "a well-known fact that you drank one quart of brandy per day, at my expense," Carver observed. "Is not this a supply of liquor for dinner and supper?" In his landlord's eyes, Paine had tried to destroy his own "domestic tranquility" by insulting Mrs. Carver—"one of the foolish epithets you attempted to stigmatize her with was that she originally was only the character of a servant."[48]

Carver offered to render an accounting of the costs of services to justify the price. He claimed $150.60 for thirty-four weeks' board, and he reminded the author of *The Rights of Man* of one source of the value he had received: "You know very well when you came I told you I must hire a servant girl if you staid with me. This I did for five months time at five dollars per month and her board." Beyond the servant's wages of $25 and found, Carver and Paine quarreled over the just price of accommodations, heat, food, liquor, and respect.[49]

While the market relation between householders and boarders may have preserved vestiges—however strained—of the integrated household, it also laid a new foundation for the intersection of the household economy and the wage economy. In his reminiscences, the nailmaker Grant Thorburn described the experience of arriving in the city in 1794 and negotiating the twin market conditions of employment and housing. Thorburn claimed that he and his brother landed with 6½ cents in their pockets; their first action was to secure money through wages. If the Thorburns had not been able to find employment quickly, they probably would have stayed at a waterfront boardinghouse and used their trunk and other possessions as security for the delayed payment of rent.

A devout Presbyterian, Grant Thorburn considered it the working of Providence that he did not go on shore the first day his ship docked. When people came on board "inquiring for friends or news," Thorburn made his own inquiries. "I asked an Edinburgh man who came on board and who had been in New York above a year if he thought my brother and I could get employment to make nails; he said he thought not, as they had just got a machine set up for cutting nails out of iron hoops." Such new inventions threatened to render worthless the skills that some journeymen had spent years acquiring. When three other gentlemen came on board, however, Thorburn's fortune turned. "The first enquired for a farmer's servant, the second for a servant woman, and C. asked if there were any nailmakers on board." "C." was a hardware merchant who supplied work space and materials and paid his employees for nails to be sold in his store. Like many merchants, he undertook to control the production of the merchandise he needed, but only as a subsidiary enterprise.[50]

When the Thorburns ventured forth the next day to pursue this lead, they encountered another kind of artisan entrepreneur, a man who ran a shop with places for twelve nailmakers to work. The Thorburns examined the shop and found only one person working there, "all his men having gone to sea about two weeks before at the raising of the embargo." Even as employers competed with one another for workers, shipping pulled many good hands out to sea. To attract new employees, the second nailmaker was forced to raise his prices, offering "a penny a pound [more] for making nails than ever had been given before." But Thorburn and his brother preferred their first offer because the proprietor and his wife were "Scotch folk" and the brothers could have a shop to themselves, thereby avoiding being "exposed to bad company." Making their decision on the basis of working conditions, the brothers also bargained up the price of their labor by persuading "C." to meet his competitor's bid.[51]

Having secured employment, the Thorburns then engaged to board with the family of a Scotch journeyman carpenter whose "wife kept a few boarders." The shoemaker who owned the house and occupied the first floor at first objected to his upstairs tenants' taking boarders. Thorburn remembered that "our appearance and the appearance of a cart stopping at the door loaded with our moveables [a large chest containing clothes, a box of books, and a mattress] drew out the wrath tongue and body of Mr. B [the shoemaker] to the street. He declared that our trash should not enter the house, that B—n [the carpenter] hired the rooms above from him and he should not bring any of his dirty Irish into the house." "Had he called us lousy Scotch I would have forgot it," Thorburn concluded, "but I could not swallow being called dirty Irish."[52]

The Thorburn brothers shared the attic with three of the carpenter's sons: "B—n's people were poor and as they had not a spare bed," the Thorburns "laid our mattress on the floor and made a bed with our clothes." The Thorburns moved in on June 18, but on the first of August the journeyman carpenter and his family "moved to the upper part of the city," to the vicinity of Chambers Street. The brothers then found board with "an old American lady, a widow, and her daughter [and granddaughter] who lived in an old wood shed" at the unpaved western end of Liberty Street, two blocks from the workshop. Thorburn remembered that he found these women far better cooks than those in his previous household, but this second household too partook of "the rage for moving uptown" (to St. James Street, three-fourths of a mile north), so in October the brothers were again seeking domestic accommodations.[53]

Thorburn described the third boarding arrangement he made in his first six months in the city as a further manifestation of Providence, for it led to his first marriage. In the morning on his way to the nailshop, he had noticed a woman turning the corner on Broadway to go to the

Battery for fresh air before starting her working day in a mantua maker's shop. Later, when he observed her father's funeral, Thorburn saw an opportunity for housing: "I thought to myself thus: The widow is poor, the daughter is of age, they must have two beds while the husband lived; now the mother and daughter may sleep in one, and perhaps they may board and lodge us to assist them getting a living." A carriagemaker who occupied the ground floor of the widow's house arranged for the Thorburns to board, but rather than persuade the women to reorder their own sleeping arrangements, the brothers received quarters in the attic.[54]

The households in which the Thorburns found accommodations did not conform to the system that merged property and labor relations under the authority of a male head. Both the American widow and the Scotch shoemaker rented the property they occupied and in turn took boarders to supplement their income. In Thorburn's experience—as in Tom Paine's—keeping boarders was an enterprise in which women exercised household authority. Boarding was also a transient housing condition. Moving uptown to escape yellow fever or the high rents of the wharf district, the Thorburns' landlords felt no obligation to consult their boarders or to give long notice. Similarly, journeymen boarders had little to say about the quality of their food or sleeping accommodations; young wage earners were not expected to require much personal space.

The Thorburn brothers had themselves traveled as a "household," determined to establish each other's security. For two years they consulted each other, made nails together, boarded together, and pooled their labor, expenses, and earnings. When Grant's brother became ill, they "hired a small store, having saved about $100; we laid it out in small hardware and got $50 more on credit consisting of pens, needles sissors knives etc. My brother was to attend the store and I was to make nails to support us." The brother, however, "got tired of attending the store and went off to Philadelphia." Faced with the prospect of going it alone, Thorburn courted his landlady's daughter, "calculating that if I got married I would have a shopkeeper of my own." For Thorburn, as for many New York wage earners, control of a wife's labor represented a key strategy for transforming the conditional proprietorship of tenancy into personal independence.[55]

Setting up "housekeeping" and a workshop, Thorburn found quarters to rent in "a small wooden building #22 Nassau street having only a ground floor." He partitioned the space into "a store, kitchen and bedroom which also served for our parlour." Thorburn allowed 6 by 12 feet for "the room in which we lived," furnished with "a bed and bedstead, one pine table (value fifty cents), three Windsor chairs, a soup pot, tea kettle, six cups and saucers, a griddle, frying pan and brander." He continued to make nails while his wife served customers (in addition, of course, to performing the other household "duties" for which Thorburn had paid as a boarder). When his wife died three years later, leaving Thorburn with a two-year-old son as well as "the care of a house and store," he decided "it more credible and wise to marry a wife than hire a housekeeper, [and] again entered into that state in 1801."[56]

Writing the narrative of his life in the Franklinesque tradition, Thorburn sought to demonstrate that hard work, personal virtue, and Providence had combined to pave his way to wealth as a seed merchant. Far from viewing the conditions of labor and property as antagonistic, he, like most New Yorkers of his generation, understood them to be necessarily integrated within a personal economy that subsumed the individuality of dependent family members. The "private economical relations" of the household still stood at the heart of social economic relations. Such individuals regarded tenancy as a temporary condition. But within the city's larger social landscape, the expansion of tenancy marked new divisions of city property and labor relations.

The Emergence of Tenant Housing

The houses that New Yorkers moved through accommodated two labor systems—found and waged employment—throughout much of the nineteenth century. The ascendancy of the free labor market and cash boarding, however, laid one foundation for the formation of New York City's rental housing market. The wages of thousands of "unattached" journeymen and laborers represented a new source of rent revenues to rentiers and landlords.

The dissolving social relations of integrated household economies, and particularly the demise of proprietors' authority, also introduced new problems in the management of the labor and housing markets. Just as employers sought to assert a new order of "industrial work discipline" in place of craft customs, landlords needed a system of disciplined rent collection. Even in the eighteenth century, New York had been a difficult town in which to collect rents. The rental market was especially chaotic during the war years, when Trinity Church's rent collection, for example, had dropped from £1,040 to £63 in three years, and the British had seized patriots' houses and assigned them to royalist refugees. The war's fires and cessation of construction had precipitated a major housing shortage in the late 1780s, when waves of people began to settle in the city.[57]

Boarding, which provided householders with cash income in an inflationary economy, also provided rentiers and landlords with a resident rental agent to collect young wage earners' rents. Thus boarding linked subdivided house spaces into the tiered tenure system that passed rents up the economic ladder from house tenant to leaseholder to landowner. At the same time, by breaking down the unified household economy, cash boarding introduced new flexibility into the use of houses.

Boarding's designation of separate rooms to produce rental income prefigured the systematic separation of quarters within houses for unrelated tenants. Following the Revolution, house owners and leaseholders accelerated the process of subdividing and marketing separate parts of houses. Advertisements, especially for houses in the city's lower wards, reveal this process of "filtering" and internal adaptation. In 1800, for example, a householder advertised a "furnished drawing room with a bed room and use of a kitchen"; and a notice in 1806 announced the availability of "the upper part of that convenient three story house 98 Cherry Street with the use of the kitchen." Another advertisement also reflected the shift from boarding to lodging by offering "a front Compting room and also parlour and two bedrooms with or without board in a respectable family," making no reference to kitchen privileges. Many shopkeepers and artisans rented out floors or rooms in houses that they themselves continued to use either as shops, domestic quarters, or both. In 1807 the booksellers J. and T. Ronalds advertised the "upper and back part of the House 188 Pearl Street" where they had their shop. The part for rent contained "ten large rooms, a very convenient kitchen and cellar. The house has been new painted and paper[ed,] with a new slate roof over the whole; and is worth the attention of a private family or person keeping Boarders." The booksellers either owned or leased domestic quarters in another area of the city. Though most of the buildings advertised had been built to the same floor plans in the same area of the city within the same twenty-five-year period, there was little uniformity in their patterns of occupancy.[58]

The reorganization of houses for the rental market also prompted the addition of kitchens for separate families, as we can see in an 1809 notice for a "neat convenient house in which are six rooms and two cellar kitchens." Some existing housing stock was adapted to multiple occupancy by, as one advertisement noted with respect to a two-story house with six rooms and a garret, being "so constructed that it may be raised another story." The change in the internal spatial organization of houses and the creation of rental apartments was seen in new houses as well as in subdivided old ones. In 1800, "several very genteel rooms and a kitchen" were advertised for rent within a "new three Story house."[59]

Eighteenth-century artisans and laborers had frequently shared houses and shops as a strategy to meet rents, but the filtering of houses into separate apartments introduced a new relation among persons who occupied the same house. Tenants who rented rooms with access to the kitchen or with no provision for board had no ties to the proprietor's household. Even when the landlord resided on the premises, the payment of cash rents and the recognition of distinct quarters established the conditions of market "anonymity" between the "producers" and purchasers of domestic quarters. And increasingly, house owners and leaseholders were nonresident landlords who managed their properties as investments and subdivided old housing stock when they could not find a single tenant to take the entire premises.

Boarding and the subdivision of houses for multiple tenants met the needs of growing numbers of New Yorkers for domestic quarters in the twenty-five years following the Revolution. At the same time, flexibility within the housing market and in the use of buildings allowed such tenants as Thorburn to maintain an integrated household economy and to use housing for their trade without encountering prescriptive definitions of "the home" as a specialized domestic space. T. M. Brantigam expressed the uncertainty of the mixed commercial and domestic rental market and the indeterminacy of housing forms when he advertised "a good front Store, different floors in a central stair case, and large dry cellar, and large Stable and warehouse with good lofts over," and then added, "May at very little expense be made a comfortable dwelling house and store."[60]

Despite their flexibility and ad hoc character, wage earners' housing arrangements in the decades following the Revolution became a systematic source of rental income for the city's landlords. While the city's most prosperous citizens concentrated on land investments, rental housing attracted the more modest savings of the city's successful artisans and shopkeepers, as well as of merchants. In the early decades of the nineteenth century, tenant districts rose from within wooden and brick-front houses erected by independent artisan households that had once leased land and built houses to accommodate their own integrated trade and domestic economies. Although the housing market emerged out of traditional practices within the city's "productive classes," the flow of rental revenues—like the labor market itself—differentiated the economic positions of artisans within the same trade.

Although wage earners' rents for domestic quarters delivered new profits out of land and housing, the housing market was dominated by those New Yorkers who, in separating their domestic and trade quarters, could afford to control the property of both. Wage-earning tenants encountered their employers and their landlords as members of the same proprietary class, a class that journeymen expected to join with age and pursuit of a well-managed, virtuous life. Yet even as propertied New Yorkers themselves embraced "modern dwellings" as a new kind of commodity, it became apparent that the landlord's power to appropriate part of the value of a tenant's wage in rent was also the power to reduce the tenant's income and savings. As the prices of land and housing rose, competition for steady employment increased, and apprentice training declined, more and more wage-earning New Yorkers faced landed property not as a means but as an obstacle to personal independence. In the first quarter of the nineteenth century, the contours of these new property relations became most readily visible in the formation of New York City's first "residential" neighborhoods.

CHAPTER 3

"Unlike Republican Simplicity":
The Shaping of a New Social Landscape

IN THE EARLY DECADES of the nineteenth century, European travelers wrote numerous accounts of the American experiment in republican democracy. Visitors to New York City tried to imagine themselves moving into the social economy of the port and offered prospective emigrants their assessment of the attractions and problems of settling in the city. The reviews were mixed: some travelers reported a wealth of opportunity for hard-working artisans and their families; others, such as Isaac Holmes, wondered whether in the end an emigrant could improve on conditions at home. Peter Nielson, a visitor who took as emblematic the elegant dwelling of a grocer—with silk curtains "worth half a ton of bacon"—could only conclude that the appearance of city houses was "very unlike Republican simplicity."[1]

European visitors commented ironically on visible domestic luxury that contradicted their expectations for a society rhetorically committed to republican principles. During the Revolution, patriots had defined themselves in opposition to the privilege and rank that bred parasitism and corruption in the imperial system. Patriots' strategies of nonimportation and domestic production, as well as their rejection of sartorial display, the theater, and other customs of formal socializing, all projected a republican aesthetic of simplicity. Thus Europeans expressed surprise at displays of wealth that suggested a presumption, albeit on more parochial grounds, to an Old World social hierarchy. Yet, despite the popularly expressed contempt for privilege, not many American patriots could be characterized as levelers. By the 1790s, radical New York republicans' brief venture into the redistribution of wealth—the confiscation of loyalists' land to dismantle Hudson Valley monopolies and to punish supporters of the Crown—had been contained within the constitutional abolition of "feudal tenures," primogeniture, and entail as unrepublican constraints on the circulation of property.[2]

The republican language of independence extended from colonial liberation to personal opportunities for a comfortable livelihood. Such patriot leaders as Tom Paine and Thomas Jefferson had rested their vision of civic independence—a social order in which virtuous citizens worked as equals to contribute to the commonwealth—on the bedrock of individual proprietorship. In a more pietistic mode that drew on dissenting Protestant discourse, republican thought identified three personal attributes as necessary if a man was to achieve the material conditions of civic independence. Skill and application at a trade provided the admission ticket to the republic. Another moral economic precept called on citizens to organize and manage their domestic economies with habits of thrift that secured savings. Finally, republican citizenship required that individuals maintain their personal character with dignity and establish a reputation for honesty, which also secured access to credit. With earned income, savings, and credit a citizen could attain and maintain proprietary independence as the just reward of virtue and industry.[3]

Republican speakers attacked rank, privilege, hoarding, parasitism, monopoly, engrossment, and usury. The accumulation of property through providence and hard work, however, stood outside republican censure. Rather, wealth carried with it heightened obligations of public service and benevolence.[4] Nor did many republican leaders question closely the relation of proprietary independence to the enforced dependency of others, be they wives, children, servants, or slaves.

In eighteenth-century natural rights theory, men's exclusive rights in the property of their own labor established the legitimacy of the social institution of private property. Yet by the early nineteenth century, "property" itself represented increasingly complex relations as claims to the uses and benefits of resources assumed competing and often antagonistic forms. The tortured republicanism of southern agrarians—as well as that of many New Yorkers—invoked white supremacy and planter paternalism to overcome the contradictions of a system that rendered the property of human labor "chattel." Northeastern agrarian republicans, though continuing to speak of property—primarily land and livestock—as the means of sustenance, faced the prior claims of creditors, tax collectors, and, in New York, rentiers. Among merchants, letters of credit had dissolved property rights in commodities into an exchange of promises.[5]

Throughout the Eastern Seaboard, the organization of land as "real estate"—just another commodity to be bought cheap and sold dear—

Corner of Greenwich Street. Watercolor and pencil on paper by Baroness Hyde de Neuville, 1810. Phelps Stokes Collection; Miriam and Ira D. Wallach Division of Art, Prints, and Photographs; The New York Public Library; Astor, Lenox, and Tilden Foundations.

stood at odds with a faith that viewed proprietorship as a necessary condition of independent living and as the "fruit" of labor. Republican leaders generally embraced the land market as a neutral institution that, by maintaining equality of *access*, overcame the corruptions of rank, family monopoly, and fraud popularly associated with imperial land grants and colonial rentiers. But the social tensions between a land market propelled by ambition for profit on the one hand and common people's aspiration for proprietary independence on the other were nowhere more apparent than in New York City.

As travelers quickly found, New York City's volatile commercial expansion set especially uncertain terms for securing an independent living through proprietorship. Despite sustained expansion of population, shipping, employment, and wealth, New York's aggregate economy fluctuated dramatically in the years 1790 to 1820. In general, the town economy prospered, and it even boomed in 1795–1796, 1800–1801, and 1805. But in 1792, 1798, 1802, 1808, and 1818–1819, recessions, trade embargoes, and foreign wars lowered wages, prices, and profits.[6]

The dominant shipping industry ran vertically through all occupational groups, from merchants, clerks, and shopkeepers to shipbuilders, dockworkers, and mariners. The city suffered massive unemployment during the 1808 embargo and again during the War of 1812. Population not only ceased to grow between 1812 and 1816 but actually declined as wage earners migrated in search of employment. Nonetheless, some sectors—nascent textile manufactures and shoemaking—thrived with the closing off of importation, only to suffer again with the dumping of British goods through the auction system.[7]

Mixed prosperity and uneven development within different sectors of the economy make it difficult to disaggregate the sources and distribution of the republican port's new wealth, which quadrupled per capita between 1800 and 1820. Importers, commission merchants, and artisan entrepreneurs in shipbuilding, tanning, and meatpacking united to form the town's economic and political leadership. Frequently they invoked the language of republican commonwealth to urge that producers and merchants had a mutual interest in fostering economic growth through the simultaneous expansion of foreign and domestic markets and of local craft production. That proposed unity of interest repeatedly broke down in disputes over political representation, foreign policy, the tariff, the auction system, credit, and bank charters. Prospering merchants and artisans, however, found common ground in local real estate investments, ranging from rentiers' subdivision of farmlands and circulation of ground leases to the acquisition of rental housing. In the first quarter of the nineteenth century, with one-third of the city's taxpayers controlling three-fourths of the city's wealth, control of real property separated artisan leaders as well as merchants from the city's mechanics and placed both groups as landlords in a new relation to the town's wage earners. The expansion of opportunity for some New Yorkers rested on the constriction of opportunity for others.[8]

As master carpenters, shoemakers, cabinetmakers, and printers embraced the competitive free labor market, journeymen in those trades protested the demise of traditional craft prerogatives and contested wage levels that failed to meet the rising cost of living.[9] Journeymen charged masters with betraying principles of craft cooperation and thereby threatening the foundations of civic and personal independence. But profit-minded employers did not alone introduce the conditions that established a new polarity between an independent bourgeoisie and dependent working classes. The intersection of the labor market and the land and housing markets introduced social divisions that reached from craft workshops to the domestic work space of new tenant quarters.

Changes in household property and labor relations which transformed the internal organization of New York City housing also altered the social relations among households. At one end of the economic scale, propertied New Yorkers directed accumulated wealth, including rental income, into a new institution of domestic property, the dwelling. At the other end, wage-earning New Yorkers paid out household earnings for domestic space in boarding and tenant houses. Though the integrated house and shop survived, it was these new domestic institutions that attracted the attention of travelers, who saw in their social organization a contradiction to republican principles. Social inequality was not new; the concentration of wealth in New York City had emerged as a century-old trend. But in the years 1790 to 1820, the formation of neighborhoods of propertied and propertyless New Yorkers—and the flow of rent from one to the other—revealed a new structure of class relations within the city's social landscape.

The power to command rents was also the power to reduce the value of wages and of savings. Through the real estate market, propertied New Yorkers exercised powers over the material conditions of life by setting the price of independence and comfortable subsistence. That class economic power, organized through prior social monopolies of land, through new investment strategies, and through the exercise of competitive purchasing power for both commercial and domestic property, restructured the city's social geography. Within three decades, a process that began as geographic displacement—the removal of independent artisans from the territory of the eighteenth-century port— had assumed the new meaning of social displacement, the removal of New York's "productive classes" from control of real property as a means of gaining a living.

Even as a new political economy of wages and rents was reshaping the social geography of lower Manhattan, New York's republican leaders made their boldest statement of faith in equal access to property by ordering land to the north. The 1811 grid plan for the laying out of streets promised to erase the distinctions and powers of prior land monopolies by subjecting private property to a "public good," defined by the Streets Commission. The grid organized the civic landscape to facilitate the distribution of land as well as the circulation of commodities, to accommodate the "habitations of men," and to promote economic growth in which all might share. Yet, as the visions of a republican commonwealth shaded into utilitarianism, the marketing of the egalitarian grid paved the way for the further spatial articulation of new class relations within the Manhattan landscape.

Reordering Lower Manhattan

In eighteenth-century New York City, merchant households had controlled the most visible wealth of the town—the slips, piers, and storehouses that formed the core of the port in the East and Dock wards. Colonial merchants had built their houses and offices on Wall, Broad, Whitehall, State, and Water streets, adjacent to or in sight of their wharves and stores. When in 1769 the sugar trader Nicholas Roosevelt advertised for sale a typical merchant house at "the Lower end of Thames Street, on the wharf fronting the North River," his description stressed the relation of the house to the proprietor's business:

> The conveniency and commodiousness of the situation excells any on the river. It fronts two slips, one of which is near 100 feet broad, and the greatest part of the year is filled with boats and crafts from the Jersies and North River. The house will suit a merchant or shopkeeper, and great quantities of rum, sugar, molasses and salt, with all manner of dry goods, have a ready sale. It is a roomy and convenient house, with seven fireplaces, a large yard in which is a pump and cistern, and a garden and grass plot.[10]

Seeking to attract purchasers previously oriented to the East River wharves, Roosevelt clearly considered his house to be recommended by its value for trade.

Common parlance characterized a shipper's entire business operation as that of a particular "house." Though occupying a smaller proportion of the house than a craft workshop, a merchant's first-floor office and counting room had further maintained the household integration of trade and domestic work space. The most substantial merchant houses organized drawing rooms, parlors, and spacious halls to accommodate the public and family traffic that accompanied successful enterprise and social prominence. Far from ensuring the luxury of domestic privacy, wealth often created its own demands for sharing space with extended kin and visiting agents or officials. Eighteenth-century merchant houses had been among the largest work establishments in the city and had relied on slave, waged, and family labor to serve both the transit of commodities and household maintenance.[11]

Yet, if an adjacent storehouse or a counting room within a merchant's house represented the personal nature of the shipping business, those traditional arrangements also suggested the confinement of family enterprise. As Manhattan shipping boomed in the 1790s and early 1800s, private accumulation itself became an increasingly corporate (though not incorporated) project. Importers and commission merchants who consolidated their operations and their capital into partnerships commissioned new brick warehouses along the East River both for their own use and as rental properties. By 1810, the opening of new markets in the western interior prompted commercial development along the Hudson River as well. Landfill had extended lower Manhattan over two hundred feet on both shores of the island, creating Front and South streets on the east and Greenwich, Washington, and West streets on the west.[12]

With increasing competition for strategically located wholesale and retail establishments, merchant proprietors organized their new building investments to tap the purchasing power of commerce. The pattern on one typical shoreline block on Front Street, between Wall Street and the Old Slip, where eight merchants owned 75 percent of the property, suggests that new buildings such as Isaac Gouverneur's double store, valued at £1,600 ($4,400), were replacing brick-front coopers' and blacksmiths' houses valued at £400. In pursuing profits not simply from the increased volume of trade but also from fixed capital investments in stores, wharves, and houses, Manhattan's merchant proprietors asserted a distinctive class interest in the organization of the city's geography which bore down on the town's "productive" classes. This local deployment of merchant capital impinged not on the organization of craft production per se but rather on the conditions of craft independence. Artisans either had to pay higher, "competitive" rents to maintain their shops or to move to a new location and hope to carry their customers with them.[13]

The expansion of Manhattan commercial interests also involved the development and circulation of instruments of credit and finance— bonds, letters of credit, insurance policies, stocks, and banknotes. Before the building of the Exchange (opened in 1827), New York merchants maintained regular exchange hours, boards of directors held weekly meetings, and brokers and auctioneers conducted scheduled auctions at the coffeehouses of Wall Street. The Tontine Coffee House, built in 1792 at the foot of Wall Street by merchants' subscriptions, became the landmark by which all other commercial activity sited itself for the next twenty-five years. Merchants also established separate offices and counting rooms within subdivided wharf-district town houses to accommodate insurance companies, brokerage houses, and lawyers and accountants. Advertisements in the 1803 *Commercial Advertiser,* such as those offering a "Front Room, particularly fit for an office in Broad Street, near City Hall," and an "Office and Cellar in Pearl Street near the Coffee Houses," identified the streets at either end of Wall Street, which marked the axis of an emerging financial district.[14]

Whether through stores or offices, mercantile specialization of land use pushed many proprietary artisan households out of the East, South, and Dock wards in the 1790s. The merchants themselves, however, persisted. In the first twenty-five years following the Revolution, New York's most prosperous citizens sought to maintain the advantages of residential proximity to the wharf district. At the same time, to distinguish and separate their households from the city's commercial traffic, merchants dramatically increased their level of investment in domestic property.

The city's most prominent merchants and gentlemen investors were the first to express a new sense of collective identity in the siting and organization of their town dwellings. In 1786 a newspaper notice drew the public's attention to the social qualities of the city's first "recreational park," at Bowling Green: "the situation is one of the most elegant in the city," the advertisement declared, "and promises to be, for a short time, the center of residence in the fashionable world . . . the large green in front pleases the eye." The commanding four-story federal-style facades that framed the Green identified it as the residential focal point of the lower mercantile wards. The "neighborhood" spilled over to lower Greenwich Street to the west, to State Street on the southeast, and up Broadway to Trinity Church. By 1795, assessors valued twelve houses on Bowling Green and lower Broadway at between $10,000 and $15,000, with one house rated as high as $25,000—

more than ten times the average value of a Manhattan house and over twice that of the most substantial brick storehouses.[15]

The social life and business affairs of proprietors on Bowling Green and lower Broadway linked their dwellings to prominent merchant houses on Wall Street, Water Street, and Hanover Square. The structure of port business continued to depend on merchants' access not only to their East River stores and Wall Street coffeehouses but to one another's domestic establishments as well. Household hospitality maintained the informal social ties and kin networks that underwrote both commerce and the management of family estates through trusts.

The mothers, wives, and daughters of wealth had a vested interest in entertaining the men who managed their property. In her diary from 1799 to 1804, Elizabeth Bleecker McDonald, daughter of a wealthy Manhattan auctioneer and resident of lower Broadway, noted the daily visiting of her merchant father, brothers, husband, and their associates, who carried on business transactions over tea and dinner as well as in their offices. Another wealthy New York woman similarly fulfilled interlocking domestic and business obligations but under extraordinary circumstances: In 1803, Janet Roosevelt Inderwick separated from her husband, a director of the Bank of New York, and moved into a respectable boardinghouse on lower Broadway. Though she and her husband were not on speaking terms, she returned to his Cortlandt Street house to preside at dinners for his business associates. Her efforts paid off when in 1805 she became one of the city's wealthiest widows.[16]

Dwellings that offered privacy for business and family negotiations also displayed visual evidence to the larger community of their proprietors' ability to acquire and maintain property. In the colonial era personal wealth had been as readily revealed in a slave labor force, in adjacent stores filled with merchandise, or in the luxury of personal possessions—furnishings, clothing, and equestrian equipment. By the 1790s, however, domestic property was taking on its own distinctive characteristics. Merchants' new requirements for town housing were reflected in an 1801 newspaper notice:

> HOUSE, COACH HOUSE AND STABLE, Wall Street, the largest elegant new house, No. 17 for Sale; situated in the most pleasant part of the street, built in the modern stile, with very spacious rooms and lofty ceilings, and finished in the most complete manner. The drawing room is uncommonly large and highly ornamented with stucco work. The porch and window sills and arches are of white marble, and the front of the best Philadelphia stock brick. The yard contains (besides the usual buildings) a brick smoke house,

pump and cistern, liquor vault and ice-house. The whole of the buildings are replete with conveniences for a large genteel family. . . . A Coach-house and Stable, in the rear of the lot, may be had with the house, or not, as the purchaser may choose.[17]

Unlike town-house notices of the previous generation, the advertisement featured the residential qualities of the house—its "modern stile," spacious and ornamented drawing room, marble trimmings, and lofty ceilings. The yard with its carriage house, smokehouse, liquor vault, private pump, and icehouse supported the household's domestic self-sufficiency. Furthermore, notice of the house's situation in a "pleasant part of the street" marked a heightened consciousness of the environs of such houses. Above all else, the "conveniences" of the house for a "large genteel family" rather than for trade marked the creation of a new exclusive identity of the house as dwelling.

Though most town houses in lower Manhattan were still narrow and small by European standards, even the dwellings of lesser merchants expanded the rooms given over to entertainment and domestic work. In 1809 Richard Tucker advertised a typical genteel house, "well calculated for a large family," with a "large dining room and front room for a counting room or office, a large drawing room, five bedrooms, besides two servant rooms, three large and convenient pantries, two store rooms below, a very good cellar and cellar kitchen and two liquor closets." Specification of servants' rooms suggested less a departure from a common use of house space than an uncommonly self-conscious presentation of labor relations within propertied households. It contrasted with the implicit interchangeability of quarters for servants, boarders, and family members in the unheated attic rooms of artisan houses. Another notice suggests other changes in the organization of genteel houses by offering "a convenient well furnished nursery on the first floor," where the office might have stood a generation earlier.[18]

In the early 1800s such artisan-entrepreneurs as the tanner Jacob Lorillard, the shipbuilder Noah Brown, and the furniture maker Duncan Phyfe, as well as lawyers and agents, joined the city's merchants in investing in "modern stile" dwellings and seeking pleasant siting as well as a convenient location. Proprietors of dwellings on Broadway (above Cortlandt Street) found that the width of the city's most prominent thoroughfare could absorb heavy traffic, provide ready access to downtown, and give fronting houses a commanding prospect. Other propertied households escaped congestion by locating their houses along open public spaces—the new City Hall common or the Columbia College campus—that enhanced the ventilation, light, and real estate values of their fronting houses. Merchants and shipbuilders also built dwellings on the elevated ground of Pearl, Rutgers, and Cherry streets, at the northeastern edge of the port.[19]

Still, many merchant houses continued to incorporate the trade space of an office, and Duncan Phyfe situated his extensive furniture workshop next door to his fashionable town house. When we read that in 1800 "the Count Room of Loomis and Tillinghast" removed with Mr. Tillinghast to his new "Dwelling House" on Jay Street, or that in 1812 the merchant Dirck Ten Broeck "removed his office from Wall Street to his Dwelling in Stuyvesant Street," we don't know whether these remergers of commercial and domestic space were aimed at serving their proprietors' own convenience or saving them a second rent.[20] But for most members of the city's emergent bourgeois class, the ability and the need to pay a second rent for housing was part of the restructuring of both commercial and domestic relations with other New York households. And these changing relations in turn entered into the further cultural elaboration of housing necessities, which included secure, controlled, and healthy environs.

In the late eighteenth century, New York's leading merchants began to elaborate their domestic quarters as part of their investment in wharf-district property. Unlike most artisan households, they could afford to maintain domestic establishments in areas that commanded "commercial rents." But whatever the convenience of proximity to stores, offices, coffeehouses, and business associates' dwellings, in the face of commercial expansion merchants encountered problems in controlling the pleasant environs that constituted part of the value of their domestic property.

One source of tension arose from popular uses of lower-Manhattan streets. In the context of the struggle for independence and a volatile postwar economy, New York artisans' and laborers' traditional deference to merchants had given way to assertions of political and social equality. Grant Thorburn recalled one confrontation in which a "mob" of French-sympathizing republican mechanics ("clammen, boatmen, oystermen and cartmen") flooded Wall and Broad streets to demonstrate against the 1794 conciliatory Jay Treaty with England. A group of gentlemen merchants had "looked on the multitude like affectionate fathers beholding with sorrow the frantic tricks of their erring children," Thorburn remembered, and when Alexander Hamilton stepped forward to address the crowd, he was "dragged from the stoop and hustled through the street." In the revolutionary period, propertied leaders had often orchestrated popular crowd politics; but mechanics' expression of collective autonomy in such incidents suggested that merchants and gentlemen could no longer count on the rituals of social deference to regulate their interaction with the town's growing numbers of craft, dock, and transport workers.[21]

The conversion of older merchant houses and stores into mariners' boardinghouses and workshops further limited merchants' social authority within the environs of their lower-Manhattan dwellings. Prosperous artisans who imported wood, hides, and other raw materials for their shops found that they could profitably use warehouse lofts for production. An 1807 notice for a house on Water Street, near the city's busiest pier, suggested such new trade uses of lower-Manhattan property by noting that an alley that rendered the lot "very accessible in the rear makes it peculiarly accommodating for a factory of any description." A former shoe manufacturer, however, recalled the hostility that initially greeted such tradesmen when they tried to convert merchant storehouses into extensive workshops: "Scarcely a decent store could be got for the business. Lofts or cellars were looked on as good enough." When "an old and worthy" leather merchant inquired about renting a store on Pearl Street, "the agent inquired for what purpose it was wanted. Being told the shoe trade, he said the store was the property of a widow and orphan children and he was sure neither he nor they would consent to have it used for such a business, and he added the shoe trade should never have been permitted beyond the limits of the swamp [the colonial center of tanning]." As landlords, most merchants and their agents cared more about the level and security of rents than about the identities and activities of their tenants, but as neighbors, they were concerned that such competing trade uses eroded the advantages of their command of prime domestic and commercial territory.[22]

Although lower Manhattan's wealthy residents were buffered from the traffic of the city's commercial streets by set-back houses and fronting open spaces, their new-style dwellings could not fully insulate them. Elizabeth Bleecker's diary further illustrates the intrusions of city life upon domestic establishments and the tensions of maintaining gentility in the midst of commerce, industry, and poverty. In 1802 Bleecker recorded a bizarre incident that by its very abruptness suggests the unpredictability of encounters: "The girls received a little fright at Mama's [on lower Broadway] as they were sitting in the front room below, some person from the street threw open one of the windows, threw up the sash, and burst open the blind at the same moment—they could not discover who it was." In 1799 Bleecker had discovered that three greatcoats had disappeared from the front entry "that had been unlocked for a little while"; and the diary records

repeated incidents of burglaries at the dwellings of friends and neighbors, particularly the theft of brass doorknobs. Another day Bleecker
came home to find "a mob at the door occasioned by a black woman
who was intoxicated and had a little malotoe [sic] girl with her whom
she had given liquor." Such incidents placed a social tax on merchants'
favored locations and challenged the image of inviolability projected by
their prominent town houses.[23]

The minor assaults on private property recorded by Bleecker had
their counterparts in felt insults to public propriety. Bowling Green,
the focal point of lower Manhattan's first loosely constructed elite residential district, fulfilled the curious prophecy of its own 1786 advertisement and remained fashionable a relatively "short time." By 1807
an observer remarked that "the [City Hall] park and the Battery have
become too common." The proximity to trade and popular use of open
spaces made it increasingly difficult to preserve emerging standards of
domestic decorum alongside convenient access to the wharves and
Wall Street.[24]

The intrusion of the city's laboring people on the domestic establishments of the elite extended beyond unpleasant incidents of burglary
and the boisterousness of Sunday crowds. In 1799 Bleecker reported
that "a black man came up our alley and laid himself down on the
ground." The man was dying of yellow fever, and though he was
quickly removed to the city hospital, countless others remained in the
streets and boardinghouses near the waterfront. Having sited their
houses for maximum convenience to the centers of commerce, merchants faced the deadly threat of summer epidemics along with the rest
of the port's population. In 1792, 1796, 1799, 1803, and 1805 yellow
fever raged in the lower wards of Manhattan, ravaging the sailors'
boardinghouses along Water, Front, and Pearl streets and the shanties
and cellar dwellings of the predominantly Irish residents of Bancker,
Dover, and Hague streets.[25]

In 1803 Elizabeth Bleecker observed the course of the epidemic in
the "lower part of the town between Murray's wharf and the old Slip,"
and noted that her brother James "moved his family out of Water
Street to mama's [on Broadway]—several persons have died near him
with the fever." A week later her brothers removed their offices from
Water Street as well, and Bleecker cut short a shopping trip because
"we are afraid to stay much longer in William Street, having one or two
cases of the fever near us." Leaving the city's health officials to debate
whether the fever was contagious, the Bleeckers followed their friends
and neighbors out of town. While those who could afford to leave re-
established their households and businesses in upper Manhattan, in

Westchester County, or on Long Island during August and September, more than 600 people died of the fever in town.[26]

In 1805 the grim lesson of the previous decade and a newly achieved medical consensus on contagion prompted more than 15,000 New Yorkers to evacuate the lower wards of the city, and altogether over one-third of the city's population retired from the port during the epidemic months of September and October that year. Such massive relocation required extensive temporary housing; city officials evacuated contaminated streets and provided ad hoc housing in tents and barracks in Greenwich Village and at Bellevue for people who could not afford to rent temporary quarters. The two-thirds of the population that remained behind, however, could not afford to abandon their households and trades, whatever the risks.[27]

Although notices for New York's first generation of "modern dwellings" continued to feature the advantages of easy access to the coffeehouses and the Exchange, gradually convenience took on the new connotation of not having to relocate during the summer. "Healthiness of situation" recurred as a dominant motif in housing notices between 1790 and 1825. In the spring months especially, newspapers advertised "summer homes" and building lots beyond the wharf district. Even highly successful New York merchants and entrepreneurs could not afford to suspend the regular operation of their domestic establishments for two months a year. In 1803 the merchant John Murray appealed to the new concern when he advertised his house on Broadway: "These premises are calculated for a large family and possess many conveniences not commonly met with, besides being in so healthy and airy a situation as to render retirement to the country unnecessary during the summer." From the other side of the market, in 1807, a "small genteel family" advertised its desire for "part of a house with use of a kitchen—not only the family but the neighborhood must be respectable and in a healthy part of the city where it would not be necessary to remove in the event of the fever." By the second decade of the nineteenth century, to propertied New Yorkers a "respectable" neighborhood was by definition healthy.[28]

Well-to-do New Yorkers had begun to elaborate both the interiors and the environs of domestic property to accommodate the socializing that was inseparable from business. But epidemics cast the social uses and environs of houses in a new light and reinforced propertied New Yorkers' ideas of what it meant *not* to be respectable. The geography of disease followed a geography of boarding and tenant houses that accommodated growing numbers of craft wage earners alongside the port's inevitable and increasing crowds of mariners. Though individually these mechanics might conform to republican prescriptions of hard work and thrift, in merchants' eyes they had collectively lost proprietary masters' paternal protection and certification of a respectable trade identity. Single-family dwellings drew new boundaries between those households that could control domestic property and work conditions in order to regulate larger patterns of social interaction and those households that remained immediately vulnerable to market determinations of health and safety.

As repeated epidemics reoriented New York's wealthy and more modestly propertied citizens away from the wharf district and toward undeveloped land north of City Hall, the experience of yearly evacuations reunited the port and the countryside, the preserve of New York City's landowning elite. In 1794 a traveler had recalled this countryside, with "every commanding eminence . . . occupied by Gentlemen's houses, some of them most delightfully situated." A 1795 survey of the city's "finest houses" listed forty such dwellings located beyond the city limits. Some of the merchants, professionals, and entrepreneurs who laid claim to the countryside may have associated the new geography of their dwellings with the gentility of these eighteenth-century country houses. Yet emulation is not a sufficient explanation for the process by which the city's propertied ranks expressed a new "preference" and associated a new set of cultural meanings with domestic property. A standard of living that to an earlier generation had represented luxury emerged in the early nineteenth century as a new necessity for establishing and securing social respect. That feeling of need came as much from perceptions of the conditions of tenant houses and boardinghouses as from admiration and imitation of the lifestyle of an elite.[29]

New York's wealthiest citizens might have chosen to remain in lower Manhattan, paying one rent on a house attached to their store or absorbing the cost of a second rent in order to preserve the convenience that had motivated their initial location of a dwelling. In this same era in European cities undergoing as rapid growth, elite families—as well as a petty proprietary class of shopkeepers—did continue to reside in central cities. But many of New York's leading merchants and entrepreneurs had found Manhattan real estate a profitable local outlet for wealth; and they recognized both the advantages of promoting residential development and their own superior power and value as a domestic rent-paying class.

The ascendancy of the respectable dwelling and the dynamic of residential neighborhood formation merged an entrepreneurial interest in real estate with a heightened cultural interest in defining and preserving domestic respectability. These interests, predicated on the economic capacity to pay two rents, came directly to bear on housing's earlier organization as an institution of proprietary independence. Investment in domestic property introduced social competition for territory and thus threatened the very existence of the integrated house and shop as an alternative way of ordering housing, labor, and work space. If we look more closely at the impact of propertied New Yorkers' appropriation of the territory of lower Manhattan to maximize rents and their own domestic convenience, we see in the displacement of artisan proprietors a larger dynamic of class formation.

From Trade to Residential Neighborhoods

Most of the city's households enjoyed less power than the well-to-do to choose the environs of their houses. The decision of where to establish a house and shop or where to rent domestic quarters turned less on investment strategies or elaborated cultural needs than on a family's immediate cash income set against the aptly termed "going rents."

As travelers studied the New York economy and social landscape on behalf of prospective artisan immigrants, they calculated individual opportunity by balancing wages against rents. Though the demand for labor pushed New York's wage levels higher than those of other American cities, wages alone did not ensure independent living or comfortable subsistence. In the first three decades of the nineteenth century, almost every visitor to Manhattan found rents excessively high by contrast to those in Philadelphia, Glasgow, and London, and much higher than their own expectations for artisans' material well-being. English visitors especially expressed disappointment and alarm that housing costs seemed to offset the advantages of immigrating by cutting into savings. "In New York," Isaac Holmes reported in 1822, "I have met with some mechanics, who stated that the high price of fuel and house rent made their situation not better than wages of one dollar and one half per day what it was in England."[30]

To make clear to their readers the consequences of the city's high rents, travelers repeatedly elaborated on the stratification of housing according to costs. Between 1800 and 1812, when New Yorkers still defined convenience in relation to the lower wharf district, a particularly fine town house on Broadway rented for more than $1,000 a year, while a substantial brick house on a less prominent but still centrally situated street went for about $700 a year. For $450 a New Yorker could rent a two-story brick-front house across from Columbia College on Murray Street; a similar house at the corner of James and Oak streets, just north of the East River wharves, cost $300 a year, and a small wooden house in the same vicinity $50 less. Cottages on the outskirts of the built town rented for just under $100. Within lower Manhattan, one or two rooms ranged from $35 for a share of an attic to $75 for chambers. Respectable room and board could run as high as $250 a year, while mariners' boardinghouses—accommodating four to six men to a room—charged closer to $50 a year.[31]

The most successful independent artisans, who might earn between $1,000 and $2,000 a year from their trade, generally had enough income to pay rent on a two-story brick-front house and shop north of the wharves or west of Broadway. Skilled journeymen, if steadily employed, might earn roughly $300 to $400 a year. Thus the pooled income of four or five skilled mechanics' households was required to lease the same house that their employer's household might occupy for both trade and domestic use. Laborers, who earned less than journeymen and worked less regularly, might—at approximately $1 a day with maximum employment—be able to pay from $50 to $70 rent, or the cost of a one- or two-room apartment, or a one-story wooden rear house.[32]

This range of wages and rents sorted out the proprietors and tenants of trade neighborhoods within a mile of the wharves in the first decade of the nineteenth century. Locational rent stratifications, of course, had emerged well before the Revolution, particularly in relation to the waterfront. What worried travelers as much as the extremes of rent differentiation within the housing market was that rising rents put accommodations they considered reasonable increasingly beyond the reach of free laboring people and at the same time made it harder for journeymen to save toward the future independence of self-employment. Alongside rising commercial rents and propertied New Yorkers' investment in dwellings, intersecting labor and housing markets were gradually reshaping the city's older trade neighborhoods into tenant districts that presaged new social identities.

In the 1790s, the majority of New York City's paved streets had contained a mixture of buildings and trades with no one house type dominating to the exclusion of others. Many households still maintained workshops and offices alongside domestic quarters; and though property ownership had declined, two-fifths of the city's voters held freeholds worth at least $50. In the decades following the Revolution, New Yorkers had accommodated the bulk of population growth within the territory of the eighteenth-century town by developing previously vacant lots or by building new houses on lots after earlier leaseholders had removed their buildings at the expiration of their leases. But as clusterings of single-family and two-family dwellings (without work-shops or offices) and concentrations of boarding and tenant houses to-gether appeared on blocks to the north of the "central business district," they brought the property of the integrated house and shop into competition with a new market in domestic property.

We can see the social process that translated travelers' calculus of individual wages and rents into a new residential geography by follow-ing the development of one street that stood on the threshold of change. In 1800, Chambers Street—running east and west and facing the city common—offered a prime location for city trade households. It was also considered a respectable address. In that year Harriet Trumbull, staying "the season" in the city, assured her Connecticut parents, "We live in quite a pleasant street—tho it is *quite* retired—they have a very comfortable small brick house." The street was a mile north of the fashionable households on lower Broadway with which Trumbull socialized.[33]

Twenty years earlier, barracks, the bridewell, the almshouse, the hospital, and subdivided vacant lots had stood on the then unpaved Chambers Street and marked the northern edge of the port. After 1785, when Trinity Church leased out lots on the street west of Broad-way for twenty-one years at ground rents that progressed in seven-year intervals from £2 ($5) to £6 ($15), grocers, carters, carpenters, masons, merchants, and laborers all took up leases for both single and multiple lots. The street was paved in the early 1790s, and by 1800 the city directory listed seventy-six houses on Chambers.[34]

The majority of these houses in 1800 accommodated a craft, and more than twenty-five trades were represented on the street. For the coachmaker, wheelwright, and joiner who built their houses and shops on the street, low ground rents perhaps permitted them to direct their resources to more extensive work space. For carters and building arti-sans, Chambers Street offered a strategic location for a journey to work either in lower Manhattan or to the north. Some artisan proprietors, while maintaining their status as independent producers, supple-mented their incomes from trade with wage earners' rents. But with resident leaseholders or landowners occupying approximately two-thirds of the houses and virtually all of the one- and two-household houses, Chambers Street approximated the republican idea of a com-munity of independent proprietors.

Though the houses were scattered on two sides of three blocks—Broadway to Greenwich Street (still under water)—different types of houses were concentrated at opposite ends of the street. Most of the houses occupied by one household stood on the blocks between

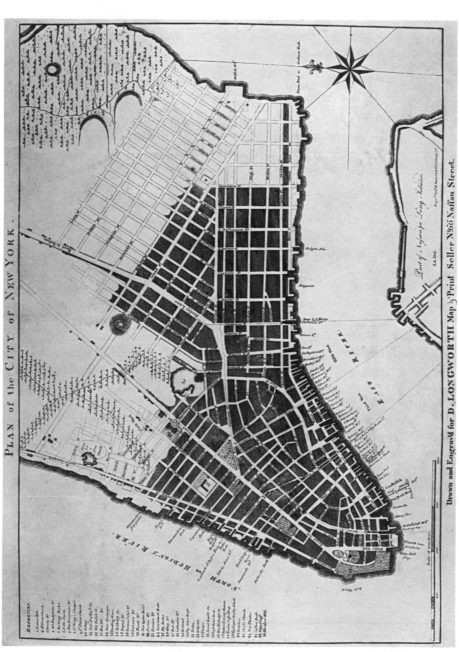

Plan of the City of New York. Engraving by P. R. Maverick, c. 1798. Eno Collection; Miriam and Ira D. Wallach Division of Art, Prints, and Photographs; The New York Public Library; Astor, Lenox, and Tilden Foundations.

Broadway and Chapel Street (West Broadway), with easy access down Broadway to the wharf district. Houses sheltering three, four, or five boarder or tenant households clustered at the western ends of the streets, near the Hudson River. Occupancy patterns were determined as much by level of income or wealth as by occupation. The residents of single-family houses ranged from the widow of the bankrupt financier William Duer (who boarded Harriet Trumbull for a season) to the successful carter Michael Standford, who held the lease to more than one lot on the street.

In a pattern repeated on many of the Trinity Church farm lots, artisans owned and occupied most of the houses that listed three or more boarder/tenant households, but the very listing of multiple residents also reveals the restructuring of previous generations' integrated household economies. If journeymen smiths and wheelwrights who boarded on Chambers near Christian Pullis's carriage shop perpetuated the close association of trade and domestic quarters, the carpenters, marble polishers, masons, carters, and oystermen who boarded together constituted "housefuls" on the street with no common craft ties. A mason and a carpenter provided widows with room and board, and the widow Stillwell boarded an oysterman and a carpenter. Domestics found employment and housing in servicing boarders. Members of the same families—two brothers, a widow and her adult son—also boarded together, pooling wages and domestic labor.

Between 1800 and 1812, the social composition and spatial organization of Chambers Street houses changed, and that change illustrates both the formation of a residential neighborhood on a mixed trade street and the process of geographic displacement. In the intervening decade, proprietors of large or multiple vacant lots on the street subdivided and sold or subleased the land for new construction. In 1806, when Trinity's 1784–1785 leases expired, new leases contained covenants requiring leaseholders to build "substantial" brick or brick-front houses. Merchants and shopkeepers who could afford to commission such housing, as well as speculative builders, took up the new leases.[35]

The 1812 city directory listed 106 houses fronting Chambers Street, 30 more than in 1800.[36] With additional houses evenly divided between single-family dwellings and multitenant houses and with five fewer two-family houses, the trade character of the street had changed. Between Broadway and Chapel, merchants' houses formed a solid residential block front. In the wake of a decade of epidemics, the street offered a healthy location and a ten-minute walk to the business district. The designation of Chambers as a desirable location for new brick dwellings increased rents on the street. The one- and two-family houses of masons, carters, carpenters, and bakers disappeared. No more than five of the street's earlier artisan proprietors remained there in 1812. One, a carpenter, became a venetian-blind manufacturer. Another, a carter who in 1800 had shared his house with one other carter, had taken in three additional boarders by 1812. In all likelihood, some of the proprietary artisans of 1800 moved voluntarily after getting a good price for their ground leases or houses. But the very conversion of Chambers Street east of Chapel to respectable residential status dictated the exclusion of new artisan houses and shops.

As significant as the rising investment in domestic property at the eastern end of Chambers was the intensification of multitenant occupancy at the western end of the street, where fewer new houses had been added between 1800 and 1812. Houses that had held two or three boarders or tenants in 1800 accommodated from four to six households by 1812. Though proprietary carters and carpenters had moved out of the street, wage-earning tenant households in those trades persisted. They were joined as boarders or tenants by families of journeymen cabinetmakers, tailors, and stonecutters. Thus one end of Chambers, west of Chapel, became an increasingly dense tenant block—earning ground rents from wage-earning tenants rather than from households engaged in a trade on the premises—while the other end formed an enclave of respectable dwellings. Only the latter was visible to the eyes of contemporary New York commentators, and Chambers Street remained a reputable address for three decades.[37]

A similar pattern of ad hoc residential development recurred on streets throughout lower Manhattan in the years 1790 to 1820. Blocks facing the City Hall common and the Columbia campus on the old church farm claimed a new status with the construction of dwellings; such church farm streets as Church and Chapel followed the western end of Chambers in the shift from a mixed trade to a tenant identity with the subdivision of older craft houses.

Mulberry and Orange (Baxter) streets, northeast of Chambers in the vicinity of the Collect (Fresh Pond), experienced a brief ten-to-fifteen-year history as a convenient location for modest trade houses and shops interspersed with manufactories. The social identity of these streets, like that of Chambers, arose from the interlocking variables of landowners' strategies, the material quality of the houses, and the density and income of their residents. Trinity's covenants requiring proprietors to build "substantial" houses (which "ran with the land") transformed the eastern end of Chambers Street. Land titles, ground leases, and houses on Mulberry and Orange streets, in contrast, had been distributed without restriction through the market since the Revolution, and

many of the modest wooden houses built by the first generation of proprietary artisans remained there twenty years later. Being slightly less
convenient than Chambers to the town core and closer to the Fresh
Pond manufacturing district with its breweries, potteries, and tobacco
manufactories, Orange and Mulberry streets had attracted grocers, tavernkeepers, and boardinghouse keepers who accommodated a laboring
population. Absentee landlords purchased old artisan houses cheaply
and subdivided them for more intensive occupancy, or they built new
houses of wood with ground-floor and basement stores and taverns.
Edward Livingston, the city's first Jeffersonian mayor, for example,
owned eight wooden tenant houses on Orange Street.[38]

In contrast to Chambers, where three-fourths of the dwellings and
shops accommodated one or two households in 1812, fewer than half of
the 107 listed houses on Mulberry were occupied by one or two families. These proprietary households tended to cluster in groups of three
to six, set apart from the houses with from three to seven tenant households which framed them on either side. Not only did Mulberry contain more mechanics' boardinghouses than Chambers; the households
of wage-earning carters, shoemakers, carpenters, blacksmiths, and laborers who had migrated to the western edge or away from Chambers
Street by 1812 continued to dominate Mulberry and Orange streets.
By 1820 these streets formed the spine of Five Points, which was to
become the city's most notorious tenant district.[39]

The history of these streets illustrates three aspects of the formation
of residential neighborhoods in the early nineteenth century. First,
within lower Manhattan, wedges of both single-family dwellings and
boarding or tenant houses replaced an older generation's integrated
houses and shops on mixed trade streets. Second, the steady rise in
land prices and rents which accompanied the twin processes of commercial and residential specialization pushed proprietary artisans to
take in more boarders, to subdivide their houses, or to move to entirely new areas of the city. "Commercial" and "residential" rents, however, remained ambiguous categories: if such landowners as Trinity
Church recognized that substantial brick dwellings generated higher
returns than artisans' wooden houses and shops, in some investors'
eyes subdivided tenant houses were a form of commercial property
that competed with stores and dwellings through the sheer concentration of domestic rents. Finally, the ad hoc interjection of residential
clusters in streets with trade histories placed sharply constrasting domestic quarters within close proximity of one another.

The spatial and social reordering of lower Manhattan in the late eighteenth and early nineteenth centuries set the stage for patterns of

residential development to the north. By 1825 the geographic center
of New York's population had moved well beyond the concentration
at the port. Whereas in 1800 nearly two-fifths of the city's 60,000
people lived in the lower four wards (below Chambers), by 1825 only
one-fourth of the city's 166,000 people lived there.[40] The process of relocation, settlement, and neighborhood formation north of
Chambers began in the same incremental and ad hoc manner as
the filling in of lower Manhattan; proprietary artisans led the way,
building houses and shops and boarding aspiring journeymen. But as
the market for respectable dwellings gained strength, merchants
and artisan entrepreneurs as a class exercised their purchasing power
to claim particular blocks for exclusive domestic use. And as land
prices rose, skilled wage earners as a class lost purchasing power, that
is, the means to establish and maintain the trade neighborhoods that
embodied the ideal of proprietary independence. New and competing uses of city land structured a real estate market that subverted
and recast the republican ideal of independent proprietorship. Still in
1811, as officials prepared the terrain north of Chambers for new settlement by adopting a street plan, they embraced that market as the
surest mechanism for guaranteeing access to the resources of land and
housing.

The Vision of a Republican Landscape

As population growth, rising rents, and the quest for healthy or controlled residential environs pushed New Yorkers beyond Chambers
Street after 1800, city aldermen confronted the problem of how to organize and open new streets. Through the 1780s and 1790s, the uncertainty of competing surveys and plans and fluctuations in the real
estate market had made street openings an especially acrimonious local
issue. Furthermore, rentiers who controlled large estates had drawn
up their own plans and in some cases opened "private streets" that
directly challenged public authority and sovereignty. Uncertain of their
ability to claim or enforce the municipal corporation's power over street
regulation, aldermen turned to the New York State Legislature for
help. In 1807 New York lawmakers established a commission with "exclusive power to lay out streets, roads, and public squares" above
Chambers Street in a manner that "shall seem most conducive to public good," and "to shut up or direct to be shut up any streets or parts
thereof which have been heretofore laid out and not accepted by the
Common Council."[41]

The strategy of turning over to an administrative body power to make permanent decisions regarding the organization of the city landscape was reminiscent of the politics that had led to the appointment of a Commission of Forfeitures to oversee the confiscation of loyalists' estates. Assuming a quasi-judicial role, a commission could declare itself above politics and special interests. Indeed, the Streets Commission could claim unusual bipartisan support. In a period marked by intense factionalism, the Jeffersonian governor Morgan Lewis appointed three Federalists recommended by the Board of Aldermen: former New York senator (and ambassador to France) Gouverneur Morris; the state surveyor, Simeon De Witt; and John Rutherford, a former New Jersey senator who had also served as clerk to the Trinity Church vestry. Such men could most easily command the respect (and acquiescence) of the large Manhattan landowners whose prospects they were determining.[42]

In 1811 the street commissioners filed the plan that prescribed the pattern of Manhattan's future development. Twelve avenues 100 feet wide running north and south were to be crossed at right angles by streets 50 to 60 feet wide running east and west (with fifteen cross streets of 100-foot width placed at roughly half-mile intervals). These streets created rectangular city blocks of approximately 200 by 610 to 920 feet, which could accommodate from fifty to seventy standard town lots (of 20 to 25 by 100 feet). In adopting the grid, the commissioners followed and extended the twenty-year precedent established by aldermen, as well as by many large landholders below 14th Street, who had demonstrated a predisposition for rectilinear streets.[43] But in their remarks explaining the plan, the commissioners went beyond an appeal to precedent and laid out the principles that they believed should govern public policy for organizing the city landscape.

If the social prominence of the commissioners reinforced their authority with New York City's rentiers, the plan they submitted surely established their republican credentials with the city's lesser proprietors. As a political and aesthetic statement, the grid plan embodied the principles of republican simplicity. The grid's national and agrarian equivalent, the 1785 Northwest Ordinance, contrasted sharply with the irregularities of politics and boundaries which had accompanied land-appropriation schemes under royal governors. Themselves substantial landholders, the commissioners embraced the logic of New York's agrarian freeholders: land should be ordered to clarify boundaries, to facilitate distribution, and to be brought into productive use through independent proprietorship. That these goals also served entrepreneurial interests suggests the ambiguity of the republican conception of the market as a neutral social mechanism.[44]

The grid's geometry suggested a revival of classical taste, which found beauty in symmetry and balance. Its spatial economy, organized around the twin principles of convenient movement and efficient land use, reflected more practical considerations of the city's commercial activity and inflated real estate market. Rectilinear streets simplified travel and clarified location by eliminating curvilinear roads and irregular intersections. Furthermore, rectangular blocks eliminated the waste of unintegrated "gores" of oddly shaped pieces of land. Defending the plan's limited number of public squares, the commissioners suggested that any land removed from productive use was an unaffordable luxury, for "the price of land is so uncommonly great, it seemed proper to admit the principles of economy to greater influence than might under circumstances of a different kind, have consisted with the dictates of prudence and the sense of duty."[45]

Later historians, planners, and critics have denounced the grid as a "speculator's landscape," a mechanical (and monotonous) organization of land which ignored topography and encouraged rapid turnover. Yet if the market served speculators' interests, in the eyes of contemporaries it also preserved small proprietors' access to land by replacing the social powers of inherited monopoly with a "neutral" agent for land distribution. The plan, of course, did create new opportunities for speculation by grounding investors' and speculators' need to know the future relation of lots to the streets. Yet speculators would have benefited from *any* permanent street plan, and many might have preferred a street system that identified more clearly particularly desirable site advantages.[46]

As the commissioners made quite explicit, the grid design for Manhattan streets spared them the political task of justifying to all landholders the privileging of particular sites or features within the city. Anticipating objections, the commissioners expanded on their own "plain and simple" intentions. It was probably Gouverneur Morris (who was familiar with European cities) who felt obliged to explain that the commission *had* considered "those supposed improvements by circles, ovals and stars which certainly embellish a plan, whatever be their effects to convenience and utility"; but the commission concluded "that a city is to be principally composed of the habitations of men, and that straight-sided and right-angled houses are the most cheap to build and the most convenient to live in."[47]

Though the commissioners abstracted land from its topographical features as well as from territories of private ownership, the varying widths of streets and avenues did establish certain locational advantages. For property owners bent on attracting commercial tenants, the flow of traffic defined the relative value—the "convenience"—of particular locations. Avenue widths thus implicitly invited commercial development, but the prospect and accessibility of these major thoroughfares also attracted prominent dwellings. Nor did the plan insulate residential land use: with the exception of already-opened interior streets in Greenwich Village and on the Lower East Side, wide avenues framed every block of the city. With residential containment seldom extending more than a block or two at a time, most Manhattan streets and neighborhoods in the first half of the century retained the distinctively eighteenth-century urban trademark of mixed land use. And in this respect, the commissioners' spatial imagination reflected the historical experience of integrated trade neighborhoods as much as speculators' new interest in development of the "environs" of domestic property.

The commissioners' interest in ordering the city's spatial economy to facilitate circulation and avoid waste extended beyond the ordering of streets and houses; they applied the same principles of "economy," "convenience," and "utility" to propose a restructuring of the city's food markets. In place of the neighborhood markets with limited stall licenses for butchers and produce sellers, they recommended a new system of wholesale and retail linkages. "Dealers" and "those from whom they purchase" would find it convenient "to meet at one general mart; this has a tendency to fix and equalize prices over the whole city," the commissioners explained, and "necessity would teach inhabitants the advantage of deriving their supplies . . . from shops in the neighborhood."[48]

As was true of so much of republican thinking, the commissioners' logic blurred the conception of an aggregate public interest in avoiding waste—"it being no trifling consideration that by this mode of supplying the wants of large cities, there is to be a great saving of time and of articles consumed"—with the principles of personal economy. Showing perhaps particular sympathy with busy merchants who, like most men in this period, undertook much of the household's food marketing, and more important, revealing an entrepreneurial consciousness of waste as a matter of lost opportunity, the commissioners identified as particular beneficiaries a new class of citizens—"consumers": "To a person engaged in profitable business, one hour spent in market is frequently worth more than the whole of what he purchases, and he is sometimes obliged to purchase a larger quantity than he has occasion to use so that the surplus is wasted."[49]

However welcome the grid's spatial economy in promoting access to land or "cheap houses" may have been to independent artisans, New

Yorkers engaged in food marketing—and particularly the politically influential butchers—were not prepared to surrender their control of
trade licensing to "consumers' " personal economies of time. The Common Council rejected the commissioners' proposal for a general food
mart and instead steadily increased the number of neighborhood markets. The significance of the food market proposal lies in the commissioners' faith that a citywide market—whether in land or in food—could,
by dismantling the constraints of prior monopolies, operate as an agent
of efficiency and savings that served a larger public good.[50]

The grid symbolically broke the monopoly of large estate holders,
who had designed "private roads" and their own plans for subdivision,
and it rejected the preemptive advantages that would accompany the
favoring of particular topographical sites. Promoting standard lot sizes,
in conception the grid was an egalitarian plan that opened a neutrally
regulated Manhattan countryside to all comers. Still, city land development did not rest on clarified spatial location alone. Rather, a combination of factors—topography, rentiers' and developers' strategies, and,
most important, the intersecting structures of the labor and housing
markets together introduced wrinkles into the neutral grid which contradicted the commissioners' "plain and simple" vision of row upon
row, block upon block of hard-working citizens' neat right-angled "habitations." Nothing is so striking as the pristine classical order of the
1811 plan set against the spatial fluidity of emerging social patterns of
land use.

Despite the commissioners' claim for the grid's essential economy,
the terrain north of Chambers dictated that it was an economy that
could be achieved only at enormous expense. As part of the project of
organizing Manhattan's future development through its street system,
city officials undertook to reshape the island's natural topography to
support those streets. Hills, rocks, marshlands, ponds, springs, and
sunken lots all threatened to disrupt the commissioners' levelheaded
program for city development by interrupting the flow of traffic and by
erratically elevating and depressing both land and its value.

Grade variations had emerged as one early determinant of Manhattan land use: the eighteenth-century Manhattan gentry had coveted
the prospect of bluffs and river views for their country homes, and the
eighteenth-century poor had inherited the sunken lots. Along the East
River and in the vicinity of the Collect Pond, lots at and even below
water level had spawned the city's yellow fever epidemics. Investigating the geography of the 1796 epidemic, Noah Webster found that Dover Street, which had "been raised, several feet, since the buildings
which are mainly low, were erected," was "up to the middle of lower

story windows, leaving the cellars of the houses and the cellar kitchens without communication to the street" and forming a dike that flooded the yards with contaminated water. Sunken lots and marshes not only bred disease, they also impeded development. For twenty-five years following the Revolution, the springs, marshes, and ponds in the central area of the island between Chambers and Canal streets had blocked the even distribution of population northward, as had the marshes of Rutgers' farm to the northeast.[51]

City officials proposed to do away with these invidious natural discriminations within the grid by leveling the hills and filling in the wetlands. From 1800 to 1815, a series of major public works projects filled in Fresh Pond, Lispenard Meadows, and sunken lots along both shores with rocks and soil taken from adjacent bluffs. By providing laborers with employment and property owners with new land, public officials broadened the base of support for internal improvements. During the 1807 embargo, for example, a Jeffersonian Common Council showed its support for the national policy by hiring unemployed mariners. Though landfill made property usable, however, it did not in all cases render it desirable.[52]

To the extent that natural topography could not be transcended, it formed a purgatory for residential developers. Throughout the nineteenth century the city issued ordinances to compel private proprietors to fill in individual sunken lots, frequently without success. In 1819 the city inspector described "sundry lots on Thompson Street [Lispenard Meadows] as great nuisances in so much that some new houses built on that street are in danger of having their foundations undermined and the buildings thereby impaired or destroyed." With the water level on landfilled lots less than eight feet below the surface, moreover, the cellars of their buildings flooded regularly. The problem of rapid deterioration of houses on sunken lots was solved socially by the expedient of letting the laboring poor continue to reside on streets that fell from investors' grace. The city's black households found the only housing they could afford on streets of the Fifth Ward (Lispenard Meadows) and of the Sixth Ward which had never been securely reclaimed from marshes, springs, and the Collect.[53]

The leveled grid plan presented a different kind of problem to members of the city's elite and to the speculative builders who sought to tap and organize the new market for respectable dwellings. Uniform rectangular blocks offered little in the way of distinctive sitings or protection from commercial intrusions. Though dwellings fronting Bowling Green and the City Hall common had demonstrated the advantage of open spaces, the only public square designated by the 1811 plan south of 34th Street was the paupers' burial ground of Washington Square. It fell on landowners and builders to create vistas of respectability through architecture and private covenants and eventually (as we shall see) through modification of the city street plan. This process marked the rapid shift in the conception of "utility" from the commissioners' emphasis on "cheap and convenient" housing to the deliberate promotion of rising land values and elite residential development as a key arena of local economic growth.

In 1804 the Trinity Church vestrymen, always alert to new possibilities in the real estate market, had introduced a model for the development of respectable neighborhoods based on London's Georgian residential parks. Deciding to build St. John's Church in a still-swampy area of the old church farm occupied by scattered artisan houses and shops, the vestry had petitioned the Common Council for permission to enclose a square. In 1807 the council recognized "Hudson Square" (later referred to as "St. John's Park"), bounded by Laight, Vesey, Beach, and Hudson streets, for the exclusive use of residents fronting the park. The church offered house lots on ninety-nine-year leases that included restrictive covenants governing the quality of the structures and proscribing "nuisance industries." The park did not immediately succeed; in 1812, stonecutters and other building artisans continued to reside in the vicinity. But by the early 1820s, Hudson Square emerged as the prototype for genteel residential blocks to the north. "That charming promenade called St. John's appears to be as exclusive as the most fastidious could desire," reported the democratic advocate and publisher Asa Green a decade later. "Belonging we believe to certain persons connected with St. John's Church, its gates are opened only to proprietors, their family or their friends." That is to say, the residential park was not open to the neighborhood.[54]

"All the People of a Certain Sort"

With the opening of new streets, more and more merchant, professional, and entrepreneurial families moved north from lower Manhattan in the first quarter of the nineteenth century. Skipping over the sunken lots and tenant houses of the Fifth Ward, they settled primarily along blocks west of Broadway or on the East Side, along the graded bluffs of the Rutgers farm. In areas that had also attracted artisans' houses, workshops, and boardinghouses, rentiers and developers elaborated their restrictive covenants—in effect private zoning—to distinguish and preserve the "respectability" of blocks within the grid.

Where developers could not provide a fronting park, they created the effect of open space by setting uniform row houses back ten to twelve feet from the street, and they prohibited such nuisance trades as breweries, slaughterhouses, bakeries, and stables, and any "offensive establishment whatsoever."[55]

The use of restrictive covenants to govern land use as well as the structural quality of buildings perhaps seemed especially necessary when the city's elite and artisan households moved north together and thus rendered the social organization of new territories uncertain. When pushed out of the port district in the years 1800 to 1820, craft proprietors, like those who had once lived on Chambers, had turned to cheaper land to the north and established new trade neighborhoods near Corlear's Hook, at the Bowery Village, and in Greenwich Village. Manhattan's Lower East Side developed as a center of shipbuilding and maritime crafts, attracting the households of shipwrights, coopers, chandlers, joiners, and sail- and ropemakers to houses near the Montgomery Street and Corlear's Hook shipyards. Other artisans—printers and stationers, furniture makers and upholsterers, suppliers of building materials and house painters, carriage or wagon makers and hardware merchants—repeated this pattern of craft clustering along particular streets. Such clusterings attracted a common pool of customers to the district and maintained artisans' own convenient access to the materials and skills necessary for the collaborative production of goods. In some areas, prior patterns of land use shaped subsequent histories. The persistence of such "nuisance" processing industries as brewing and candlemaking in Wards 6 and 14, between the Bowery and Broadway, for example, "devalued" the area for uses other than the cheap housing and entertainment of laborers. In other trade neighborhoods, social "devaluation" occurred as part of the process of restructuring craft production.[56]

The most successful master artisans established domestic quarters apart from their workshops in the early decades of the nineteenth century. But artisan employers who did not view domestic respectability as incompatible with trade associations often continued to reside in the immediate vicinity of their shops, and their presence reinforced the distinctive craft identities of particular districts. This seems to have been especially the case in the Seventh Ward, where the strength of the shipbuilding industry within the larger city economy generated high commercial rents from the waterfront yards, and prosperous shipbuilders, sailmakers, and coopers built houses on nearby lots leased from Henry Rutgers. The security offered by Rutgers' restrictive covenants (requiring brick or brick-front houses and forbidding rear houses), as well as the status imparted by Rutgers' own country house, also attracted merchants and professionals to join shipbuilders on such prominent blocks as East Broadway, Rutgers Street, and Monroe Street. The families of small masters and journeymen in the ship-building and ship-repair trades found accommodations in two- or three-family dwellings and boardinghouses erected on nearby re-claimed marshland.[57]

The shipbuilders who dominated the Seventh Ward (like the butch-ers along the Bowery) participated in neighborhood cultures that re-volved around craft rituals and benevolent associations, as well as such civic institutions as fire companies and the militia. Thus, even with the development of separate domestic quarters, masters and journeymen extended elements of craft cooperation into neighborhood relations. The most important element of that continuity, however, was skilled journeymen's own expectations of succeeding to the status of master or to the independence of a "comfortable subsistence." Meanwhile, in the eyes of outside observers, the persistence of employers in the generally neat brick-front houses of Rutgers' Seventh Ward property preserved that area's reputation for respectability into the late 1820s.[58]

The eclectic mixture of wooden and brick-front houses on the old De Lancey property immediately to the northwest of Rutgers' land (the Tenth Ward and later the Thirteenth) followed a different pattern of development, one that more closely resembled the earlier history of Mulberry and Orange streets. Whereas Rutgers sought to use long-term leases to maintain control over land use, speculators who pur-chased the confiscated De Lancey estate sold or leased lots to resident artisans and to absentee landlords who frequently erected inexpen-sive wooden houses and shops. In the late teens, for example, John R. Livingston sold off lots to carpenters, butchers, grocers, ship joiners, and carters as well as to wealthier merchant speculators. In 1824, sixty-one wooden houses went up on four streets of the De Lancey Lower East Side, whereas only three brick and sixteen brick-front buildings were erected on those same streets. Some of these wooden houses were very small; a typical notice described a "neat frame house in Hester Street, containing two chambers, one bedroom, kitchen—with three fireplaces."[59]

The generally less expensive houses of the Tenth Ward De Lancey farm initially sheltered both small shops (with their resident family and apprentice labor force) and boarding mechanics in the construction and shipbuilding trades. Some houses that featured first-floor workshops accommodated tenants unconnected to the trade on the upper sto-ries. Relatively low-priced land and the concentration of wage workers attracted manufacturers to the area. In 1816, for example, a notice advertised wooden buildings at the corner of Arundel and Rivington which were "large and convenient and well adapted to a factory or any other business where horse power might be requisite."[60]

Yet unlike merchants, the city's early manufacturers did not invest heavily in fixed capital improvements. Rather New York's light industry developed out of crafts through the subdivision of labor and expansion of small workshops and lofts, and especially through subcontracting or "putting out." In Manhattan the resource to be tapped was not water power but undifferentiated labor power. Early tenant neighborhoods thus became "industrial" districts in the first third of the nineteenth century as much through the process of house filtering, which concentrated wage earners geographically, as through systematic factory location. To meet high rents and maintain their own independence, proprietary artisans in mechanic wards took in boarders or rented out portions of their houses; absentee landlords managed multifamily tenant houses; and many of the poorest tenant families earned their rents at shoemaking or tailoring in their domestic quarters as well as at neighborhood workshops.[61]

Through these patterns of occupancy, wage-earning mechanics claimed particular blocks and effectively removed whole neighborhoods from the market for respectable dwellings. That power of possession, however, did not represent the craft independence that supported journeymen's expectations in earlier trade neighborhoods. By the second decade of the nineteenth century, the economic stratification of employers, skilled workers, and unskilled laborers was becoming both more pronounced and more systematic. The historian Howard Rock has shown that in six major "conflict" trades—shoemaking, masonry, carpentry, tailoring, cabinetmaking, and printing—both the real income and the social status of journeymen declined dramatically in the years 1800 to 1825. Whereas on average nearly three-fourths of the masters in all six trades earned enough real or personal property to be taxed, only 5.9 percent of the journeymen controlled taxable property, the savings with which they might set up their own shops.[62]

Even for those who did attain personal independence, the struggle was becoming harder and longer. Not only did the ratio of wage-earning employees to artisan masters rise dramatically in the first quarter of the nineteenth century, the average age of journeymen also increased. For more and more city residents, the resources of land and housing no longer represented the means to make an independent living; the only property they owned was their labor. Furthermore, as a class, formerly "self-employed" master artisans in these trades were themselves either becoming contractors or entrepreneurs or dropping back into the ranks of workers.[63]

As the conditions of craft employment changed and the numbers of wage-earning families grew, it was the increasing density of housing and visibly deteriorating conditions of domestic work space, as much as the presence of particular crafts or industries, that shaped the social identities of neighborhoods. In the eyes of commentators, streets in "mechanic wards" took on the social characteristics of their transient wage-earning tenants and boarders rather than those of proprietary masters or specific trades. And by the late 1820s, the dwellings of more and more native-born artisan employers were to be found clustered within predominantly residential blocks, particularly in the Ninth Ward in Greenwich Village, separated from the neighborhoods of their workshops and employees.[64]

As trade neighborhoods dissolved into tenant neighborhoods, "displacement" took on a new meaning. Thousands of New York wage earners changed their place of residence almost annually as their fortunes—the ratio of wages to rents—changed and as their families increased or decreased in size. Most wage earners moved within blocks of their previous residences. Before 1840, the rent bargain rather than the distance from the workshop (what geographers call the "journey to work") probably determined mechanics' choice of location. And as shoemakers, tailors, carpenters, and laborers scattered on blocks between Chambers and Houston streets, the dispersal and interchangeability of trade and domestic accommodations contrasted sharply with the qualities that propertied New Yorkers sought in "respectable" residential blocks. With the withdrawal of employers and the constant turnover of wage earners, groceries, taverns, and boardinghouses came to anchor tenant neighborhoods.[65]

By the 1820s, the process of the republican grid's social differentiation was well under way. Far from fulfilling the egalitarian potential of abundant land distributed to independent proprietors, the neutral market had carried a new class dynamic into the process of residential neighborhood formation, and it persisted throughout the rest of the century. This dynamic rested on three conditions: the artificial scarcity created by concentrated ownership of vast stretches of vacant land; the structure of the competitive housing market and particularly the purchasing power that permitted elite New Yorkers to claim particular blocks for their exclusive use; and the diminishing power of mechanic families to acquire property—in other words, the power of property to reduce the value of labor.

The grid's dissolution of preemptive monopolies—proprietors' power to open private streets—did not alter the conditions of market monopolies. The concentrated landownership that restricted supply rested both on the inherited position of Manhattan's largest "rural" landholding families and on the new acquisitions of investors and speculators. Landowners chose when and how to subdivide and distribute new town lots for housing. Republican sanctions against hoarding did not extend to what were considered to be sound land investment strategies by large and small proprietors. The grid plan offered the possibility of rapid distribution, but New Yorkers who managed real estate as a commodity had little interest in flooding their own market. Landowners pushed land prices up both by the restrictive requirements of their ground leases and—particularly before the 1830s, when the carrying costs of land remained relatively low—by simply holding on to estates when the market was weak.

Then, too, the advantages of accumulated and pooled wealth helped to establish the ground of market competition from the demand side. The vast bulk of wealth from the city's remarkable commercial expansion between 1790 and 1825 flowed into the hands of a select group of propertied merchants and entrepreneurs. Having claimed lower Manhattan for commercial use, this group constituted themselves as a "consumer class" within the land market north of Chambers Street by choosing to direct a portion of that wealth into domestic property. The strength of this new demand for dwellings supported the rapid rise of land prices north of the port and determined investors' expectations for the return on land and housing. Artisans and mechanics who sought space to live and work competed with a propertied class that had the means to pay as well as the power to collect separated commercial and domestic rents. Only through the concentration of wage earners' rents in boarding and tenant houses or through the mixing (rather than the integration) of workshop and housing rents could the city's "producers" generate the social income to establish their claims on land.

Propertied New Yorkers' control of the land supply and ability to determine effective demand raised the price of proprietary independence for the city's artisans. Master artisans' acquisitive ambitions did not alone prompt the restructuring of craft labor relations. New economic pressures closed down alternatives, particularly the alternative of independent household production. In large measure these pressures to reduce production costs arose from competition with foreign manufacturers and with other American trade centers. But pressures also arose from conditions within the local economy: where trades competed with a strong commercial sector for land and credit, employers found that holding down labor costs was the surest means of securing their own "independence."

Within artisan ranks the ambiguous expression of class antagonisms in the first quarter of the nineteenth century rested on the ambiguity of class powers and expectations. The majority of master artisans exercised much less control over the social means of production than the city's merchant landholding elites, and many of those artisans who joined the ranks of the city's bourgeoisie before 1830 owed their rise as much to their position as landowners and landlords as to their status as employers. Only during the depression that followed the 1837 panic did the city's manufacturers establish their power vis-à-vis a merchant rentier elite, and by that time the value of labor had been redefined through a "standard of living" that precluded most wage earners' expectations for personal independence.

By the 1820s, it was clear that the grid's accommodation of the "habitations of men" had failed to fulfill the republican vision of a civic order founded on independent proprietorship. Not coincidentally, it was also in that decade that genteel New Yorkers began an attack on the plan's spatial "avarice" and "monotony" which has continued into the present. "The scythe of equality" had moved over the island, William Duer observed in 1848, ruining its variety and leveling country seats. Perhaps equality does risk monotony, but the failure of the grid plan was more social than aesthetic. Far from establishing the landscape of commonwealth, the grid's development revealed new forces of competition within the land, housing, and labor markets. Market equilibrium failed as an agent of social equilibrium.[66]

Unlike the industrial cities where patterns of class separation emerged in the second half of the nineteenth century, antebellum Manhattan did not develop a highly differentiated class geography reinforced by transportation systems. Yet the forces that determined the initial processes of residential relocation or displacement from lower Manhattan continued to shape distinctive social neighborhoods to the north—sometimes no more than a block or two at a time. New York's economic elite had only reluctantly surrendered their claims to lower Manhattan for residence as well as for business. In the years 1810 to 1840, as they constructed a market for respectable dwellings that merged their interests as both investors and consumers, they chose their locations and restricted their neighborhoods with one eye on the location of the city's laboring people.

Historians have sometimes argued that spatial proximities within early-nineteenth-century "walking cities" reinforced customs of social deference and assuaged class tensions; that through close interaction, rich and poor understood the demands that they could make on one another. There is no question that before 1840, when merchants dominated New York's economy and political system, they exercised enormous influence on both artisan entrepreneurs and wage earners, who were tied into clientage, credit, and patronage relations. Yet economic ties are not necessarily the same thing as social ties. New York City between Chambers and 14th streets remained a walking city, with classes residing on separate blocks still in close proximity to one another. Relations that could not be defined through physical distance, however, could be expressed and clarified through new ways of asserting social distance.[67]

In his 1838 novel *Home as Found*, James Fenimore Cooper suggested the ways in which perceptions and customs of social distance, as much as geographic separation, structured respectable New Yorkers' encounter with the rest of the city by creating the channels of social discourse and obligation.

> "How do you know, my dear, that any one does think himself our better?" demanded the husband.
> "Why do they not all visit us then?"
> "Why do you not visit everybody yourself? A pretty household we should have if you did nothing but visit everyone who lives in the street!"
> "You surely would not have me visiting the grocers' wives at the corners, and all that other rubbish in the neighborhood! What I mean is that all the people of a certain sort ought to visit all the other people of a certain sort, in the same town."
> "You will surely make an exception, at least on account of numbers. I saw number three thousand six hundred and fifty this very day on a cart, and if the wives of all these carmen should visit one another, each would have to make ten visits daily in order to get through the list in a twelvemonth."[68]

Even as Cooper mocked upwardly mobile New Yorkers for abandoning what he believed to be the propriety of deference to rank, he formulated the subjective experience of new class identifications: it was inappropriate for the wife of a prosperous businessman to visit the wife of a grocer or a cartman, though they might be neighbors; and it was altogether ludicrous to imagine the wives of 3,650 cartmen undertaking formal visits. In the early nineteenth century, Cooper suggests, when New York City's propertied citizens could not always control the kinds of households that shared their neighborhoods—"everyone who lives on the street"—they created a community of those entitled to visit one another's houses—"all the people of a certain sort." Thus the gradual melding of social and spatial neighborhoods in the republican city laid the ground for new modes of class interaction.

As Manhattan's land-tenure and labor relations changed dramatically in the fifty years following the American Revolution, the institutions of domestic property—"modern dwellings" and tenant houses—opened new fields of real estate investment that contributed to the closing down of earlier institutions of proprietary independence. The process of neighborhood formation added a new spatial dimension to the marketing of land, housing, and domestic services for profit. The housing market rested not simply on the demand for shelter but on demand for particular kinds of shelter in particular locations. The definitions of these needs in turn rested on cultural perceptions of the meaning of new domestic property and labor relations. Having looked at how the housing market first formed, we now turn to the question of how it was interpreted, and particularly at how the republican rhetorical tradition of proprietary independence was transformed into a new vocabulary of domestic respectability.

CHAPTER 4

The Social Meanings
of Housing, 1800–1840

As THE SOCIAL relations and spatial organization of New York City housing changed in the first third of the nineteenth century, so did its cultural meanings—the values, beliefs, customs, and rules that housing arrangements represented to a larger community. Control over a dwelling—a realm *rhetorically* set apart from the site and activity of work—emerged as a new measure of personal independence and respectability. In 1816 the New York insurance clerk John Pintard, who had once been a wealthy merchant, invoked the language of republican simplicity to express this new sensibility. "I hope you will be able to get up the Frame of your new tenement," Pintard wrote his daughter Eliza Davidson in New Orleans upon hearing of her family's plans to build a dwelling. "A Log House is very comfortable and doubly so when it is one's own. Better a hut to ones self than to dwell in a palace of another. Sweet Independence what a blessing in the cup of Existence."[1]

Pintard's yearning for the "sweet independence" of a private dwelling stemmed from the frustrations of his own situation in New York City. Pintard had endorsed the notes of the financier William Duer, and he lost his mercantile fortune and spent time in debtors' prison when Duer went bankrupt. Pintard later recovered his social status and held positions as city clerk and as secretary to various insurance companies and benevolent organizations. But unlike many of the prominent citizens with whom he did business, Pintard could not afford "a hut to ones self." The trustees of the Mutual Insurance Company had repeatedly rejected their sixty-year-old secretary's request that he, his wife, and their younger daughter, Louisa, be allowed to move from their "found" quarters above the Wall Street office to a separate dwelling.[2]

Even if he could secure permission, "the excessive high price of houses in any favorable street," Pintard reported to Eliza in 1818, "almost makes me despair of being able to purchase one to our liking and we must have patience I fear another year." By the following year, Pintard's plaint had grown more poignant: "I had hoped this year to have provided a tenement, if not to live, to die in. But buildings are so high that nothing like a house in a decent street can be obtained under $10,000, a sum almost insuperable for me." Concluding that he would again seek to negotiate "with my Directors to allow me a compensation for the house I live in, which I fear will be attended with difficulty," Pintard persisted in his "hope of better accommodations for Mama and Sister, who are nearly prisoners during the hours of business in Wall street."[3]

Why did Pintard attach such value to a separate residence in a "decent street"? What was the relation between his perception of the dwelling as an emblem of personal independence and earlier concepts of proprietary independence attached to an integrated house and shop, house and office, or house and adjacent store? How had an earlier generation's ideas about the convenience of a Wall Street location given way to Pintard's feelings of imprisonment? Thinking about the changing cultural meanings and uses of housing requires us to look at the historical values associated with an institution—the home—that many contemporary Americans take for granted.

Historians have often described the "separation" of workplace and home as an automatic part of the process of industrialization in the first half of the nineteenth century. According to the conventional interpretation, as men found employment in expanding workshops, factories, stores, and offices, housing lost its economic function and became a "sphere" set apart from productive relations. All too often historians' representation of "the home"—and particularly of women's activities within it—have assumed a universality of experience and meaning that offers no way to think concretely about how housing relations changed, how new housing needs or desires were socially defined, and how "the home's" new economic and cultural meanings were themselves historically constructed.[4]

"Modern dwellings" and tenant houses were still *new* institutions in the early nineteenth century, and New Yorkers situated, valued, and interpreted them with reference to other social institutions, ranging from the labor and marriage markets to religion and politics. How did different ways of organizing housing to serve different material needs shape New Yorkers' understandings of shared or divided social goals? What place did housing occupy in explanations of city residents'

Broadway from the Bowling Green. Aquatint by W. J. Bennett, c. 1826. Eno Collection; Miriam and Ira D. Wallach Division of Art, Prints, and Photographs; The New York Public Library; Astor, Lenox, and Tilden Foundations.

powers, interests, and obligations in relation to one another? Why did "the home" come to figure so prominently in some New Yorkers' discussions of personal aspirations and social order, and what did housing mean to those New Yorkers who left no record of their home lives?

Before we explore these questions, it is perhaps necessary to reiterate the ways in which housing and home life remained immersed in economic relations. For not the least problem with conventional interpretations of the "industrialization" of nineteenth-century cities is the tendency to treat housing as a derivative cultural "sphere" or arena of "consumption" that merely reflected rather than helped construct the new material social relations of capitalist society.

Far from being "removed" from the marketplace, the home stood at the heart of new property and labor relations. As Chapter 3 suggested, propertied New Yorkers' simultaneous investment in commercial and domestic property structured the city's real estate market, raised the price of independent proprietorship, and undermined the economic viability of the traditional house and shop with its integrated household labor force. High rents kept thousands of wage-earning households in permanent tenancy and generated investment capital for the city's merchants and entrepreneurs. As rent revenues flowed from tenant households into landlords' more comfortable budgets, the resulting housing relations established new conditions of competition, opportunity, and vulnerability within the real estate market and altered domestic working conditions for both groups.

The home—whether within a dwelling or a tenant house—remained a workplace; housework was still an essential part of securing and maintaining a livelihood. At one end of the economy, the historian Jeanne Boydston argues, employers implicitly calculated the economic value of housework when they set the "living wage": cash income *and* the value of women's unpaid domestic labor determined the level of a household's subsistence. Deteriorating working conditions within tenant houses devalued the wage and devalued women's unpaid contribution by increasing their work load. At the other end of the social scale, within a housing market organized to accommodate and display new concepts of respectability, property values rested in part on the labor of maintaining or embellishing dwellings. If her merchant husband succeeded in his "just and natural" desire to purchase a dwelling, Pintard informed his daughter, "then indeed it will look like indep[end]ence & you will not bestow your care & labor on other people's property."[5]

Beyond determining the conditions of labor necessary to maintain both family and property, the houses of both rich and poor New Yorkers continued to shelter *paid* labor. The creation and maintenance of dwellings expanded domestic service as a major field of waged employment and established a new arena of labor conflict. The prevalence of boarding preserved the cash nexus within thousands of homes. And through the outwork system, shoemakers and needleworkers paid employers' overhead costs in their own housing rents. Like the conditions of unpaid family work, these "productive" labor relations within and between New York's houses molded new understandings of the power and value of domestic property as a labor institution.

In some respects, it is not surprising that social historians so seldom analyze these economic relations of housing and home life, for despite lively discussions of high rents, greedy landlords, spendthrift wives, idle servants, starving needleworkers, immoral boardinghouses, and diseased neighborhoods, antebellum New Yorkers themselves seldom directly confronted the question of what these housing issues had to do with the larger structures of social power. Rather, in newspapers, letters, novels, diaries, advice manuals, and city ordinances, New Yorkers presented housing conditions as manifestations of individual or collective morality and maturity.

The nineteenth-century language of housing came to rest on polarized categories—home and workplace, private and public, respectable and immoral, necessity and luxury—that sought to define and fix the cultural value of one of the city's most unstable and tension-worn social institutions. By defining what home life should and should not be, these categories offered a way of classifying and judging people, behavior, and spaces without reference to either social practice or the conditions of social power. All New York houses sheltered work; most were no less public than other institutions—churches, saloons—that accommodated a constant (if sometimes selective) social traffic; and the costs of maintaining a respectable home life encouraged entrepreneurial strategies that surely seemed immoral to their victims. Other concepts incorporated in the cultural definition of a proper "home life"—including a "mature" male provider and a "virtuous" female caretaker—were themselves the products of historical debates. Yet, precisely because rhetorical oppositions deny qualifications and contradictions, they offer a powerful means of affirming shared cultural values in the face of uncertainties and repeated challenges. Indeed, so effective was the language of housing in classifying and prescribing social attributes while denying social conflicts that by the mid-nineteenth century its vocabulary had become a mainstay of the bourgeois language of both class and gender.[6]

In order to understand how these categories assumed their social meanings and cultural authority we must think about the historical process and occasion of their construction. Some concepts of what housing represented (for example, Pintard's invocation of "sweet independence") drew on and recast earlier housing values and practices; others (Pintard's concern with a "favorable street") emerged in relation to New York's new and multiple housing forms and uses. Unfortunately, a twentieth-century social historian writing about the cultural meanings of housing inherits the social distances of the past in the kinds of sources that survive. Thus, whereas the city's most prominent citizens left records that tell us something about how they valued their own home lives and judged those of others, evidence of how the city's middling ranks and especially its laboring people interpreted housing is more fragmentary. It is perhaps a measure of the cultural power of the propertied classes that their definitions of housing's cultural meaning dominated nineteenth-century language and texts; on the other hand, it may have been the tenacity of wage-earning tenants' alternative practices and values that pushed respectable New Yorkers to expend so much energy in asserting the universal moral validity and social utility of their own experience and aspirations.

The Value of Independent Housekeeping

By the second decade of the nineteenth century, New York's most successful merchants, entrepreneurs, lawyers, and doctors allocated a significant portion of their prosperity to the acquisition of housing amenities. Self-defined "respectable" New Yorkers had created a new market for "modern dwellings" in new locations. Controlling neighborhood land use through restrictive covenants, siting, and architecture, the wealthiest developers and homeowners sought to ensure dwellings against the social encroachments that they had encountered in lower Manhattan. Economic and cultural motives went hand in hand: that the project of reorganizing the city's social geography to accommodate new domestic values should also enhance land values seemed proof of the soundness of both.

The process of constructing new standards of domestic respectability, however, involved more than new real estate investment opportunities. The formation of a market for dwellings required widespread recognition and acceptance of the cultural value—indeed, the necessity—of new arrangements for specifically domestic convenience or comfort. What exactly did domestic respectability represent and entail? As new standards of "independent housekeeping" emerged, what happened to housing's earlier cultural identity as a workplace?

Prosperous New Yorkers' increasing capital investment in domestic construction, and particularly in utilities and equipment, dramatically improved the physical conditions of housework. Private cisterns and pumps guaranteed clean water and eased the work of water hauling; the development of first wood-burning and then coal-burning stoves and furnaces made household heating more efficient and cooking less dangerous. Set-back dwellings screened the dust of the streets, and more important, the ventilation, sanitation, and light of substantial town houses contributed to their healthiness and reduced the intense labor of nursing the sick. In the 1830s and 1840s, gas lighting, early plumbing, and central heating further distinguished new dwellings from the town houses of an earlier generation.[7]

Women, who assumed primary responsibility for the production of household services, were the immediate beneficiaries of these improvements. Indeed, the rising investment in domestic establishments marked new terms of negotiation between husbands and wives over the allocation of family financial resources. Wealthy wives contributed directly to those resources through dowries and legacies, which included household equipment and furnishings as well as cash and, less commonly, land. Propertied wives also brought to their marriages social and family connections that opened channels of credit and business cooperation. Such contributions had long established husbands' obligations of reciprocity, but the balance of marital exchange appears to have shifted in favor of propertied wives in the early nineteenth century. New York women who transferred Knickerbocker wealth and local contacts through marriage to migrating Yankee merchants provided the starting-up capital for many a successful port enterprise. Although they were clearly not the only beneficiaries of housing amenities, these prosperous wives claimed new cultural authority in collecting their return in the improved working conditions of dwellings.[8]

For John Pintard, a city-born descendant of French Huguenots who married into the well-to-do Brasher family, the obligation of being a provider was weighted with the guilt of becoming in effect a family debtor. In losing his own and his wife's fortune and making Elizabeth Brasher Pintard a "prisoner" of their Wall Street quarters, Pintard felt he had failed as a husband as well as a banker. And when he failed in negotiations with his employers, Elizabeth Pintard herself ("with her usual masculine resolution") intervened to confront the insurance company's directors and demand that they give her husband an increase in pay (in place of "found" housing) and permit the family to move. In all likelihood Elizabeth represented herself to the directors more as a Brasher than as a Pintard.[9]

Family name, property, and social connections were not the only bargaining chips that wives could use to define and claim new standards of "independent housekeeping." Negotiations over family investment in dwellings as domestic work sites went hand in hand with the restructuring of household labor relations. The abolition of slavery and the demise of found labor transformed the cultural meaning of housing's "private economical relations" and required families to reposition themselves in relation to the free labor market. Even such families as the Pintards, who could not afford improved dwellings, could claim the essential housing credentials of family respectability and independence by hiring servants.

The eighteenth-century definition of a family's (and a wife's) independent social position had rested on the hierarchical organization and integration of trade and domestic labor. In the most successful colonial merchant and artisan households, wives had supervised slaves, who undertook the heavy labor that made houses habitable. Even before the passage of New York's gradual manumission law in 1799, as the price of slaves increased and antislavery sentiment grew, prominent families had begun to hire free servants (as well as slaves) to perform domestic work. Within middling artisan households, daughters had worked alongside young white women servants, who frequently came from neighboring or rural households of comparable social status. For daughters and servants who expected to become artisans' wives (and indeed were regarded as "apprentices"), such employment marked a life-cycle rather than a class position. But as both the fixed status of slavery and the interchangeability of hired "help" and family labor gave way to a free labor market, social hierarchies based on sex, age, and race incorporated new distinctions of wage status.[10]

With the rise of a specifically female labor market, some New Yorkers began to redefine the status of wives' dependency with reference to the emerging conditions of wage dependency. Identifying women's moral character with their social and economic position, republican rhetoric celebrated the virtues of the skillful and dutiful wife as a manager of domestic economy and even invoked marital unity as a model of civic cooperation. By contrast, the waged domestic worker was scorned as an abjectly dependent figure who lacked the capacity for virtue. Thus, when Tom Paine sought to insult his landlord, the blacksmith William Carver, he charged that Mrs. Carver's character "was no better than that of a servant"; and in 1801, journeymen shoemakers complained that master tanners who required that a journeyman get "a regular discharge in writing from the Bause he had worked for last" placed him "on the same footing with a hired negro wench, that must get a recommendation before she can get a place."[11]

European travelers invariably commented on the contempt with which Americans viewed domestic service, which was popularly associated with slavery on the one hand and with the privileges of an unnatural aristocracy on the other. Fueled by mysogynist as well as racist attitudes, daily gestures of contempt enacted ideological aversions to the conditions of waged dependency which domestic service embodied. Women engaged in the coarse work of hauling water and firewood, throwing out waste and garbage, and washing clothes over open fires were exposed to abusive insults in a culture of republican simplicity which imagined female virtue to consist of modest, clean, and "naturally" deferential decorum and attire.[12]

For an independent citizen to require a mother, wife, daughter, or sister to do heavy and exposed domestic labor associated with slavery or "hiring" was to place her outside his own class, implicitly contradicting his own claims to independence as measured by his obligations as a provider. Hiring domestic labor, on the other hand, placed women in a social position comparable to that of the entrepreneurial fathers and husbands who were assuming new social authority as members of an employing class. The realization of women's familial identity as republican wives and mothers further depended on securing their household positions as employers: how could a woman whose own laboring condition contradicted the virtuous qualities of personal independence retain the respect of her husband and children? The presence of servants, then, was essential to maintaining the new values of domestic respectability, which were defined in opposition to the "promiscuous" and dependent conditions of female wage labor. And whereas waged servants performed "work," the wives and daughters who supervised or worked alongside them performed "duties."[13]

In the period 1800–1850, as a new residential geography emerged in New York, domestic labor remained the city's single largest field of employment. As such, it helped shape propertied New Yorkers' cultural perceptions and interpretations of the necessary ingredients of respectability and their relation to a new class of wage workers.

The harsh conditions of waged domestic work, as well as the volatile and often antagonistic relations of domestic employers and employees, contradict images of the home as a tranquil realm set apart from the labor market. Servants were on call twenty-four hours a day; they did the dirtiest and heaviest tasks of housework; their wages were among the lowest in the city; they could not freely socialize outside their employer's house. But as waged workers, servants also asserted their own interests. At one extreme, employers confronted outright rebellion, as when Elizabeth Bleecker's "negro girl" deliberately set fire to their attic. At the other, householders faced the chronic "servant problem" of labor turnover.[14]

In 1818 and 1819, John Pintard expressed one employer's anger at workers who took full advantage of their "freedom" within the labor market. Acknowledging "how much ones existence depends on domestics," Pintard wrote his daughter Eliza that he was "distressed beyond description by unfaithful, ungrateful" servants. It was "vexatious in the extreme" when Sophia left "without notice or reason . . . just when she had become acquainted with our habits," leaving only the "tolerably handy but heedless" fourteen-year-old Susan, who had been brought from New Jersey at $2 a month and found. In the absence of servants, Pintard's wife and younger daughter, Louisa, had "performed every drudgery above stairs," while he himself "had to make office, kitchen and parlor fires, hang on the tea kettles, bring up all the wood and coals, sweep the entries etc." Four months later he complained of Sophia's successors that "life has been embittered and I have felt more like a boarder than a member of a family, afraid to give exception [or] even ordinary commands, not knowing but that at midnight we might have been robbed and deserted by the worthless trollopes."[15]

In Pintard's view, given labor market competition and aggressive employment agencies that "decoyed" away good servants, his problem was one of market position: "Our abode is not very favorable to make domestics contented, being attended with many inconveniences in consequence of the office, wh[ich] supports me." Although it would require exaggeration to argue that New Yorkers invested in new dwellings in order to keep domestics "contented," servants were essential to a respectable household's operation; and Pintard, for one, believed that servants carefully calculated their own interests in securing the best working conditions available. The prominence of "servants' rooms" in advertisements for new dwellings suggests more than the clear demarcation of status within households. Such separate quarters offered both employers and workers the option of spatial retreat within the battleground of the home.[16]

The historical use of slave and indentured labor for household maintenance, the interchangeability of domestic work with free female "family labor," and reliance on youth established the field's low wage scales. Excluded from skilled crafts, Afro-Americans (including men who worked as house porters, cooks, waiters, and butlers) constituted one core of the early-nineteenth-century waged domestic labor force.

The city's prominent families pointed to the history of slavery to assert that Afro-Americans' dependent and servile "nature" made them especially "good servants"; in light of this logic, New Yorkers were all the more mistrustful and contemptuous of white women who crossed the color line of republican independence to work as servants. Although black domestic workers were paid less than whites, they sometimes could turn such prejudices to their own advantage in order to secure work in dwellings that contained new utilities and wealthy employers' ample "leavings" of food and clothing. Indeed, one ongoing source of tension between the city's white and black laborers was the white workers' perceptions of the "patronage" that blacks received from elite (generally Federalist and/or former slaveholding) families.[17]

Knowing their own "value," some black domestic workers (who were more likely to be married or have children than white servants) further negotiated employers' control over their time and personal lives. Pintard's servant Hannah, for example, clearly mastered her employer's prejudices and won the concession of keeping her infant children with her until she decided to leave his household to join her recently emancipated husband. "Destitute of servants and dreading the constant change of unprincipled, unqualified and thieving white women," Pintard sought out another Afro-American servant, Tamar, who had left the family after eight years of employment. Tamar "at length" agreed to return on the condition that the Pintards also hire her daughter Nancy. Even then, Pintard felt he had lost the battle to discipline wage labor within the family circle. Nothing but Tamar's "integrity and care of the House in case of our absence," he had reported after her first departure, "c[oul]d have suffered me to endure and put up with her violent temper."[18]

Pintard was perhaps exceptionally vicious in his constant representation of servants as "worthless trollopes," unprincipled thieves, and "insect vexations." In other households, older customs of paternalism and deference may have absorbed some of the tensions between employers and servants. Yet such characterizations carried larger social implications. Prompted no doubt in part by rage at women who could not be disciplined, employers also impugned the morality of men who "permitted" their daughters or sisters to enter domestic service. That New Yorkers had to rely heavily on the countryside as well as on the city's Afro-American and immigrant (especially Irish) population for its domestic labor pool suggests that both women and men of native-born white mechanic families viewed the domestic employment of daughters as demeaning to themselves. Such a judgment in turn reinforced cultural cleavages within the city's working classes.[19]

Domestic labor relations had other implications for New Yorkers' perceptions and interpretations of social relations in a free market economy. By erasing housing's cultural identity as a workplace and replacing it with the "home," respectable New Yorkers could preserve wives' and daughters' independent status and at the same time reassert women's ongoing obligations to perform domestic work as "family duties." Housing's definition as a cultural rather than an economic institution in turn shaped explanations of the antagonisms between employers and workers. Rather than address issues of the value of domestic lator—including pay and hours—employers framed the "servant problem" as one of morality and discipline. Thus, for example, Pintard joined a "society for improving the character and usefulness of domestic servants," which in 1826 offered a prize for the best tract on servants' "moral and religious duty."[20]

Domestic employers' angry preoccupation with "the moral condition of a class found in the bosom of every family; of fellow creatures heretofore totally neglected and with whom . . . daily and hourly comforts are identified," revealed both their essential dependence on waged workers to preserve the conditions of their own self-respect and a new psychology of class relations. Like all strategies of blaming the victim, attacks on servants as trollops, thieves, and idlers established employers' distance and directed attention away from their own moral accountability for exploitative labor conditions within "the bosom of every family."[21]

The "moral condition of a class" (primarily of women) became a familiar refrain in antebellum discussions of social relations, and although this class language also drew on evangelical discourse, its terms were rehearsed daily in respectable New Yorkers' homes. Republican rhetoric in the early nineteenth century paid tribute to the "manliness" of virtuous mechanics' industry and skills. Despite common law sanctions against trade unions, journeymen could draw on this regard for craft (and white male) independence to assert the legitimacy of their claims against employers. In contrast, repeated characterization of servants as immoral and ungrateful distinguished them as a wage-earning class both from their employers and from the industrious "productive classes." The same accusatory language with which Pintard labeled and confronted his servants reappeared in the 1820s and 1830s in discussions of poverty as the consequence of personal failings of character. Indeed, reformers' roster of the "undeserving poor"—blacks, prostitutes, and idle vagrants—mirrored employers' descriptions of the domestic labor pool. Although white journeymen showed little interest in aligning themselves with black or female wage workers, by the 1850s they too found themselves subject to moral classifications that discounted their economic needs and interests.[22]

The cultural codes of independent housekeeping classified householders as well as workers, but the terms were far less stable. The respectability of the wealthiest New Yorkers, as of the independent artisans of the eighteenth century, rested on the bedrock of property and a dependent labor force—a dwelling and servants. But secure control over these resources was as exceptional in early-nineteenth-century New York as housing arrangements were diverse. Many New Yorkers could readily produce other evidence of their claim to social respect— family or firm name, craft skill, religious affiliation, proper dress and manners. But few could afford a private house; and many could not afford to hire servants. Thus New Yorkers either selectively conformed to cultural prescriptions (often explaining their position with reference to age or life-cycle conditions) or drew on earlier cultural understandings of the meaning and value of independent housekeeping to assert alternative standards of judgment.

The employment of servants was by no means limited to New York's elite households. By 1855, in a city of nearly 43,000 "houses," 32,000 women worked as domestics.[23] Among modestly "independent" artisan or professional households that shared a house with one or two other families, the ability to hire (or share) a servant could signal recognition of the new code of domestic respectability. And possibly the need to spare wives certain kinds of "humiliating labor" entered into understandings of "comfortable subsistence," the artisan term that came to replace proprietary "independence" (which implied a master's control over an integrated house and shop). But many nonelite households that hired servants also took in boarders, and boarding captured the ambiguities of New Yorkers' cultural definition of housing as workplace and home.

For most boarders, boarding represented a temporary "home," that is, a place culturally defined in opposition to a place of paid work as well as to "independent housekeeping." Although the vast majority of boarders were male wage earners who had no other means of securing domestic services, European visitors expressed surprise that many newly married "respectable" New York couples also chose to board rather than to set up housekeeping. When hiring domestics could add from $50 to $100 annually to already high rents, boarding offered a practical economy to couples whose incomes did not match their cultural expectations for maintaining a wife's social position. Elite New Yorkers regarded such a strategy as appropriate only for young couples; the Pintards, for example, consciously rejected boarding as a means of escaping their Wall Street "prison." But the life-cycle strategy of couples who boarded also contrasted with that of young married mechanics such as the nailmaker Grant Thorburn, who pursued the republican virtue of personal independence by renting domestic quarters and substituting a wife's labor for that of a landlady.[24]

By the 1840s, the physian-reformer John Griscom urged the construction industry to introduce new housing utilities in order to spare such modest households what he regarded as the necessity of hiring domestic labor. "Many highly respectable, but poor persons, now feel obliged to spend a considerable portion of their small incomes in paying the wages, board, and for lodging rooms, of servants," he reported, "but if houses had water-pipes and drain pipes so that there should be no need of going into the streets to perform the mortifying duty of carrying water and emptying refuse, these persons would prefer to do their domestic work themselves." Griscom suggested that hiring servants came at the expense of "wholesome food, better rooms, better education for their children, and other things needful for their happiness"; and he lamented the fate of women of poorer families who "are compelled to appear in the streets under these mortifying circumstances, and in consequence, however wrong it may be, sometimes lose acquaintances whom they value, and sometimes even their own self-respect and courage."[25]

It is difficult to know whether these women themselves found such heavy domestic labor "mortifying" or simply exhausting. There remained alternative understandings of housing's cultural value as a workplace *and* home. For many mechanic families (including those headed by women), the conditions of housekeeping represented less an issue of maintaining valuable acquaintances than of securing the economic value of household labor. Whether or not the family hired servants, New York's wives, daughters, and widows expected to contribute to their households by domestic work that included a range of cash-generating and cash-saving activities. Only "with care and frugality" within a well-managed domestic economy could a young mechanic get ahead, the traveler Isaac Holmes reported in 1823. Skilled journeymen might "save a considerable part of their earnings," he noted, and "do well, particularly if he have a wife and children who are capable of contributing, not merely to the consuming but to the earning also of the common stock." Mechanics' wives who were spared heavy domestic labor by the hiring of servants could more readily contribute other skills to the household economy. The more boarders a household accommodated, for example, the more likely women were to have the assistance of hired servants, particularly young girls.[26]

The wage-earning family's goal of maintaining the wife's position as a helpmate contrasted with propertied New Yorkers' concern to establish the wife as a member of an "independent" employing class and with "highly respectable but poor" New Yorkers' need to preserve the acquaintances they valued. And the bargaining power that women derived from the labor of keeping boarders differed significantly from that of women who brought property or social connections to a marriage. A mechanic's wife's contribution to family resources might increase savings, provide security against a slow season or unemployment, and even offer the means to acquire household furnishings and equipment. But such labor could establish few claims on the deployment of capital—investment in new housing utilities—to improve domestic working conditions and "save labor."

To a large extent wage-earning tenant households from 1800 to 1840 did not share in the material improvements that distinguished the "new modern dwelling" as a domestic workplace. Tenant quarters subdivided out of an earlier generation's artisan houses seemed interchangeable in their lack of space (although their occupants no doubt valued specific qualities and details of construction, siting, and level of repair, which varied with the quality and age of the building). Rear houses and courts further eliminated the yard as an extension of household work space, and close quarters did not offer the healthful amenities of light and air. Female working-class tenants (including boardinghouse servants) generally performed household labor without a pump, facilities for the storage of food and fuel, or improved kitchen equipment, and later without plumbing, a central heating system, or gas lighting. The most important change in tenant house utilities came in the 1830s, when coal burners replaced hearths and wood-burning stoves; this change, necessitated by the spiraling price of firewood, also increased fumes and dust.[27]

Despite mechanics' recognition of housekeeping's value to the family's comfortable subsistence, by the third decade of the nineteenth century, housing conditions for wage-earning families in and of themselves devalued unpaid domestic labor. That is to say, women in tenant houses were able to realize less for their labor in household savings, family health, and domestic comfort than propertied women in dwellings or artisans' wives in shared houses.[28]

Few sources survive to tell us how wage-earning New Yorkers regarded the changing conditions of housekeeping. New York's early labor movement focused on changing craft working conditions—on training, hours, work rules, and wages. Although early labor newspapers readily affirmed the value and virtue of home life, they seldom directly discussed the physical conditions or relations of unpaid house-work. Occasionally New York's striking journeymen presented house-hold budgets to demonstrate to the public the justice of their wage demands. Or, as in the 1830s, they suggested their domestic vulnera-bility and denounced employers who cut wages "in the middle of an inclement and unusually tedious winter, when provisions, fuel, and ev-ery domestic requisite, rose to an unprecedented price hitherto un-known in the city of New York, and rents not only already high, but rising the coming year to an average of 20 percent!"[29]

It was in the context of addressing the dangers of competition from women operatives and outworkers in the needle and shoe trades as well as in cloth manufacturing—"the system of Female Labor"—that workingmen most strongly expressed concerns about changing domes-tic relations. In the face of "ruinous competition" from female opera-tives, "the parent or the husband, or the brother is deprived of a sufficient subsistence to support himself and family . . . in decency and [keep] his wife or relative at home to perform the duties of the household." In a sense, unionists charged "speculators and monopo-lists" with appropriating not only the value of their own labor but also their proprietary interest in their wives' and daughters' domestic labor. Indirectly criticizing employers' wives by addressing the concern that women kept "at home" would be "idle," the journeymen invoked hous-ing's traditional cultural identity as an integrated workplace. In "the early ages," they reported, "women were usefully, healthily, and industriously employed, although differently engaged from their present occupations."[30]

Rather than embrace new concepts of domesticity attached to the dwelling, journeymen sought to preserve traditional values of artisan housekeeping. But the conditions of tenant housing undermined wives' and daughters' ability "to contribute to the earning of the common stock" through customary forms of "female industry," including assis-tance to male family members in their own trade work. As declining wages and rising rents reduced affordable space, there was less oppor-tunity to take in boarders. Women who faced an increasing burden of domestic maintenance under deteriorating physical conditions could not fulfill the chief "duty of the household" by providing for their fam-ilies' health. For laboring families, the alternative that loomed largest was not housing's new cultural identity as a "home" but rather its new economic identity as a sweatshop.

The outwork system in shoemaking and the needle trades built on shoemakers' and tailors' traditional claims to their wives' and children's labor. Like domestic service, such work was valued in accordance with a baseline of "family labor" that cost nothing. This measure, as well as the ideology of female dependency, kept outwork wages desperately low. The "system" of sweated female labor within the home was also a travesty of earlier housing relations of integrated domestic and trade work. Male household heads had retained obligations for their family members' subsistence. Employers paid starvation wages and further required workers to pay shop overhead in domestic rents. From the perspective of New York's laboring classes, the conditions of sweated labor provided the strongest message of what happened when a "home" became a "workplace."[31]

The conditions of male independence became increasingly uncertain in antebellum New York; succession within crafts was losing its security, skills did not necessarily secure wages that permitted savings, the costs of setting up a shop or business increased, the expansion of credit created more risks. Men who controlled real property gained power to command the labor of those who had none, and control of labor represented both security and the means to accumulate more property. Whether owned or rented, domestic quarters, no less than the integrated house and shop of an earlier generation, established conditions for controlling female labor. When women's dependency was posited through the legal doctrine of marital unity, a wife's condition represented that of her husband. In sparing a wife heavy labor or "protecting" her from the vulnerabilities and predations of the specifically female labor market, a husband preserved his self-respect as provider and his claims on a wife for other forms of family and household labor. And when journeymen's and laborers' wages reduced their control over housing, they lost control over the value of unpaid female labor and became increasingly vulnerable as a class.

Given the conditions of female economic dependency, women held their own distinctive interest in the emerging system of cultural meaning that situated "home life" within the larger frame of capitalist property and labor relations. Antebellum women as a class had limited rights in property and limited means to acquire it, and without property they could make few claims on labor. The female labor market—most immediately visible in the conditions of domestic service and outwork—determined that women's "property" in their own labor would produce more value than it could ever earn. Paid female labor did not represent a viable means of independence. The majority of women, then, had few options but to place claims on fathers and husbands for the best working conditions possible, that is, to assert the value of their labor through familial obligations of the "home" rather than the market relations of the "workplace."

The cultural construction of housing as a home separated from a workplace did not emerge simply with reference to men's departure to workshops, offices, and stores. Female family members who performed household "duties" were culturally defined against the figures of both "immoral and ungrateful" servants who grudgingly performed "work" and female outworkers who "took work away from men." Although the points of reference were vastly different for propertied and working-class New Yorkers, the language with which they interpreted housing relations was often the same. Unable to eliminate the tensions of waged employment, keeping boarders, or sweated labor within their domestic quarters, New Yorkers insisted on housing's identity as a home, defined family work as a labor of love, and spoke of domestic relations as they "ought" to be.

Labor relations were not the only field of housing's cultural redefinition. The home as a social institution also ordered new understandings of obligations within the community. As with the rhetorical opposition of home and work, the categories of private and public did not describe social reality. Rather these categories helped to establish new measures of personal morality and social maturity, the qualities necessary for social respect.

The "Public" Home

No institution in nineteenth-century America received more literary attention than the home. So many sermons, speeches, toasts, songs, novels, and articles extolled its virtues and satisfactions that the cultural value of home life seems self-evident. The home was the site of a loving family circle, of simple pleasures and intimacies, of cooperation and mutual trust. As in literary constructions of other ideal places—the wilderness, the country—the concrete referent, a physical site, its people, labors, and conflicts, often disappeared into abstract qualities. Housing's literary and ideological removal from the market and the "public sphere" underscored male privilege and denied class privilege by naturalizing gender prescriptions into a psychological landscape: men who braved the wilds of the marketplace could return to the safety and comforts of a hearth tended by women, be it in a hut, a log cabin, or a palace. For rich and poor, women and men, the home that sheltered the heart represented the possibility of human relations unqualified by a price.[32]

We in the twentieth century have inherited this elusive concept of the home as an emotional refuge that transcends specific conditions and relations of housing. And because the home is a place that exists primarily in imagination or in memory, because it represents such a depth of emotional attachment or longing, we tend to accept its inherently personal or private nature. But real homes have always had to exist in physical spaces, those spaces have been socially constructed, and they have changed their forms, uses, and meanings over time. Whatever the depth of psychological needs individuals brought to the construction of home life in antebellum New York City, they organized their housing to serve a wide range of social activities that differed from those of earlier generations and varied according to material means. In order to consider how particular cultural values and expectations shaped housing as a new social institution, we must move beyond its characterization as a "private sphere" and explore the publicity of new housing practices.

Dwellings and tenant houses evolved out of an earlier housing institution that, though private property, had not assumed the ideological attributes of a separate private sphere. Eighteenth-century integrated houses did not operate on a principle of exclusivity; sheltering trades or business alongside housework, they accommodated the traffic of customers and business associates as well as neighbors and kin. New Yorkers had ritually affirmed their "open houses" through the custom of New Year's visits. On January first, men and younger family members visited the houses of relatives and neighbors to wish the residents a prosperous new year; women stayed home to serve buffets of traditional liquors and sweets to members of the "community" who called to pay their respects. Nor were "private economical relations" opposed to public obligations: household heads' accountability for their dependents and the duties of public service attached housing to the civic order. And though family—and specifically conjugal—relations suggest personal privacy within houses, even domestic intimacy was not entirely free from exposure or publicity in a culture that sought to enforce a particular code of sexual morality and proscribed, for example, miscegenation and "unnatural" sexual acts as transgressions of social order.[33]

The only thing clearly private about eighteenth-century housing was proprietors' exclusive rights to the value of household resources and dependents' labor. The Bill of Rights, by protecting citizens' houses along with their persons, papers, and effects from unreasonable searches and seizures and by proscribing the quartering of soldiers, linked these property rights with political rights. But boundaries drawn between public and private with respect to state power and personal political rights did not construct spatial boundaries of social use or obligation. Rather, new boundaries were culturally constructed through custom, ritual, and prescription.

Even with the demise of trade uses, housing remained an intensely social, highly visible institution. Their rhetorical opposition notwithstanding, public and private "spheres" did not operate as either spatial or social polarities. In the eyes of propertied New Yorkers, respectable public and private spaces constructed one another through *continuities* of social traffic, activity, and conduct which established and maintained circles of obligation and trust beyond the family. The cultural definition of respectable housing opposed itself less to a "public sphere" than to perceptions of disreputable public and private continuities within tenant housing and neighborhoods.

Through its use for entertainment, meetings, religious life, and the marriage market, the dwelling stood at the center of circles of selective socializing that shaped public and private associational life into a class culture. A respectable home life suggested a person's capacity to enter into and to meet obligations within the community. In an era when New Yorkers were only beginning to establish financial institutions, they used kin networks, business associates, and acquaintances to certify reputation, and through reputation to gain access to property and credit. Propertied New Yorkers established their social standing and claims through rituals that affirmed their reciprocal obligations. Unlike the fixed contractural relations of a cash bargain or a dated loan, the reciprocity enacted through home hospitality laid the ground for ongoing social exchanges and cooperation. In this respect, bourgeois New Yorkers did seek to distinguish the social world that moved through their homes from the anonymous "public" market and to store up social credit that could withstand sudden turns of fortune.

The dwelling's value as a social institution that organized acquaintanceship and certified public character emerged in contradistinction to the perceived limitations and dangers of alternative housing forms. In contrast to the carefully regulated social traffic of home hospitality, boarding and tenant houses appeared socially promiscuous, nonselective, and immediately vulnerable to market determinations of personal worth. Such housing was commercial; it operated through the conversion of wages into rents and suggested money's power to resolve all social relations into cash bargains and to dissolve future obligations. A world in which all domestic services—shelter, maintenance, meals, entertainment, and even sex—were available for a price rendered domestic manifestations of character irrelevant. Through home hospitality, respectable New Yorkers could enforce codes of reputable conduct by withholding invitations. Tenant housing relations, in contrast, they perceived as imposing no social accountability for moral transgressions.

In the eyes of genteel New Yorkers, the "liberty" of boarding especially represented a condition of social immaturity that rejected the
principles of family duty and selective obligation. The cultural characteristics attributed to unmarried boarders—youth, transience, freedom
from family ties and long-term commitments—became all the more
problematic in multifamily tenant housing. Viewed from a distance, the
sharing of domestic space seemed to break down any one household's
powers to define and order its relations with other households. What
respectable New Yorkers overlooked, of course, were wage-earning
tenants' own rituals and networks of obligation and sociability, often
established through the very neighborhood institutions that most
threatened the emerging bourgeois cultural definition of "proper"
home life.

The elaboration of New York houses as centers of selective socializing
had begun in the eighteenth century. Downtown merchant houses with
offices and adjacent stores had operated as practical centers of intersecting business and kinship obligations; and informal hospitality provided occasions for negotiations, the exchange of information, and
affirmation of shared interests. Still, only the houses of the city's colonial officials and most prominent merchants contained space for formal
entertaining—dining rooms, drawing rooms, and less commonly, ball-
rooms. The owners of these exceptional houses extended patronage to
elicit deference rather than to establish reciprocal obligations; few
guests could afford to match their style of entertainment. Those merchants who could afford to entertain associates at dinner generally did
so at taverns. Inns or pleasure gardens accommodated such heterosocial amusements as dances and receptions. It was only after the Revolution that new city dwellings systematically expanded the space given
over to receiving visitors and established the value of home hospitality
in defining the circles of obligation and regulating social interaction.[34]

In embracing "modern style" dwellings that differentiated formal
"front" and family "back" parlors and featured dining rooms, prosperous New Yorkers expressed their perceptions of the necessity of public
entertainment as much as a new impulse toward family privacy. If the
level of investment in furniture and decoration is any indication of cultural priorities, a family's comfort in the "private" space of its back parlor mattered less than the accommodation of visitors. The city's social
elite established the importance of dwellings as social institutions most
clearly through the exchange of dinners, teas, receptions, and formal
visits that rendered the new domestic standards of an emergent bourgeois class visible to itself. "In fashionable, as in mercantile life," the
editor Samuel Woodworth observed in 1824, "there is a regular debit
and credit. A paying and receiving of visits, a giving and a going to

parties, and the former are as tenacious and strict in the rules of fashion as the latter are in the transactions of commerce." Furthermore,
the observance of codes of conduct that certified good character in domestic society were essential to the transactions of commerce as a collective project.[35]

With the expansion of domestic space and furnishings for entertainment, modern dwellings gained importance in the organization of
propertied men's associational activities. Even as the practice of holding private dinners for thirty or more men at taverns or hotels persisted, entertaining associates at home afforded gentlemen new
distinction. In his retrospective novel of manners, *Home as Found*,
James Fenimore Cooper sketched a typical dinner party: "Two rows of
men clad in dark dresses, a solitary female at the head of the table, or
if fortunate, with a supporter of the same sex near her, invariably composed the *convives*." When the gentlemen were seated, "the conversa-
tion turned on the prices of lots, speculations in towns, or the
currency." Women, aside from the hostess, were not commonly included in such dinner parties in the first quarter of the nineteenth
century. Their absence suggests both the persistence of older customs
of male sociability and men's recognition of the particular value of the
home to their own business affairs.[36]

In more subtle ways, propertied men used home hospitality to affirm
among themselves the continuities of public and private responsibilities, values, and manners. Members of benevolent and political organizations generally assembled at such public sites as Tammany Hall, the
New York Institution (the converted almshouse on Chambers Street),
hotels, and taverns, but the formal and informal committees that managed these associations were as likely to meet in one another's parlors.
Thus in 1818 John Pintard, De Witt Clinton, and Dr. Alexander Hosack organized a club of "6 to 9 who are to mee[t] every Sat[urda]y
ev[ening] probably at each others houses, a converzazione, to promote
useful objects . . . In these associations the various hints and projects
for the benefit of Society can be discussed improved and converted to
the best interest of the community." Always sensitive to the power of
money alone to define social standing or to inflate the requirements of
reciprocal hospitality, Pintard informed his daughter that "to prevent a
competition of luxury," the gentlemen had agreed to limit refreshments
to "Coffee, sliced Tongue, Saucisson, a pickled Oyster, Wine and porter, with Segars."[37]

If socializing within dwellings permitted propertied men to affirm a
sense of mutual obligation and display qualities of magnanimity and
character that redounded to their business and civic credit, women had

a greater stake in constructing interlocking codes of public and private respectability. Only as the modern dwelling was understood to be a cultural necessity could women secure their claims on men for the improvement of housing as their workplace. As men used dwellings to form and confirm their business and civic networks, women defined the value of home life in relation to another social institution, the church.

Insofar as New York's oldest established churches oriented themselves primarily to propertied congregations, church and home developed a symbiotic relationship. Elite families that attended Episcopal, Dutch Reformed, and Presbyterian churches purchased church pews as a form of "domestic property" and regarded home prayers as an essential religious observance. Indeed, one might argue that churches helped establish the legitimacy of dwellings that could easily be regarded—in the era of republican simplicity—as undemocratic luxuries. The location of new churches north of the wharf district (starting with St. John's in Hudson Square) readily identified the "moral character" of the new residential districts that sprang up around them. Conversely, New Yorkers viewed the scarcity of churches in the tenant neighborhoods of the Lower East Side as symptomatic of the dangers of working-class immorality.[38]

Though revivals sporadically rechurched men, by the 1820s women dominated New York's congregations, and in their church activities women asserted a public presence that is sometimes lost in historians' projections of social isolation onto the "private sphere." Women organized their own associational life through parlor prayer, Bible reading, and charity meetings, which reinforced the ties between the social duties of home life and religious practice. Confronting an ideological tradition that asserted their natural inferiority, women drew on the cultural authority of religion to articulate new standards by which to measure men's reciprocal obligations to wives and daughters. No less than employers whose evangelicalism promoted disciplined work habits among employees, women sought to link the virtues of male self-discipline and temperance to the benefits of a comfortable home life. And by making home life part of the evidence of disciplined moral character, women elaborated the cultural and material requirements of male maturity.[39]

In the early decades of the nineteenth century the ritual Sunday promenade from church to tea at home symbolized continuities between public and private spaces and values which extended well beyond elite circles. Among the evangelical women and men of more modest merchant, shopkeeping, and artisan families, domestic quarters accommodated a close congregational life that supported both religious observance and selective social networks. The architect Joseph Probyn, who maintained a ground-floor office in his house, regularly entertained both visiting Baptist ministers and fellow vestrymen in his "upstairs parlor," where they discussed and plotted church affairs. In the 1830s, Michael Floy, a perhaps exceptionally pious young man who in his early thirties became a partner in his father's nursery establishment, attended two Methodist services on Sunday as well as weekly Bible classes; and he taught Sunday school both at his own Bowery Village Church and at African Methodist churches. After services Floy regularly repaired to the parlors of other church members for tea. He and other young adult church members met for prayer meetings and held choir practice and singing parties at their parents' houses. Indeed, the parlors of Methodist church members served as the centers of Michael Floy's flirtatious bachelor social life.[40]

Through such visiting among middling households as well as those of elite families, domestic quarters were "on view" to a larger community. In an earlier generation, many rules of proper conduct—cleanliness and grooming, sobriety, refraining from profanity and spitting, a quiet demeanor—had been reserved for church attendance and observance of the Sabbath, or they had been associated with genteel rank. Such manners took on an everyday life and new codes of behavior were introduced, rehearsed, and disseminated through domestic socializing. "Among the hospitable circles which reciprocate good and cheerful entertainments a man would be marked who should retire intoxicated, indeed, except among the young and jovial, convivial parties are all decent & sober," John Pintard reported to his daughter of one change in manners. Pintard attributed the new restraint to the presence of women and credited this style of domestic entertainment in turn to the French, "who never expell Ladies from the dinner table." But New York women surely asserted their own authority in "importing" such manners to establish and enforce new temperance standards.[41]

In the early decades of the nineteenth-century, New Yorkers (like other Americans) were intensely self-conscious and often critical of domestic rituals or personal manners that smacked of European tastes. Beyond elite circles, much of the home's emerging cultural authority derived from perceptions that new codes of respectability revived, enacted, and recast precepts of family duty, Protestant piety, and republican virtue. But as they had done when the home was defined in opposition to a workplace, New Yorkers of different classes negotiated the meanings of "private" home life in relation to different arenas and forms of public interaction.

The conditions of housekeeping, for example, structured different kinds of public and private continuities for bourgeois and working-class women's activities. On the city's wealthiest clearly bounded residential blocks, town houses pulled back from the street and servants frequently acted as household agents to mediate relations with the neighborhood by performing errands and screening people who came to the door. The conceptual categories that defined the home as a private sphere (while incorporating church, charity, visiting, shopping, entertainment, *and* supervision of waged labor) drew a veil around bourgeois women's housework. The ability to assume that veil "in public" through particular styles of street dress and manners implicitly testified to "private" conditions of home life.

For most New Yorkers in tenant neighborhoods, there was a growing disjuncture between such codes and the conditions of housing, the physical environment in which wives, mothers, landladies, and servants secured household maintenance. The grounds of domestic work space in trade and tenant neighborhoods extended from the house and yard to the street and markets. Tenant women's domestic skills at bargaining for both goods and credit required personal familiarity with the neighborhood's social and economic resources and the "character" of particular shopkeepers and peddlers. Tenant women's housekeeping and socializing activities were thus more readily interchangeable.[42]

Disregard for new rules of feminine propriety worried such observers as the nursery journeyman Michael Floy, who lived in the mixed-trade neighborhood of Bowery Village. Floy used his diary to rehearse social comments that situated his own feelings of respectability by distancing him from neighbors and cohorts. "Every morning we see Mrs. Mountain, bare-headed, dishevelled hair, carrying a great boy in her arms, coming to visit our woman [servant]," he complained. Certain that there was nothing "more odious than to behold an idle gadabout woman visiting the neighbors, carrying about a squalling creature wherever she goes," Floy was especially offended that Mrs. Mountain brought her child with her when she came visiting. "She would be bad enough without the baby, but when we see her wherever she goes lugging about a child in her arms when she ought to be at home, the sight is intolerable; it sickens me completely. Then it is that characters suffer; scandal is dealt out by the mouthful, and the baby in her arms makes her look ten times more hateful."[43]

Household servants who could assist with child care and run errands, of course, permitted a respectable woman to leave her children behind when she went out visiting. And except on Sundays, housewives such as the bareheaded Mrs. Mountain did not observe the proprieties of dressing "to go out." Such women doubtless observed their own rules and routines as they dropped in at one another's kitchens to exchange gossip and information. But these codes were not organized to be legible to any observer as evidence of a woman's social position—or of the quality of her home life.

In other contexts, the cultural concept of the private home assumed a different meaning. In the city's mixed-trade neighborhoods, the households of small masters and shopkeepers and wage-earning boarders and tenants (situated amid taverns, workshops, and groceries) maintained a sometimes uneasy coexistence as they negotiated the continuities and boundaries of private and public conduct. The "comfortable subsistence" that was replacing trade proprietorship as a marker of male maturity introduced new points of reference in establishing social accountability. The home's "private," "moral" character contrasted with more "public" housing arrangements, particularly boardinghouses, which in their alliance with commercial institutions threatened the traditional authority of household (and trade) hierarchies in maintaining social order.

Although households that took boarders were arrayed along the city's economic ladder, boardinghouses had customarily been identified with transience and youth. Already suffering censure from their association with sailors and wharf-district epidemics, boardinghouses became a dominant housing form within the city's mechanic neighborhoods in the early decades of the nineteenth century. Boarding solved the problems of domestic maintenance for many young single men (and, to a far lesser extent, women) by liberating them from its labor. Boardinghouses frequently accommodated workers of the same trade or nationality, and meals served as an occasion for socializing; but the boardinghouse was less a center of social obligation to many residents than the place for meals and sleep within a daily circuit that included workshop and corner tavern. "The room in which we sleep," the journeyman printer Thomas Chamberlain noted in his diary, "is the back room of the first floor, it contains 2 double beds and 2 single beds, we have a double bed and there is at present three young men besides in the room. The ground floor of the house is a grocery store." Given such quarters, boarders readily turned to neighborhood resources.[44]

Boarding subsumed certain categories of living expenses—housekeeping and furnishings as well as food—into a fixed price. That part of a worker's wage not surrendered for rent formed "disposable income" (ranging from perhaps 50 cents to the traveler Isaac Holmes's generous estimate of $5 a week for skilled journeymen),[45] which could be saved, spent on clothing and entertainment, gambled, contributed to the church or other voluntary associations, or shared with family members in the city, in the countryside, or abroad. One category of spending did not of course exclude the others. But boarders used disposable cash to support a system of housing services and recreational pursuits that citizens within their own neighborhoods charged were destroying the republican city's virtue.

A household head of an earlier generation could discipline employees as well as family members. Master artisans as a class set the "moral tone" of trade neighborhoods. When new issues concerning the regulation of public behavior emerged early in the nineteenth century, city officials had initially looked to household heads to preserve order (holding masters responsible, for example, for journeymen's kite flying and shooting of guns). But rapidly expanding numbers of young boarding wage earners were not accountable to employers or parents—or to their boardinghouse landlords—for their public conduct. Their popular amusements—gambling, drinking, cockfights, boxing, bear baiting, fire fighting, and the boisterousness that accompanied these activities— were not new. What was distinctively new was the concentration of young men between the ages of fourteen and twenty-five who had the personal "liberty" to engage in these recreational pursuits.[46]

Through the early decades of the century evangelical artisan householders in the city's mechanic wards (Wards 5, 6, 7, 10, and 14) joined more influential citizens in repeatedly appealing to the Common Council to control young men's rowdiness and disrespect, particularly on Sundays, when churchgoing, the promenade, and labor's day of rest brought New Yorkers together onto the streets. In one typical petition, "proprietors and residents" in the Fourteenth Ward complained of the neighborhood "boys [who] assemble at and about . . . [the fire] Engine House, but more especially . . . of great noise on the Sabbath day, insulting females, and sometimes fighting and using most indecent and profane language."[47]

Artisan householders who may not have identified with bourgeois codes of respectability nonetheless sought to preserve their own moral standards (and particularly their religious values) within their neighborhoods. In 1812, for example, an aldermanic "Committee for Suppressing Immorality," composed of a lawyer, a sailmaker, and a tanner from the predominantly artisan Wards 6, 8, and 10, responded to this constituency as much as to the city's merchants when they investigated a "long and offensive catalogue of abounding immoralities" that included Blue Law violations by grocers and tavernkeepers, Sunday skating, ball playing, and horse racing, and "the Droves of Youth who on that day resort to the outskirts of the City, and commit depredations on

the property and too frequently insult the persons of the Inhabitants."
Though the aldermen acknowledged that one reason for Sunday commercial activity was that "laboring men . . . cannot get pay for their
Weeks work until late on Saturday night," the aldermen were as much
concerned with the "manifest injustice" to those grocers who did close
on Sundays, "inasmuch as they soon lose their most profitable customers." The state legislature responded to the aldermen's request for
more stringent laws regulating morality, but even the aldermen had
confessed that they were "not so enthusiastic as to believe it within the
reach of this Board, or any other Human power to eradicate the vices
which usually prevail in populous and commercial Cities."[48]

The tensions between those shopkeepers and artisans who upheld
the new codes of public propriety and those who ignored them reveal
competing economic interests as well as moral values. Proprietors who
sold "home" services as well as shelter to thousands of boarders and
tenants depended on young wage earners' spending for their own livelihoods. By 1827, for example, more than three thousand licensed grocers and tavernkeepers provided the city's journeymen and laborers not
merely with drink and food but also with heat and amusements lacking
in their domestic accommodations. By 1836 the temperance movement
had reduced the number of liquor licenses (most precipitously in
Wards 6, 8, and 10), but aldermen still charged that there was one
licensed tavern for every fifty inhabitants over the age of fifteen. "It is
in these places," the aldermen asserted in the common formulation of
the era, "that many of the youth of this city are first led from paths of
virtue and prepared for a course that must lead to ruin."[49]

In reformers' imagination, virtue's ruin came from mechanics' waste
of earnings, abandonment of ambition, and denial of moral obligation.
The institutions of journeymen's sociability, the saloons that could be
found on virtually every block, operated as wage earners' parlors; and
drinking, treating, and games may have fulfilled their own need for
rituals of mutuality. But such cultural practices—and indeed whole
neighborhoods—that revolved around cash transactions and short-term
debts suggested the rejection of long-term goals and commitments.
The pursuit of temporary pleasures seemed to undermine a social order constructed on reciprocal duties, an order so readily identified
with and orchestrated through the private home.[50]

The tensions raised by young male boarders' "ruin" proved all the
more problematic with respect to young single women. The majority of
female wage earners worked as domestics and lived under the watchful
eyes of their employers. Furthermore, given their wages, other women
probably spent in labor, and particularly in sewing late into the night,

the hours that male wage earners spent in entertainment and informal socializing. Rougher neighborhood amusements were restricted to men, but young wage-earning women participated in heterosocial institutions—taverns, dance halls, and Bowery promenades—that served a distinctive working-class sexual economy. The "liberty" of female boardinghouses was readily (and often accurately) associated with prostitution. Within the city's proliferating "parlor house" brothels, even the most sacred of home intimacies was available for a price. Only a proper home life could insulate women and men from the vices of casual exchange and regulate their intimacy.[51]

In the early decades of the century, the sociability of a male boarding youth culture (and such mixed civic and recreational institutions as fire and militia companies) had cut across class lines. By the 1830s, more and more independent artisans (contractors and employers) were locating their homes (often in shared houses) on blocks of like-minded households, particularly on the West Side. This spatial separation further framed the perceptions of the private home as a distinct arena apart from "public" workshops, boardinghouses, and institutions of workers' leisure, including the basement groceries that anchored so many tenant houses.[52]

Older styles of interclass fraternization, particularly when it was thought to be promoted by housing arrangements, also worried wealthier New Yorkers, who feared for the corruption of their sons. Young "gentlemen" who boarded in effect lost their domestic certification of character. "Boarding houses are not *home*. The circle is too large and miscellaneous to be sacred and affectionate." Thus a "bachelor" described to *Mirror* readers the strains of living in a boardinghouse, "always superintended by women whom in most instances poverty and misfortune have driven to this precarious and unhappy occupation." Feeling "ready to resort to any artifice to escape from solitude and self-examination," the boarding bachelor would turn to "theaters, gambling houses, saloons, clubs, a thousand dazzling attractions."[53]

In the 1830s, hotels such as the one built by Seth Greer on Broadway and occupied "by gentlemen exclusively" emerged as an alternative housing institution for single men who valued their reputations. Respectable young couples also turned from boardinghouses to hotels: suites with private parlors permitted exclusive entertaining of visitors while still sparing housekeeping expenses. Hotels regulated their clientele with their prices, and they supported their claims to respectability by offering the latest in domestic conveniences and comforts, ranging from new plumbing to elegant furnishings. On the surface, at least, the trappings signaled their residents' observation of the minimal codes of propriety. Although most independent households regarded hotels with ambivalence, few doubted the superiority of hotel life to that of boarding.[54]

Far from being a spatially or socially circumscribed "private sphere," the social institution of the home assumed a new public presence in the first half of the nineteenth century. As housing lost its association with a proprietor's rank or trade, New Yorkers turned to new points of reference and situated "the home" between church and saloon, between civic order and public rowdiness. These cultural associations took the home's "private" character as a statement of commitment to public responsibility and morality. The definition and display of respectable home life, by placing individualism within the frame of family duty, offered moral sanction to acquisitive and competitive impulses. Yet this definition of respectability also carried a price. As an earlier generation's housing "luxuries" became "necessities," negotiations over their price and cultural value ranged from the personal contract of marriage to the social contract of community obligation.

"The Progress of Luxury"

In the nineteenth century, domestic and social duties, Thornstein Veblen observed in his study of conspicuous consumption, became "a species of service performed not so much for the individual behoof of the head of household as for the reputability of the household taken as a corporate unit—a group of which the housewife is a member on a footing of ostensible equality." As managers of a "corporate" household, bourgeois women assumed duties ranging from the nurturing and training of children in what Veblen called the "mandatory codes of decency" to representing family interests and obligations within a larger community. Neither the definition of domestic responsibilities nor the legitimacy of women's claims to an "ostensible equality" in their management of household resources, however, had been obvious in the early nineteenth century. Against the backdrop of new mansions and tenant houses, New York women and men engaged in intense debate over the definition of household "necessities" that established the "reputability" of a corporate unit and the cultural requirements of a new "standard of living."[55]

Often we think about domesticity—the activity within domestic quarters—primarily with reference to a particular stage of the family life cycle, the relation of parents—and especially mothers—to young children. Early-nineteenth-century writers stressed this dimension of home life in order to revise an earlier generation's view of childhood as a condition to be suppressed. With the demise of apprenticeships and the prolongation of childhood within propertied families, children did assume a new centrality within the corporate unit. But nurturing and training young children constituted only one phase of a household's life cycle, and only one aspect of domesticity. If the creation of nurseries within dwellings suggests the central place of children in antebellum family life, it also points to the practical containment of children's needs and activities within the "new modern" house.[56]

The characterization of the home as a sacred family center emerged in the context of a lively public discussion of the reach, purpose, and effects of new levels of personal investment in domestic property, housekeeping, and entertainment. The very means by which respectable New Yorkers affirmed their shared valuation of independent housekeeping as evidence of social maturity—visiting and hospitality—opened the door to charges that "fashion" was corrupting republican virtue.[57]

Many New Yorkers who had been raised to identify "republican simplicity" as a distinctive American value viewed the increasingly visible private wealth of housing with ambivalence. Welcoming material prosperity, they nonetheless saw a new danger in the importation of "aristocratic" tastes and manners that imparted false measures of self-importance, increased pressures of competition, and drew wealth away from the obligations of civic benevolence. As genteel New Yorkers adopted the use of visiting cards as part of their rituals of social exchange in the 1820s, for example, a correspondent to the *Mirror* complained that "empty ceremony and heartless formality have usurped the place of friendly attention and social intercourse." Answering a gentleman who proposed that the use of visiting cards "answers every purpose of a visit and is far less trouble," the critic thought the custom convenient when confined "to its legitimate use, to obviate the carelessness or forgetfulness of servants, but when made the instrument of idle ceremony and deceitful professions, it's certainly reprehensible and may be classed with the follies and crimes of the age."[58]

Changes in older customs of New Year's visiting in the late 1820s and early 1830s further pointed up internal tensions within the ranks of propertied New Yorkers who were redefining the obligations of social patronage and exchange. Members of old New York families complained that a new generation of "would-be nobility" and "people who have no ancestry themselves" were abandoning open houses and community-wide visiting on January 1. The editor George Morris, a self-appointed arbiter of taste in the 1830s, cited the concern of those who felt "the custom must be general, or it will be entirely broken up. We must know that wherever we go we shall be welcomed, or else we shall pause before each dwelling with a doubtful and misgiving heart and look in every face for a sign of displeasure." Urging his readers not to "be too indiscriminate in censuring those tastes and wishes not similar to our own," he nonetheless concluded, "if it is the pride of wealth and aristocracy which would destroy this pleasant holiday, then let him who advances against it be known as the enemy of innocent enjoyment."[59]

On January 2, 1837, Philip Hone noted a different problem: "Mr. Lawrence, the Mayor, kept open house yesterday, according to the custom from time immemorable, but the manners as well as the times have sadly changed." In contrast to a time when "one out of twenty perhaps [took] a single glass of wine or cherry bounce," the New Year's visitors "used his house as a Five Points tavern," and the ensuing brawl prompted the mayor to call the police and close his house.[60]

Against such anxieties over fashionable circles' "pride of wealth" on the one hand and the "common man's" disrespect on the other, the image of the intimate family hearth imparted a transcendent social value to dwellings, one that existed independently of a stratified society shaped by market forces. Then, too, such a focus on the familial virtues of dwellings drew attention away from the problematic presence, importance, and strains of unrelated household members (whether servants or boarders) within most houses.

Yet another specifically familial concern and ambition—the desire to "place" young adult children in society—motivated and structured many of the rituals of home hospitality and entertainment. In a city where leading merchants had for over a century defined their collective interests and loyalties through kinship ties, the tensions that accompanied the definition of new standards of respectable housekeeping became most apparent in the negotiations to establish new homes, particularly in the marriage market. Few women or men in the volatile economy of the early nineteenth century could afford to embrace the romantic ideal of marriage for love and companionship irrespective of material considerations. Ambitious young men saw in "successful" marriage an avenue for social mobility. Since marriage determined the future conditions of their labor, young women sought to preserve or improve upon the domestic gains of their mothers, and to protect their reputation and any property they brought with them. Parents, having long since lost the power to select their children's partners, nonetheless took responsibility for arranging "opportunities" for suitable introductions and acquaintances.[61]

For many evangelical New Yorkers, the link between church and home provided the best prospects for identifying suitable mates. Michael Floy's diary regularly referred to courting activity at parlor prayer meetings and singing parties. Intensely self-conscious about his own prospects, Floy took to heart his father's admonition that it "was the business of women to study men's character." When he met his own future wife at church, Floy conducted the courtship by escorting her home to tea after services. Yet Floy also had to overcome obstacles: her parents slept in the front "parlor" room, so that it was necessary to continue the courtship in the evenings outside the front door.[62]

Earlier, as he shopped around for a wife, Floy's doubts about one woman's domestic virtues had led him to break an engagement. Other negotiations over the formation of new homes landed in the courts, where juries weighed and evaluated the "affections engaged, expectations excited, and future prospects blasted" upon the breaking of engagements. In one particularly prominent case, the mantua maker Jane Mount sued James Bogert for $10,000 in damages for failure to fulfill his promise of marriage. From 1807 to 1816, Bogert, the middle-aged son of a wealthy merchant, had conducted his courtship by visiting Mount in the parlors of houses in which she boarded and by escorting her home from church services. But Bogert's family and friends worried that he was being duped. When his father died and left him a fortune, they urged him to break off his "engagement." Jane Mount's lawyers brought a series of witnesses who testified to Bogert's unfailing devotion to the mantua maker as she moved from house to house, and the judge noted in his instructions that "heavy and exemplary damages ought to be awarded" when the breach of a civil contract "could be inferred from the circumstances." But the case had extenuating circumstances. The defendent's witnesses testified that Mount had repeatedly "ridiculed and reviled" her suitor, thereby calling into doubt the validity of a contract that required parties to "mutually agree" to its terms. Deciding that Bogert's attentions had indeed established Mount's expectations but that her conduct could not be regarded as that "of a woman towards a man who had engaged to make her his wife," the jury awarded her only $400 in damages.[63]

The marriage market of the city's wealthy, self-conscious "society" revolved around a winter season, "with Balls Theatres Concerts and private parties," which, John Pintard complained during the panic of 1819, abounded "in proportion to the pecuniary embarrassments of the country." Pintard worried about his younger daughter's position and prospects within this world, "for such is the state of Society here, that a young lady, without money, has a hopeless prospect of a settlement, no personal merits can compensate for this difficulty." Pintard was re-lieved that family connections could serve his daughter. Reporting that a Brasher cousin "who has grown up a very genteel youth and very correct" had escorted Mrs. Pintard and Louisa to the theater, he ex-pressed hope that "next season he will be able to act a brothers part and attend Sister to such parties and places as may introduce her a little into Society." Nonetheless, Pintard saw "but little benefit, in the way of matches, resulting from all these public fairs where young ladies are exhibited for market." Of the 1819 winter of "extravagant entertain-ments," he bitterly concluded, "The Beauty of it is, that not a single marriage, of all the young ladies exposed for sale, at these entertain-ments has taken place this season." The men were "too profligate," and "the young ladies too extravagant to admit of matches," Pintard ob-served, and recalling the conditions of his own courtship, he looked "with astonishment on the changes of habits, the progress of luxury and conception of morals that have taken place in my day."[64]

Pintard need not have worried. Louisa married a cotton merchant, Thomas Servoss, whom she met while visiting her sister in New Or-leans. Furthermore, in his mid-sixties Pintard finally achieved the long-sought "sweet independence" of a private house: in 1828 he and his wife moved with Louisa and Thomas Servoss to a $13,000 three-story dwelling at the corner of Broome and Crosby streets. Thus he escaped the "prison" of Wall Street, which he had declared was "no longer a residence for females." For Elizabeth Brasher Pintard, how-ever, "the change from a housekeeper to an inmate" did not represent the same achievement. "For myself I feel quite easy and comfortable under [Mr. Servoss's] roof," Pintard told Eliza, "and regret most poignantly that poor dear Mothers pride of Indpendence does not per-mit her to do the same." As tensions mounted with her son-in-law, Elizabeth Pintard "persist[ed] to go to housekeeping again," and two years later Pintard reluctantly announced that he "would make every effort to gratify her," though he himself wished that "instead of house-keeping, plague of servants & all the worrying incident thereto, . . . she wd consent to go to lodging in some neat family, where our comfort wd be greater, & our expenses defined."[65]

For all the particular anxieties of his personal situation, Pintard was not alone in his anger at the "progress of luxury" or in his frustrations at marital tensions that arose over the meaning of domestic indepen-dence. From the early decades of the century, rising housekeeping expenses and the inherent antagonism between "extravagant women" and "profligate men" recurred as themes in an expanding literature of domesticity. Newspaper articles and stories opposed the new requirements of maintaining a respectable dwelling to the traditional male prerogative of controlling family property. "The really prudent and somewhat homebred man," the editor Samuel Woodworth warned in 1824, "feels obliged to relinquish the idea of marriage altogether or defer it to a later period because it is justly considered a hazard to many on the score of supporting the expenses of modern living."[66] Though committed to and profiting from the cultural construction of the home, men seem also to have resented the ascendency of dwellings as social institutions that claimed a substantial share of household income and a public status equal to that of business, religion, or government.

More often than not, women were blamed for the new expenses of housekeeping; "many a female, because she has been educated at boarding-school[,] returns, not to assist her mother but to support her pretensions to gentility." Though few commentators doubted the necessity of servants to do heavy household labor, "gentility" connoted social ambitions that pushed households into social obligations they could not readily afford, at the expense of more practical contributions to home comfort, even to subsistence. An educated daughter, having tasted the pleasures of an expanded cultural life, would not willingly retreat back into the position of dutiful housewife: "She conceives herself to be degraded by domestic occupation and expects to lose her credit if she is known to be industrious." Such a daughter's ambition was, the *Mirror* noted, "an evil which pervades all classes in some degree, but which is peculiarly injurious to those of the middle ranks."[67]

Men of the middle ranks denounced what they regarded as women's susceptibility to the seductions of new household luxuries. In 1811 a "tradesman" wrote to the *Independent Mechanic* to share his story of domestic woes. During his courtship he had announced his prospects and "entreated" his fiancée "to maturely consider whether she would be content to live in the manner that she might expect." But after three months of marriage, when visiting took her into houses that displayed Turkish carpets instead of rag rugs, muslin rather than calico curtains, china in place of pottery, and painted rush-bottom chairs, his wife had announced that she was "quite ashamed to ask a few ladies to tea" and that "every article in the house [was] . . . a disgrace to a decent family." When the tradesman decided "to lock up money, and forbid her to run me in to debt," his wife had in effect gone on strike. "She discharged our servant girl, declaring that if she could not appear like a Christian (as she termed it) she would not be seen out of the house, and would be completely the mope I wanted her." Insisting that his wife's desires for domestic amenities and fashionable clothing were "unbecoming a tradesman's wife," the husband nonetheless found that he was now "ashamed that any one should see her." Her revenge expressed her "total disregard" both for his happiness and for "the opinion of the world at large."[68]

Female authors frequently drew on the language of republican virtue and domestic economy "to vindicate [women's] character from illiberal aspersions." In their eyes, women's claims to a comfortable home life opposed rather than promoted the temptations of new wealth on the one hand and of moral dissipation on the other. They charged that untrustworthy men looked only to marry women with property and then squandered the family's resources in gambling, drinking, and speculation. Thus in advising one another on "how to choose a husband," they denounced the seductions of male flattery and insisted that women had a right to investigate a husband's economic standing. And in what quickly emerged as a new literary genre, women wrote fiction and advice manuals that provided hints for efficient household organization, demonstrating how a wife might "save the fruits of [her husband's] labor and by her industry add to their little income."[69]

The prescriptive literature of domesticity, then, must be understood as an ongoing "contractual" debate between women and men over the allocation and management of household resources. This debate began as a process of reconceptualizing household property and labor relations between spouses who expected to achieve a comfortable subsistence. The strains of marital negotiations prompted a growing consciousness of women's vulnerability to men's control of household resources and led some women to question for the first time their economic dependency. At the same time, the blame directed toward women who asserted an "ostensible equality" of interest and authority in the organization of housing and home life also directed attention away from larger social and economic changes. Wealth was viewed as a problem of social competition and inflated ambitions rather than as a problem of the powers of appropriation. Thus reflecting on the "fatal inroads of want and distress" during the 1829 recession, the *Mirror* identified the "wasteful expenditure of money" by the rich, "imitated by the next descending ranks," as the cause of poverty and urged wealthier New Yorkers to set an example of "prudence, economy, and temperance." "Extravagance is the ruling evil—indulgence in sensuality the prevailing vice. These must be corrected. The poor will want less—the rich will have more. The former will not then experience the degradation of suing for relief—the latter the mortification of denying it."[70]

If women and men in the city's middling ranks struggled over the economic claims and social authority of "the home," comparable tensions emerged among women and men whose household budgets had less margin to support such quarrels. When a workingman retained primary control over the family's cash and household goods, his food, drink, and recreation could come at the expense of his wife's and children's clothing and food. Examining the extreme cases of wife assault and even murder, the historian Christine Stansell concludes that in court "records of most domestic quarrels, conflicts over practical household arrangements unleashed men's rage." In the less extreme case, working-class "boys' " sport of insulting well-dressed ladies aired hostility toward women who implicitly set the terms for manhood by displaying their own material standards and expectations for "respectable" womanhood.[71]

Cultural negotiations over women's and men's "domestic" obligations to each other spilled over into interpretations of the social meaning of domestic arrangements throughout the city. When high rents kept housekeeping conditions from meeting literary prescriptions, tensions over "the expenses of modern living" revealed especially the vulnerability of the city's middling families to their own investment in "the opinion of the world at large." Thus, although James Fenimore Cooper had confidently declared in his *Notions of the Americans* that "no American who is at all comfortable in life will share his dwelling with another," by the 1830s many New Yorkers who prided themselves on having achieved a comfortable subsistence nonetheless shared houses with other families. Evangelical families such as the Floys could invoke religious principles to reject "fashion"; families of "tradesmen" could call forth values of republican simplicity and economy; the *Mirror* could denounce "empty ceremony." Yet in their very vulnerability, the city's middling ranks looked to the values of respectable home life to clarify their distance from the thousands of New Yorkers who exercised even less control over the conditions of housing.[72]

Amidst ongoing personal quarrels over the expenses of modern living, middling New Yorkers turned to two social rituals—promenades and visiting the poor—to affirm and enact their common domestic values. "Our public promenades are becoming more fashionable," announced the *Mirror* in 1825. The Sunday stroll had taken on new life as a secular amusement. The *Mirror* vigorously campaigned for the Common Council's improvement of the Battery, which quickly became a place of "popular resort." To families whose parlors and neighborhoods fell short of prescription, promenades offered an alternative arena of "visiting" and structured spontaneous encounters on "safe ground." Self-conscious promenade crowds maintained codes of propriety— from proper dress to rituals for introductions—that had evolved alongside domestic hospitality. Indeed, modern dwellings provided both a touchstone and a backdrop for this public ritual. Instructing its readers in the rules of the promenade (keep to the right), the *Mirror* recommended sites that would "repay the admirers of fine scenery." "It is not known to all our townsmen that the spot formerly occupied by Vauxhall gardens is at present converted into a spacious and stately street, ornamented with the most costly private dwelling houses," it advised. "These structures attract crowds of spectators, and are deservedly objects of attention." The *Mirror*'s editors were confident that figuratively and literally, New Yorkers would unite in their admiration of modern dwellings that defined their common standards and goals.[73]

The custom of visiting the poor, which also assumed a new ritual form in the 1820s and 1830s, further allowed respectable New Yorkers to define their own minimum standards of "moral" home life. Although men led such key charities as the Society for the Prevention of Pauperism, women organized their own societies for relieving widows and orphans, advocating temperance, and campaigning against prostitution. Expressing some sense of gender loyalty in their charity work on behalf of "indigent females," respectable women also used benevolence to articulate and defend their own expectations and claims to men's support. Moral reform campaigns extended inextricably linked home and religious duties to the civic arena and found evidence for the depravity of the city's laboring classes in their "domestic habits." Perceptions of the quality of home life as evidence of moral quality structured class interactions by permitting "respectable" New Yorkers to define "undeserving" tenant families as outside the community of mutual obligation.[74]

Systematically excluded from many of the benefits of a new "standard of living," New York's laboring families preferred, when possible, independent poverty to the charity of reformers who in visiting—often without invitation or notice—determined recipients' worthiness by observing their domestic habits. Poor families exercised little control over domestic property; they lived in a world of cash, credit, and personal property—possessions that gained much of their value from their ability to be traded, pawned, or sold. Living within budgets that constantly forced choices between purchases of food, fuel, furnishings, clothing, and entertainment, wage-earning families often rejected middle-class prescriptions. Household furnishings mattered less than clothing and shoes; hospitality within tenant houses followed different codes, and clothing could provide more efficient heating than fuel and a more readily visible expression of self-esteem.[75]

Despite visitors' insistence on home life as evidence of moral character, laboring New Yorkers could not afford to rest their own feelings of social respect on housing conditions. The poor, after all, knew the social circumstances of their own poverty: the death that had removed an essential family member from the household economy; low wages whose value diminished further in the face of high rents and expensive fuel; restrictions of employment based on race and nationality. And knowing their employers, they probably understood the extent to which the value of their own labor was realized in someone else's virtuous home life. Poor New Yorkers had other means of affirming common loyalties and obligations, ranging from the camaraderie of saloons and street life to Afro-Americans' churches. Yet the bourgeois cultural definition of a proper home life—building on and recasting the republican language of personal independence, male protection, female virtue, and corporate family interests—became a powerful concept, one that introduced new ways of measuring the legitimacy of claims to public respect and assistance.

"A standard of living is of the nature of habit," Veblen observed.[76] Those standards included habits of interpretation as well as of consumption. The transition to industrial capitalism did not deliver an improved standard of living on a silver platter. New Yorkers in the first quarter of the nineteenth century struggled to define the necessary ingredients of their own self-respect and particularly the cultural value of "independent housekeeping." By placing the conflicting economic interests of domestic employers and servants, landlords and boarders, husbands and wives, and rich and poor within the frame of morality, they clarified their own standards of judgment as well as of need. Interpreted as a measure of personal virtue, proper home life became the social yardstick that marked out the distance between the city's "respectable" citizens and its laboring classes.

Even as respectable New Yorkers were acquiring the habit of explaining social inequality as the consequence of moral failings, they saw in deteriorating tenant neighborhoods a larger threat to their own values. The Democrat Asa Green satirically pointed to housing's status as the emblem of social order when he proposed a remedy to the riots that had marked the 1830s in New York City. He reminded readers of his 1837 city guide of the riot act:

> I charge ye all, no more foment
> This feud, but keep the peace . . .
> And to those places straight repair
> Where your respective dwellings are.

"Were a magistrate in New York to read the riot act out in the words of our model," Green concluded, "it might safely be answered: 'We have no "dwellings," how then can we repair to them?' Those who have houses of their own are seldom inclined to leave them for the purpose of demolishing the houses of their neighbors." By the late 1840s, a Whig editor saw more radical implications in the housing relations of working-class neighborhoods. "An immense proportion of the present misery of the poor," he insisted, "arises from the associated community—the practical *Fourierism* in which they are forced to live and which does far more than any other cause to destroy those feelings of attachment and of moral responsibility, which belong to the idea of the home."[77]

The "progress of luxury" had found its justification in the "idea of the home." Yet the habit of mind that understood modern dwellings as institutions of public order itself was formed by debates that arose when government officials, developers, and wealthy householders carried the precepts of private home life into public policy. In the face of a public campaign to improve the *city's* "character" and with it the value of real estate, housing's republican meaning as an institution of independent livelihood gave way to the "liberal" equation of respectability and prosperity.

CHAPTER 5

Public, Private, and Common:
The Regulation of Streets and Neighborhoods

"I AM WELL PERSUADED that the plans now in progress by our [municipal] corporation for ornamenting and improving the city must meet the approbation of every person who feels an interest in its character and prosperity," a "communication" to the *Mirror* observed in 1826. "It is indeed gratifying to perceive the evidence of a more enlightened view and a more liberal spirit than were prevalent at former and even some more recent periods."[1]

Such confidence in a "more liberal spirit" came from many directions in the 1820s. With the adoption of universal white manhood suffrage, democratic republicans dismantled the political privileges of landed property and rank. Economically, the opening of the state-sponsored Erie Canal spurred the development of western markets and launched a decade of economic expansion in New York City. Descriptions of "the age of egalitarianism" often conflate the liberalism of democratic politics and laissez-faire economics, but we do well to note contradictory "liberal" tendencies in these two developments, a contradiction pointed up by the object of the *Mirror* correspondent's praise. In applauding "a more enlightened view" he was referring not to the withdrawal of government from the workings of the market but to the municipal corporation's expanded program for building new streets, promenades, and squares. And this "liberal"—generous—public intervention in the city's spatial economy marked an expanded conception of local government's responsibility in organizing the city landscape to accommodate citizens' needs.

In the context of the Revolution, republicans had opposed their vision of commonwealth to the inherited privileges associated with imperial rule. And for a generation following the Revolution (the "former period" noted by the *Mirror*'s correspondent) the meaning and political organization of the commonwealth—and particularly the relation of proprietorship and political rights—remained subjects of intense debate. New Yorkers who advocated abolition of the political privileges attached to landownership also expressed new confidence in the power of an unregulated market to preserve access to real property as the means of personal and civic independence. Thus, in intervening in the local spatial economy, the street commissioners who designed the grid had envisioned a city landscape that would accommodate a mixed petty proprietary and commercial economy and facilitate the circulation of all commodities, including land and housing. The "utility" of the 1811 grid lay in its assertion of social and political neutrality.

The adoption of universal white manhood suffrage further denied freeholders' claims to special privileges and special virtues in determining state policy and the public good. But if landownership could no longer establish political status, it continued to shape local political practices. In the 1820s, domestic property—housing—assumed a new preeminence in the real estate market, in the lives of propertied New Yorkers, and in local governmental policy. And popularly elected city officials (Whigs and Democrats alike) found a new utility in the government's promotion of local economic expansion through public improvements—new or widened streets and open squares—which enhanced particular residential neighborhoods and raised aggregate land values. This utilitarian policy assigned status to land and housing not as a means or measure of personal independence but as a vital investment sector of the city's commercial economy; and it embraced a vision of houses and neighborhoods organized not as productive resources but as social settings that testified to residents' moral character.

Precisely because on its face the abolition of the propertied franchise opened the political process to egalitarian possibilities, we must examine how negotiations over the uses of state authority entered into the construction of new property and housing relations. Propertied New Yorkers who competed within the real estate market pursued often antagonistic strategies to maximize their individual gains. But the use of state power—particularly when local government laid claim to the legitimacy of a larger "public interest"—offered one means of coordinating and arbitrating individual and class interests in the organization of the city's social geography.

In the same way that householders, developers, and journalists defined the respectability of dwellings by contrasting them with multi-tenant housing, bourgeois New Yorkers measured the city's value as a place to do business and reside by contrasting its amenities with those of other cities, particularly of European capitals. Whatever the arguments on behalf of government disengagement from the economy, in practice public improvement policies in the 1820s and 1830s sanctioned and even subsidized elite residential development and condoned the omission of new amenities and utilities in working-class neighborhoods. These policies, which saw an interlocking public good in encouraging respectable home life and rising land values, bore down on the household and neighborhood economies of the city's wage-earning people. With the intersecting vocabularies of "character" and "prosperity" so characteristic of housing discussions emerging again and again in proposals to reshape the public landscape, that unity of conception revealed a darker side of New York City's "liberal spirit."

Even as developers, householders, and city officials argued for the "public" benefit of ornamented residential neighborhoods and rising land values, poor New Yorkers gave new shape to an older concept of common rights—the rights of citizens not to be excluded from the benefits of community resources. In the 1820s and 1830s, propertyless New Yorkers' practice of common rights, their use of the streets to extract a living from unlicensed peddling, prostitution, foraging, gambling, or theft, prompted aldermen to adopt new strategies to enforce public authority and private property rights. Thus city officials introduced redevelopment policies to eliminate older impoverished tenant neighborhoods that relied on the street economy's marginal (and "immoral") pursuits and implicitly contradicted a city improvement program premised on the correlation of character and prosperity. Yet, in the end, these early slum-clearance efforts also revealed a larger contradiction that stood at the heart of the city's emerging social landscape: for some landowners and landlords, the "immoral" conditions of poverty had become a source of prosperity.

In order to understand local government's role in the formation of capitalist property and housing relations, we must first examine the political faith that a redefinition of the political public—the "commonalty" of New York City—would open that polity to all white men, unite them in an understanding of shared public and private goals, and remove the question of landed property's social power from the political agenda. This faith emerged in the process of local political negotiation at the very moment when real estate was assuming a new centrality within the local economy.

"The Nature of Government Must Change": Redefining the Commonalty

Although we associate American revolutionary politics with the formation of a new nation-state, the constitution of republican sovereignty also transformed the structure of the local polity. Charters issued by royal governors in 1686 and 1730 had constituted New York City's political public as a closed municipal corporation composed of the "Mayor, Aldermen and Commonalty of the City." "Commonalty" was not an inclusive term: in order to gain membership in the corporation and the right to vote in city elections, a man was required to own land or pay a fee to become a "freeman," a status granted to artisans whose skills were essential to the colonial port economy. Nor was the municipal corporation viewed primarily as an agent of governance. The chief responsibility of its officers, as it had been for directors of the West Indies Company, was to organize and administer the town's infrastructure—its streets, docks, and markets—in such a way as to promote and facilitate imperial trade. "The strength and increase of our good subjects in . . . our frontier province of New York," Governor John Montgomerie had reasoned in his 1730 charter, "does in great measure depend on the welfare and prosperity of our said city, wherein the trade and navigation thereof are chiefly and principally carried on . . . and we . . . are very desirous and willing to give encouragement to the said city."[2]

Toward the goal of developing the colonial port, charters had endowed the municipal corporation with extensive property—exclusive rights in common lands and in shoreline water lots that accommodated slips and wharves. Public authority derived primarily from management of these municipal properties, and most public revenues came from license fees and quitrents. Elected and appointed officials had promoted and regulated the port's expansion by issuing conditional grants, leases, and licenses; by directing the construction of streets, wharves, and markets; and by restricting traffic obstructions or "public" nuisances. Proprietors, who reaped the dividends of port development, paid for the construction of streets and wharves that adjoined their land. Though the city corporation had been chartered primarily to serve the interests of an "imperial class" of English officials and merchants, its operation, like that of the colonial system as a whole, was instrumental in the formation of New York's local ruling class. The development of water lots into wharves and landfilled streets had especially merged the interests of the municipal corporation and the city's merchant elite.[3]

The imported English practice of assigning public welfare and disciplinary responsibilities to church officials and householders limited the obligations of the municipal corporation to the city's propertyless residents. The Anglican church administered the almshouse and, through church wardens, managed outdoor relief to needy New Yorkers who could demonstrate that they were legitimately "settled" within the community. Municipal authorities also looked to the household system of governance and the authority of household heads to preserve public order. Every householder in the mid–eighteenth century, for example, was expected to contribute to the maintenance of the night watch by assigning household members to perform that duty.[4]

Colonial New Yorkers had understood membership in the "commonalty" as a status analogous to that of a shareholder in a chartered corporation. In the context of the Revolution, however, "public" acquired a more inclusive and generalized meaning. In forming Committees for Public Safety, for example, patriots implicitly identified and claimed sovereignty on behalf of a commonalty that extended beyond chartered or enfranchised status. In New York, it was just this implication of an open citizenry that prompted conservative patriots to reconfirm New York City's royal charter in the 1777 state constitution, that is, to preserve the autonomy and privileges of the closed municipal corporation. Yet the ascendancy of republican theories of commonwealth also prompted a redefinition of the relationship of the public corporation, the sovereign state, and city residents. Fearful of New Yorkers "who viewed corporate power as inherently corrupt," the historian Hendrik Hartog has argued, late-eighteenth-century municipal officials sought state legislative sanction for their right to determine the common good and to govern the republican city.[5]

In many respects, the scope of the Common Council's activities and public authority did not change significantly with the republican shift from an administrative to a governing identity. Minutes of the Board of Aldermen in the four decades following the Revolution suggest the breadth of regulatory powers derived from the mercantile tradition. City officials licensed butchers, carters, and boardinghouse keepers; rented out market stalls; hired inspectors of wood, meat, flour, and lime; maintained the assize on bread; granted ferry and carting franchises; issued ordinances on the removal of refuse, the filling of sunken lots, and the construction of new wharves and streets; and responded to a steady stream of petitions for appointments, tax and assessment relief, and dispensations. Thus aldermen continued to manage local markets alongside public properties. Still, the Common Council's operation as a representative body rather than a closed corporation changed the conception of local government and posed new questions regarding city residents' rights to participate in the political process.[6]

The reach of municipal regulatory powers had long supported a system of political patronage and deference—the constant brokerage of favors, votes, jobs, and influence—which in turn organized the local political process into factional competition. In the context of the Revolution, however, political factions engaged in a larger debate over the nature of the polity itself, and particularly over the definition and reach of democratic political rights. By the late 1790s, New York Federalists and Democratic-Republicans (Jeffersonians) engaged in bitter struggles to control the state legislature and the municipal corporation (as well as the national government). Seeking to affix a clear and dangerous social identity to their political opponents, each group addressed the meaning of property relations in the definition of citizenship. Jeffersonian merchants and artisans accused Federalists of being aristocrats who betrayed republican principles by preserving landed and monopolistic privileges, including the propertied franchise. Federalist "gentlemen of property and standing" in turn charged that liberal republican leaders, disregarding the distinctions of property, would unleash the mob.[7]

As debates over opening the political public to propertyless citizens moved from the high ground of party principle to the low ground of party interest, practical victory on either side depended on recruiting loyal followers who elected party leaders. Even as they debated property qualifications and the status of "freemen," both Federalists and Jeffersonians showed their willingness to manipulate the New York City franchise to serve their own political ends. Thus Federalist mayors effectively abolished the category of unpropertied municipal voters by refusing to grant freeman status to new city artisans.[8] And since men who held land in more than one ward customarily voted for more than one alderman, Jeffersonians tried to enlist additional voters through joint ownership schemes. Thus in 1801 Federalist aldermen contested Jeffersonian votes in the Fourth Ward, where thirty-nine "tenants in common" jointly purchased a house just before the election to qualify as voters; and in the Fifth Ward seventy-four "freeholders" had claimed equal shares of a house valued at $4,000 to meet the $50 property requirement. Only after heated debate did a Federalist majority on the Board of Aldermen disallow these "combinations."[9]

Aldermen's further efforts that year to examine the qualifications of voters whose claims to proprietorship were tied up in family estates or debt exposed other practical problems with freeholding as a definitive political condition. What was the "stake in property" that established a claim to political rights? Could a man vote if he possessed a vested remainder in fee on his mother's life estate in real property? No. Could he vote if property had been conveyed to his mother in trust for him? Yes. Could a man vote if he had contracted to purchase property and paid £20 "as interest on the purchase money which he considered part of the consideration"? No. Could he vote if he had paid the purchase money for a deed executed in another grantee's name? Yes. The 1801 "scrutiny" of contested voters revealed the ambiguities of membership in the commonalty and the uncertainties of propertied status as a measure of a man's public worth.[10]

The political privileges of landownership were giving way in the face of market relations that ideologically served republican affirmations of equal access to proprietary independence and pragmatically undermined the condition—and hence the authority—of absolute proprietorship. Yet perhaps what is most striking about such controversies was the ease with which leaders of both parties abandoned political principles derived from a landed social order in the interest of expanding the base of public power.

In the first two decades of the nineteenth century, propertyless men—with the support of party leaders seeking their votes—continued to struggle for admission to the sovereign public, for the full rights and powers of citizenship. At New York's 1821 constitutional convention, debates over the abolition of property qualifications for the state senate franchise echoed earlier Federalist-Jeffersonian exchanges. Thus Chancellor James Kent, a Federalist, conjured up the danger of "men of no property, together with the crowds of dependents connected with great manufacturing and commercial establishments, and the motley and undefinable population of crowded ports" dominating the Legislature. "The tendency of universal suffrage," he concluded, "is to jeopardize the rights of property and the principles of liberty."[11] Still, much of the groundwork for democratic arguments on behalf of opening New York's political public to all white men had been laid by the market dissolution of traditional meanings of landed property.

If all adult men had *access* to land, the status of being propertied or unpropertied did not represent a fundamental or permanent—and hence politically meaningful—social division. Nor, within Democratic-Republican thought, did those two opposed conditions necessarily represent opposed interests. "The desire of acquiring property is a universal passion," declared the delegate David Buel, Jr. Given this common ambition, Buel dismissed the Federalist "supposition that, at some future day, when the poor shall become numerous, they may imitate the radicals of England or the jacobins of France; that they may rise, in the majesty of their strength, and usurp the property of the landholders." Such a specter was "so unlikely to be realized," Buel confidently concluded, that "before [it] can happen, wealth must lose all its influence; public morals must be destroyed; and the nature of our government changed."[12]

For Buel and other advocates of abolishing land-based political privileges, private property's claim on the state ended with the right to be
"made secure," and such a basic right did not require special representation. Nor could it claim special virtue. Affirming that all men's aspiration to proprietary independence within the commonwealth would
unite them as a public, delegates to New York's 1821 constitutional
convention voted to enfranchise adult male taxpayers and those who
had served in the militia. For purposes of taxation and voting, owning
personal property was as good as owning land.[13]

The new constitution, however, introduced one exception. Delegates
imposed a new property qualification of $250 on Afro-American male
voters. The intention of disenfranchising all black men was evident; the
particular requirement "add[ed] mockery to injustice," charged a dissenting delegate, since the convention knew that "with rare exceptions,
[blacks] have not the means of purchasing a freehold." Prohibited for
nearly a century to own property, New York's Afro-Americans had secured the legal right to devise or inherit land only in 1809. The majority of the delegates, however, implicitly endorsed the position that
when blacks were not "permitted to a social intercourse with the
whites . . . the distinction of color is well understood. . . . It is unnecessary to disguise it, and we ought to shape our constitution to
meet the public sentiment." Whatever the appeal to racist sentiments,
the 1821 constitution itself defined the distinction of color as one
of property.[14]

Whether proclaiming men's "natural rights" to the property of their
own labor while condoning slavery until 1827 or imposing property
barriers to exclude free blacks from citizenship, New York republicans'
investment in white supremacy contradicted their own highest egalitarian aspirations. By mandating Afro-Americans' inferior political status,
delegates especially accommodated the "public sentiment" of city craft
workers who feared labor competition and of city householders who
desired a cheap, "servile" domestic labor force. It was not the only
contradiction in egalitarian thought, but surely at that historical moment—the moment at which the issue was confronted—the very confidence that property qualifications would effectively exclude blacks
from the polity exposed white New Yorkers' determination to maintain
their social privileges in the face of a new "democratic" political order.
That is to say, at that moment delegates self-consciously reached back
to the conventions of landed society to make political rights contingent
on economic power.

Fifty years of debate over the political status of proprietorship culminated in 1826 with the New York State Legislature's passage of
universal white manhood suffrage. In New York City, a new charter

further opened the municipal corporation by providing for the popular election of the mayor. With the exception made on the basis of race, the overt rule of landed property for men had come to an end.[15]

In New York City, however, landed interests continued to define and determine the "public interest." As the delegate David Buel had predicted, the very nature of government restricted the reach of local popular sovereignty. The political authority of propertied citizens stemmed in part from the mercantile origins of the municipal corporation itself, particularly the long-standing identification of local governance with the maintenance of the municipal corporation's properties and the city's commercial infrastructure. How public officials fulfilled their obligation to organize streets, wharves, and markets was a matter of immediate concern to the city's traders, who transported goods, and to adjacent proprietors, who both bore the costs and reaped the financial benefits of government's actions in organizing the built environment.

Traditional mercantilist understandings of the municipal corporation's public duties and authority intersected with new perceptions of the Common Council as the representative body not simply of voters but of taxpayers. By the 1820s, municipal finance had shifted from rents and fees collected from public properties to taxes on private property. The legitimacy of local governments' actions depended on the broad consent of citizens whose money supported public expenditures. Despite propertyless white men's participation in city elections, merchants, proprietors, and taxpayers maintained the closed character of the local political process by controlling the agenda, budget, and policies of city government.[16]

During the 1821 constitutional debates, Martin Van Buren, though rejecting Chancellor Kent's arguments on behalf of the property franchise, had pragmatically acknowledged that landed interests would remain at the core of politics. "Basing representation on property," he had argued, was desirable only "to protect property against property. . . . It is when improvements are contemplated at the public expense and when for those and other objects, new impositions are to be put upon property, then it is that the interest of different sections of the [city] come into contact—and then it is that their respective weight in the legislature becomes important to them."[17] Propertied citizens did not need protection from propertyless voters; because people without property were not subject to government's "impositions," their claims on government's powers would remain marginal. Different "sections" of propertied New Yorkers, in contrast, engaged in intense competition over state policies that directly impinged on their material interests.

Within a government organized to arbitrate the competition of "property against property," how did propertyless New Yorkers (including women and children) make claims on the social resources that sustained the city's political economy? Their labor produced much of the city's "common" wealth, but the nature of government restricted their political claims. Despite the bold experiment of the Working Men's Party in 1829, journeymen and laborers who formed the ranks of the Jacksonian party looked primarily to local government—as they had done for half a century—for job patronage. Or they campaigned for public services (free schools) or protections (lien legislation) that only indirectly addressed the shifting balance of economic power. The historical and constitutional definition of local government's limited powers and responsibilities, the party system, and workingmen's own commitment to private property constrained both the organization and the expression of the overt class politics that posed propertyless against propertied in antebellum New York City. [18]

In a sense, then, the arguments of advocates of universal white male suffrage were borne out. The emerging social antagonisms of the market economy, between employers and workers, landlords and tenants, did not move onto the formal political agenda as *overt* issues that fell within the range of legitimate governmental action. Still, by their very presence within the community and through the occupation and uses of space, growing numbers of propertyless New Yorkers exerted indirect pressures on the process of city government and on the political negotiations of property against property. As housing conditions cast class relations into a new social geography in the 1820s and 1830s, most struggles over local public policies did not take place in the electoral arena. Rather, landowners, leaseholders, tenants, and "vagrants" asserted their conflicting interests and needs in response to the Common Council's day-to-day decisions regarding city development, public welfare, and the preservation of public order. These "administrative" issues overlapped in the regulation of public property, particularly the making and uses of the city's streets.

"Wealth Must Lose Its Influence": Public Improvements

The streets of New York were the city's common ground, the place where people of all walks of life encountered one another as they worked, socialized, or simply passed by. But the streets were not common property. Not all citizens had equal claims to the uses and the benefits of the streets. Rather, streets were public property, owned by the municipal corporation. From the early eighteenth century, the underlying aim of the corporation's street policies was to promote commerce in the very literal sense of facilitating the unimpeded circulation of commodities. In addition to passing ordinances to open new streets, the Common Council proscribed stoops, awning poles, and piled building materials or merchandise that obstructed traffic; and aldermen regulated the activities of licensed hawkers, carters, and even leaseholders in moving their houses. Eighteenth-century municipal officials had seldom found it necessary to explain the advantages of the corporation's policies to port proprietors.[19]

Into the early nineteenth century, aldermen drew on this mercantile tradition to present their reasons for mandating particular improvements in simple formulaic terms that asserted an unelaborated "public convenience," "advantage," or "utility" to the neighborhood. In dissolving the institutions of mercantile monopoly, however, aldermen in the republican city had found it necessary to emphasize their commitment to the redefined *general* public good. Thus, when breaking a ferry franchise monopoly, one committee had explained that "the convenience, safety and accommodation of the Community are the principal objects to be attained," and further, that it was "perfectly immaterial and totally foreign to the principles which should govern the decisions of this board, to enquire whose property is benefitted or is not benefitted by [improvements]."[20]

Whatever their professed interest in accommodating the "Community" as a whole, in determining where and when to build new streets or utilities aldermen did have to inquire whose property was benefited, for such calculation became the basis of paying for public works. According to the benefits assessment system, adjacent proprietors were assigned the costs of opening streets or public squares (and later of introducing sewers and water and gas lines) because whatever the larger public advantages, proprietors immediately gained from the enhanced convenience, rents, and land values that accompanied new traffic and development. The assessment system and local property taxation established an essential principle of reciprocity between private and public interests and benefit; in doing so, it also divided the interests of propertied and propertyless New Yorkers by establishing the former's greater claims on local government's policies.[21]

In the decades following the Revolution, settlement north of Chambers Street drew more and more proprietors into negotiation with city officials as to when and at whose expense vacant land would be brought into "productive use," that is, rendered accessible for development. The 1811 grid plan had prescribed the street layout, but the Common

Council determined the timing of taking land, assessing damages and costs, and grading, paving, and widening streets. The Board of Aldermen (and later the Board of Assistant Aldermen) made daily decisions largely in response to petitions and remonstrances. Proprietors—landowners and long-term leaseholders—engaged in fierce personal and political competition over the locations and costs of street improvements. Much of the conflict turned on varying real estate investment strategies set against particular neighborhood histories of land use. Since any proposal regarding the streets immediately met with remonstrances, the aldermen identified and counted signatures on both sides of any proposal and often accepted majority rule; the majority that mattered, however, was not a street's residents but rather the people who held title to the property or had a long-term interest in it.[22]

With the real estate market booming between 1825 and 1835 (despite a recession in 1829), city officials found that there were often conflicting interests even in the same piece of land. Large landowners generally passed on tax and assessment costs to their long-term leaseholders, claiming that the latter enjoyed the immediate benefits of public improvements. But sometimes long-term leaseholders risked losing everything to this principle. In one extreme but perhaps telling 1827 case, a judge described the situation of the leaseholder of John Jacob Astor's Vauxhall Gardens, a popular pleasure ground: "Madden, the tenant of Astor, had a lease for fourteen years on the garden; and was bound [by covenant] to occupy it as a garden and nothing else; he was obliged to pay $750 rent at all events, and to pay assessments for opening streets through his garden, thereby destroying the property for the only use to which he could apply it." The damage to Madden was great, the judge acknowledged, but Astor experienced no loss, as he still could collect rent, and furthermore, "the property would be returned to him and instead of a garden he would have a great many building lots with the street already made at the expense of Madden, whose interest was destroyed by it."[23] The case, affecting one of the most popular resorts in the city, became something of a local cause célèbre and went through numerous appeals until Madden's estate won its case. But though Astor ultimately had to share some of the assessment costs, he alone reaped the capital gains of land developed into the impressive colonnaded row houses of Lafayette Place.[24]

Such protracted controversies and the willingness of some proprietors to challenge assessments in court pushed city officials to elaborate ad hoc judgments as to the convenience and utility of particular improvements into larger policy statements. Early in the century aldermen had justified assessments by reminding proprietors that they would benefit from improvements. In the 1820s, however, city officials began to reverse the logic of the relation between public and private benefit to stress that public improvements were desirable *because* they increased the value of private property. Often aldermen blurred the lines of argument, as when they recommended the extension of Lispenard Street to Broadway because "the street will be much improved and the property materially advanced in value."[25] But by the 1830s, aldermen's recommendations (like judges' opinions) often incorporated petitioners' arguments and viewed street openings and modifications through the lens of the competitive real estate market. Thus when advocating the widening of Chapel Street in 1836, aldermen reported that "it is a well known fact that for a great many years past, property in the neighborhood has been in a very low and depressed situation [literally as well as financially] . . . and while the price of land in other parts of the city has doubled, trebled or even quadrupled in value, this land has not at all advanced in price. . . . Hence arose the proposal for widening the street."[26]

The shift in emphasis revealed a new way of looking at the city's landscape and in effect commuted land's use value into exchange value: the goal of public improvements was not simply to facilitate the circulation of traffic and commodities but rather to encourage the profitable circulation and use of real estate itself as a commodity. The "public" was to benefit not simply in traffic convenience but in the city's promotion of a particular economic sector. Thus officials rhetorically constructed an entrepreneurial public that identified its collective interest as aggregate economic growth and placed the real estate market at the center of the local economic expansion.

The shift from mercantile to commonwealth to utilitarian conceptions of public improvement policy derived in part from the shift in the municipal corporation's own goals as a proprietor and an institution. In 1813 the comptroller had suggested the city's immediate identification with private property owners when he explained that he was "at all times desirous to enhance the value of the public property and to render it more productive," and recommended a project that would serve the corporation's own proprietary interests "and also improve the City."[27] In other words, the city, like any other proprietor, measured the value of an improvement by its immediate impact on land use and productivity. But as the source of public revenues shifted from fees, licenses, and rents to taxes, the Common Council's interest in improving its own property gave way to policies aimed at increasing the tax base, a political strategy that also represented an effort not to increase the tax *rate*. This "self-interest" of the municipal corporation in submerging the costs of its operation in the profitability of real estate investment blended easily with utilitarian arguments that rising land values were in and of themselves a "public good" that perforce "improved the City."[28]

If the municipal corporation's expanded program of public improvements in the 1820s derived its legitimacy from an earlier mercantile tradition, it also signaled the formation of new "political" coalitions that were identified less by party affiliation than by common interests in real estate development. At the center of these coalitions stood various groups of investing proprietors. Some lower Manhattan merchants and landlords urged street widenings that initiated the commercial upgrading of older blocks of stores and artisan houses and shops. Petitioning rentiers and developers were subdividing and distributing large "farm" tracts north of the central business district to tap the burgeoning residential market. And hundreds of lesser proprietors who purchased or leased vacant lots from rentiers or developers supported the opening of streets that would permit them to realize the value of their petty investments and speculations. As property taxes attached new carrying costs to landownership, these "sectional" real estate interests intersected with city proprietors' more general interest in a policy that kept the general tax rate down by enlarging the aggregate base. Even downtown merchants who owned property primarily for their own enterprises welcomed policies that spread the tax burden away from the lower wards, where land values were highest.[29]

Support for local governments' promotion of real estate as an investment sector was not limited to investing proprietors or taxpayers. New York's petty artisan proprietors (for example, Greenwich Village weavers) most suffered the impact of public improvements when rising rents pushed them out of their neighborhoods. But for many wage earners the inconvenience of moving when rents rose mattered less than opportunities for employment on street projects. In 1818, the Chelsea rentier Clement Moore attacked these laborers when he protested public improvement policies that required him to help pay for the grading and opening of streets through his cherished country estate. In Moore's mind, the whole "liberal" policy of street improvements arose not from city officials' alliance with real estate interests but rather from artisan officeholders' concessions to a propertyless constituency.

"Sometimes a considerable portion of our corporation are mechanics," Moore charged in an angry pamphlet, "and persons whose influence is principally among those classes of the community to whom it is indifferent what the eventual result of their industry may be to society

Junction of Broadway and the Bowery. Engraving by George M. Bourne, 1831. Phelps Stokes Collection; Miriam and Ira D. Wallach Division of Art, Prints, and Photographs; The New York Public Library; Astor, Lenox, and Tilden Foundations.

if they but obtain employment and are well paid out of the pockets of their richer fellow citizens." Contemplating the expense of opening new streets on his Chelsea farm, Moore envisioned a conspiracy of "cartmen, carpenters, masons, pavers and all their host of attendant laborers" who "would find their account in having the streets of the city yearly ploughed up and dug down and filled in and in moving the houses pulled to pieces and rebuilt as fast as hands could be found and money obtained for these purposes." Before the depression of the 1840s, public officials seldom explicitly acknowledged the link between public works and jobs. But the long history of party patronage suggests that, for all his bitterness, Moore had correctly identified a key issue in some propertyless New Yorkers' support for a policy that by promoting rising land values also endorsed rising rents.[30]

Rentiers such as Moore complained that public works were defacing Manhattan's natural beauty. But another loosely constructed "political" coalition saw in a utilitarian policy of public improvements an opportunity to enhance their own residential neighborhoods. This group—who might be identified as the producers and consumers of ornamental city improvements—drew on the rhetoric and values of home life to advocate the construction and embellishment of "respectable" neighborhoods, public squares, and promenades. Identifying their own material and cultural interests with the city's status vis-à-vis other cities, developers and elite householders presented themselves as *the* public whose "good" required such amenities as those found in European capitals. Such newspapers as the *Evening Post* and the *New-York Mirror* (whose editors identified themselves as "orthodox in our morals, our religion and our politics") actively lobbied for programs that brought the city's image up to new standards of "convenience, taste and elegance." New York's "embellishment and beauty," the *Mirror*'s Samuel Woodworth declared in 1825, "will give her a fair claim to rank among the most elegant cities in the world."[31]

In the late 1820s, policies to improve the city's public image went hand in hand with new strategies for investment in residential real estate. To embellish the "monotonous" interchangeable city blocks, proprietors and developers combined restrictive covenants with an accelerated campaign for government favors. In 1828, for example, when Isaac Pearson offered for sale at $12,000 the row houses he had erected on Bleecker Street between Greene and Mercer, the purchasers were required to covenant that the "ten feet between Bleecker Street and the front walls of the dwelling houses there erected shall forever hereafter be and remain open court or space and not appropriated or occupied by any edifice or wall nor in any manner obstructed otherwise than by an ornamental fence or railing enclosing the same."[32] Having created the effect of a uniform residential park, Pearson gained the Board of Aldermen's permission to rename his Bleecker Street block Leroy Place. The Common Council also endorsed the private zoning of Lafayette Place, Waverly Place, Irving Place, and University Place, granting developers permission to enclose parts of the block with railings and/or to adopt new names to distinguish their addresses from the streets they occupied.[33]

The trend toward "enclosed" residential blocks threatened to transform the city's street system. Thus in 1834, faced with proposals for "Lorillard Place" and "Rutgers Place," Jacksonian aldermen reconsidered the public interest in converting streets into "places." At issue was not whether the local government should encourage elite residential development, for the aldermen "expressed unfeigned gratification at the very great and beautiful changes which within a few years past

Leroy Place. Drawing by A. J. Davis, engraved by Dick, c. 1830. From *Fay's Views of New York*. Courtesy of The New-York Historical Society, New York City.

have taken place in the style of buildings for the city." Rather they worried that such "refinements" posed an inconvenience to visitors and residents trying to follow street directions. The already established "places" remained as publicly sanctioned class enclaves within the egalitarian grid.[34]

If commercial interests in convenient traffic directions occasionally overrode residential elegance, other projects revealed public officials' essential sympathy with efforts to organize the real estate market to support new class values. Correlating the appreciation of beauty and land values, the developer Samuel Ruggles was especially successful in persuading the Common Council to modify the city street plan and even to provide subsidies for his elite residential parks—Irving Place, Gramercy Park, and Union Square. In 1831, in response to Ruggles' petition to create Gramercy Park, the Street Committee concurred that they "ought not only to lay out more public squares but also to facilitate enterprising individuals in laying out private squares." Accordingly the committee recommended a special tax apportionment for land on which Ruggles "intend[ed] to prevent the purchasers . . . from erecting other buildings than private dwelling houses. He also propos[ed] to enclose the square with an ornamental iron fence, maintain the same at his own expense, and keep it forever unoccupied so as to admit the free circulation of air."[35] Ruggles did not intend to admit the free circulation of the public. As with St. John's Park, only the proprietors of its bordering houses held keys to Gramercy Park. In the case of Ruggles' development of Union Square, the city itself supplied the ornamental fence to create a park out of the "shapeless ill-looking place devoid of symmetry," and again explained its logic by reference to the twin benefits of public beauty and advanced land values.[36]

The alliance of real estate developers, bourgeois householders, and public officials gained its greatest momentum with the speculative construction of residential parks and "places" on the city's periphery. Tax money went to transform such spaces as the old paupers' burial ground of Washington Square and to create new spaces such as Tompkins Park; and even without subsidies or special dispensations, the high prices and rents of new luxury dwellings covered the private assessment costs of ornamenting such spaces as Gramercy Park. Then, too, once a new tone to the neighborhood had been established, aldermen received sympathetically petitions such as the one from the developer Dudley Selden, urging that a sliver of land be taken to widen Art Street in Greenwich Village. Selden, who had "made liberal offers" to the blacksmith who owned the land, complained that the blacksmith's shop was "a wretched hovel . . . [and] a great nuisance to the neighborhood and must of course very materially lessen the value of his [Selden's] property." The aldermen concurred in the "propriety" of taking the protesting blacksmith's lot "for public purposes."[37]

In the city's older, commercially and residentially mixed neighborhoods, the economic calculus of public improvements rested on a different ground. The 1832 cholera epidemic, for example, prompted petitions to establish a park at Corlear's Hook, the center of the shipbuilding industry. The Committee on Public Lands regretfully responded that although they were "fully aware of the importance of public and open places in large and populous cities and would always recommend their establishment when such measures [could] be accomplished without too much individual sacrifice," they found the Corlear's Hook proposal "too inexpedient inasmuch as the cost would be enormous . . . [and] there would be but a small portion of the land sufficiently benefitted to induce the owner [the industrialist James Allaire] to encounter the large assessments." A park in a working-class neighborhood could yield only a limited return in increased rents. In addition to the landowner's veto power, the aldermen also pointed to merchants' need to reserve shoreline property for commercial uses.[38]

City officials and real estate developers recast the rule of property in New York City in the first third of the nineteenth century by mobilizing public authority to support private proprietors' pursuit of profit in real estate. Like the British Board of Trade, city officials offered encouragement to the city's entrepreneurs, but they did so in the name of a democratic public and addressed themselves to the market circulation of land and houses rather than goods. In the twentieth century, this logic of public improvements for the sake of private accumulation has become firmly entrenched in prevalent versions both of "human nature" (the necessity of incentives) and of rational economic behavior (efficient allocations of land use). But what were the implications of this *new* government policy that encouraged and even subsidized real estate development in the early nineteenth century?

With the population steadily expanding, new streets needed to be opened, and in theory access to vacant lands on the city's periphery would ultimately reduce house prices and rents for propertyless New Yorkers by increasing the supply of buildings. Indeed, in theory all New Yorkers should have benefited equally from the squares opened in the 1830s and the sewers and water lines laid in the 1840s and 1850s. But some New Yorkers were more equal than others.

As had been true on Chambers Street two decades earlier, the building of elite residential blocks in the vicinity of Washington Square and Union Square removed the scattered houses and shops of artisan landowners and leaseholders. And as promised by the very logic of the assessment system, landholders who footed the bills for public improvements recouped those costs in advanced land prices and rents. In an era when investors were only beginning to define the prospects for profits in the housing market, returns from the residential parks and "places" north of Canal Street fueled investors' expectations and speculations on other "uptown" streets. "The exceeding rapid increase of our population, and the measures which have been taken to lay out and form public squares," the aldermen explained, "have so much enhanced the value of lots in their vicinity as to render it desirable for persons of lesser means to turn their attention to situations somewhat more removed . . . where lots can be purchased at such a moderate rate as to come within their means." But as aggregate land values rose, fewer and fewer New Yorkers could gain access to proprietorship or afford the space for independent housekeeping.[39]

Unlike the "private improvement" of Chambers Street, the new patterns and relations of city land use were actively shaped by the local government. The political process offered neither precedent nor means for consulting the propertyless public on how the city's landscape should be organized. Decisions regarding the locations of new amenities and utilities rested on the aldermen's weighing of proprietors' competing petitions; the inconvenience of relocating tenants—and the larger implications of social displacement—seldom tipped the policy scales. Furthermore, the exclusion of propertyless New Yorkers from the decision-making process, as well as their relative weakness within the real estate market itself, meant that wage-earning tenant families could not share in new public utilities and amenities. Landlords, who saw little prospect of recouping from wage-earning tenants the assessment costs of sewers and water and gas lines, generally opposed the introduction of utilities into the city's working-class neighborhoods and tenant houses.[40]

The inequities of power revealed in city policy, however, reached much deeper than whether propertyless New Yorkers could participate in the decision-making process or enjoy the benefits of parks, sewers, and water in their neighborhoods. The priority assigned to investment—the abstraction of land use into competitive returns on costs—marked the final abandonment of the republican vision of independent proprietorship as a common political goal and a new accommodation of land's circulation as capital. This policy, which promoted rising land values and separated the claims of investment from those of customary or prior use, left the city with a new problem: "Where are the poor to go?"[41]

The aldermen who rhetorically entertained this question when they considered petitions to widen and "enhance" Chapel Street quickly concluded that "go where they may, they cannot do worse." But the poor could do worse. The answer to the aldermen's question was that poor New Yorkers would go into denser and denser tenant houses and into the city's streets. Even as the Common Council asserted increasing confidence in its power to improve the city through the regulation of the streets, conflicts over definition and uses of public space grew sharper in the late 1820s and 1830s. And as they did so, the struggles of "property against property" over the moral agenda and costs of public improvements revealed counteralliances among propertied New Yorkers whose income or profits came from the "street economy" of the city's poorest neighborhoods.

"Public Morals Must Be Destroyed": Neighborhood Renewal

New York City's housing and property relations were changing within a contradictory political context. On the one hand, the granting of universal white male suffrage suggested that landed property had lost its power to control the social and economic order. On the other, new claims of landed property to profit had gained local government's endorsement. Thus the utilitarian alliance promoted the "public interest" of rising land values and subsidized elite residential development. But New York's public—the body of the city's residents—was larger than the constituency that set policy.

The policy of improvements had immediate implications for city residents who stood outside emerging utilitarian coalitions. Such "gentry" rentiers as Clement Moore surrendered their exclusive control over the organization and use of their country estates to the grid's entrepreneurial development. Small independent proprietors, such as the Art Street blacksmith who was forced to move, surrendered the benefits of prior uses and personal investments in neighborhood networks and customary traffic. But the full implications of local government's endorsement of real estate as an investment sector became most evident in the condition of propertyless New Yorkers. Although largely excluded and invisible in the lobbying, negotiations, and decision making that shaped the city's landscape, the laboring poor became politically visible in their uses of the streets, especially in the city's oldest tenant neighborhoods.

By the 1820s the growing ranks of New York's laboring poor— swelled by recently emancipated blacks, Irish immigrants, single women, and dependent children—forced city officials and taxpapers alike to redefine the political relation of New Yorkers who controlled property to those who had none. People who had no shelter and no livelihood were traditionally defined as vagrants. Distinguished from slaves, who were themselves property; from "dependents," who came under the authority of householders; and from the indigent but settled poor who could legitimately claim the assistance of citizens, "vagrants" had no rights within the community.[42]

New Yorkers' campaigns against vagrants dated from the eighteenth century, when church wardens could warn paupers out of town. After the Revolution, city officials had taken over the task of conducting periodic sweeps of the streets to "bring up for examination all vagrants, negroes, common prostitutes and other persons likely to become chargeable, whom they may suspect have not gained a legal settlement to the end that they may be removed before the winter sets in." This 1807 conflation of social categories typified the social perceptions of the era. Fears of vagrancy among blacks had recurred in debates over gradual emancipation and prompted requirements that owners have their slaves "certified" as self-sufficient by the Almshouse. Indigent single women without male protectors—implicitly "common prostitutes"—stood as a second class of people who had no claims on a social order that viewed access to property as essential to social standing.[43]

When such sweeps of vagrants could not clear the city of poverty, city officials and private citizens expressed increasing anger at the rising costs of poor relief. In 1817, officials charged with "providing for the Poor" complained that "many hundreds of poor persons, from different parts of this and the neighboring States, resort to New York, especially in winter to throw themselves upon the bounty of the citizens . . . produc[ing] an intolerable burden upon private and public charity."[44] But in the context of periodic depressions, seasonal unemployment, Irish immigration, and the migration of blacks from Long Island, Westchester, and New Jersey after being emancipated without resources—particularly during harsh winters—transient "paupers" as a class were increasingly indistinguishable from the city's "settled" laboring poor. By the 1820s, accusations against "outsiders" who unfairly claimed New Yorkers' assistance were giving way to new perceptions and fears of the poor as a permanent presence within the city's social landscape.

Spurred by evangelicism, the temperance movement, and the increasing visibility of poverty, middle-class New Yorkers organized new charities and paid higher taxes to reform and relieve the poor.[45] But the larger problem that poverty posed to the liberal program of city improvement lay not simply in claims on the purse but in the claims of the propertyless on the uses of public property—on the streets—and by extension on the rights of private property. According to both traditional definitions of private property rights and new utilitarian concepts, one issue in regard to the use of the streets by the poor revolved around the "injury" they did to adjacent proprietors' exclusive interests in the benefits of their houses and shops.

New York's propertied and unpropertied citizens asserted different claims on the public landscape. Propertied New Yorkers proposed to order streets primarily in accordance with principles that enhanced the convenience and value of private property: principles of traffic efficiency and public image. For respectable householders, the rights of private property included protection from unwanted intrusions from the streets; through restrictive covenants they sought to extend this protection to exclude "incompatible" uses of their blocks and thus to secure their investments. For traders and shopkeepers, those rights rested on customers' unobstructed access to their shops and the restriction of competition from transients.

As peddlers, ragpickers, prostitutes, scavengers, beggers, and sometimes criminals, New York's casual laboring people used the streets as a common landscape that subverted private property's exclusionary powers. The street economy rested on the elimination of shop rents and the spontaneity of encounters. Without "overhead" payments to a landlord, it was possible to gain or supplement subsistence by peddling fruits, oysters, hardware, used clothing, or sexual favors. Scavenging, gambling, and the illicit activities of shoplifting and pawning petty merchandise could further extend wages. No less than foraging on rural common land, the "liberty" of the streets supported the city's poorest residents.[46]

As the street economy of the laboring poor expanded, petitioners complained in 1829 that peddlers "did injury" to the "fair and regular traders" of the city. Their offenses, as rehearsed in a petition urging the state legislature to "prohibit the practice of hawking and peddling articles of merchandise through the streets of the city," were at once economic and moral:

1) The evil tendency of such mode of dealing upon public morals, many children and minors being engaged in it and it being a vagrant mode of life.
2) The facility it affords for disposing of stolen property and the opportunities it presents to commit thefts without detection or punishment.

3) The gross imposition to which it exposes many persons and families in the quality of goods thus offered for sale.
4) Total want of responsibility on the part of persons engaged in the mode of dealing and the injury it does to fair and regular traders who pay rent for stores. [47]

In using the language of vagrancy, the petitioners invoked the customary definition of people without rights in the community. Peddlers who did not "pay rent for stores," who were frequently children, who stole to secure life's necessities, and who did not respect the rights of the city's "fair and regular traders" challenged the social authority of private property. The small shopkeepers who sought protection from such competition welcomed local government's intervention to enforce their claims as both private proprietors and members of the legitimate public to the rights and benefits of the streets by keeping them clear of people who pursued a "vagrant mode of life."

Such conflicts between petty proprietors and the laboring poor within mechanic neighborhoods extended outward into the relations between neighborhoods. For if the peddling and foraging of the transient poor impinged on private proprietors' rights, so much greater were perceptions of the injury that the "settled" street economy of poor tenant neighborhoods did to respectable New Yorkers' investments in the larger city's improvement. Thus alongside renewed efforts to restrict the activities of public drinking, peddling, and prostitution, officials began to focus their attention on particular tenant neighborhoods that they perceived to be breeding grounds of the "vagrant mode of life." As the municipal corporation launched a program of regrading, widening, and repaving the streets of lower Manhattan, petitioning citizens and city officials proposed a new remedy for the perceived dangers of such neighborhoods: slum clearance.

New York City's experiments in slum clearance through the widening or closing of particular streets began in the spring of 1829, when the Common Council received several petitions to clear a triangle of land in the Five Points neighborhood of tenants, taverns, and "horrors too awful to mention." Noting that Five Points "is a place of great disorder and crime and it would be particularly desirable to rid the city of the Nuisance complained of," some 2,400 memorialists from outside the neighborhood urged the city to exercise its powers of eminent domain to take the land and to build a new city jail on the site. [48] City officials' claims to the unity of their moral and economic responsibility in ordering the city's streets brought them up against competing private interests, and on the same day two aldermanic committees split sharply in response to petitions to clear the Five Points triangle.

The Street Committee, finding "that nearly all the buildings occupying the ground are in ruinous Condition of but Little value and occupied by the lowest description and most degraded and abandoned of the human species," recommended that the triangle's intersecting streets be widened to forty feet each, "the remainder of the ground to be appropriated for Public purposes."[49] The Police and Jail and Bridewell committees, on the other hand, jointly rejected their petition, reasoning that the low landfilled ground at Five Points would produce "great Mortality in a crowded prison." The incarceration committee observed further that however offensive its style, Five Points paid its own way: they knew "of no public use which this block, if taken, could be put to, [and] it would probably be valued very high to the Corporation as it produces a great rent on account of its being a good location for small retailers of liquor who have located themselves in the vicinity. What may be considered a nuisance has in reality increased the value of the property."[50]

Here was a central tension in the liberal agenda for simultaneously enhancing the city landscape and promoting aggregate economic growth. The economic advantages of respectable neighborhoods at the city's periphery lay in the rate at which land apppreciated in value; landlowners and developers realized the benefits of new or renamed streets and public squares by constructing buildings of high quality which attracted the city's wealthiest residents. Once a respectable residential block had been established, investment depended on preserving the neighborhood's reputation. As the buildings of the city's older neighborhoods decayed over time, land values did not advance so rapidly. The value of such buildings to investing landowners rested less on the calculus of rates of appreciation than on the level of rents collected over and above costs. The very deterioration of old buildings reduced landlords' tax and maintenance costs; and subdivision for more tenants increased rents.

By the 1830s, Five Points and the Lispenard Meadows territory of the old Trinity Church farm were the oldest and most densely occupied neighborhoods in the city. When landlords found they could not attract "respectable" tenants, they had turned the houses over to leaseholders who operated them as brothels, gambling houses, and taverns, thus producing "commercial rents" that far exceeded what the houses would generate solely as multitenant residences. Afro-American New Yorkers, excluded from legitimate trades and unable to afford housing in other neighborhoods, often operated these "red light" establish-

Five Points, 1827. Lithograph from *Valentine's Manual*, 1855. Courtesy of The New-York Historical Society, New York City.

ments, even as they preserved their respectable church and associational life within the same territory. These neighborhoods also accommodated new waves of Irish laboring families. And since it was poverty rather than race that placed people in these neighborhoods, the spatial mixing of poor whites and blacks fanned fears of "amalgamation."[51]

The issue of race relations—or more precisely, the issue of blacks and whites freely socializing with one another—ran as a subtext through much of the discussion of poverty in the 1820s and 1830s. The imposition of the property qualification on black voters had revealed white New Yorkers' assumption and determination that Afro-Americans would remain among the city's poorest residents and that the cost of that poverty would be their right to vote, their very membership in the sovereign public. Northern masters who emancipated slaves frequently left them without resources; dockworkers, carters and other artisans repeatedly reasserted the color line in their trades. But the crowding and physical contamination familiar to the city's indigent blacks were also conditions that might be encountered by laboring white families confronted by chronic unemployment, the death of a primary wage earner, or separation from a family support network. Precisely because they belied assertions of the "distinction of color," poor neighborhoods with an "amalgamated" racial population became the city's most threatening emblem of poverty's "contagion." Even before racial and antislavery tensions erupted in the 1834 anti-abolition riots, city officials sympathetically entertained new proposals for the "remedy" of clearance.

The initiative for extending the city's power of eminent domain to clear the Five Points triangle came from outside the neighborhood, because it was respectable outsiders who perceived the neighborhood as a danger to the city as a whole. The particularly offensive block contained, an 1831 report noted, nine houses "all old and mostly built of wood" and three small brick-front houses. The residents numbered "about 175 of whom more than two-thirds are vagrants, having no visible or honest means of livelihood." Furthermore, there were about 80 black tenants and 120 females, "all of whom, with the exception of perhaps 10–15, are proper objects for a Magdalen asylum."[52] Despite the ambiguous arithmetic, it was a familiar catalogue of people without rights in the community. By their presence, petitioners claimed, the Five Points tenants obstructed (and tempted) the flow of respectable social traffic through city streets. Thus reformers presented an argument on behalf of slum clearance which has persisted for more than a century and a half, claiming that "experience has shown that it is only by widening the streets in the vicinity and thereby inducing capitalists to invest their funds in the erection of spacious buildings that any effectual or competent remedy can be effected."[53]

Five Points was certainly not the city's only poor, densely crowded, physically deteriorated, and racially mixed neighborhood; it was simply the most visible. Its proximity to Broadway and City Hall, as well as to the expanding commercial district of Chatham and Pearl streets, contradicted popular images of the city's "enhancement" and progress. And Five Points occupied prime territory between the city's commercial center and some of its finest East Side residential blocks. The 1831 clearance proposal, like that of 1829, was blocked by the remonstrance of Five Points leaseholders, who pointed out that "taking the property in question will only send the inhabitants to the neighborhood buildings and thereby crowd the greater number of the same class together." But reformers persisted, and in 1833 the triangle was cleared.[54]

The campaign against Five Points had only begun, and by the mid-1830s similar arguments were being marshalled in efforts to widen other lower Manhattan streets to clear out "nuisances," particularly on such streets as Chapel and Anthony, which had a concentration of black residents, taverns, and brothels. In 1836, advocates of widening Anthony Street (which intersected the Five Points neighborhood) expressed both immediate personal and more broadly conceived class interests in redeveloping the neighborhood. Among the most ardent petitioners for redevelopment were several merchants, a shipwright, a master builder, a brass manufacturer, a surveyor, and a clothier who resided on East Broadway and Monroe Street. By the 1830s, these blocks formed an island of respectability among the subdivided artisan houses of Henry Rutgers' farmland. The prominent householders were offended by the boisterous street life of the adjacent neighborhood to the east, which devalued their own environs and culturally isolated them from the rest of the city. The issue was not traffic flow per se but rather the unpleasant experience of traveling through Anthony Street to reach Pearl Street, Broadway, or any of the city's new residential parks and places. Widening and extending Anthony Street through the Points, petitioners insisted, "will afford a very commodious as well as convenient street, at present so much required by the public, which when completed can be travelled at all times by our wives and children alone, without interruption or insult, which cannot now be done without a protector."[55]

The East Broadway and Monroe Street householders were joined by bank and insurance company presidents, substantial retailers in

Chatham Square and Pearl Street, merchants with property intersecting Anthony Street on Broadway, and investors who held lots on Anthony itself. Retailers in this second group also urged the widening of Anthony to remove the "most disgraceful barrier" of tenant houses and brothels, which they believed deterred respectable traffic between Chatham Square and the "elegant buildings" on Broadway. Commercial proprietors and investors who supported the street's widening knew that individual initiatives in converting single lots to more lucrative use were insufficient to realize the advantages of a geographically prime location. Only through the assertion of a broad public interest could they succeed in transforming the area and along the way capture a windfall gain in land prices and rents. "Breaking up this haunt of infamy," they argued, would encourage "proprietors of adjacent ground to build houses for respectable families," which would "greatly benefit the owners of lots" and "achieve a moral improvement more effective for public safety."[56]

Petitions for Anthony Street's clearance mobilized remonstrances from neighborhood proprietors and landlords faced with the prospect of assessments and a change in the neighborhood's economy. Three groups came to the defense of the Anthony Street neighborhood: independent proprietors, small landlords, and rentiers. Although they had different reasons for resisting the demand for clearance, they represented a coalition of propertied interests that in the end was as central to the operation of the city's real estate market as that of merchants, developers, and respectable householders.

Some of the protesters were independent householders, shopkeepers, and mechanics—a stonecutter, a carter, a laborer/shoemaker, a black fruitier, a milliner, a boardinghouse keeper, grocers, and the widows of a wheelwright and a carter, who lived and worked at houses they had erected or purchased on leased land; they were less interested in the investment value of their lots and houses than in protecting the site of their livelihood or independent housekeeping. Beyond the burden of assessments for improvements they didn't want, both the age and condition of their own houses and that of adjacent tenant houses kept tax costs in the neighborhood low. The brothers N. C. Platt and George W. Platt, jeweler and thimblemaker, respectively, complained that renewal would force them to relocate. The former held a "favorable lease" on a house at 17 Mulberry Street, "which will be taken away from me by such alteration, and thus subject me to the necessity of removing my residence farther from my business, which would be an item of no small importance and loss of much time, as my Clerks reside with me, and the scarcity of dwellings nearer my business would oblige me to remove farther from it." Such householders had made their own peace with their poorer neighbors.[57]

The small proprietors and householders aligned themselves with a group that had a different kind of interest in the neighborhood. This second group consisted of the leaseholding landlords of tenant houses, many of which were used as brothels and taverns. The grocers Patrick Collins and Elijah Valentine, for example, owned four tenant houses; the undertaker Abram Florentine owned two houses as well as a livery stable and his own house in the neighborhood; the widow A. Guion ran a china shop and owned three neighboring houses. These petty landlords also objected that they could not afford the assessment costs assigned them under long-term leases for improvements that would remove the very tenants (wage earners and prostitutes) on whose rents the landlords depended.[58]

The small proprietors and landlords of Anthony Street and Five Points were joined by a group of rentiers who included some of the most prominent men in the city—Benjamin Romaine, Henry Remsen, John L. Livingston, and Peter Lorillard. In defending the "haunt of infamy" from the improving impulses of other respectable citizens, they found themselves in a somewhat awkward position. Although doubtless aware of the illicit activities that generated their rents, they defended their interests and their reputations as honorable men with paternalistic protestations on behalf of their less-secure leaseholders and charged that the moral campaign against Anthony Street was itself tainted by the crude material interests of real estate speculators. The "plan of the speculation of a few," they insisted, "would cause the beggary and ruin of many widows and orphans, as also those who hold leases, and who are bound to pay all assessments." Peter Lorillard promised that "when the leases of his property expire, he will erect good substantial houses," but reiterated his concern for his present leaseholders' risk of "ruin."[59]

This alliance of large and small proprietors came to the defense of the neighborhood's poor and transient wage-earning tenants, who were ultimately the source of revenues and profits from Anthony Street's houses. "We are not disposed to join in the crusade which is carried on by the speculator against the poor," they declared at a "large meeting" at the Sixth Ward Hotel, "and are not reconciled to measures that drive hundreds from their homes under the specious plea of improving a neighborhood." After all, if there was a "vicious class" in Five Points, "we desire to be informed to what location such a class can be driven more desirable than the vicinity of our criminal courts and offices of detention."[60]

Revealing the economic interdependency and shared vulnerability of New York City's petty proprietors, small landlords, and poorest laboring tenants, as well as the opportunism of rentiers, the meeting also reiterated charges of speculation and corruption. Thus the meeting's remonstrance stressed—probably with reference to Alderman Myndert Van Schaick, who owned three lots on Anthony and had signed a petition for its clearance—that "such [of] our fellow citizens as hold seats in the City Council, ought never to allow themselves to vote upon, much less to be active in urging measures in which they have a direct pecuniary interest." "A few interested and influential individuals," far from seeking to serve the public good, were making "exertions" for Anthony Street's clearance in order "to obtain special legislation for their private pecuniary advancement."[61]

Such struggles over the poorest tenant neighborhoods revealed underlying structures—the methods of "private pecuniary advancement"—that stood at the heart of the city's simultaneous drive for improvement and the steady deterioration of housing. Proprietors' and reformers' debates over widening streets and thus clearing lower Manhattan's older artisan/tenant neighborhoods arose in tandem with the beautification of elite residential blocks. "Moral improvement" won out in the initial struggle over Anthony Street's widening, but the neighborhood proprietors were able to overturn the aldermen's decision when the 1837 panic brought real estate investment and government redevelopment policy to a temporary halt. The "sudden reverse," another group of backpedaling improvers explained, meant that improvements that they had once enthusiastically advocated "would put them to great expense and destroy the present usefulness of their property."[62]

During the depression that followed, new market dynamics took over the redevelopment process in lower Manhattan. Faced with reduced rents, some proprietors made up their losses by adding rear houses and tenements, or by crowding in more tenants. With economic recovery other investors who had acquired land and houses at depressed prices began to build warehouses and stores. The persistence of tenant houses and the introduction of new commercial structures on streets below Canal Street precluded the building of the "elegant dwellings" envisioned by earlier reformers. Respectable New Yorkers had learned that the most socially secure neighborhoods were those on the city's periphery, and developers abandoned the effort to persuade them otherwise.[63]

By the 1840s, Five Points' tenant houses, brothels, and saloons had become, to many citizens' dismay, a major tourist attraction as the center of the city's lowlife. New York's claims to the status of a European city were backhandedly achieved when Charles Dickens likened the Points to London's own notorious East End. Meanwhile, the campaign to clear the heart and history of Five Points continued well into the twentieth century, until it was finally won when courthouses and the Police Plaza were constructed on its site.[64]

On one level conflicts over the uses of streets and the social life of New York's poorest tenant neighborhoods revealed not the divisions between propertied and propertyless residents but rather the tensions within the local politics of property against property. Manhattan landowners and leaseholders exercised the power of their political and economic standing to petition public officials to accommodate their needs and interests in the organization of the public landscape. Their differences revolved around different modes of securing a living or realizing profits from real estate. At this level, the struggle over clearance revealed the underlying conditions of the city's emerging capitalist housing market: the vulnerability of small independent proprietors and a dual structure of profits that could be extracted out of elite residential blocks and out of crowded tenant neighborhoods. And in this respect, tenant neighborhood life, however demoralized, was integral to the city's larger economy: it both sustained the laboring classes and generated profits for a landlord class.

On another level, such struggles suggest that poor New Yorkers' survival strategies (and the very culture of a street economy) formed one arena of resistance to propertied New Yorkers' authority to define and control the public agenda for the city's "improvement." No less than the utilitarian alliances that shaped the logic of improvement policy, the street economy of the poorest tenant neighborhoods established fluid and indeterminate boundaries between public and private spaces and interests. By using the streets to secure their livelihoods, however illicit in the eyes of respectable citizens, poor New Yorkers restored the claims of common property—the right not to be excluded from the city's resources. Outside the polity, the city's poor could make few claims other than the practical possession of territory.

Public officials' impulse to find spatial solutions to the city's growing poverty was not confined to campaigns for neighborhood redevelopment. When it was not possible to remove indigent neighborhoods, city officials hoped to remove the people. By the mid-1830s, the Almshouse, Bridewell, City Hospital, and Debtor's Prison had all exceeded their physical capacities to accommodate the city's sick, indigent, and criminal residents, three categories that frequently overlapped in the eyes of men empowered to incarcerate them. Even as aldermen heard mid-Manhattan residents' objections to placing these institutions in their neighborhoods, in 1837 the Almshouse Commissioners offered a new tactic for isolating New Yorkers who stood outside the dominant public order. "The increase in paupers keeping pace with population and receiving great addition from the want of present employment for the producing classes, together with excessive immigration from Europe," the commissioners observed, "renders it expedient to revive consideration of erecting another establishment for paupers." The aldermen agreed that it was "not improper explicitly to state . . . that great advantage would be gained by locating such establishment on an *island* separated from that on which the city is built."[65]

Yet, as real wages steadily declined, there was no way to remove the presence of poor people who made up the labor pool of New York City's industrializing economy. Although city officials continued to entertain proposals for public street improvements that spurred redevelopment, they increasingly turned their attention to regulating the laboring poor through police surveillance. When day watches failed to preserve the peace, city officials looked to other cities, particularly London, for new models of law enforcement, and after a decade of debate, in 1845, they instituted a new citywide police force.[66]

Not the least problem for the police in preserving order and protecting private property rights was the definition of public offense. One typical mid-century police report on persons taken into custody during the past three months listed 14,662 arrests (roughly three arrests for every hundred city residents). Slightly over 10 percent of those persons were arrested for, or on suspicion of, crimes against persons or property. Over 80 percent had been taken into police custody for various forms of "immoral conduct" (including 4,241 for intoxication, disorderly conduct, or both) or for "crimes" of condition (7,659 "indigents," 74 "lodgers," 431 lost children, and 428 "vagrants"). The report suggests, as reformers had claimed a decade earlier, that the everyday "nuisance" of life in poor tenant neighborhoods—the crime of poverty itself—posed the greatest threat to respectable citizens' feelings of safety and command of city streets.[67]

When in 1819 John Pintard decried the new "conception of morals" in New York City, he pointed to the drive for wealth and the corruption of luxury.[68] But when Delegate Buel listed the destruction of public morals as one condition for the political mobilizaton of the propertyless against the propertied, he contemplated the end of respect for private property. The difference in their emphases was more apparent than real, yet the utilitarian conception of public and private morals, by positing unqualified good in expanded competition and aggregate economic growth, sanctioned the accumulative impulse without confronting its social consequences. Worrying that poverty impinged on (as well as produced) the benefits of private property, respectable New Yorkers could label it as immoral or even criminal. And the very definition of poverty's public immorality limited propertyless New Yorkers' powers to challenge the rights of private appropriation. The fact that profit itself came out of the immoral exercise of private property rights did not lessen proprietors' claims to public protection. The nature of government did not change, wealth did not lose its influence, and propertyless New Yorkers did not rise up "to usurp the property of landholders."

The antebellum language of property and morality, of "prosperity and character," moved fluidly from pulpits and parlors to the offices of aldermen and real estate investors. Offended by the living conditions of the city's poorest neighborhoods, New Yorkers in the 1820s and 1830s blamed neither employers nor landlords but rather the tenants themselves. To the extent that bourgeois New Yorkers regarded a new institution of property—the home—as the measure of society's material and moral progress, it is not surprising that politicians in the 1820s and 1830s readily accommodated proposals to enhance elite residential neighborhoods and reform immoral tenant neighborhoods. The assumption that shaped propertied New Yorkers' and public officials' perceptions of poverty—that the laboring poor lacked character as well as money—also determined investment strategies within the housing market. In the liberal age of egalitarianism, rentiers and builders encountered little political resistance as they went about the business of systematically constructing a class-divided city landscape.

CHAPTER 6

Building a Housing Crisis

"IT IS STATED that a finished house without a tenant is not to be found in this great city," the *Niles Weekly Register* noted in 1825, "and that well-dressed families are observed to be occupying houses of which the builders do not appear to have accomplished the work so far as to have fully closed them in by doors and windows." Again and again in the early decades of the nineteenth century, newspapers, visitors, and residents reported that the city did not have enough housing, indeed that in some seasons a "private house" was "not to be had for love or money." By the 1840s, the tone of such complaints had gained a new urgency. New York City's chronic housing shortage did more than inconvenience "well-dressed families"; it permanently altered the city's social fabric. "Thousands and tens of thousands," reported the *Morning Courier* in 1847, "are compelled to exist from day to day under the constant, crushing pressure of . . . terrible sufferings resulting directly from the miserable houses in which they live." Families were sleeping in cellars under basement apartments; people without shelter were crowding the precinct houses where they were taken as "vagrants" or "indigent lodgers"; the city's mortality rate, particularly in working-class wards, was climbing. New York City faced its first major housing crisis.[1]

On the face of things, New York City did not lack the resources to build new housing. In the first quarter of the nineteenth century, speculative building emerged as one of the port's largest capitalist enterprises. By the 1820s, two-fifths of the city's artisans worked in the building trades, producing more than a thousand buildings a year. A decade later, the capital invested in new construction exceeded $3 million a year, rivaling the production of ships, clothing, and shoes as a major New York industry. Yet in those same years, building failed abysmally to keep pace with the growth of New York's population, and the quality of new dwellings—their designs, locations, and prices—did not match the needs and means of the majority of city residents.[2]

More than any other industry in the first half of the nineteenth century, speculative building brought home to all New Yorkers the new conditions of capitalist production. What determined new construction was not the social need for housing but the rate and security of profits. And what determined profit was not simply the costs of land, labor, materials, and capital, but the larger set of social relations that determined those costs; the income of would-be tenants; the organization of the building industry; the felt cultural need for particular forms of housing; and the competitive advantages of alternative investments.

Contemporary observers, who had no doubts as to the demand, readily acknowledged the overwhelming determinative power of capital's drive for profit in the building of new housing. "Surely our wealthy and enterprising citizens would find it answers their object," the *Mirror* argued, "were they to invest their surplus capital in building by which they would insure a good and secure interest for their money."[3] Yet they were at a loss to address the underlying conditions that determined a "good and secure interest" and shaped investors' strategies within the housing market. As an easily accessible arena of local investment, speculative building did attract the savings and capital of hundreds of New Yorkers in the early decades of the nineteenth century. This influx of investment capital transformed the organization of the building trades, spurring the development of the "industrial" contract system. But speculative construction was also fraught with risks: neither the building process nor the product was easily subjected to the predictability and discipline of factory production.

In the eyes of most investors, the greatest risk was the uncertain economic ability or willingness of the city's residents to purchase new housing, whether for their own occupancy or as rental properties. Through the 1830s, credit-dependent builders, who could ill afford the carrying costs of unsold inventories, tailored their product to the seemingly most reliable market—merchants, manufacturers, professionals, and the most successful artisans. Indeed, the extraordinary boom in new town houses, which created the city's respectable residential neighborhoods, testified to the value that middle-class New Yorkers attached to domestic property as a necessary ingredient of their social identity.

For New York's growing number of wage-earning tenants, however, new housing, though "ready-made," remained a luxury good. "Capitalists who alone possess the means for erecting better buildings," one housing reformer explained in 1853, "appear not to have known how much the laboring class suffered" and had not built new tenant housing because "the opinion . . . long prevailed that such property was unproductive."[4] But if builders and investing landlords alike regarded *new* working-class housing as "unproductive" in the 1820s and 1830s, its very shortage guaranteed the "productivity" of subdivided old housing stock.

The 1837–1843 depression devastated the construction industry. Such a "crisis" often marks a culmination or turning point. The recovery of Manhattan residential building, however, prompted less a redirection than the fulfillment of a logic that had emerged out of the city's rental housing market. Antebellum builders, like other manufacturers, sought to increase their profits by reducing production costs, especially the costs of labor. Yet as real income declined for growing numbers of workers, so did the level of effective demand, that is, the level of income that could be directed toward the rents that secured builders' profits. The restricted supply of working-class housing created effective demand through crowding, and the subdivision of old housing stock became landlords' surest hedge against the vicissitudes of New York City's industrial wage economy. In the 1840s, tenements—the first purposely built multifamily housing—rationalized three decades of tenants' ad hoc crowding into a new housing form.

In order to understand the pattern of new construction in antebellum Manhattan, we must look more closely at why the city's capitalists did not "find that it answered their object" to build more housing and at how New Yorkers responded to the housing crisis as a permanent feature of the city's nineteenth-century landscape.

The Rise of Speculative Building

The production of houses in New York City underwent dramatic changes at the turn of the nineteenth century. In colonial Manhattan, builders, like most artisans, had generally created their product for a known customer. And most customers commissioned new housing for occupancy on land they owned or leased. A local economy of simple commodity exchange—the owner/occupier's saved, borrowed, or inherited cash for the builder's labor—had formed one basis of colonial artisans' proprietary independence. In the first half of the eighteenth century, carpenters and masons had built from 20 to 50 houses a year as the population increased from 7,000 people (in 800 to 1,000 houses) in 1700 to 25,000 people (in approximately 2,500 houses) in 1770. In the two decades following independence, as the population rose to 69,000 people, builders raised from 500 to 700 new buildings a year. Not only had much of the town's old building stock burned or deteriorated during the war years; successful merchants and artisans had turned to "modern dwellings" as a new measure of personal independence.[5]

The dramatic increase in building registered population growth and rising levels of personal wealth, and in turn propelled the rapid appreciation of land values. Furthermore, the formation of a new residential market encouraged New York landholders and builders to produce houses as ready-made commodities for general sale to unknown customers, including landlords. Between 1785 and 1815, in a process that introduced residential wedges into old trade neighborhoods and established new residential blocks, speculative ventures generally raised from one to five houses at a time. Thus a typical notice in 1807 offered "four new houses" "to be sold together or separate," and in 1810 the "gentleman" George Clinton sold a row of three dwellings for the substantial sum of $4,075 each to a grocer, a tin plate worker, and a cabinetmaker. In 1813 John Jacob Astor, in one of his few ventures into residential construction, entered into a contract with the builder John West for five brick-front houses on Spring Street at $1,388.87 each.[6]

In contrast to the uncertainty of postrevolutionary Manhattan land speculation, speculative building, which promised returns from the sale of domestic space in a general market, also guaranteed land's appreciation. Rentiers had acknowledged this advantage of development when they introduced covenants requiring leaseholders to build "substantial houses." As landownership declined in the first quarter of the century and land values and house rents increased, leaseholding landlords joined homeowners in bolstering the market for new dwellings intended as rental properties.[7]

Building multiple houses required substantial amounts of advance cash to pay for labor and materials. Capital for speculative construction projects came from the profits of shipping and such manufacturing enterprises as tanning and brewing, from ground rents, from estate annuities, and especially through credit. New Yorkers used mortgages both to purchase land and to raise the capital to improve their landholdings. Like business itself, the channels of credit were more personal than institutional in the early decades of the century. In 1800, for example, Leonard Bleecker, an auctioneer, agent, and early real estate broker, had made a typical offer of "money to loan": "One sum of 1000 dollars, one of 2000 dollars and one of 10,000 dollars may be had at common interest for a term of years by mortgage of real estate in this city."

Three years later, when Bleecker advertised his wish to borrow money, probably for a client, he reversed the mortgage offer: "Wanted on loan, $15,000 on approved real estate in the city for one or two years." Most mortgages (whether to arrange a sale or raise capital) were for short terms, running from one to five years at 6 percent interest. A typical notice offered for sale eight lots at "20% [down] and 20% annually with interest, to be secured by mortgage"; in 1803 a relatively inexpensive "two story framed building, containing four rooms with fireplaces," might be purchased for "one half purchase money May 1; other half may remain on mortgage eight or ten years."[8]

Large and small investors who purchased or leased "building lots" generally used that land as collateral to raise the funds to improve it. A leaseholder who paid an annual ground rent ranging from $20 to $50 in the early decades of the nineteenth century could raise from $500 to $1,000—one-third to one-half the cost of constructing a house—on the value of that appreciating twenty-one year ground lease.[9] The mortgage and leasehold systems together expanded the ranks of small investors as shopkeepers and successful artisans joined merchants in taking multiple ground leases on the port's periphery to pursue building investments. Master carpenters and masons also used mortgages to finance their speculative ventures.

Master builders who were expanding their trade and hundreds of small landowners and leaseholders produced the first generation of rental houses. By pursuing new opportunities for profits in the housing market, these petty entrepreneurs threw their political support as well as their dollars behind the ideology of a competitive free market as the path to a democratic social order. Yet the participation of small entrepreneurs in this market rested on an unacknowledged alliance with and deference to traditions and practices of landed monopoly. Major capitalists in the system remained New York's merchant rentiers, such as John Jacob Astor. Astor's position as both rentier and creditor allowed him to collect rising ground rents and interest while leaseholders went about the business of developing the long-term profitability of his extensive Manhattan properties. The interchangeability of land and credit which underwrote speculative construction further extended the class powers of landed monopoly into the new arena of finance capital.[10]

Construction capital in the early nineteenth century came from institutions as well as from individual creditors. Between 1795 and 1820, the New York Legislature chartered twenty-four city fire insurance companies with a total capital worth of $9.85 million. Charters often prohibited these insurance companies from placing their capital in financial intangibles, such as stocks and bonds, but permitted them to hold well-secured mortgages. The city's early banks, in contrast, tended to concentrate on commercial loans. Still, as late as 1830, only one-third of the capital invested in new construction came from chartered corporations. In the housing market's formative years, real estate remained a highly diffuse and personal investment sector. As such, it reflected the judgments and prejudices of individual landowners, creditors, and builders, who developed their strategies by watching one another's successes and failures and who readily identified people such as themselves as the most "productive" in New York's housing market.[11]

The rise of speculative building prompted changes in the organization of the building process. Most eighteenth-century building contracts had arranged for the owners' payments in exchange for the "measure and value" of each builder's work. When John G. Leake arranged to have a house built on Park Row in 1804, for example, he drew up separate contracts with a master mason and a master carpenter. These master builders were directly accountable to Leake for the hours and wages of the "day labor" they hired. Owners such as Leake or their personal agents closely supervised the building process. Though the contract generally specified an estimated price as well as a timetable, the owner and builders could adjust costs and payments as the work proceeded. In 1812 William Rhinelander, for example, deducted wages from his carpenter's bill when he was dissatisfied with the workmanship on a new house.[12]

Many owners and leaseholders who undertook multiple building projects considered it a nuisance to obtain materials and hire and supervise separate artisans for each phase of construction. Thus they began to arrange contracts with one builder, who in exchange for a fixed price and according to a prescribed timetable supplied materials and labor and arranged subcontracts with other artisans. For this service, contractors received a commission. If the contractors themselves worked on the building—as they often did in the early nineteenth century—the cost of their skilled labor was figured along with that of their employees.[13]

Most contracts specified installment payments as the building went up and reserved final payment until the building was completed and an outside judge had certified that the finished product complied with the contract's specifications. When the building contract set a fixed price, entrepreneurially minded contractors who reduced the true production costs below that estimate could claim any favorable difference as their own profit. Owners who surrendered control of the building process sought to protect their interests in the quality of new houses by specifying in detail the materials, manner, and timing of construction. In the absence of an express contract stipulation, for example, a contractor might use pine instead of the more expensive oak timber that an owner expected. Specifications for room dimensions and finishings prevented builders from literally cutting corners. The costs of specified materials could be fixed with recent market information and generally remained inelastic. The variable cost during the construction process was that of labor.[14]

In the early decades of the nineteenth century the contract system varied as to the division of owners' and contractors' responsibilities and control, but it fundamentally altered the relations of contracting builders and their employees. Eighteenth-century master builders had regulated their own competition by organizing trade associations to set minimum wages for their workers each season, and the price was then passed on to the owner/customer. But as the pace of new construction accelerated and the contract system intensified competition, shrewd builders sought to cite the season's standard labor price to owners and then hire workers for less. The cheapest workers were also the least skilled.[15]

The expansion of New York's free labor market eroded the rights, training, and status of journeymen who had affiliated with a single master builder. Journeymen builders—especially carpenters—organized to protest these changes in their trade. As early as 1785, "a considerable number of Principal Journeymen Carpenters" had felt it was

incumbent upon them to lay before the impartial public the following imposition which the Masters have practiced: The Master Carpenters have long made it a practice to employ Journeymen (so very ignorant of their business, that some of them have been at a loss to know the right end of their tools) upon very low wages, while they charge the employer 12s per day, the wages only paid to good workmen, and from which they have 1s 6d per day [commission]; for what reason? Because their ignorant journeymen are taught by us, what the Master ought to instruct them in. About 12 of these Master Carpenters having agreed to reduce our wages to 9s per day, but still charging the employer 10s 6d and positively insist on having the above allowance made to them even should wages be reduced to 6s a day, we now submit our case to every candid Reader.

Against this expropriation, the journeymen carpenters proposed that "employers" (owners) hire them directly for their labor at nine shillings a day, "as we should sooner receive our money from the Employer than from any of those Masters whose ungenerous conduct justly merits our contempt." Despite such resistance, however, the conduct of more and more masters within the industrializing building crafts suggested that neither "generosity" nor craft paternalism could be reconciled with successful competition.[16]

Speculative builders, whether working on their own or as contractors, worked against time and money, for the mortgage compounded the two. In order to convert interest on loans into profits, investors pushed their builders to produce as quickly as possible. Competing with one another, builders in turn pushed their own hired workers to build more quickly at less expense. The consequences of such competitive strategies troubled many consumers and producers. Those owners and builders who shared journeymen's contempt for contractors' use of "ignorant workers" continued to link quality to the older system of day labor. Through the mid–nineteenth century, advertisers noted a dwelling's construction by day labor as a selling point, and editors regularly indicted speculative builders for shabby products "built to sell," such as six buildings on Reed Street which, being only one brick thick, collapsed in 1825.[17]

Though some independent builders made personal fortunes through the traditional craft system in the first half of the nineteenth century, within the larger industry the champions of day labor were gradually losing control of the building process. The ascendant contract system frequently led to legal conflicts when owners dissatisfied with the quality of work refused to pay final installments on buildings that failed to meet specifications. Contractors in turn demanded compensation for the "measure and value" of labor that gave the owner a valuable product, even if it deviated from the agreed-upon standards. Since New York judges tended to enforce building contracts strictly in support of owners, some contractors faced with cost overruns abandoned projects before completion. Others completed the job but failed to pay their subcontractors, hired workers, or materials suppliers.[18]

Organizing to protect their interest in being paid, construction workers brought the ongoing disputes over the rights and obligations of owners, contractors, and wage earners to a head in the late 1820s. Building mechanics focused on the industry's "merchant capitalists," who supplied the cash for land, materials, and labor, owned and distributed the product, and determined the overarching conditions of production. Joining the Workingmen's movement, carpenters, masons, and stonecutters demanded that the owners of new buildings be held accountable for contractors' obligations to pay their employees. New York's building workers campaigned for lien legislation that would place an encumbrance, comparable to a mortgage, on a new building until all workers on the project had been paid. Such a law would, in effect, take new houses hostage for contractors' obligations to workers and materials suppliers. The owner had to pay off the lien in order to establish clean title to a new building.[19]

Through the lien law, independent builders and journeymen sought to hold contractors accountable to their workers and by implication to the community. Competition at any price was not a public good. But men of property, embracing the utilitarian logic of an ever-expanding market, argued that the community could best preserve its claims on local capital by protecting and encouraging competition, whatever its form or price. Thus in 1829 the Whig *Morning Courier* weighed the advantages of a lien law "aimed at protecting the mechanic and at the same time preserving uninjured the capitalist who invests his money in houses" by stressing the mechanic's own interest in an unregulated and unencumbered market. Such a law would discourage investment, the newspaper warned, and "a few master builders of large property who could give ample security [to the owner] for the payment of their workmen" would dominate the building industry, destroy competition, force prices up, and send capitalists scurrying from construction. Appealing to artisans' pronounced sentiment against monopoly, the newspaper stressed that holding owners liable for conditions of employment within the building trades would destroy the favorable investment climate on which the community as a whole depended for its new housing. The *Courier*'s warnings about the dangers of "monopoly" did not extend to the concentrated ownership of land or control of credit.[20]

State judges shared the *Courier*'s concerns that liens would disrupt the contract building system. New York's lien law, first passed by Jacksonian legislators seeking to capture workingmen's support, went through five revisions between 1831 and 1855, but the courts repeatedly construed it narrowly to protect owners' interests. Strict rules governed the posting of a lien and the liability of succeeding owners, and whatever protection the lien did give workers under a contract did not extend to subcontracted workers or materials suppliers without a further legislative struggle. In the eyes of judges, to hold owners liable for the conduct of contractors would result in "virtually compelling an owner to pay all money directly to the laborer, and to the material man, to do away with all building by contract, and compel all improvements of lots to be done and paid by the owner by 'day's work' . . . [a development] in the end as prejudicial to mechanics and laborers, by discouraging improvements, as it would be inconvenient and hazardous to the owner."[21]

New York's building workers remained among the best organized and most militant in the city as they struggled against employers over hours, wages, and control over the work process. But in the eyes of New York's entrepreneurial class, construction as an industrial enterprise required the protection not of its workers but of investors. Promoting competition to reduce costs and shielding owners from contractors' mistakes and exploitations seemed essential to *encourage* new construction. The underlying contradiction remained, however, that workers who did not get paid or whose real wages fell could not afford to purchase the new "industrial" goods that they produced. Though housing was a social necessity, city residents had no claim other than their purchasing power on the way accumulated local wealth would be deployed. Within twenty years of the lien controversy, editors and reformers found themselves reinvoking a traditional concept of social and moral "duty" to urge capitalists to construct more housing. Their efforts were defeated by the logic of the competitive profit motive, which they themselves had so firmly embraced as the best means to guarantee that new housing would be built.

The Logic of Residential Construction

In New York's eighteenth-century mercantile economy, merchants who turned to land as a relatively secure long-term investment had settled for returns that often fell short of the 5 percent interest rate. In the early nineteenth century, landowners who looked for substantial short-term profits from building new housing also found that real estate was highly vulnerable to other sectors of the economy which determined both production costs and the level of income that supported demand. As an overall trend, housing absorbed a significant portion of the city's rising per capita wealth in the early decades of the century. But however culturally important the new institution of the home was becoming, the ability of New Yorkers to pay for "modern dwellings" and the willingness of capitalists to invest in construction depended on the state of the city's larger economy.[22]

The pace of new construction tended to follow business cycles. New building stagnated, for example, from 1812 to 1815, during and immediately following the war with England; but when population growth and shipping recovered, the construction industry boomed. "Many buildings are going up in the city," *Niles Weekly Register* reported in 1818, "materials are high and mechanics find plenty of employment and good wages." Furthermore, "a gentleman of leisure who has examined every street in the city [reported] that there is now erecting and finishing, south of Spring Street, no less than 1969 buildings, upwards of 1000 of which are intended as dwelling houses." Yet in November of that year the insurance clerk John Pintard, viewing this activity with an experienced eye, wrote his daughter that "February will show whether we are not overbuilt. The commercial world has suffered extremely from the unprecedented scarcity of money and the depression of stocks is beyond everything before known." The following April, Pintard reported that "on walking thro' a great number of streets I found an unusual proportion of Houses with bills to let, which proves what I apprehended, that there would be more building than tenants this spring. . . . Rents . . . must fall with the fall of trade."[23]

The panic of 1819 hit real estate especially hard, and in 1820 *Longworth's Almanac* took the unusual measure of reporting 400 vacant houses in the city. The reported vacancies suggest just how elastic consumer demand for new dwellings was, despite population growth and rising per capita income. Housing investments did not return to the 1818 level until 1824.[24]

In the face of such market uncertainties, investors and builders concentrated their energies and their capital on producing new row houses for families most shielded from unemployment and most willing and able to pay for new housing. While the elegant three- and four-story town houses on Bond Street, Hudson Square, and Leroy Place dramatically displayed propertied New Yorkers' new standards and tastes in housing, the great bulk of residential construction accommodated more modest "respectable" renters. In the decade 1825 to 1835, as New Yorkers surged to new dwellings between Chambers and 14th streets, standard brick or brick-front houses cost from $2,000 to $3,500 to build on lots that ranged in price from $500 to $1,000. Such new houses were generally occupied by one or two families, their servants, and occasionally boarders.[25]

In the summer of 1831, the Westchester rentier Richard B. Morris undertook a speculation typical for the period and contracted with the builder Samuel Martin to construct "four good and substantial two story brick dwelling houses" on Suffolk Street, part of the old De Lancey farm. Morris agreed to pay Martin $10,400 for the houses, $2,600 each, and Martin in turn agreed to begin building immediately and to finish the houses by November. According to the specifications, each house was to be 18 feet, 9 inches wide and 40 feet long, typical dimensions for New York's modest row houses.[26]

The carefully drawn specifications for the houses suggest the twin requirements of respectability: utilities that enhanced domestic working conditions and ornamental details that satisfied architectural taste. Thus Martin agreed to "make and completely furnish the cistern, pumps, fences and privies," and to provide the front stoop, vaults, grates and iron railings as well as paneled doors, venetian blinds, and a "front door trimmed with neat pattern column and fan light." Morris himself supplied eight marble mantles and eight pairs of fireplace brasses, but at $45 each they did not depart from the basic economy of the houses. Though the contract did not specify the expected use of interior rooms, typical row houses contained a kitchen and dining room (or, alternatively, a bedroom) in the basement, front and back parlors (or an upstairs dining room) on the first floor, chambers on the second floor, and (unlike the Morris houses) attics or half-stories for servants or boarders. Two-story houses generally had from three or four bedrooms, and three-story dwellings contained from five to eight bedrooms. Such houses built as rental properties might contain two kitchens, and closet chambers supplied additional sleeping space.[27]

Morris, acting as an estate trustee, financed the project with a mortgage for $10,991.75 at 6 percent from the landowner John Jay. Even before paying Martin the last installment for finishing construction, Morris had arranged to lease one of the houses. He collected $275 rent a year on each house, a 10 percent return against 6 percent interest. Paying $100 a year in taxes and insurance, Morris recovered the cost of building in eleven years. If he had had to purchase the lots, the additional $2,400 expense would have added three years for full recovery of the investment. Such a return contrasted with eighteenth-century expectations of a 5 percent return, or "twenty years' purchase price" to recover the cost of an investment.[28]

The rents of $275 to $500 a year on most new dwellings required that tenants have an annual income of $1,000 to $2,000—the income of a professional, small merchant or successful artisan or shopkeeper. Securely employed skilled mechanic households (earning from $400 to $600 a year) might also afford new brick-front houses if they took in boarders or shared quarters with another family. So long as investors and builders could obtain rents in this middling bracket (that is, rents that secured a 7 to 10 percent return on land and building costs), they had no incentive to alter the basic town-house design. Builders who entered the much smaller luxury housing market—such as the $13,000 dwelling purchased by John Pintard's merchant son-in-law in 1828—risked more capital for higher returns.[29]

Speculative construction of typical town houses occurred at three levels in the decade 1825 to 1835. The first involved modest independent builders who might raise one to three houses a year, either by using long-term leases or, if they were more prosperous, by purchasing building lots. In the late 1820s the carpenter Henry Bayard, for example, developed five to eight lots on twenty-one-year leases from Trinity Church, raising the capital primarily through mortgages from the Phoenix Insurance Company. Bayard also mortgaged leases to a hardware merchant and a New Jersey wheelwright; builders going out on their own often found one or two such backers willing to advance money on mortgage without entering directly into the speculation by purchasing land or contracting for labor. Small-scale independent builders, who were most likely to produce housing aimed at an artisan market, were especially reluctant to experiment with the successful formula of a known product. Initiating their own projects and financing them through small mortgages, they played very close to the margins: a sudden increase in the prices of land or materials or a sudden contraction in the consumer market for their finished houses could send them into the Court of Chancery on a foreclosure proceeding. Bayard, for example, withdrew from independent speculative building following the 1829 recession.[30]

Master builders also worked as contractors for the second group of speculators, whose ventures filled in the city landscape from Canal to 14th Street. Lawyers, merchants, shopkeepers, and craft entrepreneurs directed their savings into the construction of from one to fifteen houses over a ten-year period—investments worth from $3,500 to $40,000. Such investors as the druggist Benjamin Underhill, who developed more than ten lots leased from Henry Rutgers; the bakers Charles and Barant Deklyn, who purchased and developed five building lots on Christopher Street; and the lawyer Thomas Wells, who underwrote the development of Waverly Place, usually arranged contracts with one or two builders to raise houses both for sale and for rent.[31] Like independent builders, these investors relied on mortgages to raise building capital, but they also had their own reserves—frequently in the form of multiple building lots and a steady income from business—to cushion the risks of their construction investments. The proliferation of modest speculative projects created new business for brokers, who managed the sale of both land and houses. Those investors who met with success in one area of the city often formed partnerships to consolidate their resources and undertake larger schemes. Thomas Wells and the merchant/insurance broker Thomas Mercein, for example, moved from projects on Waverly Place to Gramercy Park.[32]

Such old landed families as the Moores, the Stuyvesants, and the Livingstons, and such new rentiers as the pressmaker Alfred Pell, the shipbuilder Henry Eckford, and the tobacconist George Lorillard also participated in speculative building both by leasing lots under restrictive covenants and by developing their own land. Morgan Lewis, for example, built and rented out more than twenty two-story houses on his De Lancey farm property, using housing rents and the interest on mortgages he held to pay for new construction. John Jacob Astor, in contrast, left residential development entirely to his leaseholders.[33]

New York's most successful independent builders entered into joint speculations with landowners to form the third group, developers, distinguished primarily by the extent and turnover of their landholdings and construction projects. In the late 1820s, the lawyer and developer Samuel Ruggles began his real estate ventures (with a small inheritance and his wife's money) by buying up building lots (under covenant) on Waverly Place in Greenwich Village and reconveying them to builder-entrepreneurs. As Manhattan's population moved north, many of the multiple inheritors of eighteenth-century farms found the management and carrying costs of those estates a burden, especially after 1825, as taxes rose and street assessments were levied. Ruggles, who offered assurance as to both the profitability and the respectability of his projects, purchased farmland from the Watts, Williams, Stuyvesant, and Burling families and in turn drew members of those families into financing some of his ventures. In managing land acquisition, finance, construction, and sales, Ruggles established an informal business network of creditors, brokers, contractors, and agents which formed a model for the mid-nineteenth-century consolidation of building and real estate companies.[34]

In the 1830s, as the city prospered from booming commerce with the West, Ruggles and other developers adopted a new strategy that transformed the building contract into a conveyance. The developing landowner and the builder entered into a contract for the construction of a house which included a covenant requiring the builder to purchase the house upon its completion at a price that incorporated the costs of both the land and construction. Such buyback building contracts firmly linked the production of housing to the production of new city neighborhoods. The developer, who usually bought up multiacre tracts and then subdivided them into building lots, gained the advantage of a certain buyer and price for a particular lot—a price enhanced by the improvement. The contract also gave the developer control over each building's design, which was crucial for the successful transformation of large land tracts into the uniform block fronts that stabilized land values. The builder under these contracts gained both the funds to undertake the project and the possibility of substantial profits when he resold the land and building. If the property was transferred to the contractor before a lien had been properly posted, judges held, such building contracts also circumvented mechanics' liens. Using conveyance building contracts, Ruggles and the builders Moody Cummings, John Nichols, and George Furst—among the city's wealthiest contractors—erected rows of town houses in Greenwich Village, between 14th and 23d streets, and on Third and Fourth avenues.[35]

The projects of independent builders, small investors, and developers combined with rentiers' strategies to shape the city's new residential landscape. Through the 1820s most middling families continued to share dwellings, to take one or two boarders, or to house relatives; but with commercial prosperity after the opening of the Erie Canal, the "single-family" town house came into its own. According to the popular theory of the antebellum period, the city's wage-earning population could inherit soundly built middle-class dwellings when the original tenants migrated to the new houses being supplied by builders to the north. Such a theory reflected the practical filtering process that had subdivided houses for multiple tenants and boarders since the late eighteenth century. It also revealed investors' and builders' underlying assumption that producing new housing for wage-earning families was—in the city inspector's phrase—"not productive."[36]

By the late 1820s, however, new social implications of this housing market logic had emerged: New York's wage-earning population, concentrated in the "industrializing wards" of the Lower East Side, was growing faster than the city's middle class. The highest rate of profit for construction was at the periphery, where the value of vacant land advanced rapidly as it underwent improvement. The rapid rate of new residential construction in the city's "upper section" (Wards 9 and 11 between Houston and 14th streets) between 1825 and 1830 did not relieve the rising density of lower-central and East Side wards (Wards 5, 6, 8, 14, and 7, 10, 13). Below Houston Street by 1830 an average of eleven people occupied each of the predominantly two-story brick-front and wooden houses of the previous two decades' construction. Above Houston an average of nine persons occupied larger houses that offered new amenities in plumbing, sanitation, and heating. The filter was breaking down.[37]

As growing numbers of wage-earning households found that individually they could afford rents only in the city's older wards, collectively they made old housing stock productive to investing landlords. The lower wards' workshops, taverns, groceries, and tenant houses occupied twice the number of lots as dwellings in the upper wards; but rents from these older buildings supported land values that were six times those of the upper section. The relatively higher prices of land in

City of New York. Map by David H. Burr, 1839. Courtesy of the New-York Historical Society New York City.

lower Manhattan's mechanic wards offered landlords and builders little incentive to replace houses. Thus through the 1830s, rentiers and leaseholders such as those on Anthony Street had often defended the poorest tenant neighborhoods from proposals for slum clearance in order to protect their own interests. Those lower Manhattan streets that were widened in the 1830s attracted investments in commercial buildings rather than new housing. The pattern of new construction, far from relieving the rising density of mechanic wards, reinforced the class bifurcation of the housing market.

The crowding of old housing stock made tenant houses profitable not only through the first conversion to multitenant occupancy but through subsequent subdivisions that increased gross rents. The reduced maintenance expenses and tax assessments that accompanied deterioration further increased landlords' net rents. The rising density of mechanic neighborhoods, in increasingly sharp contrast to new residential blocks to the north, suggested to landlords and builders alike that wage earners, who of necessity had grown accustomed to cramped quarters, needed less space than more affluent households. Landed capital's drive for profit—as much as that of industrial employers—had reduced wage earners' standard of living by reducing the quality of shelter— and of domestic working conditions.

The Collapse of the Housing Market

Builders responded to their own perceptions of the strength of demand—the purchasing power of particular customers for new dwellings—by tailoring their product to middle-class means and needs. They also decided how much housing of what kind to build and where to build it on the basis of construction costs. Even as the demand for dwellings was growing with the expansion of the city's economy, the cost of producing that housing increased. The relation between the two became most readily apparent in changes in the nature of houses being built.

The capital requirements and credit dependency of independent builders, small-scale investors, and developers rose dramatically in the 1830s with the rising cost of land, materials, and labor and with the increasing cost of credit itself. Builders invested in better construction materials and larger houses in order to secure and increase their return from expensive land. By 1834, wooden houses made up only one-fifth of the city's new dwellings, marking the end of the era when artisan leaseholders built houses for their own occupancy. Whereas in 1824 three-fourths of the new buildings were two stories high and none more than three stories, ten years later one-third of new structures were three or more stories in height. New stories rose, in part, as a consequence of enlarged commercial buildings; over two-thirds of the city's new stores (which represented 15 percent of new construction) were three or more stories high by 1834. But the decline of two-story dwellings to less than one-fourth of all new houses also exposed the impact of the land market on developers' strategies and signaled a redefinition in New York's standard dwelling form.[38]

In 1830, following the 1829 recession, land values rose by 14 percent (to approximately $87.5 million overall) and continued to rise by 7 to 10 percent annually over the next four years. Fed by commercial construction and land speculation, this steady rise further reflected and encouraged the activity of residential developers such as Ruggles, who expanded his joint speculation projects for construction at the periphery. The city's finest three- and four-story town houses were going up by the block in the vicinity of the new residential parks that had been sanctioned by city officials—Union and Washington squares—as well as up Broadway and Fifth Avenue.[39]

The trend toward building three-story houses in the mid-1830s, however, reflected more than the demand of the city's elites for more spacious dwellings. Rising land prices raised the entry costs for the small independent builders and investors who were most likely to build housing in working-class wards. With subdivision following within a decade of a house's construction, builders and landlords were beginning to recognize that two-story dwellings were economically inefficient in the city's mechanic districts. Landlords would quickly have to pay for alterations for the inevitable conversion of single- or two-family houses to denser occupancy (through the addition of a story or the partitioning of rooms). And since landlords set rents according to their desired return from construction or purchase costs, an additional story gave them more flexibility in obtaining that return, or even increasing it. Thus by the late 1830s, three-story houses had begun to appear on streets removed from the elite and middling neighborhoods of Greenwich Village, St. Mark's Place, and Union Square. Particularly on the Lower East Side, three-story houses gradually began to fill in vacant lots and to replace the two-story artisan houses of the previous three decades.[40]

Clearly intended for multifamily occupancy, many of the new three-story tenant houses continued to follow the design of older town houses: 18 to 20 feet wide by 40 feet deep with additional living quarters in the attic, basement, and even cellars. Landlords divided the interior space into more rooms—three to four rooms to a floor—and rented two-room "apartments" to one or more families. Larger barrack-style buildings, which began to appear in the Lower East Side's industrial waterfront district, extended the length of such housing to 60 feet. The industrialist James Allaire is said to have built Manhattan's first "tenement," a "four story house designed for many tenants" on Water Street near his foundry in 1833. Landlords also sought to increase the productivity of old housing stock by adding rear houses and courts. Though these new structures marked the first designed accommodation of multiple tenancy, the pace of new building in the city's older working-class neighborhoods continued to be slower than that to the north.[41]

The capital requirements of construction increased with land prices, building size and materials, and labor costs stemming from renewed organizing efforts in the building trades. Rising production costs, as well as the scale of developers' projects, in turn extended the credit webs supporting speculative construction. New York's prevailing short-term mortgages, while increasing creditors' security, also exacerbated the risks of default for delayed or overextended building projects. Creditors in the finance sector, whose business was the circulation of capital, had little interest in foreclosures on uncompleted buildings. Rentiers such as John Jacob Astor often preferred to settle for their reliable 5 percent return on ground rents (which increased with the steady climb in land values) and placed their liquid capital in commercial loans, banknotes, or mortgages for the sale of land rather than for its development. The perceived risks of construction loans in turn raised interest rates for the building industry as builders competed with new investment outlets in western land, transportation, manufacturing, and finance. Higher interest rates alongside rising land prices placed an additional burden on small investors and independent builders.[42]

To reduce the expenses of construction, editors and developers urged city officials to make new land accessible by opening streets; such land, being farther out, would cost less, and its development, they argued, would accelerate the filtering process. To encourage the city to sponsor more public improvements, Samuel Ruggles had provided the Common Council with a survey of the city's real estate and building markets. His report showed that in 1831, more than $6.5 million had been loaned on mortgages in New York City. Nearly two-thirds of this capital came from individuals residing in the city, and one-third from "incorporated companies." Two-thirds of the mortgages were at 6.0 percent interest, but nearly one-fourth brought 6.5 to 7.0 percent interest, with an additional one-tenth at 5.0 to 5.5 percent (as might be arranged in a family rather than a commercial transaction.)[43]

Ruggles presented his figures to the Common Council as evidence of the vitality of real estate investments in the city, but in other quarters he expressed a different concern. Though the city's land market thrived, developers and builders had encountered difficulties in securing capital to improve land. Even as small independent builders joined the Workingmen's movement in calling for usury laws, Ruggles wrote to Senator N. T. Talmadge in 1832 to explain why the Legislature should not set a ceiling on interest rates. Citing the rate of growth in the city between 1825 and 1831, Ruggles argued, "Now it really behooves us to look around and contrive how to find money enough to build our city."[44]

Keeping pace with population growth and maintaining existing density rates, Ruggles estimated, would cost $3 million a year to build 1,500 houses annually (an optimistic calculation of $2,000 per house). "This money we must borrow and our law givers knowing our necessities must allow us to borrow it where we can and pay for it as much as we can afford." Ruggles went on to note that in such cities as New Orleans and Cincinnati, plagued by a limited supply of specie, interest rates had climbed as high as 10—and in some instances as high as 20—percent. In his own city, Ruggles observed, "capitalists lend freely to us because we pay all that the money is worth. And why should not the city be built with borrowed money? Why should not the lender of capital be allowed to take a risk with one per cent and assist enterprising builders in improving the city and increasing its taxable property? If the risk of their loans is worth seven per cent per annum, no law or legislative enactment can reduce it to six."

A legislative limit on the interest rate, Ruggles warned, would "drive capital into other channels and out of the state." Arguing that "the only legitimate business of this city is to distribute for the country," and that therefore the "city must increase to handle [that] business," he appealed to the state's larger interest in promoting city development. Land values had increased by 45.6 million in seven years; real estate, Ruggles passionately affirmed, "is *marching onward* and *cannot stop*." In May 1837, however, the march came to an abrupt halt.

Reports that cast the results of the 1837 panic in the "most gloomy and formidable light [that] can possibly be imagined are not exaggerated," Peter G. Stuyvesant wrote Ruggles in February 1838. "It appears to me the whole community has made a strike, engagements and positive stipulations are at naught—individuals cannot from their present position make good or fulfill promises entered into with the most scrupulous fidelity."[45]

With the panic of 1837, the contraction of credit in all sectors, and the subsequent recession from 1838 to 1844, hundreds of Manhattan landowners and builders defaulted on mortgages and lost their property through foreclosure. The 1837 panic put a brake on a two-year joyride of speculation and inflation. Fueled by an accumulation of factors—cotton prices, the balance of trade with Europe, the supply of English specie, the Opium Wars in China, federal monetary policies, and the credit policies of local institutions—the panic rebuked Americans' enthusiasm for the consolidation of international capital before its time. As the "provisioner" for the rest of the country, New York City had pumped credit across the continent. Locally, the speculative disposition had manifested itself in the real estate market.[46]

Between 1830 and 1834, land values had advanced at between 8 and 10 percent a year. But as the speculative fever caught on in 1835, land values took their sharpest upswing in twenty years, increasing by nearly 17 percent; and the following year they soared by 62 percent, to $233 million. This astonishing surge reflected in part the rebuilding of lower Manhattan's commercial heart following the fire of December 1835. The fire had destroyed more than 600 stores and houses. But with 1,000 new buildings constructed outside the wharf district, housing construction, unlike the aggregate real estate market, had had a brisk but not aberrant year in 1836. Land and commercial building, not housing, had attracted capital beyond what the city's businesses or residents could pay back in rents.[47]

With the panic, the distended real estate investments of 1836 collapsed in on themselves, and values dropped by 16 percent. In 1838, land prices held steady, and in 1839 they even rose slightly. But by 1840, the real estate market lagged in tandem with the depression that crippled the city's entire economy. Business failures and massive unemployment forced landlords to reduce rents. The $116 to $139 million extended on mortgages in 1836 set off a series of defaults that continued over four years as those mortgages came due. Between 1840 and 1843, land values declined by an average of 4 percent a year. The 1843 low point still exceeded the pre-1835 level, but stagnation gave little encouragement to new construction. With economic recovery in 1844, land values hobbled forward the rest of the decade, gaining 2 to 4 percent a year. Manhattan real estate had (temporarily) lost its investment glow.[48]

Producers and consumers of new housing went down together. The small building investors—merchants, lawyers, and manufacturers—turned their efforts to preserving their own businesses. Independent builders turned to contracting; and contractors who couldn't find work tried subletting buildings or becoming landlords' agents. Building mechanics joined the city's laboring poor in the endless search for jobs and enough income to pay their rents, and some found work on the Croton water project. The survivors of the 1837 panic were those who held reserve wealth—investors who had not overextended themselves and financiers who had played both sides of the credit bubble, balancing their own speculations on borrowed capital by the loans they made to others. John Jacob Astor emerged a profiteer of wreckage. Foreclosing the mortgages he had extended on land he had sold in order to buy new lots to the north, Astor consolidated his real estate holdings and waited. Other investors who had not gone bankrupt retrenched; some took a cue from Astor and plowed their reserves back into cheaply acquired land.[49]

The prophet of real estate's drive forward, Samuel Ruggles, fared better than most. Through his own careful financial management and his substantial reserve wealth, Ruggles was able to meet his obligations by selling off land and houses. Indeed, in 1839 and 1841, he continued his development of Union Square and built his own house there and one for his daughter and son-in-law, George Templeton Strong. But Ruggles took little satisfaction in mere survival. "I am tired of being in debt," he wrote in 1840, "and of paying interest with one hand and taxes with the other." The solution was to liquidate his Manhattan real estate holdings and look elsewhere. Thus Ruggles fulfilled his own prophecy of capitalist behavior and redirected his assets "into other channels"—canals and railroads. When he returned to real estate speculation a decade later, Ruggles went bankrupt in a project to build the Brooklyn Dry Docks.[50]

After the ravages of 1837, wholesale speculative building stalled for nearly a decade in New York City. Ruggles had calculated that if the city were to grow at the rate of 15,000 people a year, it would require 1,500 new dwellings annually to maintain the 1830 citywide average density of ten persons per lot. The city grew by 100,000 people between 1835 and 1845. Although the rate of growth was uneven during the decade (slowing down following the 1837 panic and accelerating after 1842), the average number of new buildings per year, 1,059, approximated Ruggles' projected need. The average number of *dwellings*, however, did not.[51]

Not only was new housing not going up in proportion to population growth, "uninhabitable" old buildings were not being replaced. New residential buildings between 1838 and 1842 averaged 674 a year; on the basis of Ruggles' own proposed standard of density, the city's supply of houses fell behind by over 1,500 buildings in those five years alone, pushing more than 15,000 additional people into existing housing stock. In 1842 the city inspector, John Griscom, estimated that more than 14,000 New Yorkers lived in cellars, courts, and rear houses. By the mid-1840s, police records reported that "the number of destitute persons to whom lodging was given in several District Headquarters" exceeded 20,000 a year.[52]

The building industry began to recover in 1843, when the number of new houses reached 1,115. Even with recovery, however, the rate of residential construction did not approach the extent of the city's housing needs. "According to an estimate made by an experienced architect," the *Evening Post* reported in 1846, "the number of dwelling houses in this city compared to the number of inhabitants falls short of what it was four years ago [at the depth of the depression] by 1200." The supply of housing in Manhattan continued to fall further and further behind the number of new residents, and housing density continued to climb for the next twenty years, as did the mortality rate in the city's working-class wards.[53]

In one sense, the arrival of thousands of Irish and Germans after 1845 meant that New York City's housing market never recovered. Urban historians have long pointed to the sheer force of immigrant numbers to explain why New York had the worst housing conditions in the country. But numbers alone did not determine the structure of the city's housing market or the willingness of capitalists to invest in new housing. In the decades 1820 to 1840, builders had developed strategies to secure a competitive rate of profit from construction of new housing. The growing numbers of wage-earning New Yorkers prompted the rationalization of those strategies into the investment logic that determined the future supply, design, and location of working-class housing. What began as a crisis in the 1840s ended as a new way of life for the rest of the nineteenth century.

Residential Rationalization

The shakedown of the 1840s depression prompted a reorganization of the building industry and the housing market along lines that had begun to emerge a decade earlier. Although real estate remained a broadly based local investment sector (with credit permitting relatively low entry costs), modest individual projects that had produced much of the city's housing before 1837 gave way to partnerships and consolidated speculations. Developers, building companies, and real estate firms increasingly relied on institutional loans for construction capital. As a specialized sector of the local economy, builders pursued respectable residential construction on a new scale. At the same time, they rationalized the working-class crowding of earlier decades into the new housing form of the tenement.

Despite significant rent reductions in the years following the panic, landlords continued to collect substantial profits by subdividing their houses, renting out cellars, and adding rear houses to the backs of lots. By pooling rents and occupying less and less space, working-class tenants proved themselves to be a "productive" market even during a depression.[54]

When new construction picked up in the mid-1840s, landowners and builders expressed new interest in tapping the profits in working-class housing. An average of 1,714 new buildings a year went up between 1845 and 1849; and for the first time in the city's history, new construction systematically included dwellings designed for multifamily occupancy. Christian Bergh, the heir to his father's shipbuilding fortune, exemplified the new era when he erected ten five-story "model tenements" on his family's Lower East Side estate in 1843. Built with the "design of supplying laboring people with cheap lodging," three- to five-story "new tenant houses" on standard 25-by-100-foot lots typically contained from twelve to twenty-four apartments. Room dimensions varied from 12 by 14 feet in "model tenements" to 8 by 10 feet in vernacular multifamily dwellings; each contained smaller "closet" rooms for sleeping. These purpose-built multifamily tenant houses legitimated a reduced housing standard, which had emerged gradually out of two decades of filtering (greatly exacerbated by the depression) to become a new norm.[55]

In the city's lower wards, such new tenant houses appeared erratically in the mid-1840s, often as rear houses or replacements for wooden or brick-front houses lost to age or fire. Both the waves of immigrants settling on the Lower East Side and the impact of the depression had further "ripened" lots in older mechanic wards for investment in new construction. In 1845, for example, builders raised seventeen three- or four-story brick rear houses on Mott and Mulberry streets near Five Points. Five-story tenements went up in the old waterfront Fourth Ward on Cherry, Howard, Chatham, and Roosevelt streets, and the only six-story building erected in the city that year was a tenement on Oliver Street, near the East River.[56]

In the areas of most rapid development in 1845—14th to 23d streets (Wards 15, 16, and 17)—new construction patterns more clearly revealed the housing market's bifurcation. On the "native" West Side, particularly in the vicinity of Chelsea (under Clement Moore's restrictive covenants), rows of three- and four-story town houses dominated the landscape. On the East Side, "new-style" tenements went up in the increasingly immigrant 11th Ward, although still at a slower rate. In contrast to the building pattern of the 1820s and 1830s, builders anticipated the most efficient use of lots in new working-class wards. In what would become the predominantly German 17th Ward, forty-four tenements, many with first-floor or basement shops, went up on avenues A through D in 1845 alongside three manufactories. Between 23d and 30th streets, beyond the fire district and in the vicinity of the slaughterhouse, the paper mill, the cabinetmaking workshop, and the wire, turpentine, paper, and chair factories erected at the eastern and western edges of those streets in 1845, builders raised 107 wooden tenements of the kind commonly known as railroad flats.

Newspaper editors and early housing reformers initially welcomed and promoted the "new-style" tenant houses as a way of reconciling builders' expectations of profits with workers' need for housing. During the winter of 1847, for example, the staunchly Whig *Morning Courier and New York Enquirer*, alarmed at the housing conditions of the city's laboring people, declared that the "duty of providing good, whole and healthy dwellings for the poor devolves directly upon those who own the property and the houses which the poor now occupy." Explaining that "twenty or even more poor families might well be accommodated in a single tenant house erected for that special purpose," the *Courier* suggested to its readers that "houses built entirely for comfort without respect for show . . . could be erected at a very cheap rate and would command a rent sufficiently increased to cover any apprehended falling off of profits." Within this logic, any builder who erected multifamily tenant houses "without respect for show" could claim a benevolent fulfillment of duty.[57]

The *Courier*'s confidence that new tenant houses with "rents sufficiently increased" would solve the housing crisis rested on the construction of a particular marginal utility—a calculated trade-off of means and needs—for workers. "Such lodgings of themselves would enable the poor man to pay a higher rent for them for he would save the expense consequent upon that sickness which his present exposure and destitution involve." City Inspector John Griscom saw another trade-off in the close regulation of "philanthropic housing," which would resolve landlords' problems of rent collection and maintenance. "A system of tenantage might be established, at so moderate a rent," he argued, "as would form an inducement for the poor to live under it, even with such restrictions and supervision, as might be deemed necessary to maintain uniform cleanliness and good order."[58]

Griscom worried that housing conditions demoralized and undermined the ambition of the city's "bone and sinew" craft workers, who found their situation indistinguishable from that of the laboring poor.

"There are hundreds of families in depressed circumstances," he observed, "who would gladly embrace such opportunities, even at higher rents than they are now compelled to pay, to escape, with their children, the contagion of immorality and licentiousness, to say nothing of disease, which almost uniformly pervades the densely populated courts and yards of the City." Though Griscom was doubtless correct in attributing such a preference to "hundreds of families," neither skilled or unskilled laboring families could afford to pay for philanthropy.[59]

The initial fine line between vernacular and "philanthropic" or model tenements became even finer within a decade of occupancy. When New York's sanitation officials and reformers inspected housing in the late 1840s and early 1850s, they repeatedly declared "recently built tenant houses" the "best habitations for the laboring classes." Indeed, "from so promising a beginning, much that would be advantageous was expected," reported housing reformers in 1853. "But after a time an unlooked for deterioration in the character of the buildings was manifested. Many were erected on so contracted and pernicious a scale as to be inferior, as it respects the essentials of a dwelling, to the old buildings whose place they were intended to supply."[60]

Later reformers often blamed the "contracted scale" of New York's standard 25-by-100-foot lot for the inadequacies of multitenant housing. Investors who erected rows of narrow tenements, the argument went, could not provide light and air. Fragmented ownership and leaseholding patterns, uneven redevelopment strategies, and high land costs below 14th Street did hinder the assembling of land parcels that permitted healthier design; but New York's antebellum rentiers and developers who owned contiguous lots also chose to maintain the town lot unit. To the north, developers purchased whole blocks at a time. On the West Side they undertook consolidated building investments to create uniform row houses for a middle-class market. In 1847, for example, William Astor invested $700,000 in land and two hundred row houses between 44th and 47th streets. On the East Side, landowners were more likely to subdivide and distribute land in 25-by-100-foot lots for development by smaller operators. The contrasting results rested less on the custom or necessity of town lot dimensions than on calculation.[61]

Tenement builders defined the "essentials of a dwelling" according to their perceptions of their market. The experience of the preceding decade had suggested that light, air, plumbing, sewerage, and Croton water were not necessities for the city's wage-earning families. Certainly such "amenities" were unavailable in most of the subdivided tenant housing in lower wards. Indeed, in the eyes of builders, one of the things that made the construction of new-style tenements competitive with middle-class housing was the opportunity to eliminate the "variable" expenses of utilities and ventilation. Built at a bare minimum, a four-story tenement in the 17th Ward might cost $5,000 in the 1850s. Even allowing for vacancies and expenses, twenty well-employed laboring households paying $6 monthly rent (or $1,440 a year) could return that cost in less than a decade. Builders erected tenements without light, ventilation, or utilities primarily for the households of *skilled* workers whose combined rents brought back the construction industry's standard (and hence "competitive") 7 to 10 percent profit or better. By living in cellars, rear houses, and courts, and by sharing rooms with two or more families, unskilled tenant households improved that level of profit for landlords.[62]

The construction industry's consolidation contributed to the legitimation of new standards of minimalism in working-class housing. By the 1850s, building companies were beginning to incorporate under new state laws to reduce the level of personal risk and increase their attractiveness to institutional investors. Changes in the regulation of banks, particularly the entry of highly successful savings banks into the mortgage market, opened up new channels of construction capital. Within an increasingly institutionalized finance sector, construction rules of "least risk" had less to do with a builder's personal ambitions or conscience than with a bottom line sanctioned by the most powerful class in the city. And as had been true of independent builders a generation earlier, the small operators who were most likely to raise tenements also were the least likely to deviate from what had become accepted practice.[63]

The 1840s saw new levels of cultural tolerance and intolerance in New York City—tolerance for poor housing conditions and intolerance for Irish immigrants escaping famine. In a period of heightened nativism, the two attitudes mirrored and reinforced each other. Just as fears of job competition from emancipated slaves had raised the specter of poverty's racial "amalgamation" in the 1820s and 1830s, hostility to immigrant competition shaped discussion of working families' deteriorating living conditions in the 1840s. Thus reformers blamed the Irish—"accustomed to living on less"—for pushing down the standards of all workers. But even as stratification within the city's working classes continued to sort out gradations of living accommodations, New York employers capitalized on the expanding labor pool to redefine the "living wage." Builders of course saw no reason to extend their own level of investment in working-class housing beyond employers' definition of what was necessary to perpetuate their labor force.[64]

In the late 1840s and 1850s, many propertied New Yorkers expressed shock at the new social world they were constructing. Editors and reformers published annual investigations and exposés of cellar dwellings, crowded tenements, and sweated "home" labor, and they called for both more "philanthropic" building ventures and legislative regulation of building standards.[65] Still, behind such proposals echoed Samuel Ruggles' confident pronouncement that if a "risk" was "worth" 7 percent, no legislature could make a capitalist take 6 percent. If the rate of profit was not competitive, capital could always move into other channels. The city's rentiers, creditors, employers, and landlords together exercised class power thirty years in the making to create conditions that by any standard can be described only as exploitative. That such power arose out of the republican vision of proprietary independence was more than ironic. It was the essence of the capitalist transformation of housing from an institution of private property and labor relations into a commodity.

The independence associated with proprietorship rested on unrestricted rights to the uses and benefits of property, including the household head's right to appropriate the value of "dependents' " labor. The market had dissolved the patriarchal integration of property and labor relations which governed traditional housing relations, and for the first generation of New York republicans, a "neutral" market seemed to promise the dismantling of mercantile monopolies on land and political rights. But whatever the ideological promise of free market competition as a guarantor of access to proprietorship, the increasing concentration of ownership of real and personal property laid the foundation for new class powers to appropriate the value of waged *and* unwaged labor.

The housing market was built on the investment logic first introduced by city rentiers at the end of the eighteenth century. Rentiers who competed within an "oversupplied" land market had initially looked to leaseholders to improve property (and thereby increase land values) according to tenants' own needs. But those rentiers who controlled a particularly convenient location, such as Trinity Church and Henry Rutgers, had found that they could control the improvement process through restrictive covenants and building leases that governed the quality and use of new structures and guaranteed the highest rate of appreciation. The need for new kinds as well as amounts of housing, and particularly respectable New Yorkers' cultural need for modern dwellings, had structured the demand for residential construction and strengthened landowners' position beyond the wharf district. Controlling land use, rentiers organized the housing market to capture a share of the city's expanding wealth in domestic as well as ground rents. The economic and social quality of those rents in turn determined the material quality of housing.

The process of capitalist class formation in New York City was at once economic, social, and cultural. Bourgeois New Yorkers—a group who came to understand their collective identity through their control of housing as well as of productive resources—explained their own motives by recasting the republican equation of morality and economy. Artisans' goal of independent proprietorship gave way to a liberal agenda of economic growth. By the 1820s, those city residents who had lost control of the conditions of domestic as well as trade independence found themselves outside the calculus of economic, social, and political considerations which governed the organization of the city landscape, the real estate market, and the production of new housing.

Looking from a new distance across the boundaries of domestic respectability, bourgeois New Yorkers in the 1820s and 1830s had grown increasingly suspicious of a wage-earning tenant class that had seemingly abandoned private property as the cornerstone of the republican moral economy. The laboring poor's "cooperative" housing practices, their uses of public streets, their readiness to abscond when they could not pay their rent only confirmed that as a class and as a market they could not be regulated by an economic system that relied on private property rights to maintain social order and discipline. But in the period of the housing market's formation, poor New Yorkers' greatest failing as a class was that their waged-based rents were not sufficiently "productive" to landed capital to permit them to claim the benefits of new housing. In the 1840s, the city's builders discovered how to capitalize on wage earners' value as a housing market, and they did so by redefining the housing needs of working people. In the eyes of New Yorkers who had capital to invest, the preceding decade had demonstrated that working people did not need decent housing to survive. Perhaps the city inspector was right, perhaps capitalists did not know "how the working class suffered." They did not need to know. The insular logic of capitalist investment did not carry with it responsibility to examine consequences other than the rate of return.

Still, the housing conditions of the city's working classes troubled many observers. When Horace Greeley's *New-York Tribune* reprinted with satiric satisfaction the conservative *Courier*'s concession that landowners had "*no right* to allow these wretched houses to be human habitations," the *Courier* editors hastened to clarify their position. Building decent housing was a "duty imposed and required by the law of Christian charity, a law quite as emphatic and binding, and far more precise and reasonable in its requirements than that indefinite law of *nature* upon which alone the Tribune is willing to base its clamorous philanthropy. No man has any *right* to neglect this duty . . . or disregard the law of Charity . . . which seeks simply to accomplish some actual, practical and efficient good."[66]

The *Courier's* editor sought to preserve the authority and legitimacy of private property through concepts of duty and charity. The *Tribune's* editor, Horace Greeley, on the other hand, advocated agarian land reform (particularly the distribution of western public lands) as a means to restore the republican vision of all *men's* natural right to property as the fruit of their labor. Although the *Courier* condemned the *Tribune's* "socialism," Greeley shied away from confronting the interlocking structures of class power within the city or directly advocating the redistribution or abolition of private property. Like most land and labor reformers of the period, Greeley was too attached to natural rights theories and agrarian republicanism to abandon the liberal tradition of private property rights.

Building from the individual's exclusive right in the property of his own (and his "dependents' ") labor—that is, resting on the principle of exclusive appropriation—natural rights theory could not recover or articulate principles of common rights, a person's right not to be excluded from necessary social resources. And attached to the patriarchal values implicit in that tradition (and accepting the equation of labor value and cash), few labor leaders or land reformers could articulate the particular class exploitation that women suffered in the deteriorating housing that was the primary site of their productive social labor. Rejecting "speculators' " organization of agrarian land as a commodity, reformers nonetheless did not reflect on the meaning of city housing as a workplace and commodity. Within the dominant political discourse, the antebellum housing crisis provoked few arguments or actions that could lead to its resolution. Rather, city tenants found their own unarticulated ways of negotiating property relations in the daily operation of the city housing market.

CHAPTER 7

"The Quality of Pay":
Landlord–Tenant Relations

EVERY YEAR, when leases expired on May Day, thousands of New York City tenants simultaneously moved. With citywide attention fixed on the rental housing market, the prevailing perception was one of disorder. "The Spirits of anarchy and confusion might have roamed with delight through our streets on the first of May," reported the *New York Mirror* in 1825. "May Day is a day of horror," concurred the *Evening Post* ten years later. Indeed, "passing through parts of this city" on May first, another editor found that "there scarcely could have been greater confusion had the news suddenly been circulated that the British had landed on Coney Island."[1]

"The practice of all moving on one day" was "of antient custom," John Pintard explained to his daughter when he reported that 1832's rainy May Day had been particularly "unfavorable to the general moving of our great city." Looking back fifty years on the New York of his youth, Pintard observed how the conditions of the rental housing market had changed since the eighteenth century. "When the city was small and inhabitants few in numbers," he recalled, "almost everybody owned or continued for years in the same houses. Few instances of removals were seen, but now N[ew] York is literally in an uproar for several days before and after the 1st of May." A generation earlier, the city's tenure and labor relations had paced a slower rhythm for the turnover of housing: twenty-one-year ground leases had given tenants control over their houses and shops, and found labor and slavery had tied workers to a master household. Furthermore, the abundance of land had weakened eighteenth-century landlords' bargaining position and inhibited rapid rent increases. But emancipation, the demise of the household labor system, the formation of the housing market, and a chronic housing shortage had changed the meaning and impact of "antient customs." Thus every May 1, Pintard observed, "high rents, incommodious dwellings and necessity combine to crowd our streets with carts overloaded with furniture and hand barrows with sofas, chairs, sideboards, looking glasses and pictures, so as to render the sidewalks almost impassable."[2]

In a city where property trading intimately affected all who lived and worked there, the annual exchange of housing gave concrete form to the forces that drove the city real estate market, redefined tenure relations, and determined the ordering of space: the advance of land values stemmed from the continuing turnover of housing as well as from its productive use. The force of that turnover, the annual selling of use rights in a building to the highest bidder, unleashed a spatial dynamism of market competition that converted buildings and transformed city neighborhoods within a decade of their construction. Moving day itself, concentrating and resolving into one moment competing social needs for shelter, dramatized the power of the price to determine the social organization of space.

As moving day brought all other trade to a halt and focused the commercial city's attention on the single commodity of shelter, the tensions of competing needs frequently erupted in the streets. Freely flowing liquor fueled and rewarded movers' exertions through the inevitable traffic jams and moving day brawls. Refusing to give up their homes, old tenants sometimes fought with new leaseholders, each side drawing support from crowds of relatives and acquaintances.[3] Yet, even as visitors to the city wondered at the irrationality of everyone moving at once, newspaper editors and citizens alike greeted the moving day "uproar" with that distinctive New York fortitude heard in future citywide disasters, from blizzards to blackouts. And despite the disruption, the "anarchy" of the moving day carnival ultimately confirmed market rules of property relations.

With the May 1 turbulence sealing the outcome of the preceding months' negotiations over the terms of new leases, thousands of New Yorkers entered into new contractual relations that affected the conditions of their business, trade, and domestic labors. More than July Fourth's parades or January First's visiting rituals, moving day revealed bonds that held city residents together within a market economy. As a contract, the lease embodied the economic principle of free will: the right and capacity of individuals to negotiate and voluntarily enter into agreements backed by law. If the chaos that accompanied turning houses inside out arose primarily from the logistical problems of transporting furnishings, equipment, and personal property to another floor, down the block, or across town, May Day also committed people to future obligations and structured other sets of social relations.

Broadway, New York. Drawing and etching by T. Horner, aquatint by J. Hill, 1836. Eno Collection; Miriam and Ira D. Wallach Division of Art, Prints, and Photographs; The New York Public Library; Astor, Lenox, and Tilden Foundations.

As they traded places, New Yorkers assembling in the streets and in taverns could assess the year's bargain; they congratulated themselves on improvements in their accommodations or complained of new hardships; and, having calculated what they could afford in space, tenants perhaps reflected on other relations that flowed out of the lease agreements they had signed. Merchants, shopkeepers, and manufacturers could anticipate one "production cost" in their enterprises which—unlike the cost of goods, labor, or materials—would remain constant in the year ahead, and indeed, by its very certainty require adjustments in what they would bid for those other commodities. If there had been a dramatic increase in rent, employers might forecast new workers' demands. Sublandlords and boardinghouse keepers could calculate the number of wage earners' rents they would in turn have to collect to meet the terms of their new leases. Laboring tenants, knowing the portion of household earnings given over to rent, may have reflected on the balance left for other necessities. Wives and domestic servants contemplated the task of organizing a new workplace and new domestic support networks. And as new neighbors settled in and surveyed one another, peddlers, prostitutes, and youths reasserted their own territorial boundaries, letting newcomers to a block know the customs of the street's economy and culture.

The city's rentiers and landlords must have met the chaos with mixed feelings. Rental housing was only one of many investments, and moving day was clearly a nuisance that interrupted the regular flow of commerce. But May Day also closed the preceding year's accounts and fixed the value of real property for the year ahead. Wealthy landlords may well have spent the day in their offices or at the Exchange, taking stock of the flow of rent revenues. That rental income provided cash for expenditures or obligations that ranged from Mrs. Livingston's "drafts from France" and Robert Turnbull's tailor and hardware bills to C. W. Wilkes's interest on a bond and Morgan Lewis's family annuities. Over and above such prior commitments, rental income provided funds for new investments: Morgan Lewis used his rents to build more tenant houses; John Jacob Astor put ground rents into the purchase of more land; the Bayard and Johnson families applied rents to the purchase of railroad bonds and bank stocks. For half a century following the American Revolution, the flow of New York rents had formed a primary channel of local capital accumulation.[4]

On moving day New York became a city united by declarations of contractual obligation and "a community divided," as one legal commentator noted, "into two great classes of landlords and tenants."[5] Yet the opposition of landlords and tenants as parties to a lease—as sellers and buyers of use rights in shelter—also obscures historical conditions that shaped landlord–tenant relations in the antebellum city and determined an unstable and shifting balance of class power.

On the face of things, New York City landlords retained the upper hand in negotiations over the lease. Controlling the limited supply of a necessary good, landlords could set rents at whatever level would yield the return they sought on property. In raising rents annually, they exercised the power to encroach on livelihood, to poach on profits, and to turn the entire city inside out. Yet whether landlords could collect rent and realize their anticipated return was another matter, one that depended both on their legal powers of enforcement and on their social power within the larger capitalist political economy. By the 1840s, the very transformation of tenure relations into contractual market relations signaled a social compromise that placed limits on the power of New York landlords as a class.

New York's colonial proprietors had adopted the institutions and investment strategies developed by the landed society of England, where legal, social, and political power had merged to form the basis of class rule. England's agrarian landlords had controlled the economy's essential productive resource, and through the control of land, they had established their claims on labor. The common law, the law of England's seventeenth-century gentry, recognized land as a special form of property, and rules governing real property's succession, transfer, and use preserved a closed social monopoly. Although establishing the principle of landlords' and tenants' reciprocal obligations, that law favored landlords as a legal and a social class by granting them jurisdiction over tenants and unilateral powers in actions to collect rent.[6]

In comparison with English landlords, New York's eighteenth-century rentiers had never fully established their position as a ruling social class through lineaged monopolies of land and control of a dependent agricultural labor force; rather, large landowners in the country and city alike had turned to the market to realize the value of their holdings. Republicans had further dismantled the vestiges of gentry power by abolishing both hereditary constraints on the circulation of land and landowners' political privileges of voting and officeholding. But if New York's landlords had formed themselves and thrived primarily as an entrepreneurial class, they had readily availed themselves of the common law's doctrines of landlord privilege, which distinguished their position from that of other entrepreneurs. One of those privileges—appropriately enough designated by the legal term "distress"—entitled landlords to seize and sell tenants' personal property to recover unpaid rent.

The law afforded New Yorkers one arena in which to contest land-lords' power and to resolve the tensions among competing forms of property which, by the mid–nineteenth century, represented compet-ing factions of capital. In the seventy-five years following the Revolu-tion, legal challenges to landlords' power came from three directions: from agrarian republicans, who feared that social monopolies of land restricted access to proprietary independence; from commercial and in-dustrial entrepreneurs, who resented (and themselves had to pay for) landlords' economic power and special legal status as creditors; and from city tenants, who sought to hold landlords accountable for the physical conditions of leased housing. A law that placed real property above all other forms of property interfered with the profitable circula-tion or use of other kinds of commmodites—goods in transit, tools for production, and even the commodity of labor.

New Yorkers who fervently believed in private property rights drew on the language of republicanism to assert a common interest in dis-mantling landlords' special status under common law—particularly their power to seize tenants' property. Yet to argue that the exchange of real property was indistinguishable from that of other forms of property was also to imply housing's social neutrality as a commodity. And to question landlords' rights to use and maintain property as they chose was to question the same principle of absolute property rights on which the larger contractual economy rested.

By the 1840s, judges and lawmakers who embraced liberal market ideology were beginning to interpret landlord–tenant law in light of the rules of commercial contracts. New statutes and instrumental legal reasoning—the use of law to encourage economic expansion—supported tenants' victories in freeing land to an unregulated market and limiting landlords' common law powers. That same reasoning de-termined the conditions of tenants' defeat in their efforts to claim legal protection of their right to habitable housing. Within the housing mar-ket, the lease, which had once embodied the customs of a deferential landed society, came to represent no more—and no less—than the bargain struck, the express terms of agreement that could be asserted before law.

In place of the prescriptive social and political inequality of landed society stood the practical inequalities of bargaining power within the market. From year to year, the terms of new leases most immediately revealed the conditions of supply and demand which determined both the price and the quality of rental housing. Yet it was from within the interstices of the market itself that another challenge to land-lords' power arose in the mid-nineteenth century, a challenge not to landlords' *right* to rent but rather to their ability to collect it. Prosperous leaseholders, who had their own distinctive stake in orderly property relations, sought to protect their interests through lease negotiations or legal challenges to landlords' claims for rent; wage-earning tenants developed their own self-help strategies of delaying rent payments and moving. Or, caught between employers' power to set wages and landlords' power to set rent, poor tenants unilaterally removed themselves from contractual obligation and simply stepped outside the law by absconding. Such strategies undermined the predictability of profits within the rental housing market. If May Day's anarchy paid tribute to the housing contract as the instrument of order in a free market society, negotiations outside the lease revealed social contradictions that set limits on the powers of class domination.

The Limits of Landlord Privilege in a Free Market Economy

In his 1828 legal *Commentaries*, New York's chancellor, James Kent, an American spokesman for the received English common law tradition, defined rents as landowners' right "to a certain yearly profit in money, provisions, chattels or labor issuing out of land and tenements in retribution for the use, and it cannot issue out of mere privilege or easement."[7] The creation of a tenant estate required the exchange of consideration—a measure of equivalency—that both distinguished tenancy from mere license and placed landlords and tenants within a contractual relation. Yet Kent addressed the legal nature of "rent" not under contract law in his treatise but at the end of a discussion of corporeal and incorporeal hereditaments, the entitlements of inherited property. The contractual relation established through payment of rent carried with it one-sided conditions derived from the customs and powers of English landed society.

Though common law protected tenants from arbitrary termination of leases by landlords, most of the rules of law served to protect landlords' property from the effects of tenants' use, to maintain landlords' control over land and tenants, and, most important, to secure rent. Once landlords had transferred possession through a lease, they had no responsibility for the condition or the maintenance of the premises, unless such a provision was expressly stipulated in the lease. The common law of waste made tenants liable for any damages to the property or changes to it without the landlord's consent—trees cut for firewood or commercial sale, for example, or unrepaired fences—which came at the expense of the landlord's interest in preserving the land; indeed, tenants could not make alterations, except by prior agreement, even if those alterations increased the value of the property. Tenants who gave notice to quit and then remained on the premises were liable for twice the rent; landlords who changed *their* minds about termination could simply continue to accept payments. Through covenants, landlords could reserve labor service, restrict tenants' use of property, and fine tenants for selling their leases or subletting the property.[8]

Landlords' greatest legal power lay in the principle of tenants' absolute liability for the full term's rent. That legal doctrine had arisen out of the long-term tenures of an agricultural economy that understood rents to be "produced" by cultivation of land. Droughts, floods, fires, or market fluctuations might burden agricultural tenants, but the law strictly upheld landlords' absolute claims to a portion of the crops' value, by which the value of the use of the land was measured. The law put teeth into this doctrine by granting landlords "self-help" remedies to collect rent—"one of the few instances of ability," one legal historian has noted, "of a person to take law into his own hands."[9] Thus according to the legal doctrine of "distress and distraint," landlords could directly seize, hold, and even sell tenants' personal property as a pledge for the rent. Though distress could serve as a remedy to enforce other debt obligations, its broadest American use came in actions to collect unpaid rent. "The law may be deemed rather prompt and strict with respect to the interest of the landlord," Kent observed, "but I am inclined to think it is a necessary provision, and one dictated by sound policy."[10]

Kent, a Federalist, felt compelled to defend the "social policy" of common law rules and remedies that favored landlords' interests in the face of a sustained political challenge from New York republicans, who argued that "sound policy" also required the dismantling of landlords' traditional powers in order to facilitate the circulation of land. In the context of the Revolution, a coalition of rural leaseholders and city artisans had confronted the legal tradition that empowered New York's mercantile rentier elite by introducing statutory and constitutional modifications of the common law. Controlling the state legislature between 1781 and 1786, radical republicans had abolished primogeniture, entail, and "feudal tenures"—the core of a landed society based on hereditary privileges.[11]

But law that proscribed feudal tenures in the future did not clarify the status of earlier long-term lease agreements. In the early nineteenth century, a new generation of Hudson Valley rentiers claimed that they retained an interest in property leased by their forefathers "in fee," "in perpetuity," for life, or for ninety-nine years. A new generation of rural leaseholders in turn loudly protested the efforts of Stephen Van Rensselaer and other rentier heirs to collect quitrents or fines ("quarter sales") from tenants who sold their leases. It was in the context of this confrontation that New Yorkers began to reexamine the ideological grounds of the landlord–tenant relation and the legal enforcement of landlords' power.[12]

With the still-fresh memory of revolutionary principles that opposed aristocratic monopolies, the lawmaker John Woodworth made the republican case against "a rigid and unreasonable burden to tenants" in his notes to the 1812 *Revised Statutes*. Landlords' "restraint in the nature of fines, or quarter sales, against alienations are exceedingly objectionable," he observed; "whatever tends, under a government like ours, to interrupt or prevent the free course of alienating real property is opposed to sound policy and the genius of our political institutions." But as significant as Woodworth's rejection of landlords' preemptive rights to impose unilateral conditions on a tenant's use or circulation of a lease was his interpretation of the substantive principle of contract embodied in a lease. A landlord's assertion of a right to fine tenants, he argued, subverted contractual fairness, the *mutual* exchange of consideration, for a tenant gained nothing against the landlord's power to impose penalties for certain uses of the lease, including its sale. In Woodworth's mind, a social and legal policy that embraced contractual principles of free market exchange was not morally neutral. "If it should be objected that tenants enter into such kind of stipulations voluntarily, and that every man should be left free to contract in such manner as he pleases—we answer that the public is bound to protect and guard individuals from oppression."[13]

Guarding against landlords' oppression required rethinking common law remedies that enforced the principle of private property rights. In asserting their claims to quitrent or fines, Van Rensselaer and other rentiers had recourse to the remedy of distress: whatever lawmakers thought of the vestiges of feudal tenure, the common law permitted landlords to help themselves, to seize tenants' property to extract rents and fines. Furthermore, Hudson Valley rentiers were not the only landlords who relied on this legal privilege. In cities as well as in the countryside, landlords' rights and powers rested on the customs of an older social order. Thus one battle to dismantle landed privilege assumed the concrete form of a struggle to limit landlords' exercise of the power of distress.

In the first third of the nineteenth century, New York judges and legal commentators repeatedly defended landlords' powers as "founded on the reasonable and necessary principles of a lien or pledge"; but many New Yorkers shared the perception of lawmakers who observed in 1828 that the "remedy of distress for rent is one of the most severe and may be the instrument of more oppression than any other proceeding."[14] As New York tenants petitioned the legislature for relief from landlords' power to seize their property, lawmakers discovered that though the law empowered landlords as a single class, different classes of tenants sought different kinds of protection. Over the course of thirty years, rural and city tenants, who stood in very different positions with respect to their control and use of real property, in effect formed a coalition that challenged landlords' power to encroach on their livelihood, household necessities, profits, and instruments of "home morality." The battle over distress marked the gradual breaking apart of an older mercantile landed elite into class factions that could best unite around the principle of free competition and the social neutrality of all forms of property, including land, rental housing, and labor.

The most direct challenge to the common law of landlord–tenant relations came from rural areas. The struggle continued over seventy-five years before it culminated in the rent wars of the 1840s, the 1846 New York State Constitution, and major legislative reforms. Rural tenants' militancy reflected in part rural landlords' aggression. In the eighteenth century, Hudson Valley rentiers had used their political power in the Legislature to extend landlords' common law powers. Thus in 1774, an "Act for the better Security, and more easy recovery of Rents, and renewal of Leases, and to prevent Frauds committed by Tenants" had expanded the power of distress beyond English precedent. The law allowed landlords to follow and seize delinquent tenants' property even after it had left the demised premises and provided that any tenant or person who aided in "conveying away their Goods and Chattel leaving the Rent unpaid" should "forfeit and pay" to the landlord double the value of those goods. Furthermore, in a political culture highly suspicious of unlimited powers of search and seizure, landlords could "break open and enter" any house, barn, or other place to which the goods had been taken.[15]

As defined by English judges, common law itself offered tenants some minimal protections that eighteenth-century New York rentiers had often ignored. Thus the legal custom of landed society had exempted from seizure beasts of plow, certain essential household goods, and especially the implements of trade unless all other remedies had proved insufficient. Since implicitly the object of distress—the "pledge" being collected—was the crop or livestock on leased land, and since tenants thrown off the land had few resources for survival, common law restrained landlords from stripping tenants of their essential means of making a living.[16] In the 1813 revised statutes, New York lawmakers reaffirmed these common law exemptions and addressed landlords' abuses with something of a plea, legislating "that all distress made or taken for any cause whatsoever shall be reasonable and not too great and whosoever shall take great and unreasonable distress shall be punished by fine for the excess of such distress."[17]

But landlords' use of distress was not a problem for rural tenants alone. In 1814 the New York State Legislature received a petition on behalf of "certain persons in the City of New York" who "have associated together for the purpose of relieving indigent widows and females, of various descriptions, from distress." The petitioning manufacturers "represented the advantages that would arise from lending or furnishing such widows and females with articles and materials to work with," and asked that the tools and materials of the outwork system be removed from landlords' reach. Accepting the petition, the Legislature exempted "all looms, spinning wheels, and stoves . . . that shall or may be loaned or furnished by any benevolent institution or body incorporate, or by any person or persons of the same city of New York or in this state, to any widow or female of above description."[18]

In a society in which fewer and fewer tenants owned the tools of their trade, the practice of seizing household property for rent conflicted with the entrepreneurial interests of employers who supplied tools and materials. In accepting the petition of textile employers—and in effect granting protection to a nascent industry that found its labor force among indigent women—the legislature took one step toward acknowledging that changing social relations of labor had created new property transactions that competed with traditional landed property rights for the law's protection.[19]

In another struggle of "property against property," city merchants joined manufacturers in seeking to place limits on landlords' common law powers. Rentier and shipping families had been closely aligned in eighteenth-century New York. By the mid–nineteenth century, however, the ascendancy of commission merchants, wholesalers, and factors oriented to the domestic market broke apart this alliance of economic interests. Furthermore, city shopkeepers and artisans often held goods and materials that belonged to larger merchants, as well as to customers and clients. A sheriff who executed a landlord's action of distress for rent was not liable for mistakenly appropriating goods held on consignment, and the improperly seized property of third parties could be recovered only through a cumbersome legal action for trespass.[20] Particularly in New York City, merchants and entrepreneurs, who found that land monopolies pushed up commercial rents, expressed their resentment that landowners, "who are so abundantly and amply able to sustain themselves, their families and their fortunes . . . are the very persons who are made the recipients of a profuse legal bounty, which flows in no other direction, and favors no other portion of the community." An unsigned article in *Hunt's Merchant Magazine* singled out the summary action of distress as the "last lingering relic of tyrannical power," "sprung from a barbarous age."[21]

In an economy organized around deferred payments, merchants and artisans alike particularly resented the "notorious privileges possessed by the landlord over those enjoyed by any other creditor." "How often do we see the merchant after trusting his debtor for large quantities of goods" on commission, the *Hunt's* article wondered, "disappointed in his reasonable anticipation of payment by this exercise of a landlord's tyrannical prerogative? He has perhaps received nothing whatever from his debtor, and the very property he has trusted [to] him goes in satisfying the last farthing of a landlord's claim."[22] Was it because the landlord "is a wealthy man that he is invested with peculiar privileges to collect his debts?" asked the editor George Morris. "The tailor, grocer, the shoemaker, butcher and the baker are all frequently compelled to allow long credit and sometimes consequently suffer heavy losses in the course of business transactions"; landlords should bear a similar burden of risk.[23]

In contesting landlords' privileged legal status, manufacturers and merchants sought to protect their own entrepreneurial investments in tools and goods. With the expansion of New York's rental housing market, domestic tenants also found themselves distressed by their landlords' privilege of seizure for rent. Although common law's exclusion of "implements of trade" did not cover domestic possessions, the Legislature had nonetheless recognized tenants' need for certain household goods. Thus an 1815 act extended a measure of relief when it protected from distress (in addition to ten sheep, "together with their fleece and cloth manufactured from the same, one cow, two swine and the pork of the same") "all necessary wearing apparel and bedding, all cooking utensils, one table, six chairs, six knives and forks, six plates and six teacups and saucers owned by any person being a householder."[24] In the 1820s, as respectable New Yorkers elaborated on the virtues of the "home" as a protected sphere, legislators accepted householders' petitions to guard the necessary instruments of home morality—the family Bible, schoolbooks, family pictures, and the church pew. They also acknowledged the pervasive system of boarding in New York City and exempted boarders' and lodgers' personal possessions from seizure by a chief landlord.[25]

After two decades of efforts by various tenant groups to obtain their own special relief from landlords' distress, the economic crisis of 1837 and the depression of the 1840s altered the climate of discussion of landlords' privileges. In the face of bankruptcies and unemployment, the Legislature found itself called upon to protect the domestic property of thousands of households that could not pay their rent or other debts. With the demise of the integrated house and shop and the ascendancy of an ideology of domesticity, dispossession exposed the particular vulnerability of women and children held liable for the sins of husbands and fathers. Indeed, common law enforcement of landlords' and creditors' claims through distress threatened to contradict that same law's principle of coverture, the male householder's duty to protect his dependents.

"The operation of law furnishes no more painful spectacle," one investigating Senate committee reported, "than the little comforts and conveniences of life, the cheap but cherished garniture of the humble dwelling—wrought or procured by the work of the wife or which formed her scanty endowment upon marriage, all swept away upon marriage by its stern process against an unfortunate or dissipated husband." The claims of poor women as dependent members of the laboring class had been acknowledged by charitable exemptions from distress which served employers' interests in 1813. But the panic's dislocations gave new visibility to the economic position of middle-class wives as members of a tenant class. Through landlords' peremptory actions, women's claims to domestic protection could be, in the senators' view, "sacrificed amid coarse jests in the open market." Discussion of relief from distress in the 1840s, with its contradictory recognition of women's economic interests and concern with insulating "home life" from economic risks, bridged reform debates over creditor and debtor relations and married women's property rights.[26]

By the 1840s, legislators despaired of being able to meet all demands for tenants' protection. "The list of privileged property is so limited," the Senate committee complained in 1842, "as to embrace only articles of prime necessity for a small family—altogether inadequate to the absolute wants of a larger one." Reflecting on the 1815 law's exemption of dining utensils, senators wondered "what rule of adaptation limited household goods to exactly six unless it was regarded as the mystic number beyond which a poor man's household should not be enlarged." Abandoning the effort to stipulate protected necessities altogether, the Legislature commuted its distress exemptions to a cash maximum that did not distinguish the nature of tenancy. The 1842 statute allowed tenants to select their own exempted goods up to the value of $150.[27]

Even as lawmakers abandoned efforts to classify tenants' needs, they heard arguments as to the particular needs of New York City landlords. In the face of a growing housing shortage, landlords insisted that the security of distress was necessary to encourage investment in rental housing. Chancellor Kent had been one of the first to suggest that landlords' claims to profit represented a policy as well as a principle of private property rights. "It would tend to check the growth and prosperity of our cities if the law did not afford the landlords a speedy and effectual security for their rents, against the negligence, extravagance, and frauds of tenants. It is that security which encourages moneyed men to employ their capital in useful and elegant improvements." Without the power of distress, landlords would be "driven in every case to the slow process of a suit at law for their rent, it would lead to vexations and countless lawsuits, and be, in many respects, detrimental to public welfare."[28]

The Senate committee considering distress reform in the 1840s took the landlords' position seriously, for it was not their intention to limit the incentives of landed capital. "By weakening the inducement to furnish tenements to the families of the poor," senators warned, "one great object—that of preventing the dispersion of families by securing a home—might be defeated . . . and the changes thus made to work unfavorably to the interest of those whom it is intended to benefit."[29] The arguments on behalf of landlords' privileges had shifted from customary entitlements to the instrumental requirements of capitalist investment.

While legislators worried about discouraging investment in city real estate, rural leaseholders brought the issue of landlords' privileges to a political head. In late 1845, the murder of a Delaware County sheriff who was collecting personal property for distress triggered riots and prompted Governor Silas Wright to send in state troopers to restore order to the Hudson Valley. Less than six months later, "Anti-Renter" legislators led the way in reforming the fundamental remedy afforded to landlords by the common law. Abolishing landlords' distress, the 1846 law facilitated procedures for landlords' summary recovery of real property through ejectment and recovery of rents through suit. Eliminating the landlord's self-help action for rent, the Legislature also reduced tenants' security of possession by making it easier to evict them.[30]

This latter trend had already been evident in statutory reductions of the time required for notice to quit, from the common law's six months to three months and finally in 1828 to one month.[31] In agricultural economies marked by seasonal crop production, self-help remedies such as distress had been tied to the product of the land—its medium of value—and landlords' long-term notice guaranteed tenants' possession long enough to extract that value through harvest. In commercial economies, land and housing were themselves circulating commodities, especially in cities, where real property's income-producing value derived primarily from location and rents from trade- or wage-based cash. If republican logic looked to the real estate market to preserve access to proprietary independence, capitalist logic proposed a further corollary: profits were realized not from land's product but from the revenues of waged production. When the flow of those revenues was cut off by seasonal unemployment or other market turns, so too were tenants' rights to possession.

Overt political conflict, along with structural changes in the economy, pushed the Legislature to modify the common law of landlord and tenant. The abolition of the remedy of distress, primarily a concession to agrarian leaseholders, also served the city manufacturers, merchants, and domestic tenants who had lobbied on its behalf. The end of distress represented a tenant's victory, but that victory paled against landlords' other major source of legal power, the common law doctrine of tenants' absolute liability for rent. Judges and legislators, working with a law that had evolved out of an agricultural economy, were ill prepared to address its application to new issues within the city housing market: the "tenantability" of built premises and the disruption of the "peaceable enjoyment" of leased housing by building activity, fires, faulty utilities, landlords' negligence—or tenants' resistance to claims for rent on buildings they could not safely inhabit. Even as land-based privilege was giving way to an entrepreneurial ideology that no longer viewed land as a special form of property, the organization of New York City's housing market exposed the new social costs of republican law: if landlords had no social privileges within a free market economy, neither did they have any social obligations.

The Habitability of Housing

Alongside controversies over landlords' powers to enforce their claims to rent, changes in the nature of rental property posed new questions as to the contractual obligations of the landlord–tenant relation. Under common law, a tenant covenanted to pay rent, and the landlord in turn guaranteed "the quiet enjoyment of possession of the premises" during the lease term. In 1859, New York's Court of Appeals reasserted the traditional legal interpretation of these obligations with an authority that belied thirty years of dispute when it declared that "the covenant of quiet enjoyment, expressed or implied in a lease, only goes to the extent of engaging that the landlord has a good title and can give a free and unencumbered lease of the premises demised." A landlord's duties ended with the affirmation of the proper authority to lease.[32]

New York City leaseholders, who generally appeared in court as defendants in landlords' suits for rent, argued that the landlords' covenant implied a larger duty. Defending themselves in court against landlords' claims for rent, tenants sought to reinterpret their contractual right to "quiet possession." Landlords who "constructively evicted" their tenants by making it impossible for them to remain on the premises, tenants' lawyers argued, were not entitled to rent. The argument proposed that the courts examine the substance of the exchange between landlord and tenant. In 1826, when the New York Court for the Correction of Errors accepted the argument of constructive eviction in the case of *Dyett* v. *Pendleton*, it launched a new era of controversy that pitted the community's sense of fairness against the emerging judicial view of landed property's social neutrality.

John Pendleton had brought suit against his tenant Joshua Dyett for the $425 annual rent due on two third-floor rooms of a lower Manhattan corner house. In the Court of Appeals, Dyett claimed that he had abandoned the house and refused to pay rent because his landlord used other parts of the building for prostitution. Pendleton had thus "constructively evicted" his tenant by forcing Dyett to move out in order to preserve his reputation. The Court of Appeals, applying the common law rule, rejected the argument and concluded that Dyett had voluntarily abandoned the premises because the landlord had not physically entered the house and thrown him out on the street. The tenant, the court concluded, had recourse to other remedies—such as calling the police—but in any case Dyett remained fully liable for the rent.[33]

On appeal, the Court of Errors (the state's highest court, composed of members of the Senate as well as judges) viewed the matter differently. Senator John C. Spencer, writing for the majority, examined the issue as one of contract and the "dimunition of the consideration of the contract, by acts of the landlord, although those acts don't amount to a physical eviction." Finding it a "universal principle in all cases of contract that a party who deprives another of the consideration on which his obligation was founded can never recover damages for its nonfulfillment," the majority of the court decided that "whether possession was peaceable and quiet was already a question of fact for the jury."[34]

To throw the power to juries to absolve tenants of their obligation for rent opened the law of landlord–tenant relations to popular sentiment, a force that New York judges found themselves fighting on other fronts in the Jacksonian era. Juries were likely to share the sympathies of Senator John Crary, who in a concurring opinion passionately declared, "When a defendant is told that every right, when withheld, shall have a remedy, and every injury its proper redress, and that personal security, which includes reputation, is one of his absolute rights, and then told he must live in a brothel against his will, or at least pay rent for it, he cannot but see the disparity between the text and the comment, and if one is right, the other must be wrong." If lawyers could not satisfy the technical requirements of evidence of a physical eviction, Crary announced, "I should resort not to the statute law, nor to the common law, but to the great principles of morality on which both are founded."[35]

For respectable New Yorkers who were undertaking to define "great principles of morality" through their dwellings in the 1820s, reputation was itself an essential form of property. The very fact that the other residents in one's house could be prostitutes exposed the vulnerability of individual moral character within a "promiscuous" housing market. But if the majority opinion responded to the new anxieties of the city's respectable residents, other judges saw a much greater danger in abandoning the principle of tenants' absolute liability for rent.

"What was this but calling on the jury to determine the *law*, by giving a construction to legal terms?" demanded Senator Ethan B. Allen in a dissenting opinion.[36] Senator Cadwallader Colden, in another dissent, saw the seeds of chaos when judges gave juries license to decide whether a tenant "finding himself temporarily disturbed in the enjoyment of the demised premises by the misconduct or immoral practice of the [landlord] may abandon the tenement for the whole term and be exonerated from the payment of rent." The majority's acceptance of the argument of constructive eviction, Senator Colden warned, would "introduce a new and very extensive chapter in the law of landlord and tenant"; for if a landlord's "encouragement or practice of lewdness, on premises under the same roof," released a tenant from the covenant to pay rent, "there is no reason why, if the landlord should by any other means render the occupation of the premises inconvenient or uncomfortable, the same consequences might not ensue." In Colden's view, to raise the question of the quality of the landlord–tenant exchange "would be to afford grounds for litigation on which there would be perpetual contentions."[37]

Senator Colden's predictions proved accurate. Higher court judges quickly came to regret the decision in *Dyett* v. *Pendleton* and spent the next thirty years reasserting the principle of absolute tenant liability. The majority opinion in *Dyett* quickly moved into the legal literature of the period, but legal commentators such as Kent stressed that they did not regard *Dyett* as establishing a new precedent.[38] Judges of New York's appeals courts also undertook to distinguish the case from other claims of constructive eviction, explaining that *Dyett* v. *Pendleton* "shows only an application of the doctrine to an extreme case" that involved "lewd and offensive conduct of the landlord . . . so offensive to common decency and accompanied with such notoriety and out- rageous disturbances, as effectually to destroy the quiet enjoyment." But judges saw no comparable offense to justify, for example, a city jury's generous decision to release a leaseholder from his obligation to pay rent because the chief landlord had posted a "to let" notice that interfered with subtenants' quiet enjoyment and possession of the premises.[39]

Whatever juries' sympathies, much of the courts' retrenchment rested on New Yorkers' adjustment to the exigencies of the city's rental housing market and on their application of rules of commercial contract to the landlord–tenant relation. Judges, like other New Yorkers, quickly came to terms with practical conditions that resulted when landlords subdivided old housing stock and minimized maintenance costs. Although in the 1820s the landlord's "indecent and outrageous" conduct in *Dyett* v. *Pendleton* had been viewed in effect as a violation of the tenant's property right in reputation, within a decade judges had backed off from evaluating the quality of the commercial exchange of use rights in housing. If tenants valued reputation, comfort, or even health, they should pay for better housing. In *Vanderbilt* v. *Persse*, for example, the judge insisted that a tenant who had abandoned premises as "untenantable" remained liable for rent because "there was nothing in the offers to show the house to be untenantable." Overturning the jury's judgment on the matter, the appeals judges insisted that "a bad smell in the pantry, a kitchen being too hot with the stove in it, bad smells from the front window, a stagnant pond of water near the place, bad smell from fish, vermin in the bedrooms were all matters that might have given some trouble to eradicate, but none of them can be held sufficient to relieve the tenant of liability." The court went further to declare that "no case in this state has ever extended the rule of *Dyett* v. *Pendleton*."[40]

As they continued to hear landlord–tenant cases on appeal, New York judges moved their defense of the old principle of tenants' absolute liability for rent to the new ground of contract law and applied the legal rule that contracts must be construed and enforced according to their specific terms. Senator Crary had insisted in *Dyett* that "great principles of morality" required examination of the substantive value of consideration and that the landlord's actions had reduced the value of the exchanged good to the tenant. By contrast, the theory of contract held that buyers and sellers were obliged to protect their own interests in the market and could not appeal to the community's sense of fairness when they got a bad deal.[41] "The maxim *caveat emptor* [buyer beware] applies to the transfer of all property, real, personal, and mixed," asserted the Court of Appeals in an 1846 landlord–tenant case, "and the purchaser generally takes the risk of its quality and condition unless he protects himself by express agreement."[42] To treat housing like any other commodity under contract for exchange was to release landlords from any obligation to warrant their goods.

However little protection tenants had received from the common law of landlord and tenant, they received little more from contract law. Positing the equality of parties to a contract, the law overlooked practical inequalities of bargaining power and of experience in using legal instruments. The emphasis on express terms of agreement attached new importance to the lease, for judges had declared as early as 1812 that they would not "enter into any equitable consideration when the instrument speaks for itself."[43] The instrument, rather than the parties, could speak only when written. The New York Legislature, recognizing the complications of unrecorded terms of agreement or casual understanding in a commercial, mobile society, had added leases to the list of contracts that must be written in order to avoid fraud. And in theory written leases provided the opportunity for both tenants and landlords to negotiate and secure their mutual conditions. Statute, however, could not overrule the customary practices. "It is well known that in the City of New York the far greater proportion of contracts of this kind [leases] are mere parole [spoken] agreements," a judge observed in 1853, "and have, since the passage of the Revised Statutes, been continually enforced . . . as valid and binding contracts."[44]

Even if judges were disposed to enforce spoken agreements, by law they had to defer to written terms. Tenants who continued to trust their landlords' spoken word could find that trust abused by law. In an 1851 case, a tenant defending against a landlord's claim for rent charged that "both before and subsequent to signing of the agreement, and at the time, the landlord made many strong assurances that the premises would be repaired and improved, that a connection would be made with a sewer, which he affirmed was about to be constructed, that conveniences for bathing would be added." But that same shrewd landlord put none of these promises in the written lease, and the court, regretting "a case of hardship in the application of a rule," found the tenant liable for rent. On the other hand, another tenant who refused to pay rent after the landlord broke his oral promise to make repairs found jurors sympathetic to her cause. She sued the landlord for assault during a forcible eviction, and the jury awarded her $2,100.[45]

Despite the position of appeals court judges, New York City juries and lower court judges also continued to accept the legal defense that tenants did not owe rents on buildings they could not inhabit. One Court of Common Pleas judge, upholding a jury finding of constructive eviction, ignored subsequent court decisions and insisted that the *Dyett* doctrine had "commended itself to the good sense of bar and community."[46] His decision was overturned. "The jury, I think, have acted under some misapprehension or mistake, as their verdict is, in my judgment, not only one against the weight of evidence, but is without evidence to support it," a Court of Appeals judge observed in overturning another lower court decision.[47] The only evidence that would have made the landlord responsible for the condition of the building was an express clause to that effect in the lease.

There were two reasons that city tenants could not always honor the terms of their "contracts" for housing: they did not have money to pay rent, or the buildings themselves were uninhabitable. By the mid-nineteenth century, for thousands of wage-earning tenant households the two conditions were merging—they could not afford to pay rent for safe *or* unsafe housing. But habitability, property as shelter, had no legal meaning.

By common law, the responsibility for maintenance fell not to the landlord but to the tenant.[48] In the absence of a landlord's express covenant to make repairs, tenants were obliged to keep the premises in the condition in which they found them. Though enjoined to maintain leased property, transient tenants had little incentive to donate their labor to a building they might not inhabit the following year, or even the following month. Landlords, as their letters to agents show, undertook repairs primarily to protect their own investment. "Mr. Livingston desires me to say that the wooden gutter in the front area which runs the whole length of all the houses in Chapel Street will carry water, kept clean, it was constructed for that purpose, and the tenants ought to attend to it," Margaret Livingston, clearly aware of the legal rule, informed her agent, Charles Osborn. "But if they will not, a colored man can be hired for a few shillings to do the whole labor."[49]

Most landlords undertook repairs only if the expense could be made back in stable or higher rents of respectable tenants. "If in bargaining for the rent of the house it should be necessary to make reasonable repairs to procure a tenant . . . do so," William Gibbons advised his niece, who had inherited a rental property. Dr. Binsse, who tried to imitate the investment strategies of his brother-in-law, the real estate magnate Dudley Selden, calculated that his house on Greenwich Street "ought to bring $1000 by making some little necessary repairs such as painting the weather woodwork in the rear of the house—or perhaps in front also," or $1,100 a year if he repaired it throughout. Selden, Binsse observed, was collecting $200 a year more on a house on the corner of Greenwich: "The house is the same size as mine. It is true [he] is going to repair it throughout, but $200 more rent for the same size house is a great deal."[50]

If making repairs procured "good tenants" and permitted rent increases, landlords also worried about putting too much into buildings that had already reached a rental ceiling. "The present rent will . . . not justify the expense of iron shutters," Margaret Livingston informed Osborn regarding a house in Maiden Lane. "If we put them to the first floor they will immediately be demanded for the upper stories which are now more exposed to fire from the rear." Still, however reluctantly, landlords acknowledged their own interest in maintaining property regardless of rents. "The house in the rear of 131 Church," Livingston noted, "is not worth a new roof but must be repaired." Often leaving maintenance decisions to their agents, landlords offered a minimal rule: when "it is necessary for the preservation of the house it should be done," George Abbe directed his agent. Similarly, "Whenever application is made to you by the tenants to correct evils arising from cisterns and privies and I am out of town," Mrs. Livingston instructed, "let George Stoll at once attend to it without waiting for orders from me. He understands the business and I trust will do what is right and *only when it is necessary*."[51]

Maintenance "only when it is necessary" defined the prevailing landlord ethic. Whatever outrage the public expressed through juries' decisions, editorials, city inspectors' reports, and state senate investigations, private landlords saw no moral imperative to distinguish an investment in housing from any other well-managed enterprise: the goal was to maximize revenues and minimize expenses. Houses that produced more rent from a single reliable tenant received more attention in maintenance. Landlords of multitenant houses translated that attention into agents' 5 percent commission to collect rents rather than into maintenance to attract and keep tenants. Account books of landlords' agents demonstrate that low maintenance costs were essential to the profitability of working-class housing. Thus whereas 7 to 15 percent of gross annual rent from single-family or two-family dwellings might go back into maintenance, multitenant houses generally commanded less than 3 percent, if that.[52]

Contract law envisioned a free market in which buyers, exercising the power of refusal, could protect their own interests by examining the commodity before purchase. That law took no account of the social forces that determined particular markets. In the context of a massive housing shortage, New York tenants—particularly the laboring classes—exercised limited powers of choice. In incorporating the doctrine of tenants' absolute liability for rent, contract law sanctioned landlords' power to profit off the "sale" of faulty goods—houses that risked the health and safety of their occupants.

In the 1850s, even as New York's judges reached new confidence in using *caveat emptor* to defend the ancient rule of tenant liability for rent, they encountered other kinds of "extreme cases." While responsibility for maintenance could be settled by examination of the lease, what happened if the premises were utterly destroyed by accident or by actions of a third party? The common law was clear: tenants still owed rent. When a barn or a farmhouse was destroyed by fire, agricultural tenants—who often owned the building—could continue to benefit from the use of the land, and thus had no basis to evade the lease. In terms of the contract, there was essentially no failure of consideration.[53]

In the city environment, however, the destruction of rental property—usually improvements on land—by street openings, excavation, fires, or new construction, as well as by landlords' neglect, could completely deprive tenants of the benefits for which they had contracted to pay. "The operation of the inflexible common law rule . . . which requires payment of rent, although the house may be burned down or otherwise destroyed during the term, without the default of the tenant," one angry defending lawyer declared in 1854, "is repugnant to our sense of justice and equity." New York judges, however, having seen the litigious risks of doctrinal concessions, had no intention of reopening the question of equity: "Not only is the landlord not bound to repair, in any case, unless by force of express agreement," Judge John Duer answered the lawyer, "but the tenant even when the tenement demised ceases to be habitable, or is wholly destroyed, is not discharged, in whole or in part, from the payment of the rent subsequently accruing. . . . The promise of the tenant to pay the whole stipulated rent during the whole term is construed unqualified and

absolute, notwithstanding the apparent failure of consideration."
It might be that such rules "are unsuited to the present condition of society, and judged by modern notions are unequal and
oppressive," Judge Duer conceded. "But the court of justice has
no power to abolish them . . . [or] to encroach on the province of the
Legislature."[54]

Duer's position was correct from the perspective of democratic sovereignty, although New York judges had displayed few such reserva-
tions in modifying other common law rules in order to promote new
patterns of economic development. Indeed, as the historian Morton
Horwitz has demonstrated, judges had modified common law contract
principles to arrive at the doctrine that placed the fairness of the bargain beyond judicial inquiry. The state courts' unyielding endorsement
of landlords' powers through the doctrine of *caveat emptor* might be
placed in the context of the political and economic struggles of the
1840s. During the intense battle over rural tenures, the state courts,
which had upheld rentiers' claims, faced Locofoco Democrats' repeated
attacks, including calls for codification of common law and the election
of judges. But in seeking to apply the principles of commercial contracts to leases, judges themselves fulfilled the republican democratic
definition of "sound policy" by liberating land to "neutral" market rules
of self-protection. Thus the state courts' unyielding endorsement of
landlords' powers merged with a new instrumental legal concept that
"freed" all forms of property within the market and left contracting
parties to look after their own interests. Whether contractual freedom
included the right to exploit tenants who lacked the means to command
adequate shelter was placed beyond the consideration of either judges
or juries.[55]

As was the case with the struggle against landlords' powers of distress, pressure to modify common law's support of landlords' powers
did not come from the most vulnerable tenants. Rather, for more than
a decade New York City's commercial leaseholders, public health reformers, and land reformers joined in lobbying the Legislature to revise the doctrine of absolute tenant liability. In 1847 Horace Greeley
had urged the *Tribune*'s readers to sign a petition protesting tenants'
obligation to pay rent "whether [the] premises be kept in good repair
and in tenantable condition or whether they be suffered to decay and
become utterly unfit for human habitation." And in 1860 New York's
Republican lawmakers responded to their own diverse commercial and
land reform constituency and passed a law removing tenants' obligation
to pay rent on buildings "which shall, without fault or neglect on their
part, be destroyed, or so injured by the elements, or any other cause,

as to be untenantable and unfit for occupancy . . . unless otherwise expressly provided by written agreement."[56]

To a large extent, this legislative intervention on the side of fairness and common sense attested to the increasing economic and political power of certain tenant classes and the diminishing power of landlords in relation to other sectors of capitalist investment. By 1860, most of the commercial activity in New York City took place on leased property; and as commercial tenants paid the highest rents, they were the most likely to be taken to court. As had been true of the remedy of distress, merchants and industrialists (as well as householders) resented landlords' favored position under common law. Judges had held, for example, that leaseholders had to pay to protect the buildings they occupied from the effects of new construction on adjacent lots, and they still owed rent even if their buildings were destroyed. Commercial leaseholders argued that they could no longer afford to carry the entire risk of the destruction that accompanied the city's expansion and economic development. In placing landed property on an equal footing with all other forms of property, lawmakers spared the courts the "political" task of enforcing a doctrine that entrepreneurial as well as popular sentiment had found to be repugnant.[57]

The 1860 law did not place a positive obligation on landlords to repair or maintain their property. It did not require that they offer a warranty as to its habitability. Instead, it gave tenants a legal defense against the doctrine of absolute liability for rent in extreme cases. Commercial and better-off residential tenants availed themselves of this defense in court. The vast majority of wage-earning tenants had recourse only to their own "self-help" remedy of moving. It took another century for New York legislators to endorse the principle that landlords were accountable for the quality of the goods they sold.[58]

Bargaining Power

"The relations of landlord and tenant are everywhere felt; and by some, as a burden," the editor George Morris had observed in 1831. Addressing a middle-class readership, Morris explained that the problem derived from the purchasing power of New York's commercial sector. "Buildings situated in those parts of New York which are adapted to large commercial transactions command high, and sometimes indeed excessive rents. The consequence is that every person owning real estate thinks himself justified in levying a similar contribution no matter where it might be situated." Speculation exacerbated the problem, for landlords acquired property "at a price far beyond its intrinsic value; they nonetheless suppose they ought to realize a full interest for their investment without at all estimating the ability of a tenant to pay that amount." But "the fair criterion for estimating real estate," Morris insisted, "should be this: *What sum can a tenant afford to pay for the use of the premises and fulfill his contract faithfully?*" Lest this invocation of "just price" offend his entrepreneurial readers, Morris concluded by noting that his "remarks are not applicable to the majority of respectable men who hold real estate in the city, but to those few whose maneuvers to extort by unfair means a paltry increase of rent from good tenants have [deservedly] come under our observation."[59]

As a spokesman for New York's bourgeoisie, Morris placed himself in an awkward position when he demanded that landlords set their prices according to what a tenant "could *afford* to pay." Such an argument ran contrary to the neutral laws of supply and demand, to which his wealthier readers pointed in explaining the legitimate sources of their own prosperity. But the "burden" of the high rents that accompanied real estate investors' competitive quest for profit was indeed felt by all but the wealthiest New Yorkers. Throughout the early nineteenth century, the tension between propertied citizens' enthusiasm for profits and their anger at having to pay for others' pursuit of the same goal found expression in repeated attacks on "unfair" landlords in many of the city's most solidly entrepreneurial journals and newspapers.[60]

If producers and consumers of rental housing within the same class viewed one another with mistrust, intraclass interests further divided the employers and landlords of the city's wage earners. In the first third of the century, both merchants and master artisans had invested in land and houses, and rent circuits occasionally transferred money from the debit to the credit side of a family's account book. The city's diversified economy made it difficult to isolate landlords' economic interests from those of other entrepreneurs. But by the 1830s, with landed capital assuming a dominant position within the local economy, merchants, respectable householders, manufacturers, and wage earners alike had begun to speak of landlords' particular "impositions."

Real estate speculation and high rents particularly inhibited the development of local industry. Thus New York's light manufacturing, especially the needle and shoemaking trades, expanded through the outwork system rather than through factories in part because contractors could let workers pay overhead costs through their own domestic rents. At the same time, rising rents pushed down real wages and fueled the militancy of the citywide labor movement of the 1830s.[61] Indeed, in demanding higher wages, organized labor pointed up a central tension in the relation of landed and industrial capital. Overlapping though their interests frequently were, New York City's landlords and employers competed for the value of the wage: employers sought to keep wages as low as possible; landlords welcomed higher wages, which allowed them to collect higher rents. But if landlords held the upper hand in the 1830s, the panic of 1837 and the depression that followed dramatically turned the tables: New York's landlords had had to concede the determinative power of those sectors of the economy that paid out salaries and wages.

In 1842, his account books showing marked irregularities and de-faults, the landlord's agent Charles Osborn informed his clients that tenants could no longer pay the going rent. "I am aware that rents must fall," William Gibbons answered his agent, "and we must try to meet it the best way we can."[62] During the depression of the 1840s, both landlords and tenants elaborated the strategies that, whatever their respective powers at law, shaped practical negotiations within the bifurcated rental housing market.

Like investors in new construction, landlords as a group preferred to deal with reliable middle-class tenants and were most willing to make concessions to attract them. Thus Gibbons decided that in hard times there was a trade-off between the level of rent and security of pay-ment. "Those who meet the change first will get the best tenants and I would have you take that course with my houses," he wrote his agent. "If the tenant offering be a satisfactory one and a small reduction will secure him, I recommend that you make the reduction—many good tenants will be driven away by obstinate landlords and I should like them secured for me in the place of any on hand that you do not ap-prove of."[63]

Gibbons' concession throws into relief trade-offs always present in the rental housing market. What was at issue from the landlord's per-spective was not only the level but also the predictable collection of rents. Thus Gibbons reserved his own "obstinance" for tenants "on hand" whom he would willingly evict in order to secure "the best tenants," even with a reduction. The difficulty in collecting rents prompted landlords to adopt other strategies for managing rental housing, including delegating rent collection to agents, subagents, and sublandlords.

The city's largest landlords, and especially its rentiers, had long avoided the troubles of rent collection by relying on agents. Family agents—such as Oliver De Lancey, who looked after his sister's Man-hattan properties—had offered the simple advantage of sharing a com-mon interest in a well-managed estate. The tradition of employing

family members in this capacity continued well into the nineteenth
century: Richard Morris kept the accounts for his brother's New York
City holdings, and though John Jacob Astor personally supervised his
real estate, he also initiated his son William into the secrets of building
and maintaining the family fortune.[64]

By the 1820s, however, the management of rental properties had also
developed into a new business enterprise. "The only advice I can give
you is to do as I do with my house adjoining yours, put it under the
care of Charles Osborn," William Gibbons advised his niece, "and you
have the assistance of a person who makes it his profession." Charles
and George Osborn, working both in partnership and on independent
accounts, inherited the real estate business from their father, Charles
Osborn, who had managed property for business clients in the 1810s
and 1820s. The Osborn brothers kept accounts with several of New
York City's wealthiest landed families, including the Livingstons and
the Van Rensselaers. Their smaller clients included the toilet maker
Jacob Hadley, who owned three houses, and the tavernkeeper Patrick
Dolan, who owned one. Often the Osborns' clients (many of whom
were related) lived outside Manhattan—Willam Gibbons and Dr. Binsse
resided in New Jersey; Morgan Lewis, his daughter Margaret Livingston, and members of the Van Rensselaer family lived in Westchester
and Dutchess counties; and Uriah Levy lived in Monticello, Virginia.
Whereas the senior Charles Osborn had charged a 2.5 percent commission on the rents he collected, the sons charged the 5 percent
commission that had become a standard rate by the 1830s.[65]

Most New York rentiers continued to insulate themselves from the
volatile local economy through long-term leases as well as by hiring
agents. By the 1830s, however, agents themselves and smaller landlords confronted head on the uncertainty that ruled the domestic economies of New York's tenant households. The attention focused on the
May Day tidal wave belied the less predictable daily undercurrents of
New York's rental housing market. Wage-earning tenants did not organize their lives according to real estate's fiscal calendar. Many, employed in the building, textile, and other finishing trades, followed
seasonal manufacturing calendars and adjusted their household economies to unpredictable turns in income. The steady influx of new arrivals further disrupted the standard lease year. And as New York's
employers set limits on what landlords could extract in rent by setting
wage levels, tenants expressed these limits by moving.

The 1840s depression fully exposed these limits on landlords' economic power. In 1842, when giving permission to reduce rents, Gibbons cautioned his agent to "do it in a manner to keep control."[66] But

many forces, particularly tenants' assertion of their own powers of direct action and self-help, undermined landlords' control and gave tenants a measure—however constrained—of bargaining power.

By the 1840s, landlords had most dramatically lost control over the rent-payment schedule. New York's traditional lease arrangement called for tenants to make quarterly payments in advance. The May, August, November, and February due dates conformed neatly to many schedules for the distribution of annuities and dividends and for the payment of interest on bonds. Advance payment served as a form of surety. Landlords' accounts in the 1840s show merchants, grocers, brass founders, and watchmakers who occupied single- or two-family houses on Hubert, Spruce, Beekman, and Hester streets paying their quarterly rents on time; for example, the grocer, painter, engineer, and carpenter who occupied Uriah Levy's Houston Street houses at $350 a year paid $87.50 every three months.[67]

Most New York households, however, could not pay three months' rent in a lump sum. For tenants on the lower rungs of the occupational ladder, the intervals for rent collection shortened as the irregularity of payment increased. Securely employed skilled artisan households on Allen, Clinton, or Sullivan Street—carters, masons, carpenters, wheelwrights, boatmen—often broke their $70 to $80 quarterly payments into installments of $15 to $50. Rent collections were somewhat less predictable from the households of shoemakers, coopers, porters, stevedores, and hack drivers who owed $5 to $6 a month in multitenant houses on Greenwich, Sullivan, Mott, and Mulberry streets. Unnamed and unenumerated "sundry tenants" of Uriah Levy's rear house on Thompson Street yielded between $3.50 and $10.50 every two weeks. And Margaret Livingston complained that the black tenants of her Church Street rear houses "seldom paid rent at all."[68]

No doubt it was such variations that brought Gibbons to the conclusion that "the acceptance of an offer" should "depend more on the quality of the tenants and security than upon price." For "in rents as well as in other things," Gibbons explained, "the quality of pay influences the rate of price."[69] This same philosophy—the suspicion that the unreliability of rent collection rendered working-class housing by definition "unproductive"—had constrained construction of purposely designed multitenant houses before the mid-1840s. During the depression, however, even "quality" tenants encountered difficulties. Some tenants who had been paying quarterly rent switched to monthly installments and then returned to quarterly rents with the passing of whatever personal financial exigency had prompted the change. Occasionally a "reliable" but economically pressed tenant would give up part of a house to a second or third tenant to reduce the individual rent. When the carter Thomas Stephenson could no longer pay the $56.25 quarterly rent for the house he occupied on Houston, he shared the house with a porter for a year, one paying $35.00 and the other $21.25 quarterly. In 1845, Stephenson resumed single occupancy at the original rent.[70]

Tenants who disregarded the landlords' due dates implicitly set their own rents through patterns of payment. Landlords further lost control when tenants unilaterally abandoned their leases before expiration or without notice. In 1842, "Mr. Jones, tenant of the premises fronting Washington Street," who had received a rent cut in the summer, did apply to Gibbons to cancel his lease in November. "He states he has paid his rent in advance to the 1st of February and wants to move away and be discharged of further rent." Gibbons resisted, noting "that he ought not be allowed to relinquish before the 1st of May."[71]

Given such a response, tenants devised other tactics to get out of their leases. Sarah Cook, lessee and proprietor of a boardinghouse on Beekman Place, paid in irregular installments between August 1842 and May 1843. Refusing to show the house to new tenants or to give up the keys, and deducting maintenance expenses from her rent, she seemed to hold the house hostage to get out of her lease. Possession, Gibbons concluded, was nine-tenths the profit. "I recommend that you get the rent from Mrs. Sarah Cook upon the best terms that you can without going to law—you have no claim upon her for refusing to show the house and the amount of glass and keys will not pay the lawyers fees if you recover. I advise you to take the $250 and give the discharge she asked, not being the right way as being the cheapest way . . . and most prudent."[72]

In other instances Gibbons and other landlords did turn to the law for help in dispossessing tenants and recovering rents. In the year 1842–1843, for example, Gibbons spent $46 to sue or evict five tenants who owed back rent. In most cases, at least one month passed between the last rent payment and suit, as landlords waited to see if the default was temporary. The dispossession of tenants could take several weeks in the courts, and often a tenant would abscond before the final judgment. Even before the abolition of the legal remedy of distress, city landlords found that wage-earning tenants' personal property seldom met the cost of rent and legal expenses. Though an occasional landlord was successful in collecting arrears or surety after a tenant had left the premises, for many of New York's anonymous "sundry tenants," absconding provided the only solution to high rents and low wages or unemployment.[73]

From the landlord's perspective, the only thing worse than default-ing tenants was an empty rental unit. The two, of course, went hand in hand. The Osborn brothers' account books demonstrate the source of landlords' fears that laboring tenants offered a risk to systematic and predictable rent collection. Over the course of the 1845–1846 rental year, for example, sixteen households moved through nine units (renting for $3.50–6.00 a month) in the two-story front and rear houses at 111 Mulberry Street. Vacancies eliminated rent revenues for 11 of the 108 total rental months, and the Osborns collected only 84 percent of the anticipated rent from the shoemakers and laborers who rented the rooms.[74]

The landlords, however, recovered almost half of the potential loss from vacancies by carving a store and another dwelling unit out of the buildings in November of the rental year. And even without further subdivision, vacancies, defaulting tenants, and turnover did not neces-sarily render working-class housing unprofitable. The total expense of the Mulberry Street houses—including ground rent, taxes, and re-pairs—came to less than one-third of the collected rents, as compared with 50 to 60 percent of rents collected from middle-class housing.

Apparently well enough satisfied with the houses' productivity, in May 1846 the Osborns decided to purchase 111 Mulberry Street and the front and rear houses next door. They paid one-half the purchase price outright and 6 percent interest on a $3,000 bond. With purchase, the Osborns changed their management procedures. Rather than col-lect rents and keep accounts for individual tenants in all four houses, they turned the task of managing the houses over to their own agent, a carpenter named Aaron Hardman, paying him a 5 percent commission on the rents he collected. The Osborns' own accounts then showed only the sums collected by Hardman from "sundry tenants."[75]

The first year, 1846–1847, Hardman collected $1,350 in rents, $350 more than the maximum income potential of the two properties the year before. The added store accounted for $200 of this increase, and the other $150 came out of some combination of increased occupancy, increased rents, and decreased vacancies. (The additional income of $12 a month suggests that two new rental units may have been created out of the existing space.) In 1847–1848, the Osborns spent almost as much money to dispossess two tenants as they did to maintain the four tenant houses ($10.50 vs. $12.89). The advantage to the Osborns of purchasing the houses and turning their management over to Hardman became readily apparent as they further decreased expenses for main-taining the houses. By 1848–1849, more than two-thirds of the houses' gross rents came back to the landlords, and their net return represented 15 percent of the houses' market price.[76]

Master masons and carpenters were experienced as brokers of the houses they constructed, and from the eighteenth century, landlords had often employed them as rental agents. The alliance of the real estate industry and the building trades thus extended from production to distribution of housing. The carpenter Aaron Hardman did well in the business of collecting wage earners' rents, and by 1850 he had moved into partnership with Charles Osborn.[77]

Alongside subagents, the Osborns relied on both resident and absentee sublandlords, who took the lease on a building and managed its multiple tenancy themselves. This strategy can be seen in William Gibbons' four Greewich Street houses. Accounts show that at 504 Greenwich, for example, Hardman collected from $12 to $26 a month from "sundry tenants," whose total rents dropped from $282.88 to $251.33 in the two rental years 1842–1844. In June 1844 Gibbons found a single leaseholder who paid $275 rent in regular quarterly installments, and the following year he raised that rent $25. Each of Gibbons' four Greenwich Street houses continued to house multiple tenants, but Gibbons collected regular quarterly payments from the carpenter, grocer, wiremaker, and "agent" who held the leases.[78]

The subtenancy system built on, but significantly modified, a century-old practice in New York City. In the eighteenth century, the long-term ground lease had formed one basis of artisan proprietorship. Artisans who held multiple ground leases had generally sold the leases or sublet the land rather than buildings. The new sublandlords, by contrast, leased houses for one year to three years at a time, and each renewal was likely to bring an increase in rent. Few sublandlords in the 1840s and 1850s achieved the independence or the security of New York's earlier generation of artisan leaseholding landlords; like their tenants, they remained immediately vulnerable to the conditions of the labor market.

Reformers viewed sublandlords and subagents as the villains of New York's housing crisis. Thus in his 1845 report on the city's sanitary conditions, the physician John Griscom attacked the "system of tenantage to which large numbers of the poor are subject," and particularly "the merciless inflations and extortion of the *sublandlord*." Griscom accurately spelled out the logic that prompted landlords to adopt subtenancy. "A house, or a row, or court of houses is hired by some person of the owner, on a lease of several years, for a sum which will yield a fair interest on the cost," he reported. "The owner is thus relieved of the great trouble incident to the changes of tenants and the collection of rent. His income is sure from one individual, is obtained without annoyance or oppression on his part. It then becomes the object of the lessee to make and save as much as possible, with his adventure, sufficient sometimes to enable him to purchase the property in a short time."[79]

No doubt some working-class sublandlords did subject their tenants to "merciless inflation and extortion," but they also operated under the constraint of what they owed the owner or chief landlord, whose ideas concerning a "fair interest on the cost" derived from competitive investments within the larger capitalist economy. The $110 that the wheelwright Benjamin Powell could make from collecting rents on Morgan Lewis's Allen Street rear houses no doubt helped make up the $285 rent he owed for his own house, but it was a far cry from the $10,000 that Lewis himself cleared in rents that same year. And for every sublandlord or agent who, like Aaron Hardman, prospered from the system, there were countless others for whom collecting rents was simply a subsistence livelihood; or, when a husband worked at a separate trade, another form of "women's work" (in effect replacing a previous generation's strategy of taking boarders).

By removing both rentier and chief landlord from the scene, the sublandlord system obscured the flow of profits from rental housing and perhaps also defused tenant militancy against rentiers and landlords. It must have been hard to accuse a carpenter or a widow of rent racking when their own mode of living gave little evidence of unjust profits. An organized rent strike must be aimed at a particular landlord. Though all New York City knew that John Jacob Astor made his fortune out of rents (over $100,000 a year), the subtenancy system probably meant that few people, including sublandlords and tenants within his buildings, knew precisely which properties were his.

Griscom could not see some of the advantages of a housing system that, by giving some members of the working class control over rents, may also have given tenants greater leverage in day-to-day negotiations. Working-class agents and sublandlords, who often resided in the same houses as their tenants, of necessity were responsive to the contingencies of unemployment and hardship. When a "missionary" in the Seventh Ward "advance[d] rent for room in another part" to a widow with four children living in a cellar on Columbia Street in 1842, he found that "such was the kindness of her landlady, and the neighbors by whom she was surrounded and the difficulty of finding a more commodious room into which she could move, she had not yet availed herself of my offer." Working-class landlords were not likely to take tenants to court, particularly when wage earners' rents would not cover the court costs. And when tenants took landlords to court on charges of assault during eviction, juries were ready to add the weight of their judgments to landlords' restraint. In 1845, for example, John Shepherd tried to evict his tenant from her "rooms" in a house at 46 Avenue B; "when Mrs. Adams (who is an aged woman) resisted and held on to a bed which Mr. Shepherd was about throwing over the bannister," he pushed her down. The jury awarded Mrs. Adams the equivalent of eight months' rent ($49.50) in damages for assault and battery. And if wage-earning tenants were not in a position to organize rent strikes, they could nonetheless organize informal word-of-mouth boycotts of neighborhood landlords who gained reputations for being particularly difficult.[80]

In any case, to blame the sublandlords was to miss the point: given the structure of the capitalist housing market, New Yorkers' ability to secure adequate housing depended on the level of their incomes as well as on the level of rents. The tiered rent system added to the costs of housing—more gross rent had to be collected to pay the "middle agents"—but this system also circulated a portion of rental revenues back through New York's neighborhoods and thereby may have contributed to the resources of working-class communities.

As with subcontractors in the outwork needle, shoemaking, and building trades, sublandlords occupied an ambiguous position within New York's emerging class structure. Wage-earning tenants may have resented sublandlords' relative economic power, but sublandlords also joined New York's shop, tavern, and boardinghouse keepers as informal working-class creditors who extended the wage. In this sense, though they were fully integrated within the dominant capitalist economy and may have accepted its profit motive, working-class landlords also retained a loyalty to their own communities. Historians have credited the strength and relative autonomy of New York's working-class culture in the second half of the nineteenth century with sustaining labor militancy. But they have not given much attention to the economic structure of community support, which surely included delayed rent collections. The role of the working-class landlords in New York politics also remains a critical question for further investigation. It seems likely that they, like building contractors, formed one core of the local Democratic party. If working-class landlords' own economic interests prompted them to steer clear of radical politics, as party regulars they nonetheless could make claims on the city budget for their own neighbors and neighborhoods.[81]

This is not to say that wage-earning tenants wasted any affection on their landlords. Landlords, after all, were stock villains of antebellum popular melodramas. Furthermore, thousands of Irish New Yorkers carried long memories of rentier exploitation, as well a tradition of *political* opposition to landlords. "Landlordism had driven him not only out of the houses of this city," the Irish radical M. T. O'Connor declared at one tenant meeting, "but out of his house in his native land three thousand miles away, and if the people here submit to it, they will be subjected to the same treatment."[82]

In the 1840s, Irish leaders joined forces with radical labor leaders who embraced agrarian land reform as a program to recover the republican vision of independent proprietorship. Land reform, which had emerged alongside of the Workingmen's movement in the late 1820s, expanded its ranks and its analysis in 1844, when George Evans organized the National Reform movement. The national program called for limitations on the amount of property an individual could own, free distribution of western public lands "to actual settlers and to them only," and the exemption of homesteads from executions for debt. Despite the movement's agrarian focus, New York City land reformers sought to recruit local support by applying their principles to the particular exigencies of the housing market. Although most city editors worried about the housing crisis, it was land reformers who sought to organize tenants.[83]

In the late 1840s, discussion of the housing crisis heated up as landlords moved to cash in on economic recovery and intensified immigration by raising rents. In February 1848, even the Democratic *Herald*'s James Gordon Bennett, a consistent critic of all brands of radicalism, warned that landlords were preparing to raise rents and advised that tenants individually take action to protect their interests. Bennett charged that landlords fanned fears of a housing shortage "to get up an excitement" and "to create a false alarm" that justified their rent hikes. Insisting that there had not been sufficient population increase to justify increases in rents and that "a large number of houses had been built in all quarters of the city," he urged that tenants investigate their landlords' intentions and if a rent increase was in the offing, "commence May day on this very first day of February." In effect—if not by intention—Bennett was endorsing the most common tenant self-help strategy of absconding.[84]

That same February, following a meeting of the Irish Repeal Confederation, Irish radicals and land reformers assembled to urge the organization of a citywide "Tenant League." Regretting the meeting's "small attendance," the speakers eloquently called on wage-earning tenants to "understand and reflect upon their rights" vis-à-vis a "system of land-lordism . . . that was one of the most blighting curses that ever was inflicted on the human race." If the meeting's passion came from such Irish leaders as M. T. O'Connor, its resolutions encompassed the proposals of agrarian land reformers, city health reformers, and the particular grievances of the city's laboring tenants.[85]

The Tenant League called on the Legislature to restrict rents to 7 percent of assessed value. Invoking National Reform's limitation principle, they urged the Common Council to tax unimproved city lots at three times assessed value (thereby encouraging development) and to sell public "common land" only to persons not otherwise possessed of any lots. "Homesteaders" on city lots could build their own houses and pay off the purchase price gradually with their 7 percent ground rents, explained John Commerford, a veteran of the Workingmen's movement who became one of land reform's staunchest advocates. Another resolution endorsed John Griscom's repeated recommendations that the Legislature forbid the letting out of cellar apartments and the construction of courts and rear houses that left no part of their lots uncovered.

Unlike the health reformers, the meeting also called for the repeal of the fire limit law that mandated brick buildings in areas north of 14th Street; such a law, the tenants insisted, was a "scheme of speculators" which rendered "the condition of the poor much harder" by pushing Irish shanty dwellers off leased land. The tenants also separated themselves from housing reformers who saw a solution to the housing crisis in reducing the risks of consolidated building investments; thus they condemned the legislative proposal "to incorporate companies with large capital for building tenements for the poor as tending to encourage the combination of capital to oppress that class still more."

Denouncing the May Day turnover as part and parcel of landlords' conspiracy to raise rents annually and attacking landlords' right to show occupied rental quarters to prospective tenants, the Tenant League called upon the Legislature to guarantee security of possession for tenants who paid "legal rents." And offering a rousing critique of landlords, "being knit together by a common interest and feeling that there is nothing to restrain them in their exactions," they warned of the problem of "warehoused" vacant apartments, noting that whenever landlords "choose to confederate to raise the rate of rents it may be in their interest to have numbers of their houses to remain idle to secure an advance upon those they may rent."

The Tenant League made bold proposals to limit landlords' power, and although the 1848 movement faded, many of its resolutions were taken up again during the 1850s. Raising housing issues at the 1850

trade unionists' Industrial Congress, and at demonstrations by the unemployed in 1853–1854 and again in 1857, land reformers continued
their attacks on the local concentration of landed wealth and the "impositions" of city landlords. They called for the distribution of common
lands to city "homesteaders" and urged the Common Council to appropriate $500,000 to build workers' housing. Yet even as land reformers
insisted on city tenants' right to housing, their greatest commitment
was to the restoration of independent proprietorship through western
migration. Maintaining a sometimes uneasy alliance with the city's
trade unions, they were open to charges both of opportunism in dominating labor councils and of irrelevance in coming to terms with the
conditions faced by the city's working people. Land reformers were
less successful in organizing working-class tenants than in joining the
coalition of insurance companies, health reformers, and Republican
lawmakers who placed the housing question on the state legislative
agenda.[86]

In recent years, labor historians have demonstrated the importance
of direct economic action in determining the balance of power between
employers and workers in antebellum industrializing cities. Drawing on
the distinctive cooperative values of artisan republicanism, mechanics
resisted the degradation of labor within the new industrial economy.
Against a common law tradition that declared unions illegal, wage earners organized and went on strike to secure living wages, shorter hours,
control over the work process, and the very right to engage in collective action to protect their interests. The early labor movement also
developed a vocabulary that challenged the legitimacy of the wage relation within an industrial capitalist economy. At the heart of workers'
struggle, historians have argued, was a new political consciousness of
class identity which permanently transformed American labor
relations.[87]

Changing housing relations in New York City in the first half of the
nineteenth century also revolved around changing relations between
capital and labor, but the struggle over housing—and the conditions of
domestic labor—did not assume the same clear class opposition. For
the most part, New York City's antebellum wage-earning tenants did
not organize collectively to confront landlords' power. In this sense,
they did not articulate or extend a class politics into all sectors of the
emerging industrial capitalist economy. Nor did they directly challenge
the principle of private property rights on which that power rested, a
failure that had important implications for radical politics for the rest of
the nineteenth century.

It was not for want of cause, vision, or concrete remedies that a city tenant movement never successfully organized itself in the antebellum period. Rather, tenants found that the most effective action against landlords was voting with their feet. In the same way that antebellum laborers' informal work customs contested the formation of a new system of industrial discipline, tenants resisted landlords' control of the housing market. Tenants' mobility and absconding undermined the predictability of (and on some occasions limited the level of) profit that could be extracted from housing. As a form of historical agency, such self-help tactics tell us less about the possibilities of working-class political consciousness than about practical strategies of survival. Nonetheless, in the face of enormous constraints and little economic power, in the day-to-day, year-to-year, and decade-to-decade negotiations of the nineteenth-century housing market, New York City's tenants did what they could to make landlords work for their profits.

Conclusion:
The Housing Question

BY 1850, NEW YORK CITY'S capitalist housing market had transformed the spatial organization of everyday life and with it the social relations of real property. Landownership had lost its association with the conditions of independent proprietorship, and houses no longer sheltered and integrated trade and domestic labor. Though the proprietary house and shop persisted as a residual form, particularly in family-operated taverns, groceries, and handicraft shops, the vast majority of New York households had moved onto the cash nexus of wages and rent. The social distribution of shelter, like that of any other commodity produced for profit, measured economic power; and in the years 1785 to 1850, New York City's working people had lost power, their collective claims on the city's resources, including the value that they created as workers and as tenants. No matter how many individual families might move up and down the economic ladder, the housing market organized class divisions as permanent features of the city's social landscape.

In a culture that vigorously denied fundamental class antagonisms and celebrated "society's" progress, the construction and preservation of social distance through distinct residential neighborhoods had become a key strategy for ordering city land use into profitable investment. The displacement of older institutions of proprietary independence was only one part of a larger process that did yield the progress of an increasing social capacity to produce new material wealth. Where for centuries control of land and housing had represented the primary means of controlling labor, the organization of property relations as market relations that measured value through exchange dissolved traditional structures of social hierarchy, monopoly, and appropriation. But in New York City, control over land and housing had assumed new social meanings and represented a new kind of social power.

By the mid–nineteenth century, landed property relations in New York City had changed in part through a change in the social composition and goals of landowners. New investors, particularly speculators and developers who bought up large tracts for construction at the city's periphery, joined and gradually replaced an older generation of merchant rentier families. These real estate entrepreneurs did not expect to attach their names to the landscape, to pass on the stored wealth of prestigious country estates to sons or daughters, or to claim political privileges. Rather they looked to sell or to develop land in a favorable market and quickly reinvest the returns. And when they asserted political power, it was through the influence of their money and strategic coalitions rather than through propertied status.[1]

Manhattan real estate continued to be distributed through a tiered system of long-term ground leases, building leases, and subleases. If exposés of Trinity Church's slum housing in the 1840s and 1850s and again in the 1870s prompted that venerable institution to divest portions of its eighteenth-century land grants, other rentier families and new entrepreneurs retained and distributed large tracts through ground leases.[2] Still, property taxes and assessments for streets and utilities made the holding of Manhattan land a luxury that could be afforded—even when the land was inherited—only through close calculation of opportunity costs: interest and taxes set against rent revenues or alternative investment outlets. Political economic theory reconceptualized "ground rent" itself to analyze not only revenues collected from tenants but even land's "cost" to an owner-occupier who might pursue alternative investments. Whereas historically land investments had been central to the formation of the city's bourgeoisie, by 1860 real estate represented one choice—and not necessarily the most lucrative—among many outlets for accumulated capital or savings, including finance, industry, transportation, and western lands.

Even as social calculations of land's value changed, fluctuations in the real estate market continued to register the health of the city's larger economy. Thus the experience of 1837 was replayed in 1857 and again in the mid-1870s. Though real estate remained a relatively open sector and continued to absorb the petty capital of small entrepreneurs, each depression reinforced the trend toward institutional consolidation. By the 1870s, real estate brokerage and management firms, incorporated building companies, financial institutions, and neighborhood real estate associations sought to coordinate competition and further landed interests in particular locales, and trade journals imparted strategic wisdom alongside recent market information.[3]

Some elements of that wisdom had emerged from the trials and errors of the first half of the century. As in the 1820s and 1830s, new residential construction was liveliest at the edges of the built town. For this very reason, by the 1870s Manhattan real estate investments were closely linked to transportation systems, first to the horse-drawn railways and later to the elevated railroads and subways. Having learned the benefit of public open ground in establishing residential districts, in the 1850s uptown landowners and developers embraced the creation of Central Park, more than 800 acres of landscaped beauty guaranteed to increase the value of lots and buildings in its vicinity. But the rapid growth of Brooklyn and New Jersey towns also expanded the field of real estate competition.[4]

Then, too, after decades of debate over the problematic respectability of multifamily dwellings, by the late 1870s Manhattan developers were shifting from single- and two-family row houses to apartments. In doing so they followed the same logic of absorbing land costs through intensified occupancy which had prompted the production of "tenements." To overcome middle-class New Yorkers' suspicions of a housing form historically associated with poverty, builders added amenities lacking in tenements—new utilities and ornamentation—and promoted the value of prestigious addresses and the "convenience" of yet a new style of "modern housekeeping." No less than the single-family dwelling, the emergence of middle-class apartments restructured domestic labor relations by reducing the need for live-in servants to guarantee the home's smooth operation and respectability. And as with the management of tenant houses, the introduction of new tiers of agents and managers whose work it was to collect middle-class rents added another layer of housing cost, even as it created another sector of managerial employment.[5]

Still, despite these industry-wide strategies, specific conditions of landownership, prior land use, commercial competition, neighborhood succession, and the uncertain rhythm of building cycles continued to shape the history of particular Manhattan blocks. Not until the twentieth century did government support of the residential real estate market discover in zoning a new means of regulating land use to stabilize neighborhoods and enforce spatial and social uniformity as a primary public goal. And not until the emergence of Harlem in the early decades of the twentieth century did the Manhattan real estate market take race—as distinguished from poverty—as a primary category of spatial organization.[6]

Even as new uptown housing absorbed the revenues of the city's middling and elite families in the years 1850 to 1880, the city's laboring people remained concentrated in territories first claimed by the families of artisans and journeymen, especially on the Lower East Side. As each depression ripened downtown lots on the old Rutgers, De Lancey, and Stuyvesant lands by reducing acquisition costs, builders replaced earlier generations of subdivided tenant houses with tenements and launched a new cycle of filtering from within. Some of the city's older artisan neighborhoods gave way to commercial redevelopment—particularly the West Side Fifth and Eighth wards, which became the warehouse district now known as SoHo, with expanded sweatshops above the stores in cast-iron buildings. In the 1850s, as metal shops, gashouses, and factories located along Manhattan's shores, new Irish and German working-class neighborhoods extended north into Hell's Kitchen on the West Side and Yorktown on the East Side.[7]

At the heart of the housing market remained the essential strategy of securing demand by restricting supply. The permanent housing crisis moved in waves, exacerbated by swells of immigration following each depression. Doubtless for thousands who settled in the city, as for the Irish in the 1840s and 1850s, tenements, however crowded, represented an improvement over the living conditions they left behind. Each generation of new arrivals adapted their housekeeping to the exigencies of crowding and mobility. And working-class families developed cooperative strategies to maintain their standard of living against repeated encroachments from landlords and employers alike—from low wages and rent hikes that in reducing housing space intensified the requirements and reduced the value of domestic labor. However frequent their change in domestic quarters, wage-earning New Yorkers created neighborhood institutions—informal credit networks, saloons, ward clubhouses, benevolent societies, unions, and church congregations—which transformed the territories of hardship into the staging grounds of ongoing social contest.[8]

If investment maps and the logic of the bifurcated housing market systematically created class territories, New Yorkers drew their own boundaries through the daily patterns of social traffic and interaction. By the 1850s, a new literature of "guides" that "uncovered" and "exposed" the city to its middle-class residents testified to the irrelevance of spatial proximity to social knowledge.[9] But the practical necessities of sharing the city landscape also exposed social and spatial contradictions that could not be ignored. The questions that emerged in the mid–nineteenth century remain with us today: What were the social limits of private property rights? Who bore the social costs of unlimited rights of appropriation? How within a shared environment could any individual justly claim an exclusive interest in and control of resources necessary to all? These questions arose not from the most oppressed but from middle-class New Yorkers who saw in the city's mid-nineteenth-century housing conditions a danger to their own health, safety, and domestic tranquillity, and a threat to the social equilibrium of a free-market society. Their answers to these questions were constrained by the contradictions of the mid-nineteenth-century liberal republican response to the transformation of property relations into market relations. Regarding private property in land (as well as in labor) as the means to independent living, reformers who took up the housing question had limited ways of addressing the consequences of the circulation of land, housing, and labor as commodities.

The Politics of Property

Challenges to the Anglo-American tradition of landed property rights first emerged not in the United States but in Europe, where the privileges of crown, church, and aristocracy came under assault, and in the West Indies, where Haiti's successful slave revolution broke asunder the landed basis of racial domination. Such New Yorkers as Chancellor James Kent warned of the "Jacobin" threat to republican institutions, but it was not just radicals who had begun to question the historical foundations and justice of exclusive rights in land or enslaved labor. Steeped in a faith in natural rights and natural laws of economic behavior, liberal political thinkers could find no principle that overrode every *man's* right to the property of his own labor, and they had begun to question the legitimacy of a landed elite's monopoly of the wealth of nations.[10]

American political leaders had built and compromised their nation on contradictory principles of protecting the institution of slavery while at the same time affirming private property rights that found their justification in a person's ownership of self. The compromise collapsed, but only at that moment when the principle of labor's alienability, the free labor market, had transformed the meaning of property in labor. Labor power, not persons, not the self, could be bought and sold like any other commodity. And where, as in the South, emancipated labor had no access to the means of subsistence, landowners reasserted their control over labor through their control of land.[11]

Having embraced the principle of free labor half a century earlier, northern republican leaders sought to secure the benefits of proprietary independence by abolishing the vestigial property relations of a "feudal order." In New York, farmers drew on the language of the Revolution for seventy-five years to attack the state's "landed aristocracy." In the 1840s and 1850s, New Yorkers struck new compromises on the meaning and extent of real property rights through constitutional and legal reforms, and the last preemptive powers of a landed social order gave way to the imperatives of the market. The political debates of the mid–nineteenth century framed the possibilities for state intervention in the housing market.

The 1846 movement to write a new constitution in New York drew strength from overlapping political developments. Popular attacks on the powers of corporations chartered by special legislation, anxieties over rising taxes that bailed out state-sponsored canals, and the pressures of creditor–debtor relations following the panic of 1837 laid the ground for a bipartisan coalition that saw in a revised state constitution a new democratic charter. Although motivated by different concerns, anticanal Barnburners, Anti-Rent farmers, and reform-minded lawyers joined in dismantling an older commonwealth tradition of direct legislative involvement in the economy. Attacking state debts (which taxed individual initiative), special charters, and feudal tenures, constitutional reformers denounced "monopolies" that ran against the democratic republican grain. They simultaneously called for a reduction of government's powers and an increase in electoral participation. Thus the 1846 constitution sharply restricted the Legislature's power to incur debts for internal improvements, endorsed general incorporation laws, and abolished state inspection of commodities. New provisions for biennial Senate elections, single-member Assembly districts, the election of judges, voter referenda on state debts, and the abolition of property requirements for officeholding aimed at bringing government action more closely under citizens' control.[12]

Constitutional and legal reforms of the 1840s and 1850s endorsed a laissez-faire economy and purported to shift government's role from that of an active agent in economic development to that of the groundskeeper of the neutral playing field of contractual private property relations. But while democratic utilitarian thought embraced competition as the greatest public good, laying the legal and constitutional foundations of a free-market economy required the setting of limits on preemptive property rights. Antebellum judges had themselves initiated the process of weighing absolute private rights against public policy by modifying common law doctrines that inhibited new industrial land uses. The tensions of redefining property rights and adapting them to new market conditions without infringing on the principle of the state's responsibility to protect private property was evident in the treatment of tenure relations in the 1846 constitution.[13]

Advocates of the 1846 constitution saw its reforms as fulfilling the "policy of our government which was to favor free alienation of property, and to discourage the accumulation and perpetuation of large estates in particular families." Thus the constitution abolished feudal tenures, as had the Legislature by statute repeatedly since 1779. Furthermore, in an effort to end "feudal" conditions in leases for life or in fee, the constitution voided "all fines, quarter sales or other like restraints upon alienation reserved in any grant of land." Finally, the constitution incorporated the statutory rule against parole (oral) leases of more than a year's duration. By making written leases a matter of fundamental law, the state presumably encouraged tenants to reject unreasonable covenants and thereby protect themselves against feudal customs and even the common law.[14]

But delegates representing the cities expressed concern that these reforms on behalf of rural leaseholders would interfere with the rights and interests of urban landowners. Landlords in the "vicinity of cities" often leased their extensive speculative holdings "for agricultural purposes for long term, and in view of their being wanted hereafter for city purposes," explained one delegate, who was himself a member of a prominent Manhattan merchant landowning family. Restrictions upon the length of leases, the delegate complained, would render such lands utterly "unproductive" until such time as they might be developed for city use. Furthermore, delegates warned that proposals to restrict covenants against tenant alienation of leases "would admit of a more general construction allowing tenants to sub-rent without consent." If extended to cities, such a provision threatened the interests of landlords "who took care to know who were to be their tenants when they made leases and [who] should not be deprived of the right to do so."[15]

City landowners saw to it that reforms that established the principle of land's free alienability did not also discourage strategies that made real estate investments competitive with other sectors of capital. The 1846 constitution placed an "agricultural" qualifier on its prohibition of leases for terms of longer than twelve years, allowing city rentiers to continue speculative trading in ground leases of twenty-one years and longer. The restriction on convenants against tenant alienation of leases remained, however, and was largely ignored by city rentiers, who continued to covenant against subletting without permission.[16]

A similar ambiguity in extending private property rights by limiting traditional prerogatives of landholding emerged with the passage of

New York's first married women's property act in 1848. Despite the aggressive campaign of such of feminists as Ernestine Rose and Elizabeth Cady Stanton, most lawmakers who supported the reform saw it less as an attack on the economic foundations of patriarchy than as a measure that extended men's powers to protect dependent women. New York's wealthiest families had long used trusts to create separate estates that sheltered wives' property from husbands' obligations for debts. But reform lawyers who viewed equity jurisdiction as cumbersome and restricted in its benefits joined debtors in the campaign to place all wives' property beyond the reach of creditors. Like the mid-century general incorporation laws that replaced special legislative charters, married women's property acts can be read as part of the larger trend to promote commercial ventures by creating a personal safety net. Married women's property rights abolished the patriarchal structure of landed property and labor relations in a commercial economy that no longer questioned the rights of appropriation that those relations embodied.[17]

Alongside the 1846 constitution and 1848 Married Women's Property Act, the mid-nineteenth-century land reform movement broadened popular discussion of the republican conception of private property rights and indeed to many people represented a means of resolving the tensions between the sanctity of those rights and the problematic social powers of monopoly. The intellectual seeds of land reform were laid in England and Ireland, where Chartists, militant tenants, and liberal political economists all attacked the political and economic position of an elite landed class. David Ricardo and, a generation later, John Stuart Mill questioned the economic utility and social justice of land monopolies; class monopolies of the limited supply of natural resources, they argued, arose not from individual initiative but from inherited rank. If labor produced all value, what right did landowners have to collect in rising rents the "unearned" value that resulted from the labors of society as a whole?[18]

In the middle decades of the nineteenth century, Americans gave the principles of land reform a distinctive twist. As in Europe, radical and liberal strains of land reform found different followers. New York mechanics who embraced Owenist (and later Fourierist) associationist ideas envisioned utopian communities that, replacing competition with cooperation, would share the resource of land as common property. Although Jacksonian workingmen remained skeptical that freely distributed land could resolve the conflicts they had only begun to articulate as divided interests of capital and labor, they placed land reform on their political agenda alongside free education, lien legislation, and the abolition of banking monopolies. But when in the late 1820s such radicals as Thomas Skidmore carried Owenist principles to their logical conclusion and called for the abolition of private property, trade unionists hastened to reassure the public that they "only want to be secured in our labor and have no more intention of taking what does not belong to us than we have of taking arsenic."[19]

The stronger strain of American land reform drew on the agrarian republican tradition, which viewed individual proprietorship as the foundation of personal and civic virtue. Unlike Europe, the United States enjoyed an abundance of vacant land. When the frontier was opened to settlers, the nation would tap its natural resources without challenging the principle of private property rights in land (or, indeed, in labor). In the 1840s and 1850s, this faith mobilized popular support for the conquest of western territories and triggered lively debate over policies to distribute public lands to homesteaders. By the late 1850s, the antislavery movement had linked free soil and free labor, and the new Republican party endorsed liberal homesteading policies that reinforced the antislavery alliance of northern farmers, small producers, western merchants, railroads, and land speculators.[20]

Antebellum land reform addressed the question of the exclusive appropriative powers of landownership by promising those rights to increasing numbers of people. Attaching the republican goal of proprietary independence to migration, land reformers implicitly conceded that that goal could not be realized in eastern cities. But as taken up by the labor movement, land reform also represented a strategy to improve the conditions of working people within the free labor market: if workers' families could migrate to affordable homesteads, those who remained behind might stand in a better bargaining position. In New York City, workingmen further called on the city to distribute corporation common lands for the construction of workers' housing. At the very moment when the city took more than 800 acres of uptown land out of the market to create Central Park, unemployed demonstrators sought to apply the principles of land reform to the city's housing crisis. But with immigration accelerating, neither western migration nor cheap city lands could alleviate the condition of workers caught between employers' and landlords' drive for profit.[21]

Liberal land reformers, like the advocates of the constitutional and legal reforms of the mid–nineteenth century, saw in the distribution and unconstrained circulation of abundant land a solution to the threat that concentrated wealth posed to a democratic social order. Once positive state policy guaranteed the conditions of distribution, government could step back from the market and give private property rights free reign. But if the distribution of land embodied the goal of independent proprietorship, laissez-faire principles extended to all forms of property. Even as an older order of landed property relations finally gave way to the ideology of a free market that preserved the principle of access to proprietorship, a new system of property relations had begun to emerge. In a development prefigured by the absentee ownership of land, corporations organized individual property rights as claims not on the direct use of land, labor, or other resources but as rights to revenues, "benefits" severed from use. And even as new corporate institutions and powers of absentee ownership emerged, liberal New Yorkers began to formulate a new defense of state regulation of individual private property rights in the use of city land and housing.

Housing Reform

New York City's first housing reform movement, responding to conditions twenty years in the making, took another twenty years to achieve its legislative goals. By the 1850s, the housing crisis had received a decade of publicity from city officials faced with the task of explaining and controlling the rising mortality rate, from newspaper editors who called upon capitalists to undertake philanthropic building ventures, and from private charity leaders who found their agenda for moral reform overwhelmed by housing conditions that contradicted the very definition of morality attached to respectable home life. Whereas reformers of the 1820s and 1830s had focused on the contamination of particular neighborhoods tenanted by "vagrants," by the 1840s respectable New Yorkers were beginning to view housing conditions throughout the city as cause and symptom of new and dangerous social divisions. Indeed, housing conditions became a primary field of social interpretation and debate which incorporated a range of mid-century intellectual and political currents.

Discussions of agrarian land reform spilled over into the Whig *Courier*'s attack on the "practical Fourierism" of working-class neighborhoods and Horace Greeley's *Tribune* editorials advocating western migration. Irish and English immigrants applied their own radical brands of land reform in attacks on parasitic city landlords. Physicians, drawing on English investigations, added a scientific gloss to moral reform efforts, stressing the impact of the social environment on individual character and the value of professional medical expertise in investigations of the problem. Utilitarian merchants who defined the public interest as an ever-expanding economy warned that poor housing conditions and the social disorders they bred would scare away investors, customers, and new city residents. Manufacturers saw in high rents the fuel of worker militancy and in tenement life the corruption of disciplined work habits. Nativists and Whig politicians warned that unscrupulous Tammany politicians would exploit ethnic neighborhoods to their own advantage by trading drinks for votes.[22]

From the 1830s, commentators had readily blamed riots, disease, crime, and immorality on housing conditions; and with the depression of the 1840s, the Astor Place riot and cholera epidemic of 1849, the citywide strike wave in 1850, and the police riot and demonstrations by the unemployed in 1857, editors and reformers asserted the connection between civil disorder, epidemics, and housing conditions with increased vigor.[23] The imported European concept of "dangerous classes" gained currency in popular journals and books. Propertied New Yorkers, expressing fear that they were losing control of the city, blamed tenants for disregarding the prerogatives of private property rights and landlords for abusing them. Conditions in working-class neighborhoods, they argued, placed the entire city's physical, economic, and social well-being at risk. And because through voting, through disease, through strikes, and through riots, social politics asserted a class geography that did not respect class boundaries, reform-minded New Yorkers began to see a solution to class divisions in housing reform.

As part of the transformation of common law in the first half of the nineteenth century, judges had repeatedly weighed absolute private property rights against the social needs and benefits of development. In the arena of landlord and tenant law, however, absolutism had triumphed as the means to entrepreneurship. The contract principle of *caveat emptor* incorporated the ancient doctrine of tenants' absolute liability for rent and relieved landlords of any obligation to guarantee the habitability of housing. When the law failed to distinguish landlord–tenant relations from general contractual relations, the "consuming" city public had no legal means to restrain the mass production of tenant houses that lacked sanitation, heat, ventilation, and structural stability.

In the 1840s, City Inspector John B. Griscom marshaled utilitarian arguments to warn that landlords violated the basic principle of a republican society by maximizing their own profits at the expense of the public good. "A clearer understanding of the relative cost to the City of sickness and health among the poorer classes," Griscom suggested, "may be had by supposing a small section, as a court or block of buildings, containing a given number of inhabitants who are liable to be thrown upon public charity for support by the premature death or illness of heads of families." Furthermore, he insisted, inadequate housing undermined the growth of the larger economy by producing a chronically sick and unstable work force. In order to protect public welfare, Griscom argued, the state had to intervene in the housing market.[24]

Precedent for state regulation of real property already existed indirectly in the state's power to tax and to assess and directly in its police power and the power of eminent domain. Positive legislation required landowners to pay for public works, and preventive laws established minimum standards for building materials used in outer walls and roofs in fire districts drawn primarily according to building density. The same public authority that supervised streets, sewers, sunken lots, piers, wells, and cisterns also monitored the "private" utilities of privies and such "nuisance industries" as bone-boiling establishments, slaughterhouses, tanneries, and soap manufactories. City inspectors could order the removal from private property of "nuisances" that were regarded as public hazards by virtue of their immediate external impact but not because they threatened the well-being of occupants of the premises.[25]

John Griscom drew on these precedents to recommend legislative reform as the key to resolving New York's housing crisis. "If there is any propriety in the law regulating the construction of buildings in reference to fire," he argued, choosing a particularly sensitive subject for New Yorkers, who had suffered more than one multiblock conflagration, "equally proper would be one respecting the protection of the inmates from the pernicious influence of badly arranged houses and apartments." And he urged that the definition of "public nuisance" reach into internal housing conditions: "The power given to a magistrate to pull down a building whose risk of falling endangers the lives of the inmates and passers-by," he insisted, "may with equal reason be extended to the correction of interior conditions of tenements when dangerous to health and life. The latter should be regarded with as much solicitude as the prosperity of citizens." Drawing an analogy to federal legislation regulating the number of passengers on seagoing vessels, Griscom argued that the city, too, was justified in putting "an immediate stop to the practice of crowding so many human beings in such limited space."[26]

In the 1850s, the merchants and manufacturers who led the Association for Improving the Condition of the Poor and the physicians of the Academy of Medicine took up Griscom's recommendations and began to lobby the state legislature. But when he had recommended the legal abolition of cellar dwellings in 1845, Griscom himself had noted "that

any stringent measures forbidding the letting of underground tenements as dwellings would meet with considerable resistance from
interested parties as conflicting with their personal rights and
interests."[27] What Griscom did not say was that the "interested parties" who resisted housing reform included tenants as well as builders
and landlords.

Unlike agrarian leaseholders, New York's antebellum wage-earning
tenants did not organize systematic political resistance to landlords'
power. Though trade unionists and Irish radicals allied themselves with
middle-class land reformers in the 1850 Industrial Congress, for the
most part working-class tenants engaged in the practical politics of negotiating with particular landlords and switching landlords often. Their
actions within the housing market took on a collective aspect only insofar as they prompted new landlord strategies, including the subten-
ure system. While such reformers as Griscom attacked the rapacious
greed of working-class sublandlords, many tenants were sympathetic to
these community creditors, who, by "extending" the wage, sustained
working-class families within the bounds of the legal economy. Then,
too, tenants well knew that landlords repaired housing in order to increase rents. And finally, whereas the strongest proponents of housing
reform were first Whigs and then Republicans, the majority of city
tenants remained faithful to a Democratic party that opposed legislative reforms.[28]

In light of land reformers' preoccupation with land as a productive
resource, it is worth stressing that the calls for state regulation of the
housing market were not aimed at New York's landowners, the rentiers
who stood at the head of the housing market. For it was the very focus
on tenement landlords (the people who collected rents in order to pay
rents) and on the small builders who produced tenements that made
housing reform consistent with the view that the state existed to protect private property rights. Extension of the state's police power to
preserve civil order, health, and safety could be ideologically distinguished from direct state intervention in the economy. So long as housing was treated as a moral and social problem rather than as a political
and economic one, state action did not fundamentally challenge laissez-
faire ideology. And when the issue was clearly economic—as with insurance companies' campaigns for construction standards that reduced
fire risks—it intersected with a new disposition toward socializing risk
and limiting liability to further commercial expansion.

If the reasoning that separated the property relations of housing from
those of land, labor, and credit seems curiously compartmentalized,
the isolation of housing as a discrete public health and safety issue

helped mobilize the support of the city's manufacturers and merchants. The antebellum language of housing, which erased its identity as a workplace, reinforced this narrow focus and combined with the particular conditions of New York State and New York City politics in the 1860s to shape the city's first housing reform legislation.

When housing reformers went to the Legislature in 1856, they found lawmakers elected on nativist, antislavery, and temperance platforms receptive to their cause. The coalition that within the year would consolidate into the Republican party saw political as well as social dangers in a Democratic city. In 1856 and again in 1857, legislative committees conducted fact-finding investigations into the Manhattan and Brooklyn tenant housing problem and heard lengthy testimony from medical experts who denounced the indifference, ignorance, and incompetence of city politicians on public health matters. By merging the two cities into a new metropolitan district, the Legislature technically circumvented the issue of home rule. Still, however ready Republican lawmakers were to expose and document the extent of the city's housing crisis and blame city politicians, they were uncertain of their power to resolve it.[29]

The first housing reform legislation came indirectly. Commercial tenants capitalized on the widespread antipathy to landlords' "feudal" powers and in 1860 secured statutory modifications of the common law doctrine of tenants' liability for rent for uninhabitable buildings. And insurance companies joined in lobbying for a series of laws that extended the boundaries of fire districts, introduced new minimum construction standards, and established a new city office for building inspection. Then, too, reformers' efforts to move health wardens from the (Democratic) City Inspector's Office to the state-controlled (Republican) Metropolitan Police Department resulted in the creation of a special division of sanitary police.[30]

The pace of housing reform accelerated following the devastating draft riots in 1863, the renewed threat of cholera in 1865, and the ascendancy of the Radical Republicans, who saw in social reform legislation both a means to curtail the Democrats' power (by replacing the offices of city patronage) and a positive program for "Reconstruction at Home." Then, too, in 1864 the labor movement and the German press threw their support behind the efforts of the bipartisan (and anti-Tammany) Citizens' Association to address housing conditions. Although the social divisions that underlay the draft riots were complex, propertied New Yorkers continued to express faith that housing reform could assuage the class antagonisms that the riot had exposed.[31]

State politicians formulated the issue of housing and public health reform as questions of party power and enforcement. In 1865, lawmakers created a Metropolitan Health Board, which, like the Metropolitan Police and Fire departments before it, removed city matters from the hands of locally elected officials and authorized a new system of housing inspection. Though aimed at eradicating the physical conditions that fed the spread of cholera, to many wage-earning tenants the invasion of Board of Health inspectors represented an assault on the integrity of their neighborhoods and domestic quarters. And as the campaign for housing reform continued, so did the resistance of small builders and tenants to measures that threatened to raise construction costs and rents without fundamentally relieving the conditions of the housing market.[32]

The Radical Republicans' 1867 Tenement House Act consolidated the powers of fire and health inspection and expanded the jurisdiction of the Building Department over tenement construction and conversion. The law required the filing of building plans, and it confirmed the authority of the Board of Health to inspect tenements and take action against landlords for violation of specified minimum housing standards. In an effort to overcome the confusion of liability within the city's tiered tenure system, the law required landlords and agents to post their names and addresses conspicuously in their buildings. But despite intense debate over proposals to license subletting and regulate tenement density, the reform legislation limited itself to supervising the structural elements of housing: the number and quality of utilities (one toilet to twenty persons), room dimensions and ceiling heights, provisions for ventilation and light, and building materials. These minimum standards for new buildings were a significant gain. By standardizing the product, the law also regulated competition within the building industry. How city dwellers actually inhabited the tenement apartments, however, depended on the level of wages and rents—matters beyond the purview of law.[33]

So long as wages remained low and unemployment chronic, working-class tenants had little choice but to crowd or to move. However bad the housing, there was little reason to expect its regulation would prompt builders to produce enough multifamily dwellings to accommodate the city's laboring people at rents they could afford. Though the law limited the rights of builders and landlords, it did not positively defend the rights of tenants. At most it sought to protect tenants as members of the "public" from houses that fell down, burned up, or fostered epidemics. And after 1870, in part as a result of the party and class politics that had governed its passage, many provisions of the law went unenforced.[34]

The principle gained in the first housing reform legislation was an important one: the state could set limits on strategies of profitmaking sanctioned by private property rights. The old common law principle that restrained a landowner from using property in such a way as to injure the interests of a neighbor had been effectively recast: the city as a whole constituted the neighborhood. And in separating housing from other forms of private property, reformers sought to consider its distinctive spatial and social attributes and the consequences of inadequate shelter within a shared landscape. Yet this very separation also exposes the limits of housing reform as a solution to the social costs of capitalist property relations. The appropriative powers buried in the historical construction of "individual" property rights in land and housing, a householder's right to dependents' labor, had become class rights to the value of society's labor.

Those limits could be seen more clearly in one of the nineteenth century's most radical social movements—Henry George's campaign for a single tax on land. In his 1879 *Progress and Poverty*, George drew on antebellum land reformers' critique of the social monopoly of natural resources to argue that "the great cause of inequality in the distribution of wealth is inequality in the ownership of land." The solution therefore was to eliminate the benefits of landownership when it was severed from land use, to tax away landowners' "unearned increment," the ground rent they collected from appreciating land values. The community created that value through its labors, and no individual could claim exclusive rights in the common property of natural resources. With a single tax on land, George argued, "no one could afford to hold land that he was not using, and consequently, land not in use would be thrown open to those who would use it."[35]

It was a remarkable critique and program in a nation that had enshrined private property rights in land as its unique heritage and the foundation of republican government. George rejected the call of antebellum land reformers for the distribution of public lands through homesteading policies. Having spent time in San Francisco, he had observed at firsthand the monopolization of western lands by railroads, speculators, and mining companies. "Any measures which merely permit or facilitate the greater subdivision of land," he insisted, could not offset the "tendency to concentration." Instead, George called for a single tax that would inhibit speculation and landlordism and restore land to the people who occupied and used it; such a measure would not infringe on property rights in improvements that contributed to material progress.[36]

The abolition of rentiers' right to expropriate social wealth in ground rent, George argued, would free capitalists and workers to cooperate in the shared project of increasing that wealth. Thus, though he abandoned earlier agrarian land reformers' faith in homesteading, he shared their producerist assumptions and analysis of land's benefit to industrial workers. If the alternative of independent proprietorship was restored, "competition would no longer be one-sided. Instead of laborers competing against each other for employment and in their competition cutting down wages to the point of bare subsistence, employers would everywhere be competing for laborers, and wages would rise to the fair earnings of labor." Furthermore, employers would bid "against the ability of laborers to become their own employers upon the natural opportunities freely opened to them by the tax which prevented monopolization."[37]

George brought his program to New York City, and in 1886 he formed an alliance between the city's trade union movement and middle-class reformers and ran for mayor as the United Labor Party candidate. Few labor leaders shared his optimism that the single tax represented a permanent solution to poverty or that the elimination of land monopoly would reconcile the interests of capital and labor. Yet in the 1880s the cooperative labor movement itself, and particularly the Knights of Labor, had moved far beyond shop-floor relations to experiment with multi-issue community organizing.[38]

George's mayoral campaign found its institutional base in the independent political culture that had sprung up in the city's ethnic neighborhoods. As the historian David Scobey has shown, the George campaign organized "pledge drives, neighborhood meetings, and street-corner rallies . . . supported by informal social networks within the working-class community and by the rhetorical traditions of organized labor." Unlike efforts at housing reform twenty years earlier, the George campaign mobilized wage-earning families who saw improved housing conditions as only one of the benefits of abolishing land monopolies. And though the insurgent party was defeated, the threat of working-class militancy prompted propertied New Yorkers to renew discussion of housing reform as a solution to class conflict.[39]

Yet George's ideas were symptomatic of the larger problem of limiting a critique of private property to only one of its forms. By the late nineteenth century, rentiers who collected an unearned increment were not simply landowners, for land no longer stood at the heart of the American economy, and its unequal distribution was not the only source of social inequality. A program that captured the landed wealth of an Astor or a Vanderbilt left untouched the even greater wealth—and appropriative powers—of a Morgan, Rockefeller, or Carnegie. Nor would the abolition of property in land affect the power of the stock- and bondholders who "owned" the means of industrial production. Property relations had moved beyond the family and market relations that determined labor's access to land and housing as resources for in- dependent subsistence. Corporate absentee ownership had "socialized" the ownership of capital—and claims on the value of labor—without risking the principle of exclusive appropriation. Capitalists in effect paid landowners the private tax of ground rent in exchange for the his- torical legacy and legitimacy of private property rights. If George, no less than Karl Marx and Friedrich Engels, declared that property in land was theft, socialists took the argument the next step and called for the abolition of all private property.[40]

The first half of the nineteenth century yielded contradictory con- cepts of private property rights within the liberal tradition. On one level, the triumph of laissez-faire claims to absolute property rights re- inforced the concept that the state exists only to protect those rights. On another, nineteenth-century housing reformers formulated the con- cept of an overriding public interest that justified the expansion of the state's police power to restrain the exercise of property rights that in- fringed on the "domestic tranquillity" of the community as a whole. The two conceptions opened the way to the weighing of private inter- ests and public consequences so characteristic of land-use regulation today. And in a sense George's single-tax campaign recovered a third tradition of property rights—that of common rights in natural re- sources. New theories of social limits on private property rights have emerged when the social costs of exclusive appropriation have been felt to be too great. These debates continue as New York City once again faces a housing crisis.[41] In order to address the contemporary housing question it is necessary, as it was in the past, to look at how the larger structures of property and labor relations have emerged and worked together to determine people's access to shelter. To view these relations as having a history is also to see the possibility of their future transformation.

Appendix

THE TABLES that follow offer a schematic statistical overview of the transformation of Manhattan property and housing relations. Table 1 records the proportion of freeholders and renters among city voters and shows the steady decline in proprietors from more than two-fifths (46.9%) of the electorate in 1790 to one-fifth (19.6%) in 1821. Table 2 shows the social geography of the changing patterns of landownership and tenancy in 1807: landownership was lowest in Wards 4, 5, 6, and 7, where such rentiers as Trinity Church, Henry Rutgers, and the Roosevelt family held sway and where artisans and journeymen moved when they could no longer afford housing in the wharf-district wards (1–3).

Table 3 traces the economic cycles that governed real estate investments and the production of new housing in New York City between 1817 and 1850. It shows that land values appreciated by more than 280 percent between 1825 and 1836, when new construction reached 14th Street, and then fell off to less than 7 percent a year during the decade that followed the panic of 1837. Table 4 presents the specific social geography of the expanding housing market, particularly the rapid appreciation of land values which accompanied the construction of new single-family and two-family row houses in Wards 9 (Greenwich Village) and 11 (in the vicinity of Union Square) and the commercial conversion of lower Manhattan (Wards 1, 3, and 5). Despite the rapid rate of population growth in new areas of the city, new residential districts had the lowest density. With limited investment in new construction in the city's older mechanic neighborhoods (Wards 6, 8, and 14 and Wards 10 and 13), density rose higher than the citywide average of 9.5 persons per occupied lot. Table 5 shows the continuation of these patterns between 1834 and 1842 and the impact of the bifurcated housing market and the depression on the housing conditions of the city's poorest families, as many as 6,618 of whom resided in cellars, courts, and rear houses. Although, as Table 6 shows, the construction of new housing—and particularly of tenements—accelerated in the second half of the 1840s, it did little to relieve these conditions.

Table 7 gives us a statistical snapshot of New York City's class-divided landscape in 1855. Just short of 12 percent of the city's families owned land and lived off rents collected from their neighbors. Between 10 and 27 percent of merchants and shopkeepers continued to own the land in the lower wards where they did business. Nearly one-third of the families who resided in the elite Fifteenth Ward (Greenwich Village), from one-fourth to one-fifth of families in transitional "rural" wards north of 42d Street (Wards 12, 18, 19, 21), and one-sixth of the middle-class families in the "native-born" Ward 9 owned land. These famlies also enjoyed a density of people per house lower than the citywide average. Density and tenancy, of course, went hand in hand, particularly in the city's lower wards. But the high density and low ownership rates in working-class wards north of 14th Street (11 and 17) show the systematic building of inequity into the city's social landscape.

Table 1. Number and percentage of freeholders, renters, and others who voted in New York City elections, 1790–1821

Year	Freeholders				Renters[a]		Other electors[b]		All electors
	Property worth £100[c]	Property worth £20–100[c]	All freeholders	Percent of electorate	Number	Percent of electorate	Number	Percent of electorate	
1790	1,209	1,221	2,430	46.9%	2,661	51.3%	93	1.8%	5,184
1795	2,144	10	2,154	29.6	4,948	68.0	170	2.3	7,272
1801	2,332	19	2,351	29.1	5,693	70.4	44	0.5	8,088
1807	3,000	20	3,020	24.3	9,334	75.2	62	0.5	12,416
1814	3,141	17	3,158	22.7	10,763	77.2	20	0.1	13,941
1821	3,881	17	3,898	19.6	12,761	64.0	3,266	16.4	19,925

[a]Persons paying annual ground rent of 40 shillings ($5) or more.
[b]Freemen.
[c]£100 = $250.
Source: Franklin Hough, Statistics of the Population of the City and County of New York (New York, 1866), pp. 18–19.

Table 2. Number and percentage of freeholders and renters who voted in New York City elections, 1807, by ward

Ward	All freeholders and electors	Freeholders[a]		Renters[b]	
		Number	Percent of electorate	Number	Percent of electorate
1	1,081	374	34.4%	707	65.1%
2	1,042	355	34.1	687[c]	65.9
3	1,117	338	30.2	779	69.7
4	1,327	351	26.4	976	73.3
5	1,895	466	24.5	1,429	75.2
6	1,421	258	18.1	1,163	81.5
7	3,136	418	13.3	2,718	86.6
8	1,023	308	30.1	715	69.9
9	336	162	47.8	174	51.3
All wards	12,407[d]	3,030	24.4	9,348	75.3

[a]Owners of real property valued at £20 ($50) or more.
[b]Persons paying annual ground rent of 40 shillings ($5) or more.
[c]Corrected; last digit missing in source.
[d]Plus 29 freemen.
Source: Minutes of the Common Council, 1784–1831 (New York: Dodd, Mead, 1905), 4:650.

Table 3. Assessed values of real estate in Manhattan, 1817–1850

Year	Assessed value	Percent change	Population
1817	$ 57,799,435		
1818	59,846,185	+ 3.54%	
1819	60,490,445	+ 1.08	
1820	52,063,858	−13.93	123,706
1821	50,619,820	− 2.77	
1822	53,331,574	+ 5.36	
1823	50,184,229	− 5.90	
1824	52,019,730	+ 3.66	
1825	58,425,395	+12.31	166,086
1826	64,804,050	+10.92	
1827	72,617,770	+12.06	
1828	77,138,880	+ 6.23	
1829	76,130,430	− 1.30	
1830	87,603,580	+15.07	197,092
1831	95,594,335	+ 9.12	
1832	104,160,605	+ 8.96	
1833	114,124,566	+ 9.57	
1834	123,249,280	+ 7.99	
1835	143,742,425	+16.63	270,089
1836	233,732,303	+62.60	
1837	196,450,109	−12.19	
1838	194,543,359	− 0.97	
1839	196,940,134	+ 1.23	
1840	187,221,714	− 4.94	312,710
1841	186,359,948	− 0.46	
1842	176,513,092	− 5.28	
1843	164,955,314	− 6.55	
1844	171,937,591	+ 4.23	
1845	177,207,990	+ 3.07	371,223
1846	183,480,534	+ 3.54	
1847	187,315,386	+ 2.09	
1848	193,029,076	+ 3.05	
1849	197,741,919	+ 2.44	
1850	207,142,576	+ 4.75	515,547

Sources: 1817–1825: Board of Assistant Aldermen, Documents 4, December 5, 1831 (unbound): Appendix, table 4, in Columbia University Library; 1826–1850: David Valentine, ed., *Manual of the City of New York* (New York, 1857), p. 186.

Table 4. Assessed values of lots and population density, Manhattan, 1825 and 1830, by ward

Ward	1825		1830		Percent change		Vacant lots	1830 Assessed lots occupied	Density per lot
	Population	Assessed value	Population	Assessed value	Population	Assessed value			
1	9,926	$11,647,900	11,217	$18,415,350	+ 13%	+ 58%	79	1,898	5.9
2	9,315	7,537,000	8,202	9,434,150	− 13	+ 25	11	1,239	6.6
3	10,801	5,300,600	9,620	8,779,000	− 11	+ 66	84	1,139	8.4
4	12,240	5,243,250	12,705	6,349,450	+ 4	+ 21	21	1,423	8.9
5	15,093	5,264,900	17,722	7,616,600	+ 17	+ 45	141	1,709	10.3
6	20,061[a]	4,742,640[a]	13,569	5,590,000	− 32	+ 18	49	1,189	11.4
7	14,192	4,071,630	15,868	5,515,780	+ 12	+ 35	883	1,326	11.9
8	24,285[a]	6,197,050[a]	20,920	6,658,800	+ 08	+ 07	362	1,989	10.5
9	10,956	4,498,550	22,752	9,073,450	+ 108	+ 102	2,838	2,539	8.9
10	23,932[b]	4,314,400[b]	16,438	3,749,570	− 31	− 13	78	1,481	11.1
11	7,344	2,320,200	14,901	3,874,900	+ 103	+ 67	1,287	1,766	8.4
12[c]	7,938	3,664,980	11,901	5,178,735	+ 50	+ 41	NA	NA	NA
13	–	–	12,683	2,177,800	–	–	343	1,074	11.7
14	–	–	14,370	3,902,900	–	–	176	1,326	10.8
6, 8, 14	44,346	10,939,640	48,886	15,551,700	+ 22	+ 13	587	4,504	10.9
10, 13	23,932	4,314,400	29,076	5,927,370	+ 10	+ 42	421	2,555	11.4
All wards[d]	166,086	64,803,050	202,960	95,716,485	+ 22	+ 48	6,352	20,093	9.5

NA = Not available.
[a] Includes Ward 14.
[b] Includes Ward 13.
[c] Manhattan north of 14th Street; approximately one-third of the population between 14th and 21st streets.
[d] Figures do not yield totals given in source.

Source: Board of Assistant Aldermen Documents 1, no. 37 (December 5, 1831): 130–31; and no. 4 (unbound) (December 5, 1831), Appendix, tables 1 and 2, in Columbia University Library.

Table 5. Number of new buildings constructed in Manhattan, 1834–1842, by ward

Ward	1834	1835	1836	1837	1838	1839	1840	1841	1842	All years, 1834–1842	1842 Inhabited cellars	1842 Courts and rear buildings
1	43	106	609	59	33	42	43	25	29	989	36	16
2	32	68	102	18	27	51	50	46	15	409	1	9
3	11	55	22	11	19	15	10	10	28	181	14	30
4	11	18	24	18	28	15	37	10	10	171	35	38
5	20	12	25	32	5	17	21	21	6	159	111	96
6	34	10	9	21	8	10	25	12	44	173	56	130
7	43	80	81	45	31	30	30	41	18	399	146	81
8	36	38	26	19	14	17	40	22	26	238	89	187
9	122	105	85	52	80	46	78	102	73	743	26	91
10	49	28	44	25	17	21	13	41	53	291	104	176
11	204	249	150	77	100	82	48	104	104	1,118	240	157
12	122	274	110	89	69	59	66	66	63	918	–	–
13	40	44	43	39	25	28	46	29	21	315	252	204
14	34	35	34	28	37	26	22	18	24	258	140	189
15	75	137	140	50	80	63	60	75	80	760	–	122
16	–	–	116	180	98	75	192	215	215	1,091	–	–
17	–	–	–	77	110	77	69	134	103	570	209	201
All wards	877a	1,259	1,620	840	781	674	850	971	912	8,783	1,459	1,727

aSum given by city inspector.

Source: "Annual Report of the City Inspector on the Number and Class of New Buildings," Board of Aldermen (BA) Documents 1, no. 53: 585–88 (1834); BA Documents 2, no. 119: n.p. (1835); Board of Assistant Aldermen (BAA) Documents 3, no. 59: 193–98 (1836); BA Documents 4, no. 145: 526–31 (1837); BAA Documents 5, no. 15: 102–8 (1838); BA Documents 6, no. 63: 621–28 (1839); BA Documents 7, no. 64: 727–34 (1840); BA Documents 8, no. 74: 559–66 (1841); BAA Documents 9, no. 65: 243–250 (1842); "Annual Report on the Interments in the City and County of New York for the Year 1842, with Remarks Thereon and a Brief View of the Sanitary Condition of the City," BAA Documents 9, no. 59: 163.

Table 6. Number of new buildings and dwellings constructed in Manhattan, 1834–1850

Year	Buildings	Dwellings[a]
1834	877	654
1835	1,259	865
1836	1,826	868
1837	840	634
1838	781	626
1839	674	502
1840	850	666
1841	971	788
1842	912	775
1843	1,273	1,115
1844	1,210	925
1845	1,980	1,337
1846	1,933	1,115
1847	1,846	1,446
1848	1,191	NA
1849	1,618	NA
1850[b]	1,912	NA

NA = not available.

[a]Includes buildings listed as "store and dwelling."

[b]Nine months.

Source: "Annual Report of the City Inspector on the Number and Class of New Buildings," Board of Aldermen (BA) Documents 1, no. 53: 585–88 (1834); BA Documents 2, no. 119: n.p. (1835); Board of Assistant Aldermen (BAA) Documents 3, no. 59: 193–98 (1836); BA Documents 4, no. 145: 526–31 (1837); BAA Documents 13, no. 15: 102–8 (1838); BA Documents 6, no. 63: 621–28 (1839); BA Documents 7, no. 64: 727–34 (1840); BA Documents 8, no. 74: 559–66 (1841); BAA Documents 9, no. 65: 243–50 (1842); BA Documents 10, no. 67: 1268–79 (1843); BA Documents 11, no. 59: 625–50 (1844); BA Documents 12, no. 45: 744–70 (1845); BA Documents 13, no. 39: 463–93 (1846); BAA Documents 14, no. 22: 147–80 (1847); BA Documents 15, no. 60: 1071–98 (1848); *History of Architecture and the Building Trades of Greater New York* (New York: Union History Co., 1899), pp. 135–36.

Table 7. Number of families and of landowners and density per house, Manhattan, 1855, by ward

Ward	Population	Families	Landowners		Number of houses	Families per house	People per house
			Number	Percent of families			
1	13,486	2,646	302	11.4%	660	4.01	20.4
2	3,249	434	79	18.2	256	1.70	12.7
3	7,909	1,012	279	27.6	419	2.42	18.9
4	22,895	4,732	159	03.4	1,162	4.07	19.7
5	21,617	4,233	432	10.2	1,620	2.61	13.3
6	25,562	5,241	288	05.5	1,133	4.63	22.6
7	34,422	6,811	718	10.5	2,104	3.24	16.4
8	34,052	7,066	863	12.2	2,560	2.76	13.3
9	39,982	7,745	1,287	16.6	3,339	2.32	13.3
10	26,378	5,825	450	07.7	1,713	3.40	15.4
11	52,979	11,893	798	06.7	2,454	4.85	21.6
12	17,656	2,335	602	25.8	1,700	1.37	10.4
13	26,597	6,040	270	04.5	1,652	3.66	16.1
14	24,754	5,143	258	05.0	1,467	3.51	16.8
15	24,046	3,690	1,192	32.3	2,268	1.63	10.6
16	39,823	8,125	1,028	12.7	2,938	2.77	13.5
17	59,548	12,708	857	06.7	3,340	3.80	17.8
18	39,509[a]	7,551	1,703	22.6	2,599	2.91	15.2
19	17,796	2,796	522	18.7	1,651	1.69	10.8
20	47,055	10,178	1,025	10.1	3,250	3.13	14.5
21	27,914	5,451	995	18.3	1,968	2.77	14.2
22	22,605	4,903	650	13.3	2,355	2.08	9.6
All wards	629,904[b]	126,558[b]	14,784[b]	11.7	42,668[b]	2.97	14.8

[a]Error noted in census.
[b]Figures do not yield totals given in census.
Source: New York State Census of 1855 (Albany, 1855), pp. 8, 236–37.

Abbreviations

AICP   Association for Improving the Condition of the Poor.

Arts and Crafts   Rita Susevin Gottesman, comp., *Arts and Crafts in New York Advertisements and News Items from New York City Newspapers.* NYHS Collections 64: 1726–1775 (1938); 81: 1776–1799 (1954); 82: 1800–1804 (1965).

BA Documents   Board of Aldermen Documents, Municipal Archives, City of New York.

BA Proceedings   Proceedings of the Board of Aldermen, Municipal Archives, City of New York.

BAA Documents   Board of Assistant Aldermen Documents, Municipal Archives, City of New York.

CA   *Commercial Advertiser.*

Iconography   I. N. P. Stokes, *Iconography of Manhattan Island*, 6 vols. 1915–1928. Rpt. New York: Arno Press, 1967.

Loyalist Transcripts   Transcripts of the Manuscript Book and Papers of the Commission of Enquiry into the Losses and Services of American Loyalists, Transcribed for the New York Public Library, 1900.

MCC, 1675–1776   *Minutes of the Common Council*, 1675–1776. New York: Dodd, Mead, 1905.

MCC, 1784–1831   *Minutes of the Common Council*, 1784–1831. New York: Dodd, Mead, 1917.

NYHS   New-York Historical Society.

NYHSQ   *New-York Historical Society Quarterly.*

NYPL   New York Public Library.

RC   Register of Conveyances, New York County, Hall of Records, City of New York.

Rivington's   *Rivington's New York Newspaper: Excerpts from the Loyalist Press, 1773–1783.* NYHS Collections 3 (1870).

Valentine's Manual   David Valentine, ed., *Manual of the Corporation of the City of New York*. New York, 1852–1917.

WMQ   *William and Mary Quarterly*.

Notes

Introduction

1. C. B. Macpherson, *Property: Mainstream and Critical Positions* (Toronto: University of Toronto Press, 1978), pp. 4–6, offers cogent definitions of public, private, and common property rights; on customary rights in common lands, see also E. P. Thompson, "The Grid of Inheritance: A Comment," in Jack Goody, Joan Thirsk, and E. P. Thompson, *Family and Inheritance in Western Europe, 1200–1800* (New York: Cambridge University Press, 1976), pp. 328–60, as well as essays in the same collection by J. P. Cooper, Cicely Howell, and Margaret Spufford. On the legal history of landed property relations, see Frederick Maitland, *The History of English Law*, 2d ed. (1898; Cambridge: Cambridge University Press, 1968), pp. 10–22, 80–106; Kenelm Digby, *An Introduction to the History of the Law of Real Property* (Oxford, 1876); Marshall Harris, *Origins of the Land Tenure System of the United States* (Ames: Iowa University Press, 1953), pp. 21–61, 403–4. For the social history of English landed society, see Lawrence Stone and Jeanne Fawtier Stone, *An Open Elite: England, 1540–1880* (Oxford: Clarendon, 1984); Margaret Spufford, *Contrasting Communities: English Villages in the Sixteenth and Seventeenth Centuries* (Cambridge: Cambridge University Press, 1974), on small landholders; and Alan Mcfarlane, *Origins of English Individualism: The Family, Property, and Social Transition* (New York: Cambridge University Press, 1979), pp. 7–79, for a summary of debates over the distribution of property in England in the sixteenth and seventeenth centuries.

2. Macpherson, *Property*, p. 10.

3. John Locke, *Second Treatise of Government* (1689), chap. 5, quoted in Macpherson, *Property*, pp. 19–20. On the commercial revolution and agricultural enclosures in England, see Christopher Hill, *Reformation to Industrial Revolution, 1530–1780* (New York: Viking/Penguin, 1967, 1969), pp. 61–71, 146–56, 268–74; Joan Thirsk, ed., *The Agrarian History of England and Wales: 1500–1640*, vol. 4 (London: Cambridge University Press, 1967), pp. 200–55, 466–592; E. L. Jones, "Agriculture and Economic Growth, 1660–1750: Agricultural Change," *Journal of Economic History* 25 (March 1965): 1–18; A. H. John, "Agricultural Productivity and Economic Growth in England, 1770–1760," *Journal of Economic History* 25 (March 1965): 19–34. For the intellectual and cultural response to these changing property relations, see Raymond Williams, *The Country and the City* (New York:

Oxford University Press, 1973), pp. 42–45; C. B. Macpherson, *The Political Theory of Possessive Individualism: Hobbes to Locke* (New York: Oxford University Press, 1962), pp. 204–14. On the relation of internal economic change and colonial adventures, see Hill, *Reformation to Industrial Revolution*, pp. 72–81, 155–68; and Ralph Davis, *Rise of the Atlantic Economies* (Ithaca: Cornell University Press, 1973), pp. 264–87. On contrasting Native American and European conceptions of property rights, see Alden Vaughn, *New England Frontier: Puritans and Indians, 1620–1675*, rev. ed. (New York: Norton, 1979), pp. 104–21; and William Cronon, *Changes in the Land: Indians, Colonists, and the Ecology of New England* (New York: Hill & Wang, 1983), pp. 54–81.

4. Quote from Edmund B. O'Callaghan, *Documentary History of the State of New York* (Albany: Weed, Parsons, 1848–1851), 1:209. For various colonial systems of land distribution, see Harris, *Origins of the Land Tenure System*. On colonial land distribution and problems of controlling labor, see Edmund Morgan, *American Slavery, American Freedom: The Ordeal of Colonial Virginia* (New York: Norton, 1975), pp. 108–30, 172–73, 218–31; Allan Lee Kulikoff, *Tobacco and Slaves: The Development of Southern Cultures in the Chesapeake, 1680–1800* (Chapel Hill: University of North Carolina Press, 1986), pp. 31–33, 64–65. On servitude and the development of the institution of slavery, see Morgan, *American Slavery, American Freedom*, pp. 123–29, 216–30, 295–315, 380–81; Kulikoff, *Tobacco and Slaves*, pp. 86–92. A. Leon Higginbotham, Jr., *In the Matter of Color: Race and the American Legal Process, The Colonial Period* (New York: Oxford University Press, 1978), traces the colonial legal status and rights of slaves and free blacks. On the legal status of married women and widows as one structure of colonial household property and labor relations, see Marylynn Salmon, *Women and the Law of Property in Early America* (Chapel Hill: University of North Carolina Press, 1986). On familial structures of colonial land distribution which implicitly "paid" wives and children for their labor through inheritance and transferred land through kinship systems, see Kulikoff, *Tobacco and Slaves*, pp. 50–51, 56–92, 136–41, 158–61, 205–60; Morgan, *American Freedom, American Slavery*, pp. 165–71; George Lee Haskins, "The Beginnings of Partible Inheritance in American Colonies," *Yale Law Journal* 51 (1942): 1280–1315; Richard B. Morris, *Studies in the History of American Law, with Special Reference to the Seventeenth and Eighteenth Centuries*, 2d ed. (New York: Octagon, 1958), pp. 69–125; David Thomas Konig, *Law and Society in Puritan Massachusetts: Essex County, 1629–1692* (Chapel Hill: University of North Carolina Press, 1979), pp. 18–63, 65–69. Other valuable studies of colonial landed property relations include Kenneth Lockridge, "Land, Population, and the Evolution of New England Society, 1630–1790," *Past and Present* 39 (1968): 62–80; Philip J. Greven, Jr., *Four Generations: Population, Land, and Family in Colonial Andover, Massachusetts* (Ithaca: Cornell University Press, 1970); Sung Bok Kim, *Landlord and Tenant in Colonial New York: Manorial Society, 1664–1775* (Chapel Hill: University of North Carolina Press, 1978); James T. Lemon, *The Best Poor Man's Country* (Baltimore: Johns Hopkins University Press, 1972); Toby Ditz, *Property and Kinship: Inheritance in Early Connecticut, 1750–1820* (Princeton: Princeton University Press, 1986); and David Grayson Allen, *In English Ways: The Movement of Societies and Transferral of English Local Law and Custom to Massachusetts Bay in the Seventeenth Century* (Chapel Hill: University of North Carolina Press, 1981).

5. Cited in Sean Wilentz, *Chants Democratic: New York City and the Rise of the American Working Class, 1788–1850* (New York: Oxford University Press, 1984), p. 389.

1. *The Formation of Manhattan's Rentier and Landlord Classes*

    1. Ralph Davis, *Rise of the Atlantic Economies* (Ithaca: Cornell University Press, 1973), pp. 176–211; Thomas Condon, *New York Beginnings: The Commercial Origins of New Netherlands* (New York: New York University Press, 1968), pp. 106–7, 144–48; Oliver A. Rink, *Holland on the Hudson: An Economic and Social History of Dutch New York* (Ithaca: Cornell University Press, 1986), pp. 135–36.
    2. On Dutch settlement and culture in New York see Condon, *New York Beginnings*, pp. 139–71; Rink, *Holland on the Hudson*, pp. 166–71; Henri and Barbara van der Zee, *A Sweet and Alien Land: The Story of the Dutch in New York* (New York: Viking, 1978); Alice P. Kenney, *Stubborn for Liberty: The Dutch in New York* (Syracuse, N.Y.: Syracuse University Press, 1975).
    3. Oliver A. Rink, "Company Management or Private Trade?" *New York History* 59 (1978): 5–27; Condon, *New York Beginnings*, pp. 80–85, 93–96, 148–53.
    4. See David Valentine, "The Original Grants of Village Plots below Wall Street," in *Valentine's Manual* (1857), p. 495. I. N. P. Stokes, "The Dutch Grants," in *Iconography*, 2: 355–411, traces the distribution of 188 lots in 17 blocks. See also Harold C. Syrett, "Private Enterprise in New Amsterdam," *WMQ*, 3d ser. 9 (1954): 536–50; and on "commonalty's" challenge to company rule, Condon, *New York Beginnings*, pp. 164–72, and Rink, *Holland on the Hudson*, p. 257.
    5. Peter Nelson, "Peter Stuyvesant's Regime," in *History of the State of New York* (New York: Columbia University Press, 1933), 1: 295–321; for Dutch West Indies boweries, see Stokes, "Original Grants and Farms," in *Iconography*, 6:10–11, 78–79, 91–92, 141–43, and "Landmark Map," 6: 946–48. On land grants to "half-free" slaves in New Netherlands, see A. Leon Higginbotham, Jr., *In the Matter of Color: Race and the American Legal Process, The Colonial Period* (New York: Oxford University Press, 1978), pp. 106–8; and Stokes, *Iconography*, 6:74–75, 78, 90, 100–101, 104–6, 123–24, 136–37, 154, 160.
    David T. Valentine's "Operations in Real Estate in the City of New York in the Olden Times," in *Valentine's Manual* (1860), pp. 527–67, also describes Dutch land acquisitions and suggests the relatively stagnant seventeenth-century market for land beyond the port. See also Condon, *New York Beginnings*, pp. 95–105.
    6. For immigration after 1657, labor problems, and Dutch slavery, see Rink, *Holland on the Hudson*, pp. 160–63, 166–69, 171, 212–13; Higginbotham, *In the Matter of Color*, pp. 100–114; Edgar McManus, *A History of Negro Slavery in New York* (Syracuse, N.Y.: Syracuse University Press, 1970), pp. 3–22; Thomas Joseph Davis, "Slavery in Colonial New York City," (Ph.D. diss., Columbia University, 1974), pp. 47–53.
    7. Condon, *New York Beginnings*, pp. 129–41; Rink, *Holland on the Hudson*, pp. 94–116. On Van Rensselaer patroonship, see Sung Bok Kim, *Landlord and Tenant in Colonial New York: Manorial Society, 1664–1775* (Chapel Hill: University of North Carolina Press, 1978), pp. 6–7. On Stuyvesant lands in Manhattan, see Stokes, "Original Grants and Farms," pp. 141–42; other Dutch Manhattan grants listed in Stokes include those of Kip, p. 111; Webber, p. 170; Beekman, pp. 90–92, 110; Bayard, pp. 70–76; Van Cortlandt, pp. 6, 86, 88–93, 164–65.
    8. For Hudson Valley manors, see Kim, *Landlord and Tenant*, pp. 3–43 and frontispiece map. On provincial politics and land grants, see Robert C. Ritchie, *The Duke's Province: A Study of New York Politics and Society, 1664–1691* (Chapel Hill: University of North Carolina Press, 1977), pp. 25–252. Sung Bok Kim usefully summarizes the difference between the Hudson Valley manors and an English "feudal" model in "A New Look at the Great Landlords of Eighteenth-Century New York," *WMQ*, 3d ser., 27 (1970): 581–614.

9. The classic text on the political power of New York's landed elite is Carl Becker, *The History of Political Parties in the State of New York* (Madison: University of Wisconsin Press, 1909), pp. 10–16. For persuasive reassessments see Patricia Bonomi, *A Factious People: Politics and Society in Colonial New York* (New York: Columbia University Press, 1971), pp. 5–7, 56–59, 96–97, 189–90, 156–65, 179–228, 231–35, 241–45; and Kim, *Landlords and Tenants*, pp. 44–86, 118–22, and passim. For the British slave trade in New York, see McManus, *Negro Slavery*, pp. 23–39. For mid-eighteenth-century land grants in provincial politics, see also Stanley N. Katz, *Newcastle's New York: Anglo-American Politics, 1732–1753* (Cambridge: Harvard University Press, 1968), pp. 80–82, 143–46, 178, 232. See also William Chazanof, "Land Speculation in Eighteenth-Century New York," in Joseph Frese and Jacob Judd, eds., *Business Enterprise in Early New York* (Tarrytown: Sleepy Hollow Press, 1979).

10. For Governor Nicolls' grants on Manhattan, see Stokes, "Original Grants and Farms," pp. 69–70, 81–82, 125, 152–53. The heirs of only one of the original grantees of the 1,300-acre tract, between 41st and 89th streets, retained their share of the land into the eighteenth century. For the De Peyster/Bayard grant, see Martha Lamb, *Wall Street in History* (New York, 1883), p. 28. On town politics under the first British governors, see Thomas J. Archdeacon, *New York City, 1664–1710: Conquest and Change* (Ithaca: Cornell University Press, 1976).

11. The Dongan charter and the Montgomerie charter are reprinted in Henry E. Davies, comp., *A Compilation of Laws of the State of New York Relating to the City of New York* (New York, 1855), pp. 147–59, 162–98. For locations, maps, and subsequent distribution of the city's common lands, see George Ashton Black, *History of Municipal Ownership of Manhattan Island to . . . 1884* (New York: Columbia University Press, 1897). Black (pp. 38, 62) estimates that common lands covered 1,650 acres out of a total of 10,032 Manhattan acres (before landfill). The best discussion of the formation, powers, and eighteenth-century policies of the Corporation of the City of New York is Hendrik Hartog, *Public Property and Private Power: The Corporation of the City of New York in American Law, 1730–1870* (Chapel Hill: University of North Carolina Press, 1983), pp. 13–32, and on the distribution of water lots, 53–68; see also George Edwards, *New York as an Eighteenth-Century Municipality, 1731–1776* (New York: Longman, 1917), pp. 162–68. On franchise and politics, see Beverly McNear, "The Place of the Freeman in Old New York," *New York History* 21 (1940): 418–30; Nicholas Barga, "Election Procedures and Practices in Colonial New York," *New York History* 41 (1960): 249–77; Samuel McKee, *Labor in Colonial New York* (New York: Columbia University Press, 1935), pp. 33–41. For the social identity of aldermen, see Bruce Wilkenfield, "The New York Common Council, 1689–1800," *New York History* 52 (1971): 249–74.

12. In "Original Grants and Farms," pp. 69–177, Stokes traces the seventeenth- and eighteenth-century ownership of 79 Manhattan farms, citing original grants and subsequent conveyances, as well as descriptions of the farms derived from newspaper advertisements and family papers. I have used his reconstructions as a primary source for my analysis of changing patterns of landownership in Manhattan. Examples of late-seventeenth-century land accumulation, particularly the movement of the Dutch West Indies Company's boweries into private ownership and the consolidation of parcels that had been granted to half-manumitted Dutch slaves (the "Negro lots") can be found on pp. 74–75, 78, 80, 100–101, 104–6, 123–24, 136–37, 154, 160. Starting at the end of the seventeenth century, six influential New Yorkers purchased sections of the 1,300-acre Nicolls grant (see n. 10 above): two farmers, Wolfert Webber (1697) and Mathias Hopper (1714); two merchants,

Cornelius Dyckman (1701) and Cornelius Cosine (1725); a lawyer, Joseph Murray (1744); and Stephen De Lancey, who acquired six of the ten tracts between 1720 and 1735. With the exception of 153 acres that De Lancey's son sold to the merchant Charles Apthorp in 1763, these estates remained within the same families for forty years or more after purchase. The earliest transfers came in 1759, when Webber and Dyckman heirs sold their tracts, but one of them ended up in the hands of Dyckman's son-in-law, the merchant John Harsen. The Revolution brought the dispersal of the De Lancey estates. Four tracts remained undivided and in the same families into the nineteenth century. See Stokes, "Original Grants and Farms," pp. 170 (Webber), 106–7 (Hopper), 100–101 (Dyckman), 86 (Cosine), 125–26 (Murray), 94 (De Lancey). For succession of land grants north of 42d Street, see Henry C. Tuttle, *Abstracts of Farm Titles in the City of New York*, 3 vols. (New York: 1878, 1881), which is one source for Stokes's reconstructions.

13. For land transfers at the port, see *Original Book of New York Deeds*, NYHS Collections 46 (1913): 3–60, listing transfers between Jan. 1, 1672, and Oct. 19, 1675; and Valentine, "Operation of Real Estate," pp. 527–47. For settlement patterns in the last quarter of the seventeenth century, see *Iconography*, 1: 225–31, 236–38. On population growth before 1730, see Robert V. Wells, *The Population of the British Colonies in America before 1776: A Survey of Census Data* (Princeton: Princeton University Press, 1975), pp. 111–13. For occupational structure and settlement patterns in 1701, see Bruce Wilkenfield, "Social and Economic Structure of the City of New York, 1695–1796" (Ph.D. diss., Columbia University, 1973), pp. 21, 32, 34–36, 61. Wilkenfield stresses the port's "economic dynamism" between 1695 and 1708, but this dynamism is not reflected in the total value of property assessed, which dropped from £49,657 in 1695 to £38,670 in 1708 (pp. 58–59). One problem, of course, is changing standards for assessments.

14. Davis, "Slavery in Colonial New York City," p. 86; Vivienne L. Kruger, "Born to Run: The Slave Family in Early New York, 1626–1827" (Ph.D. diss., Columbia University, 1985), p. 428, notes that the black population of New York's six southernmost counties increased by 0.8% annually between 1698 and 1703, and by 6.2% annually between 1703 and 1723, the most rapid rate of increase during the colonial period.

15. *Weekly Post Boy*, June 7, 1764, quoted in Edgar McManus, "Negro Slavery in New York" (Ph.D. diss., Columbia University, 1959), p. 39. Slaves constituted 18.8% of the port's population in 1723; that proportion rose to 18.3% in 1731 and peaked at 20.9% in 1746. See Davis, "Slavery in Colonial New York City," table 1.1, p. 3. On employment of slave labor in crafts, see McManus, *Negro Slavery*, pp. 41–52; McKee, *Labor in Colonial New York*, pp. 114–33; and Davis, "Slavery in Colonial New York City," pp. 64–70. For use of skilled slave labor in shipbuilding, see Joseph G. Goldenberg, *Shipbuilding in Colonial America* (Charlottesville: University of Virginia Press, 1976), pp. 61–68; McKee, *Labor in Colonial New York*, p. 114. For comparison of town and rural slaveowning households in colonial New York, see Kruger, "Born to Run," pp. 90–98. For comparisons of colonial slaveholding in the North and South, see Ira Berlin, "Time, Space, and the Evolution of Afro-American Society on British Mainland North America," *American Historical Review* 85 (1980): 44–78.

16. On slaves' legal status under the British, see Higginbotham, *In the Matter of Race*, pp. 114–35 (the 1712 restriction of landownership is cited on p. 122), and Davis, "Slavery in Colonial New York City," pp. 72–81; Davis discusses the 1712 slave revolt on pp. 96–114 and the regulation of free blacks in the city on pp. 87–89. See also *MCC, 1675–1776*, 1:277, 2:102–3.

17. Davis, "Slavery in Colonial New York City," p. 114.

18. Wilkenfield, "Social and Economic Structure," p. 85. Kruger, "Born to Run," pp. 90, 92, finds that in 1703, 41.4% of city households owned slaves and that by 1790 this proportion had dropped to 19.1%.

19. Wilkenfield, "Social and Economic Structure," p. 28. See also "The Burgis View" (1716–1718) in *Iconography*, 1:239–51; and for examples of the land market, see "Operations in Real Estate in Olden Times," pp. 528–44.

20. For example, the fifteen-acre Pero farm sold for £250 in 1715 and for the same sum in 1720; the Pearsall farm sold for £173 in 1738 and was mortgaged for £160 in 1756; Stokes, "Original Grants and Farms," pp. 127–29. See also prices cited in Valentine, "Operations in Real Estate," pp. 527–67; and Black, *Municipal Ownership*, pp. 17–28. On colonial New York's population growth, see Wells, *Population of the British Colonies*, pp. 112–31, 302–3. On trade cycles, Gary Nash, *The Urban Crucible: Social Change, Political Consciousness, and the Origins of the American Revolution* (Cambridge: Harvard University Press, 1979), pp. 123–25, 177, 235–40, 248. Gerald Warden notes a similar fluctuation in the real estate market in Boston in the first half of the eighteenth century, which he links to credit cycles: "The Distribution of Property in Boston, 1692–1775," *Perspectives in American History* 10 (1976): 90–98. Stokes, "Original Grants and Farms," shows that major estate purchases in the 1740s often exceeded 100 acres; e.g., Humphrey Jones, 1740 (115–16); Admiral Peter Warren, 1740 (157–68); David Provoost, 1742 (78, 109, 124); Benjamin Vandewater, 1745 (97); Lieutenant Governor James De Lancey, 1747 (86–93); Mordecai Gomez, 1746 (151); John Watts, 1747 (170–71); Thomas Clark, 1750 (84–85); David Brevoort, 1749 (80); and Cornelius Tiebout, 1748 (144–45). A second wave of proprietors purchased farms in the 1760s, generally smaller ones; e.g., Abraham and William Beekman, 1760 (76–77); Thomas White, 1762 (156); Jacob Harsen, 1763 (164); James Duane, 1763 (98–99); John Stryker, 1764 (141); John Morin Scott, 1764 (83, 102); Richard Varian, 1769 (156); and Abraham Keteles, 1766, 1769 (109).

21. For women taxpayers, see Wilkenfield, "Social and Economic Structure," pp. 27, 86, 168, 177, 207–8. On coverture and equity, see Norma Basch, *In the Eyes of the Law: Women, Marriage, and Property in Nineteenth-Century New York* (Ithaca: Cornell University Press, 1982), pp. 17–26; Joan R. Gundersen and Gwen Victor Gampel, "Married Women's Legal Status in Eighteenth-Century New York and Virginia," *WMQ*, 3d ser., 39 (1982): 114–34. For New York City taxpaying widows between 1676 and 1730, Christine Tompsett, "A Note on the Economic Status of Widows in Colonial New York," *New York History* 55 (1974): 319–23. For a comparison of Dutch and English inheritance customs, David Evan Narrett, "Patterns of Inheritance in Colonial New York City, 1664–1775" (Ph.D. diss., Cornell University, 1981), chap. 4; Linda Briggs Biemer, *Women and Property in Colonial New York: The Transition from Dutch to English Law, 1643–1727* (Ann Arbor: University of Michigan Press, 1983). Kim includes genealogies of the patroon families in *Landlord and Tenant*, pp. 416–20. For the extended Rutgers family, see *New York Genealogy and Biographic Record*, April 1886, pp. 82–93.

Julian Gwyn, *The Enterprising Admiral: The Personal Fortune of Sir Peter Warren* (Montreal: McGill/Queen's University Press, 1974), provides an excellent case study of Oliver De Lancey's exercise of fudiciary responsibilities for his sister and nieces, Sir Peter Warren's widow and three daughters.

22. In 1752, ground rent on Warren's Turtle Bay farm yielded 7% of its purchase price because of its use as a "careening place for British naval vessels," (Gwyn, *Enterprising Admiral*, pp. 40, 43, 46–47); and his Greenwich farm, though less profitable, yielded lumber and fruit trees (pp. 47–48). Harlem proprietors—who were mostly of Dutch stock—formed one core of Manhattan's largest landowners

and controlled the Harlem common lands. See Black, *Municipal Ownership*, p. 23; James Riker, *Revised History of Harlem and Early Annals* (Elizabeth, N.J., 1904), and Kruger, "Born to Run," pp. 138–39.

23. Evert Bancker, "List of Farms in New York Island, 1780," in *NYHSQ* 1 (1917): 8–11. The original manuscript is in the Bancker Papers, NYHS. Five farms exceeded 200 acres, 22 covered from 100 to 200 acres, 23 were from 40 to 99 acres, 25 were from 20 to 39 acres, and 39 were less than 20 acres; acreage was not listed for 23 farms. To identify farm proprietors I relied on Stokes, "Original Grants and Farms"; on "List of Citizens Admitted as Freemen," in *Valentine's Manual* (1856), pp. 477–502; and on "Principal Wealthy Citizens, Sixty Years Since," in *Valentine's Manual* (1855), pp. 565–67.

24. Gwyn, *Enterprising Admiral*, pp. 96–97, 99; Virginia Harrington, "Employment of Capital," in David M. Ellis et al., *History of the State of New York* (Ithaca: Cornell University Press, 1967), 2:365–70. Examples of mortgages can be found in the land papers of William Bayard in the Bayard-Campbell-Pearsall Papers, NYPL (e.g., mortgage of a long-term lease, May 1, 1742, further secured by penal bond). Warden makes a similar argument for the "liquidity" of land in "Distribution of Property in Boston," pp. 92–96.

25. Deed, Robert Livingston to Margaret Livingston, August 4, 1772, in Bayard-Campbell-Pearsall Papers, NYPL.

26. See, e.g., Stokes, "Original Grants and Farms," pp. 169–70 (Rose Hill, Watts), 144–45 (Roxborough, Tiebout), 125–26 (Hermitage, Norton), 176–77 (Spring Valley, Youle), 108–9 (Louvre, Jones), 109 (Bellevue, Ketelas); and "Landmark Reference Key," in *Iconography*, 3:95. Esther Singleton offers a lively account of Manhattan's eighteenth-century gentry in *Social New York under the Georges, 1714–1776* (New York: Ira Friedman, 1902). See also Frederick Cople Jaher, *The Urban Establishment: Upper Strata in Boston, New York, Charleston, Chicago, and Los Angeles* (Urbana: University of Illinois Press, 1982), pp. 160–73; and Carl Bridenbaugh, *Cities in Revolt* (New York: Knopf, 1955), pp. 141–46, 163–67, 334–72.

27. Bayard's and Rutgers' acquisitions: Stokes, "Original Grants and Farms," pp. 70–76, 134–36. Eighteenth-century artisan landholders: Bancker, "List of Farms, 1780." For artisans among the city's economic elite in 1730 and 1789, see Wilkenfield, "Social and Economic Structure," pp. 93–94, 178–79; and "Principal Wealthy Citizens," which lists the names and occupations of 279 economic leaders in 1790. The line between New York's artisan entrepreneurs and merchants is sometimes hard to distinguish when production, particularly in such processing trades as brewing and sugar refining, also incorporated importation and distribution. Thomas Doerflinger discusses the "social fluidity" of Philadelphia's merchant community in *A Vigorous Spirit of Enterprise: Merchants and Economic Development in Revolutionary Philadelphia* (Chapel Hill: University of North Carolina Press, 1986), pp. 47–69; cf. Nash's excellent discussion of political tensions between New York merchants and artisans in *Urban Crucible*, pp. 363–74.

28. Black, *Municipal Ownership*, pp. 17–28. Valentine, "Operations in Real Estate," p. 527, places the first Manhattan real estate boom around 1766, but Gwyn, *Enterprising Admiral*, pp. 43, 48–49, notes that rents from Warren's city properties doubled between 1752 and 1759. A lot on lower Broadway was sold for £80 in 1734, £100 in 1737, and £300 in 1771 (RC, 40:28–36). There are no tax records for the period 1730–1760 to permit charting of rising land values. For the increase of adult white men after 1740, see Wells, *Population of the British Colonies*, pp. 118, 119, 121.

29. On the regulation of hatters, see Edward O'Callaghan, *Documentary History of New York State* (Albany, 1848–1851), 1: 516; and for examples of governors' reports (and reassurances) to the Board of Trade on the state of colonial "manufacturing," pp. 487–91 (1705), 491 (1732), 494 (1749), 513 (1761), 498–99 (1767). For economic growth, "enhanced earning power," and increased construction during the Seven Years' War, see Nash, *Urban Crucible*, pp. 233, 236–41; subsequent depression, 247, 248–51; and recovery, 313. For shipping in this period, see Wilkenfield, "Social and Economic Structure," pp. 137–51.

30. Clarke is quoted in McManus, *Negro Slavery*, p. 122; on craft competition, 48–49. Rising wages in this period (for slaves as well as for free workers), McManus argues (pp. 49–54), made the hiring out of slaves profitable and intensified competition. On the 1741 slave insurrection, see Thomas J. Davis, *A Rumor of Revolt: The "Great Negro Plot" in Colonial New York* (New York: Free Press, 1985). Davis links the shifting sex ratio to the aftermath of the revolt (pp. 185–86). For comparative black and white sex ratios, see Kruger, "Born to Run," pp. 305, 369–70. Between 1746 and 1771, the proportion of the city's people who were enslaved dropped from 20.9% to 15.8%. Davis, "Slavery in Colonial New York City," table 1.1, p. 3. Slave women, of course, also produced goods. See, e.g., the advertised skills of a 20-year-old woman who "does all sorts of House work, she can Brew, Bake, Boyle soaft Soap, Wash, Iron & Starch; and is a good Darey Woman she can Card and Spin at the great Wheel, Cotten, Lennen, and Wollen": McKee, *Labor in Colonial New York*, p. 126.

31. On the increasing concentration of landownership, see Wilkenfield, "Social and Economic Structure," p. 207. For patterns of wealth controlled by the top 2%, top 20%, and bottom 50% in 1701, 1730, and 1789, see ibid., table V–2, p. 160. For similar trends in wealth concentration in New York, Boston, and Philadelphia, see Gary Nash, "Urban Wealth and Poverty in Pre-Revolutionary America," *Journal of Interdisciplinary History* 6 (1976): 545–84; Jacob Price, "Quantifying Colonial America: A Comment on Nash and Warden," *Journal of Interdisciplinary History* 6 (1976): 701–9; James Henretta, "Economic Development and Social Structure in Colonial Boston," *WMQ*, 3d ser., 22 (1965): 75–92; and Allan Lee Kulikoff, "The Progress of Inequality in Revolutionary Boston," *WMQ*, 3d ser., 28 (1971): 376–409. For a thoughtful discussion of measuring inequality of wealth and the limits of tax records, see John J. McCusker and Russell R. Menard, *The Economy of British America* (Chapel Hill: University of North Carolina Press, 1985), pp. 270–76. See also Alice Hanson Jones, *Wealth of a Nation to Be: The American Colonies on the Eve of the Revolution* (New York: Columbia University Press, 1980), pp. 48, 209, 227, 230, 233, 268.

For the concentration of merchants in the East and Dock wards in 1730 and 1789, see Wilkenfield, "Social and Economic Structure," pp. 93, 94, 173–74. One indicator of interest in downtown land as an investment is the accelerating distribution of shoreline water lots; see Black, *Municipal Ownership*, pp. 21–22, 26; Edwards, *New York as an Eighteenth-Century Municipality*, pp. 147–54. In *Public Property and Private Powers*, pp. 53–68, Hartog explains the policy of distributing water lots to adjacent proprietors and notes that the Common Council received more petitions on this matter than on any other. For a typical water lot grant, see deed, Corporation of the City of New York to Elizabeth Rutgers, Jacob Le Roy, Anthony Rutgers, and Mary Rutgers, Nov. 13, 1772, and others in Bayard-Campbell-Pearsall Papers, NYPL. Petitions and grants can be found in *MCC*, 1675–1776.

32. "Map of the City of New York Showing the Original High Water Line and Location of Different Farms and Estates," in *Valentine's Manual* (1852); Stokes,

"Original Grants and Farms," pp. 144–45, 148–49 (Trinity Church), 134–36 (Rutgers), 86–93 (De Lancey), 141–45 (Stuyvesant), 157–68 (Warren estate), 70–76 (Bayard).

33. Lottery deed to Philip Livingston and others, December 20, 1771, RC, 39: 388. For the history of this and other parts of Bayard's estate, see Valentine, "Operations in Real Estate," pp. 553–54; and Bayard Family Deeds, 1717–1776, 1780–1845, in Nicholas Bayard Papers Pertaining to New York Real Estate, NYHS.

Long-term leases were common in England, where primogeniture, entail, and custom limited the free alienation of real property. The practice reappeared in those American proprietary colonies marked by concentrated landholdings, particularly in New York and Maryland. For a discussion of the English tenure system, see Marshall Harris, *Origin of the Land Tenure System in the United States* (Ames: Iowa State College Press, 1953), pp. 55–58. See also Beverly Bond, *The Quit Rent System in American Colonies* (New Haven: Yale University Press, 1919), comparing the uses of long-term leases in the private and public sectors.

34. Stokes, "Original Grants and Farms," pp. 144–45, 148–49; J. W. Gerard, "Anneke Jans Bogardus and Her Farm," *Harper's New Monthly Magazine* 70 (1885): 836–49; Thomas B. Wikoff, comp., *Anneke Jans Bogardus and Her New Amsterdam Estate, Past and Present* (Indianapolis, 1924), pp. 110, 113–18.

35. Wikoff, *Bogardus and Her New Amsterdam Estate*, p. 110. In the nineteenth century, Trinity exceeded the legislative limit placed on its rental income, thus prompting an ongoing controversy with the State Legislature. See *Niles Weekly Register*, Sept. 26, 1835.

36. *Iconography*, 4:536 (Aug. 14, 1734), 619 (May 1, 1750), 727 (Dec. 1, 1762), citing vestry resolutions. For 1752 and 1763 advertisements of farm and lots, see *Old New York and Trinity Church*, NYHS Collections 1 (1870): 160, 185–86.

37. For representative leases, see "Indentures, 1757–1785," in Trinity Church Papers, box 29, New York City Miscellaneous Manuscripts, NYHS. Unless otherwise indicated, all Trinity Church manuscripts come from this collection. After 1770, the church raised its ground rent by £1 for each seven-year interval. See lease to John Anderson, Aug. 30, 1770.

The Vestry Committee on Leases after 1774 expressed a more active interest in the quality of improvements when they settled conflicts between prewar and new leaseholders. Reports of the Committee on Leases, vestry minutes, 1783–1787, listed 197 lots leased before the Revolution, "the leases of which remained unexpired and the greater part of them for long terms of 50 years to come." Noting that new leaseholders "have chiefly erected valuable improvements," the committee recommended a policy of remitting rents to prewar leaseholders in order to protect those new improvements. For house-moving complaints and permissions, see, e.g., *MCC, 1784–1831*, 13:5, 26, 34, 35, 41, 53, 54, 105, 216, 235, 248, 289, 630, 700, 722, 758, 793.

38. After 1750, Oliver De Lancey leased out Warren's town lots on Broadway below Cortlandt for £8 to £12 a year, and in 1772 he valued a lot on Pearl Street near the wharves at £500, or £25 a year at the standard 5 percent ground rent: Gwyn, *Enterprising Admiral*, pp. 49, 51. William Bayard leased two houses on Queen Street for £120. See lease, William Bayard to Samuel Selby and John Johnson, Jan. 17, 1775, in Bayard-Campbell-Pearsall Papers, box 3, NYPL. Another Pearl Street house was sold by a shoemaker to a distiller for £253 in 1775: RC, 40:463. For other real estate transactions involving a blacksmith, silversmith, tailor, spinster, feltmaker, and cartman: RC, 40:440 (two lots on Ferry Street, 1775, £500), 445 (Broad Street lot, 1770, £550), 452 (William Street house, 1772, £350), 458 (two houses on Cortlandt Street west of Broadway, 1772, £430).

39. Representative advertisements for houses and lots on the church farm can be found in *Old New York and Trinity Church*, pp. 181, 305, 307, 313–14, and passim. See, e.g., leases to Nicholas Staaks, butcher, Feb. 28, 1771; George Whitton, stonecutter, Feb. 28, 1771; Alexander Clark, weaver, Feb. 28, 1771; George Stanton, house carpenter, Feb. 28, 1773; David Smart, laborer, July 8, 1773; John Van Orden, cartman, Mar. 14, 1775, in "Indentures, 1757–1785," in Trinity Church Papers, NYHS. The lease to Staaks—the earliest example of a building lease from Trinity Church that I located—provided for Staaks to build a two-story brick-front house within ten years. See also Wilkenfield, "Social and Economic Structure," tables V–5 and V–6, pp. 173–74.

40. For policies, see n. 36 above. An undated memo (c. 1787) showed a total of 695 lots on the church farm, of which 77 had been sold or reserved for sale, 200 were leased on 21-year terms, and 120 on 63- or 90-year terms, with 20 lots lost to street openings and an additional 278 apparently granted outright to church affiliates; e.g., 105 lots to Columbia College.

41. Gwyn, *Enterprising Admiral*, p. 46.

42. Wikoff, *Bogardus and Her New Amsterdam Estate*, pp. 162–63, and "Estimate of Expenditures," n.d. (c. 1783–1787), in Trinity Church Papers, NYHS. Aaron Burr acquired the Richmond Hill leasehold estate in 1767 and sold it to John Jacob Astor in 1804 for nearly $80,000. The church's ground rent for approximately 240 lots was $201.75 a year. By 1833, when Trinity's ground rent had reached $239, Astor himself was collecting ground rents that ranged from $15 to $45 on lots leased for 63 years between 1798 and 1805, and from $65 to $100 on lots leased for 11 to 21 years between 1827 and 1833: John Jacob Astor, House and Land Book, 1833, and Richmond Hill Rent Rolls, in Astor Papers, NYHS, summarizing his initial acquisitions. See also Trinity Church Vestry minutes, Aug. 8, 1787. For examples of leaseholders subleasing, see John Leake Papers, NYHS, and n. 43 below.

43. Trinity Church, memo (c. 1787), NYHS. Of the 43 multiple leaseholders listed on the memo, 17 had survived from the prerevolutionary period, but the occupational structure of multiple leaseholders does not appear to have changed significantly. Fewer than 10 of the 43 leaseholders were merchants (the memo excluded major tracts, such as Richmond Hill, given out on 63- and 99-year leases); the rest included laborers, cartmen, bricklayers, innkeepers, engravers, grocers, and house carpenters. Warden, "Distribution of Property in Boston," pp. 90–92, 102–3, has suggested that in Boston such properties served as a form of currency—security for credit—in a cash-short economy. For small-scale land investments among Philadelphia artisans, see Nash, *Urban Crucible*, pp. 122–23.

There is clear evidence of both profit upon sale and rapid turnover after the Revolution. "Gentleman" John Leake inherited a 99-year lease from Columbia College (from a Trinity Church grant) for a double lot at the corner of Murray and Greenwich streets. In 1780 the lot had been subdivided and leased for 21 years to a boatman, who in turn assigned his lease to an innkeeper. Leake's leases were confiscated and the loyalist innkeeper's sublease was sold for the remainder of its term in two parcels to a grocer in 1784. The grocer assigned one lease in April 1786 to another grocer, who sold it in May of that year to a carpenter. The carpenter sold the lease back in February 1790, presumedly having added a wooden house. The grocer then sold the lease to a ropemaker for £115 pounds ($387.50). In 1800, at the point of the lease's expiration, the ropemaker sold the house and the lease (with one year to run and a covenant for renewal) for $522. The lease to the second parcel was sold in 1788 to a stonecutter, whose widow sold it in 1791 for £50 to a grocer, who in turn transferred it for £140 to a mason in 1793. The mason sold back the lease for £490 in 1803, having added a brick or brick-front house. See leases in Leake Papers, box 2, NYHS.

44. Stokes, "Original Grants and Farms," p. 93. See also De Lancey Papers (microfilm) and Deeds, 1621–1784, NYHS; Bernard Ratzer, "Plan for the City of New York, 1766–1767," in Eno Collection, NYPL, rpt. in John A. Kouenhaven, *Columbia Historical Portrait of New York* (New York: Harper & Row, 1972), pp. 68–69; advertisement in *Iconography*, 6:742.

45. Loyalist transcripts, 41:312.

46. Ibid., 41: 292, 294–97.

47. Ibid., pp. 296–97, 274–83.

48. Ibid., p. 310.

49. Ibid., pp. 311–12. Building leases in London date from the Restoration. See Steen Eiler Ramussen, *London: The Unique City* (London: Jonathan Cape, 1936), pp. 165–201; and John Summerson, *Georgian London* (New York: Praeger, 1970), pp. 39–42.

50. Kim, *Landlords and Tenants*, explains Hudson Valley rentiers' fines for selling leases (pp. 223–29) and dissects the interlocking issues of uncertain land titles, New England migration and squatting, and "long-simmering discontent" at a particularly "autocratic" landlord which underlay rural tenants' "Great Rebellion" of 1766 (pp. 346–415). Edward Countryman, *A People in Revolution: The American Revolution and Political Society in New York, 1760–1790* (Baltimore: Johns Hopkins University Press, 1981), follows these conflicts through the Revolution (pp. 287–89) and in state politics (pp. 197–98, 262–65). See also Irving Mark, *Agrarian Conflict in Colonial New York, 1760–1790* (Baltimore: Johns Hopkins University Press, 1940). For the postrevolutionary continuation of these disputes, see chap. 7, nn. 11–13, below.

51. "Vestry Minutes," n.d. (c. 1784), listing rental revenues, 1770–1776, in Trinity Church Papers, NYHS.

52. "Estimate of the Value of the Real Estate in the Out Wards of New York Belonging to Persons in Actual Rebellion," in B. F. Stevens, comp., *Facsimiles of Manuscripts in European Archives* (London, 1888–1898), 12: no. 1234 (in NYHS).

53. Ibid. Among those patriots who owned more than five houses were Henry Rutgers, brewer, 12; Abraham Duryee, merchant, 6; Isaac Roosevelt, merchant and sugar refiner, 11; Gerardus Duyckink, glassmaker, 6; Thomas Van Eyck, merchant, 7; Samuel Gilford, merchant, 8; Henry Kipp, silversmith, 13; Evert Byvanck, merchant, 11; Gerardus De Peyster, merchant, 8. Other examples of the ownership of multiple houses are found in Virginia Harrington, *New York Merchants on the Eve of the Revolution* (Gloucester, Mass.: Peter Smith, 1964), pp. 134–35; Philip White, *The Beekmans of New York: Politics and Commerce, 1647–1877* (New York: NYHS, 1956), pp. 525–26; Gwyn, *Enterprising Admiral*, pp. 43–47. Doerflinger finds a comparable pattern of limited investment in rental housing among Philadelphia merchants, who in 1774 owned an average of 3.6 "rental properties" and collected ground rent from an average of 5.9 long-term leases: *Vigorous Spirit of Enterprise*, p. 377.

54. On economic expansion, see Sidney Pomeranz, *New York: An American City, 1783–1803* (New York: Columbia University Press, 1938), pp. 147–225. See also Jacob Price, "Economic Function and the Growth of American Port Towns in the Eighteenth Century," *Perspectives in American History* 8 (1974): 123–86. On the decline of slavery, see chap. 2, n. 29, below.

55. On the real estate market, see Pomeranz, *New York*, pp. 178–81; Pomeranz estimates that the price of "improved lands near the city" went from $50 an acre in 1785 to $250 an acre in 1800. See also Robert East, *Business Enterprise in the*

American Revolutionary Era (1938; New York: AMS Press, 1969), pp. 221–23, 235–37. Symptomatic of the passing of the eighteenth-century rentier generation were notices for the sale of the estates of Gulian Verplanck, Cornelius Roosevelt, and Gerard Bancker in *CA*, Jan. 1, 1800. For the subsequent history of the eighteenth-century farms, see John Randall, "Map of Farms, 1815, Commonly Called the Blue Book," assembled by Otto Schersdorf, in NYPL; and for farms north of 42d Street, see Tuttle, *Abstracts of Farm Titles*.

56. Harry Belder Yshope, *The Disposition of Loyalist Estates in the Southern District of the State of New York* (New York: Columbia University Press, 1939), chaps. 3–4 and pp. 154–55; and "The De Lancey Estate: Did the Revolution Democratize Land Holdings in New York?" *New York History* 17 (1936): 167–79; Stokes "Original Grants and Farms," p. 171.

57. Stokes, "Original Grants and Farms," p. 81; "Inventory of Church Lots" (1787); Edmund Willis, "Social Origins and Political Leadership in New York City from the Revolution to 1815" (Ph.D. diss., University of California, Berkeley, 1968), p. 113, and discussion of comparative growth of real and personal property, 109–12. For breaks in speculative bubbles, see also E. Wilder Spaulding, *New York in the Critical Period, 1783–1789* (New York: Columbia University Press, 1932), pp. 17, 22; and Black, *Municipal Ownership*, pp. 37–38.

58. Willis, "Social Origins," pp. 113–14. For one record of land distribution to "artisan" speculators, see the inventory of 205 lots contained in two deeds from Philip Livingston and others to Nicholas Bayard, July 31, 1772, in Johnson Papers, NYHS.

59. See, e.g., Rutgers' lease to John Morss, builder, May 1, 1826, box 2, Bayard-Campbell-Pearsall Papers, NYPL; and RC, 212:358, 214:338, 216:364. Many of Rutgers' leases dated from the 1820s, when he had filled in marshy land on his Lower East Side estate. For earlier examples of building leases, see William Bayard to John Roberts, mariner, May 2, 1780, box 3, Bayard-Campbell-Pearsall Papers, NYPL; John G. Leake to John Poalk, carpenter, Oct. 12, 1786, Leake Papers, NYHS. Newspaper notices for ground leases occasionally noted "improvements to be paid for" at the expiration of the lease; e.g., *CA*, Mar. 10, 1807, and Mar. 15, 1817.

60. Lease, May 1, 1810, RC, 91:206. For other examples of appraisal arrangements, see lease from William Bayard to Sandford and Burger, Mar. 25, 1780, box 2, Bayard-Campbell-Pearsall Papers, NYPL; *MCC, 1784–1831*, 1:33–34 (May 12, 1784).

2. The Formation of the Urban Tenancy

1. Grant Thorburn, *Forty Years' Residence in America* (Boston: Russell, Odiorne & Metcalf, 1834), pp. 20–21. I thank Warren Leon for first calling this work to my attention.

2. Sidney Pomeranz, *New York: An American City, 1783–1803* (New York: Columbia University Press, 1938), pp. 201–9; for rural migration, see Richard L. Bushman, "Family Security in the Transition from Farm to City," *Journal of Family History* 6 *(Fall* 1981): 238–44.

3. *Heads of Families: First Census of the United States, 1790* (Baltimore: Genealogical Publishing Co., 1966), pp. 116–38; Ira P. Rosenwaike, *The Population History of New York City* (Syracuse, N.Y. : Syracuse University Press, 1972), pp. 15–28. For a useful compilation of African-American demographics in New York County (Manhattan), see table 2, p. 747, and table 4, p. 924, in Vivienne L.

Kruger, "Born to Run: The Slave Family in Early New York, 1626–1827" (Ph.D. diss., Columbia University, 1985), which also gives the age structure of the white population in New York's six southernmost counties (p. 1157). Kruger estimates that 9.6% of New York County's population was of Dutch descent in 1790 (table 1, p. 742). For the youth of immigrants throughout the antebellum period, see Diane Lindstrom, "The Economy of Antebellum New York City," paper presented to the Social Science Research Council, November 1983, table 7, p. 24.

4. Pomeranz, *New York*, pp. 158–59; Robert Greenhalgh Albion, *The Rise of New York Port, 1815–1860* (1939; Boston: Northeastern University Press, 1984), pp. 8–9, and on the natural advantages of New York Harbor, 16–37. See also David T. Gilchrist, ed., *The Growth of Seaport Cities, 1790–1815* (Charlottesville: University of Virginia Press, 1966), and Diane Lindstrom, *Economic Development in the Philadelphia Region* (New York: Columbia University Press, 1978), pp. 14, 23, 30, 34–36, for an overview and comparisons with New York's economic development.

On employment in New York City during this period, see Sean Wilentz, *Chants Democratic: New York City and the Rise of the American Working Class, 1788–1850* (New York: Oxford University Press, 1984), pp. 23–60; Howard B. Rock, *Artisans of the New Republic: The Tradesmen of New York City in the Age of Jefferson* (New York: New York University Press, 1979), pp. 151–78; and Christine Stansell, *City of Women: Sex and Class in New York City, 1789–1860* (New York: Knopf, 1986), pp. 11–18.

5. Thorburn, *Forty Years' Residence*, p. 23. Excerpts of other travelers' accounts appear in Bayard Still, *Mirror for Gotham: New York as Seen by Contemporaries from Dutch Days to the Present* (New York: New York University Press, 1956), pp. 54–75. Lupton's store is advertised in *CA*, Feb. 2, 1803. For descriptions of the harbor and town during and immediately following the Revolution, see H. B. Dawson, *New York during the American Revolution* (New York, 1861), pp. 9–40; and Thomas E. V. Smith, *The City of New York in the Year of Washington's Inauguration* (1889; Riverside, Conn.: Chatham, 1973).

6. For a comparison with Liverpool, see Still, *Mirror for Gotham*, p. 64.

7. In addition to travelers' reports, this description is drawn from maps, prints, and drawings of New York City in John A. Kouenhaven, *The Columbia Historical Portrait of New York: An Essay in Graphic History* (New York: Harper & Row, 1972), pp. 29–127, and in *Iconography*, e.g., 2:418–19, 3:975–82.

8. Quoted in Still, *Mirror for Gotham*, pp. 67, 65.

9. My description of the interior organization of New York City houses during this period is based primarily on newspaper advertisements reprinted in *Arts & Crafts*, in *Rivington's*, and in "Old New York and Trinity Church," NYHS Collections 3 (1870): 147–408. In addition, I read the *Commercial Advertiser*, January to May and September to October, 1800–1820. For a fuller description of interior work spaces, see my "Housing and Property Relations in New York City, 1785–1850" (Ph.D. diss., Harvard University, 1981), pp. 156–61. For a discussion of the city's vernacular architecture in the postrevolutionary period, see Charles Lockwood, *Bricks and Brownstones: The New York Row House, 1783–1929* (New York: McGraw-Hill, 1972), pp. 1–6.

I. N. P. Stokes also compiled an extensive file of clippings giving nineteenth-century descriptions of the city, catalogued under "New York City Slums," Stokes Collection, NYPL. Some of its articles for this period are reprinted in James Ford, *Slums and Housing, with Special Reference to New York City* (Cambridge: Harvard University Press, 1936), 1:87–90.

For comparisons with rural vernacular housing, see, e.g., the descriptions in James Deetz, *In Small Things Forgotten: The Archeology of Early American Life* (New York: Doubleday, 1977), pp. 92–117; John R. Stilgoe, *Common Landscape of America, 1580–1845* (New Haven: Yale University Press, 1982), pp. 159–62.

10. Eighteenth-century housing notices frequently gave more attention to the features of the yard than to the layout of the house interior. See, e.g., *Royal Gazette*, Mar. 17, 1781; *New York Gazette*, Feb. 27, 1790; *New-York Daily Advertiser*, Jan. 5, 1797, all in *Arts & Crafts*, 81:184, 407, 342. On the widespread practice of salting the family's pork in the yard see "Recollections of an Old Citizen," in *Valentine's Manual* (1859), p. 589.

11. See n. 7 above. Carl Abbott, "The Neighborhoods of New York City, 1760–1775," *New York History* 55 (1974): 35–53, offers a good starting point for mapping the port's social geography in the postrevolutionary period. See also Bruce Wilkenfield, "Social and Economic Structure of the City of New York, 1695–1795" (Ph.D. diss., Columbia University, 1973), pp. 173–74, 196; and Smith, *City of New York*, pp. 22–54. I also used Evert Bancker's Street Surveys, 1795–1799, listing "proprietors, lessees and tenants" in the various areas of the city, esp. surveys of Chambers, Reade, Barclay, Church, and Anthony streets, c. 1799, in Bancker Papers, NYHS, in conjunction with *Longworth's American Almanac, New York Register, and City Directory*. For merchant houses attached to stores, see "Private Residences of the City, Sixty Years Ago," in *Valentine's Manual* (1855), pp. 561–64.

12. For the emergence of the wholesale and retail districts, see Isaac Israel, "New York Fifty-two Years Ago," in *Valentine's Manual* (1859), pp. 565–66; and "Assessment of Real and Personal Property of the East Ward of the City of New York," NYHS Collections 43, vol. 2 (1911): 318–83.

13. For shipyards, see John R. Morrison, *History of the New York Shipyards* (Port Washington, N.Y., 1970), pp. 21–22; and for relocation of the shipyards to Corlear's Hook after 1800, pp. 22–23. For tanners, see Frank Norcross, *A History of the New York Swamp* (New York, 1901), pp. 33–34. For the Fresh Pond area, see Smith, *City of New York*, pp. 12–13.

14. Quoted in Still, *Mirror for Gotham*, p. 67. For further discussion of the church farm, see chap. 1 above.

15. On the structure of crafts, see Wilentz, *Chants Democratic*, pp. 35–60; and Rock, *Artisans of the New Republic*, pp. 151–78. The concentration of domestic workers is inferred from the large number of women in prominent merchant households, as revealed in *Heads of Families, 1790*; pp. 116–38; see also Stansell, *City of Women*, pp. 11–20.

16. *New York Gazette and General Advertiser*, Feb. 21, 1804; *Daily Advertiser*, July 9, 1798, and Mar. 4, 1791, all in *Arts & Crafts*, 82:228; 81:127, 228.

17. Carl Kaestle, *The Evolution of an Urban School System: New York City, 1750–1850* (Cambridge: Harvard University Press, 1973), p. 31. Wilentz qualifies Kaestle's assessment in *Chants Democratic*, p. 27n. See also Wilkenfield, "Social and Economic Structure," pp. 169–70. In 1790, 31.6% of blacks in the city were free: Kruger, "Born to Run," p. 747. The proportion of the city's enslaved population declined from 8.9% in 1786 to 7.4% in 1790 to 5% in 1800: Thomas J. Davis, "Slavery in Colonial New York City" (Ph.D. diss., Columbia University, 1974), p. 218.

18. The phrase "private economical relations" comes from William Blackstone, *Commentaries on the Laws of England* (1788), ed. William Casey Jones (1915; Baton Rouge, 1976), p. 579. In their introduction to *Household and Family in Past Time* (New York: Cambridge University Press, 1972), pp. 24–28, Peter Laslett and Richard Hall define the household as a coresident domestic group sharing location,

kinship, and activity. The problem with this definition is that it does not account for journeymen or apprentices who, as "found labor" boarding at a separate location, nonetheless were members of a master's household unit. For a discussion of the household as an economic unit, see also Hans Medick, "The Proto-industrial Family Economy: The Structural Formation of Household and Family during the Transition from Peasant Society to Capitalism," *Social History* 3 (1976): 291–316.

For classic descriptions of American colonial households, see Carl Bridenbaugh, *The Colonial Craftsman* (New York: New York University Press, 1950), pp. 126–29, 136–39, 141–43; and, for the late colonial period, *Cities in Revolt: Urban Life in America, 1743–1776* (New York: Knopf, 1955), pp. 126–27. For the New England town model, see John Demos, *A Little Commonwealth: Family Life in Plymouth Colony* (New York: Oxford University Press, 1970), pp. 60–125; and Laurel Thatcher Ulrich, *Good Wives: Image and Reality in the Lives of Women in Northern New England, 1650–1750* (1982; New York: Oxford University Press, 1983), pp. 11–17.

19. For provincial vagrancy laws, see David M. Schneider, *The History of Public Welfare in New York State, 1609–1866* (Chicago: University of Chicago Press, 1938), pp. 45–50, and on New York City ordinances, pp. 51–54. On masters' accountability for apprentices, see Julius Goebel, Jr., and T. Raymond Naughton, *Law Enforcement in Colonial New York: A Study in Criminal Procedure, 1664–1776* (Montclair, N.J.: Patterson Smith, 1970), pp. 107–8n, citing cases; on the practical failure of households and institutions to preserve public order in the city, Douglas Greenberg, *Crime and Law Enforcement in the Colony of New York, 1691–1776* (Ithaca: Cornell University Press, 1976), pp. 56–57, 200.

20. Blackstone, *Commentaries*, pp. 579, 625–26. On coverture see also Norma Basch, *In the Eyes of the Law: Women, Marriage, and Property in Nineteenth-Century New York* (Ithaca: Cornell University Press, 1982), pp. 42–113. Basch notes (pp. 61–64) that by the 1820s, New York chancellor James Kent's *Commentaries on American Law* was presenting Blackstone's arguments on the marital contract in a more sentimental and moralistic tone. See also Marylynn Salmon, *Women and the Law of Property in Early America* (Chapel Hill: University of North Carolina Press, 1986), pp. 14–57; Joan R. Gundersen and Gwen Victor Gampel, "Married Women's Legal Status in Eighteenth-Century New York and Virginia," *WMQ*, 3d ser., 39 (1982): 114–34.

21. Blackstone, *Commentaries*, p. 627; Jeanne Boydston, "Home and Work: The Industrialization of Housework in the Northeastern United States from the Colonial Period to the Civil War" (Ph.D. diss., Yale University, 1984), pp. 29–77; and see Susan Strasser, *Never Done: A History of American Housework* (New York: Pantheon, 1982), chaps. 1–7, for an overview of the nineteenth century.

22. My discussion of gender and household labor relations here and throughout the book has been greatly influenced by Boydston's "Home and Work." See her Introduction, pp. 1–28, for a theoretical overview.

23. On women as husbands' agents, see e.g., Ulrich, *Goodwives*, pp. 35–55. On widows, see Christine H. Tompsett, "A Note on the Economic Status of Widows in Colonial New York," *New York History* 85 (1974): 319–23. On female traders and shopkeepers, see Jean P. Jordan, "Women Merchants in Colonial New York," *New York History* 87 (1977): 412–39; and Elizabeth Anthony Dexter, *Colonial Women of Affairs: Women in Business and the Professions in America before 1776*, 2d ed. (Boston: Houghton Mifflin, 1931), pp. 18–38, 46, 105–8. On changing inheritance provisions for wives and daughters, see David Narrett, "Patterns of Inheritance in Colonial New York City, 1664–1775: A Study in the History of the Family" (Ph.D. diss., Cornell University, 1981), chap. 4. Robert V. Wells, *The Population of the*

British Colonies in America before 1776: A Survey of Census Data (Princeton: Princeton University Press, 1975), p. 128, notes that in the early part of the century an unusually high 16% of Manhattan households were headed by women.

24. On the decline of New York women's control of taxable property, see Wilkenfield, "Social and Economic Structure," pp. 27, 30, 86, 168, 177, 207–8; and Tompsett, "Economic Status of Widows," pp. 438–39. For the decline of widows' status in relation to that of inheriting daughters, see Narrett, "Patterns of Inheritance," pp. 141, 172; cf. Carole Shammas, Marylynn Salmon, and Michel Dahlin, *Inheritance in America from Colonial Times to the Present* (New Brunswick: Rutgers University Press, 1987), pp. 57–69. On domestic cloth manufacturing, see William Bagnall, *Textile Industries of the United States* (1893; New York: A. M. Kelly, 1971), 1:52–53, 56, 81, 122–27. For St. Andrew's Society, see *Arts & Crafts*, 64:258.

For varying assessments of changes in women's status in the period 1780–1820, see Joan Hoff Wilson, "The Illusion of Change: Women and the American Revolution," in Alfred Young, ed., *The American Revolution: Explorations in the History of American Radicalism* (De Kalb, Ill.: Northern Illinois University Press, 1976), pp. 383–445; Mary Beth Norton, *Liberty's Daughters: The Revolutionary Experience of American Women, 1750–1800* (Boston: Little, Brown, 1980); and Linda Kerber, *Women of the Republic: Intellect and Ideology in Revolutionary America* (Chapel Hill: University of North Carolina Press, 1980).

25. Stansell, *City of Women*, pp. 11–20 and table 1, p. 226, showing women's occupations in 1805.

26. Blackstone, *Commentaries*, pp. 635–56. See also Philip J. Greven, Jr., *The Protestant Temperament: Patterns of Child-Rearing, Religious Experience, and the Self in Early America* (New York: New American Library, 1977), for a social-psychological study of parent-child relations. On the increasing importance attached to education and women's responsibilities for child care, see Kerber, *Women of the Republic*, pp. 199–200, 228–31.

27. For the legal status of slaves, see chap. 1, n. 16, and Blackstone, *Commentaries*, pp. 581–86; Goebel and Naughton, *Law Enforcement in Colonial New York*, pp. 118–21. For the economics of hiring out slave labor, see Edgar McManus, *A History of Negro Slavery in New York* (Syracuse, N.Y.: Syracuse University Press, 1970), pp. 43–55; and, for slaves' negotiations of customary rights, 61–62.

28. See Davis, "Slavery in Colonial New York City," table 1.1, p. 3; Kruger, "Born to Run," table 3, pp. 138–39. On the shift in the sex ratio and employment of servants in domestic work, see chap. 1, n. 30. For slaves doing spinning in the De Peyster household, see "Of the Domestic Affairs of the Inhabitants of New York Anterior to the Time of the Revolutionary War," in *Valentine's Manual* (1858), pp. 517–18, and Kruger, "Born to Run," p. 105. On the city market for hired domestic slave labor, see McManus, *Negro Slavery*, pp. 46, 53; and Samuel McKee, *Labor in Colonial New York* (New York: Columbia University Press, 1935), p. 126.

29. For a discussion of the "decline and upheaval" of slavery during the Revolutionary period, see Kruger, "Born to Run," pp. 635–91. On conditions leading to and debates over emancipation, see also A. Leon Higginbotham, Jr., *In the Matter of Color: Race and the American Legal Process, The Colonial Period* (New York: Oxford University Press, 1978), pp. 140–48; Davis, "Slavery in Colonial New York City," pp. 191–220; Arthur Zilversmit, *The First Emancipation: The Abolition of Slavery in the North* (Chicago: University of Chicago Press, 1967), pp. 147–49, 160, 176–77, 180–88; McManus, *Negro Slavery*, pp. 161–88. In 1790, 31.6% of New York County's black population were free; in 1800, 54.9% were free; and in 1810, 82.8%: Kruger, "Born to Run," pp. 131, 924.

30. "An Act to enable certain persons to take and hold estates within this state," passed February 17, 1808, *Laws of New York, 32nd Session*, chap. 44, pp. 29–30; Kruger, "Born to Run," on 1809 law, pp. 348–49, 818–30, 942–43; on eighteenth-century slave marriage in New York, 303–65; and on adult black and white sex ratios after 1800, 305. On discrimination against free black men in trades, see also Wilentz, *Chants Democratic*, p. 48 n; and Graham Hodges, *New York City Cartmen, 1667–1850* (New York: New York University Press, 1986), pp. 152–53. On New York's free black community, see Shane White, " 'We Dwell in Safety and Pursue Our Honest Callings': The Free Blacks of New York City, 1783–1810," *Journal of American History* 75 (1988): 445–70; and for later decades, Leo H. Hirsch, "The Negro and New York, 1783 to 1865," *Journal of Negro History* 16 (1931): 382–473; Rhoda Freeman, "The Free Negro in New York City in the Era before the Civil War?" (Ph.D. diss., Columbia University, 1966); and George Walker, "The Afro-American in New York City, 1827–1860" (Ph.D. diss., Columbia University, 1975). Cf. Leon Litwack, *North of Slavery* (Chicago: University of Chicago Press, 1961), on free blacks in other Eastern Seaboard cities. The rest of this chapter assumes a similar structure of household property and labor relations within the households of white and free black New Yorkers—an assumption that requires testing.

31. Kruger, "Born to Run," p. 899. See also tables, pp. 162, 897–98, 902, 911, 915–16, 945–46, for demographic data on enslaved and free blacks living in white households and in free blacks' own households in New York County to 1820.

32. Blackstone, *Commentaries*, pp. 587–88. Historians of labor in colonial cities have not given much attention to the different working conditions of indentured and free waged labor or explored journeymen's ambiguous "dependent" position as "found labor" within master households. See Richard B. Morris, *Government and Labor in Early America* (New York: Columbia University Press, 1946), pp. 363–89, on apprenticeship; 310–89 on indentured service; and 390–512 on the legal status of bound servants. McKee, *Labor in Colonial New York*, pp. 21–61, links his discussion of "free labor" to freeman status, pp. 21–61; and examines indentured servitude, 89–113. For a comparison of colonial labor systems, see Richard S. Dunn, "Servants and Slaves: The Recruitment and Employment of Labor," in Jack P. Greene and J. R. Pole, eds., *British Colonial America: Essays in the New History of the Early Modern Era* (Baltimore: Johns Hopkins University Press, 1984), pp. 157–94.

33. "Indenture of Apprentices," NYHS Collections 42 (1909): 111–99; specific examples on pp. 130, 178. See also McKee, *Labor in Colonial New York*, pp. 62–88.

34. Merchants who invested in manufacturing enterprises also "found" lodging and meals for their workers. See, e.g., "Proposal for Establishing a Glass Works in the City of New York in 1752," *NYHSQ* 10 (1926): 95–96, in which proprietors contracted to provide a glassblower with "Proper Victuels drink and lodgeing and also a Proper House for his family all which shall continue til one month after aforesaid JMG [the glassblower] shall begin to blow and make Glass in the Glass House"; and the lumber merchant John Keating's offer in 1771 of £60 a year "with meat drink washing and lodging" to "a man who understands the paper making business," in *New-York Gazette and Weekly Post Boy*, Oct. 17, 1771, in *Arts & Crafts*, 64:235.

35. *Rivington's*, p. 102 (Feb. 2, 1775). On wages, see *Iconography*, 4:861; McManus, *Negro Slavery*, pp. 53–54; McKee, *Labor in Colonial New York*, pp. 25–26, 28. Gary Nash, *The Urban Crucible: Social Change, Political Consciousness, and the Origins of the American Revolution* (Cambridge: Harvard University Press, 1979), pp. 238–41, 322–23, notes substantial wage increases during the

Seven Years' War, with ship carpenters earning 8 shillings and mariners 5 shillings a day, followed by wage cuts to "the traditional 2 to 3 pounds a month" for mariners, whereas building artisans held on to their gain of 14 to 16 shillings a day. Jackson Turner Main, *The Social Structure of Revolutionary America* (Princeton: Princeton University Press, 1965), discusses wages primarily in New England, pp. 74–78. The cost of purchasing a house in New York City was often higher than the £100 cited by Main for other colonies, pp. 132–33. Deeds in the early 1770s show artisans buying and selling houses for from £215 to £500, though houses on leased land often went for less than £100. See n. 38, chap. 1, above.

36. On slave resistance, see Thomas J. Davis, *A Rumor of Revolt: The "Great Negro Plot" in Colonial New York* (New York: Free Press, 1985); McManus, *Negro Slavery*, pp. 101–19. On legal controversies between masters and apprentices, see Richard B. Morris, *Select Cases of the Mayor's Court of New York City, 1674–1784*, American Legal Records 2 (Washington, D.C.: American Historians Association, 1935), pp. 354–56; and Goebel and Naughton, *Law Enforcement in Colonial New York*, pp. 108–9n. For notices of runaway apprentices, see *Rivington's*, pp. 34, 36, 43, 63, 81, 125–26; *Arts & Crafts*, 64:127, 143, 339, 344, 346. Apprentices also ran to Manhattan from New Jersey, Connecticut, Long Island, and Pennsylvania: *Rivington's*, pp. 68, 70–72, 74, 77. *Rivington's*, pp. 317–61 passim (1783), contains notices placed by both husbands and wives charging "abandonment." On divorce in New York, see Kerber, *Women of the Republic*, pp. 157–84, esp. 159. On the expense of contributing household labor to the watch, see *MCC, 1675–1776* 5:196–97 (June 4, 1747); *Iconography*, 4: 575, 664–65. Masters also worried about competition from workers they had trained. In 1788 the state legislature passed an act forbidding masters to compel apprentices to sign a bond or take an oath not to set up in the same trade: Smith, *City of New York*, pp. 100–101.

37. E. B. O'Callaghan, *Documentary History of the State of New York* (Albany, 1849–1851), 1:513: on mariners' work contracts, see Morris, *Government and Labor in Early America*, pp. 223–78.

38. For sharing of residence and work space by craftworkers, see, e.g., *Arts & Crafts*, 64:88, 257, 292, 366. For house sharing among carters, grocers, and tavernkeepers, see Evert Bancker, Jr., "List of Proprietors, Lessees and Tenants on Chambers, Reade, Barclay, Church and Anthony Streets," c. 1799, Bancker Papers, NYHS. For a more general discussion of the status of unskilled labor, see Main, *Social Structure of Revolutionary America*, pp. 69–74, 112–13, 131–32, 198–99; and Hodges, *New York City Cartmen*, pp. 45–49.

39. For the decline of apprenticeship, see McKee, *Labor in Colonial New York*, p. 63. For artisans forming partnerships before the Revolution as a step toward expansion of production, see *Arts & Crafts*, 53:43, 46, 53, 67, 73–74 (silversmiths); 85, 88–90, 92, 93, 98 (glassmakers); 101–2, 116, 119, 123, 127, 138 (furniture trades); 147, 152, 155, 157, 165, 179, 181–83, 185 (watchmakers); 198–223, passim (workers in heavy crafts, such as iron foundries). In his 1768 report to Lord Hillsborough, Governor Henry Moore noted local manufacture in leather tanning, cabinet and joiner work, hat- and shoemaking, ropemaking, brewing, shipbuilding, and soap- and candlemaking: O'Callaghan, *Documentary History*, 1:513–15; on other processing trades (brewing, sugar refining, and tobacco) that relied on merchant capital and free waged labor, 488–520. I have found George Unwin, *Industrial Organization in the Sixteenth and Seventeenth Centuries* (Oxford: Clarendon, 1904), useful for thinking about the reorganization of craft production.

40. *The Autobiography of Benjamin Franklin* (New Haven: Yale University Press, 1974), pp. 101–2; another strategy to save rent recommended by Franklin was shar-

ing quarters (p. 115). On attitudes toward the "freedom" of waged employment, see Fred Anderson, "A People's Army: Provincial Military Service during the Seven Years' War," *WMQ*, 3d ser., 40 (1983): 518–24.

41. Stansell, *City of Women*, pp. 12–13; Faye Dudden, *Serving Women: Household Service in Nineteenth-Century America* (Middletown, Conn.: Wesleyan University Press, 1983), pp. 12–27, on the persistence of "bound" domestic labor, and 27–35 on New England's transitional domestic labor market in the early nineteenth century. Cf. Carol Lasser, "Domestic Service in New England" (Ph.D. diss., Harvard University, 1981), pp. 7–8, 33–38, 125–39, and on black servants, 201–37.

42. *Heads of Families*, pp. 116–38, and William Duncan, *The New York Directory and Register* (New York, 1791). Households with more than four males over the age of 16 show the following distribution:

Trade of household head	Number of households	Number of males over 16 years of age				
		4	5	6	7	8+
Merchant	30	24	3	1	1	1
Tavern/ boardinghouse keeper	12	7	4	–	–	1
Shoemaker	14	8	6	–	–	–
Metal trade	15	11	3	–	–	1
Builder (mason/carpenter)	11	9	1	1	–	–
Cabinetmaker	12	7	3	–	1	1
Paint and glass/other light manufacturer	12	5	4	1	1	1
Baker	9	6	2	1	–	–
Hatter	8	7	1	–	–	–
Tailor	7	3	2	2	–	–
Grocer	5	4	1	–	–	–
Printer	4	1	1	1	–	1

The relation between the trade of the household head and the number of adult male household members is of course speculative. Many of the adult males who shared a house, especially in the West Ward, may have been boarding journeymen in a range of trades. The large size of merchant households is also related to the size of their houses. Nonetheless, the large number of adult males in artisan households might be taken as partial evidence of the persistence of the integrated household labor system. For Foster's shop, see *Arts & Crafts*, 81:228.

43. *Arts & Crafts*, 82:44–45 (engraver, 1800); 123 (cabinetmaker, 1796); 332 (organ builder's widow, 1801).

44. On the changing demography that may have contributed to the opening up of house space for boarders, see Wilson, "Illusion of Change," pp. 400–406. Between 1701 and 1730, New Yorkers maintained an average house density of 5.5 persons; by 1776, density ranged from 7.2 to 8.7 persons per house, and it appears to have averaged 7.0 persons per house by 1786. Colonial "house" counts, unfortunately, do not distinguish buildings that were used exclusively for commerce. See Wells, *Population of the British Colonies*, pp. 125–27; and Evarts B. Greene and Virginia Harrington, *The American Population before the Federal Census of 1790* (New York: Columbia University Press, 1932), pp. 92, 94, 97, 101, 102, 104.

45. *Rivington's*, p. 84 (Aug. 25, 1774); *CA*, March 9 and May 14, 1800, and passim. For women boardinghouse keepers listed in directories, see *Duncan's Directory* (1790) and *Longworth's American Almanac* (1800).

46. See, e.g., Edward Probyn, Memorandum Book, 1812–1820, NYHS (Sept. 22, 1812; Sept. 14, 1816; April 26, 1827; May 1, 1817), noting a beaver hat as part of rent payment and boarding his nephew. Similarly, in 1790, Mrs. William Duer boarded her nieces in New York: Helen Morgan, ed., *A Season in New York: Letters of Harriet and Marie Trumbull* (Pittsburgh: University of Pittsburgh Press, 1969), pp. 103, 145. The shipbuilder Noah Brown built a boardinghouse for his apprentices; another shipbuilder, Henry Eckford, allowed his apprentices $40 a year "in lieu of meat, drink, washing, lodging, clothing and all other necessities," and a wage of $2.50 a week: G. W. Sheldon, "The Old Ship Builders of New York," *Harper's New Monthly Magazine* 65 (1882): 234. On trade boardinghouses, see Howard Rock, "Independent Mechanics: Tradesmen in New York City Labor and Politics during the Jeffersonian Era" (Ph.D. diss., New York University, 1974), pp. 28–30; Wilentz, *Chants Democratic*, p. 52; and Bancker Street Surveys, c. 1799 (NYHS).

47. Paine to Carver, Nov. 25, 1806, in "The Correspondence between Thomas Paine and William Carver," in Thorburn, *Forty Years' Residence*, pp. 203–5. Thorburn, finding Paine's freethinking ideas particularly threatening to his own vision of republicanism, published the letters to discredit the pamphleteer in 1834, when the Paine legacy gave encouragement to the Workingmen's movement.

48. Carver to Paine, Dec. 2, 1806, in ibid., pp. 207, 208, 211.

49. Ibid., p. 211.

50. Thorburn, *Forty Years' Residence*, pp. 24–25.

51. Ibid., pp. 25–26.

52. Ibid., p. 27.

53. Ibid., pp. 28–29, 31–32.

54. Ibid., pp. 34–37.

55. Ibid., pp. 45–47.

56. Ibid., pp. 48, 54, 72.

57. See Vestry Minutes, n.d. (c. 1784), listing rental revenues from 1770 to 1776, in Trinity Church Papers, box 29, New York City Miscellaneous Manuscripts, NYHS; Julian Gwyn, *The Enterprising Admiral: The Personal Fortune of Sir Peter Warren* (Montreal: McGill/Queen's University Press, 1974), pp. 56–57; Esther Singleton, *Social New York under the Georges, 1714–1776* (New York: Ira Friedman 1902), p. 34. On the housing shortage following the Revolution, see Pomeranz, *New York*, pp. 226–37.

58. *CA*, Jan. 3, June 6, and Dec. 3, 1800; Mar. 9, 1806; Feb. 10, 1807. The increase in porterhouses and advertisements for board without shelter at the end of the eighteenth century further points to a shift from boarding to lodging. See, e.g., *CA*, Dec. 3, 1800; Apr. 24 and June 9, 1803; and a notice of Mar. 15, 1817, announcing that "a few gentlemen who lodge in their stores can be accommodated with board."

59. *CA*, Aug. 14, 1809; *Arts & Crafts*, 81:188 (1794); *CA*, Mar. 9, 1800; for other examples of two-family houses, see *CA*, Feb. 26, 1805; Feb.12, 1807; Mar. 6, 1817. Such notices, of course, appealed to the better-off portion of the community. For housing for the poor in the late eighteenth century (described primarily in relation to epidemics), see Ford, *Slums and Housing*, 1:33–71.

60. *CA*, May 13, 1803.

3. *"Unlike Republican Simplicity": The Shaping of a New Social Landscape*

1. For travelers' reports from 1815 to 1845, see Bayard Still, *Mirror for Gotham: New York as Seen By Contemporaries from Dutch Days to the Present* (New York: New York University Press, 1956), pp. 78–124; Isaac Holmes, *An Account of America Derived from Actual Observations during a Residence of Four Years in That Republic* (London, 1823), esp. pp. 128–29; Peter Nielson, *Recollections of Six Years' Residence in the United States of America* (Glasgow, 1830), p. 34. Foreign travelers were not the only ones to find New York City lacking in republican simplicity. Joyce Appleby reports in *Capitalism and a New Social Order: The Republican Vision of the 1790s* (New York: New York University Press, 1984), pp. 93–94, that Jefferson expressed shock in 1790 at the city's "aristocratic sympathies."

2. On nonimportation see Gary Nash, *The Urban Crucible: Social Change, Political Consciousness, and the Origins of the American Revolution* (Cambridge: Harvard University Press, 1979), pp. 321, 332, 335, 354–78. On republican rejection of luxury and gentry practices, see Rhys Isaac, *The Transformation of Virginia, 1740–1790* (Chapel Hill: University of North Carolina Press, 1982), pp. 46, 202, 247–60, 268–69; Ann Withington, "The Birth of an American Identity" (Ph.D. diss., Yale University, 1983). For specific incidents of attacks on elite institutions in New York City, see, e.g., Esther Singleton, *Social New York under the Georges, 1714–1776* (New York: Ira Friedman, 1902), pp. 280–81 (1766, theater); 371–72 (1765, Vauxhall Gardens); 358–60 (agitation on behalf of the regulation of food prices during an inflationary period). For New York after the Revolution, see Edward Countryman, *A People in Revolution: The American Revolution and Political Society in New York, 1760–1790* (Baltimore: Johns Hopkins University Press, 1981), pp. 191–279; on confiscation, 172–73, 186–87, 206–7, 214–15; and on measures to protect land's alienability, 243. Barbara Clark Smith, *After the Revolution: The Smithsonian History of Everyday Life in the Eighteenth Century* (New York: Pantheon, 1985), offers a social interpretation of the material artifacts of a republican culture of "simplicity."

3. "Republicanism" can be used so broadly to characterize American ideology during the Revolution that it runs the risk of losing any precise meaning. Gary Nash provides a cogent summary of conflicting ideological tendencies in *Urban Crucible*, pp. 340–51; see also Drew R. McCoy, "Benjamin Franklin's Vision of a Republican Political Economy for America," *WMQ*, 3d ser., 35 (1978): 605–78; Robert E. Shalhope, "Toward a Republican Synthesis: The Emergence of an Understanding of Republicanism in American Historiography," *WMQ*, 3d ser., 29 (1972): 49–80; Gordan Wood, *The Creation of the American Republic, 1776–1787* (Chapel Hill: University of North Carolina Press, 1969), pp. 46–124; Eric Foner, *Tom Paine and Revolutionary America* (New York: Oxford University Press, 1976). I find Joyce Appleby's distinction between Federalists' "classical republicanism" and Jeffersonians' "liberal republicanism"—and particularly her arguments on the ascendancy of the latter ideology after 1790—useful for thinking about republican discourse in New York City; see *Capitalism and a New Social Order*. For a characterization of New York "artisan republicanism," see Sean Wilentz, *Chants Democratic: New York City and the Rise of the American Working Class* (New York: Oxford University Press, 1984), pp. 61–103.

4. McCoy, "Franklin's Vision," pp. 618–19, 624; Wood, *Creation of the American Republic*, pp. 65 and, for tensions in thinking about wealth, 488–93, 495–99; Appleby, *Capitalism and a New Social Order*, pp. 12–19, 25–50. For examples of civic philanthropy in the first quarter of the nineteenth century, see Raymond Mohl,

Poverty in New York, 1783–1825 (New York: Oxford University Press, 1971), pp. 137–58.

5. C. B. Macpherson, *Property: Mainstream and Critical Positions* (Toronto: University of Toronto Press, 1978), pp. 200–205, and *The Political Theory of Possessive Individualism: Hobbes to Locke* (New York: Oxford University Press, 1962), pp. 204–14. On slavery and republicanism, see Edmund Morgan, *American Slavery, American Freedom* (New York: Norton, 1975), pp. 363–87. Social historians debate northeastern agrarians' view of property and market relations, but much of the discussions of *mentalité* seems to focus on the market relations that follow production without examination of the acquisition of the means of production. See James Henretta, "Families and Farms: Mentalité in Pre-industrial America," *WMQ*, 3d ser., 35 (1978): 3–32; Michael Merrill, "Cash Is Good to Eat: Self-Sufficiency and Exchange in the Rural Economy of the United States," *Radical History Review*, 1977, pp. 42–72; Christopher Clark, "The Household Economy, Market Exchange, and the Rise of Capitalism in the Connecticut Valley, 1800–1860," *Journal of Social History* 13 (1979): 172–75; Joyce Appleby, "Commercial Farming and the 'Agrarian Myth' in the Early Republic," *Journal of American History*, 1982, pp. 833–49. On merchants' legal conceptions of property, see Morton Horwitz, *The Transformation of American Law* (Cambridge: Harvard University Press, 1977), pp. 31–62.

6. Sidney Pomeranz, *New York: An American City, 1783–1803* (New York: Columbia University Press, 1938), pp. 147–225; Arthur H. Cole and Walter Smith, *Wholesale Commodity Prices in the United States, 1700–1861* (Cambridge: Harvard University Press, 1938), p. 31. Diane Lindstrom analyzes the basis of New York City's expansion and domination of foreign commerce, access to credit, and control of the long-distance circulation of information in "The Economy of Antebellum New York City," paper presented to Social Science Research Council, November 1983.

7. Robert Greenhalg Albion, *The Rise of New York Port, 1815–1860* (1939; Boston: Northeastern University Press, 1984), pp. 7–15.

8. Shipping and investment in land (as measured by the level of assessed land values) generally rose and fell together. Though the population increased by 59% in the decade after 1800, assessed wealth increased only 8%, reflecting the losses of the embargo and the leveling off of the speculative real estate boom in the 1790s. By 1810, a prosperous "middling" section of the city included artisan-entrepreneurs as well as commission merchants and wholesalers, who joined import merchants in land investments. Between 1810 and 1820, when population increased at half the rate of the previous decade (28.5%), wealth expanded 163%. See Richard S. Fisher, *A New and Complete Gazetteer* (New York, 1853), p. 579. For New York's "economic class structure," see Edmund Willis, "Social Origins and Political Leadership in New York City from the Revolution to 1815" (Ph.D. diss., University of California, Berkeley, 1968), pp. 103–32; and wealth distribution by ward for 1790, 1795, 1808, and 1818, pp. 56, 60, 62, 64. Willis finds (p. 173) that roughly two-thirds of officeholders from 1778 to 1785 were landlords with more than one tenant, that from 1811 to 1818 one-fourth were landlords, and that Republicans were slightly more likely than Federalists to be landlords. Among 283 officeholders, over half of the "mechanics" were landlords compared to 27% of the merchants and 16% of the lawyers; see table IV–18, p. 170; table IV–20, p. 173.

On the political divisions between merchants and artisans, see Staughton Lynd, "The Mechanics in New York Politics, 1774–1788," *Labor History* 5 (1964): 225–46; Alfred Young, "The Mechanics and the Jeffersonians: New York, 1789–1801," *Labor History* 5 (1964): 245–76; Howard Rock, *Artisans of the New Republic* (New

York: New York University Press, 1979), pp. 19–147; Willis, "Social Origins and Political Leadership," pp. 49–93; Wilentz, *Chants Democratic*, pp. 63–77; and Graham Hodges, *New York City Cartmen, 1667–1850* (New York: New York University Press, 1986), pp. 81–128. For New York City in the context of state politics, see Alfred Young, *The Democratic Republicans of New York: The Origins, 1763–1797* (Chapel Hill: University of North Carolina Press, 1967), pp. 68–69, 183–84, 420–21.

9. Rock, *Artisans of the New Republic*, pp. 264–94; Wilentz, *Chants Democratic*, pp. 48–53, 56–60. See also David Montgomery, "The Working Classes of the Pre-industrial American City, 1780–1830," *Labor History* 9 (1968): 3–22.

10. *New-York Gazette and Weekly Post Boy*, Jan. 30, 1769, in *Arts & Crafts*, 64 (1938): 59. For merchant concentration in the East and Dock wards in 1790 and 1796, see Bruce Wilkenfield, "Social and Economic Structure of the City of New York, 1695–1796" (Ph.D. diss., Columbia University, 1973), pp. 173–74, 196. For merchant houses and adjacent stores, see "New York Residences Sixty Years Since," in *Valentine's Manual* (1855) pp. 561–64; and "Assessment of Real and Personal Property of the East Ward of the City of New York, 1791," NYHS Collections 43 (1911), 2:318–83.

11. The sizes of merchant households in relation to those of artisans are evident from *Heads of Families: First Census of the United States, 1790* (Baltimore: Genealogical Publishing Co., 1966), pp. 116–38, particularly for the East Ward (pp. 117–19), with an average density of 6.46 persons per house vs. 5.36 persons per house in the artisan West Ward. For inventories of colonial merchants' household goods, see "Of Domestic Affairs Anterior to the Revolution," in *Valentine's Manual* (1858), pp. 517–25; and Singleton, *Social New York*, pp. 53–168. For eighteenth-century consumption patterns, see Richard Bushman, "American High-Style and Vernacular Cultures," in Jack P. Greene and J. R. Pole, eds., *Colonial British America: Essays in the New History of the Early Modern Era* (Baltimore: Johns Hopkins University Press, 1984), pp. 345–83.

12. For the impact of the landfills, see the map by J. Hills, "City of New York: (1782), in James G. Wilson, *Memorial History of the City of New York* (New York, 1893), and "Taylor-Roberts Map" (1797), in John Kouenhaven, *Columbia Historical Portrait of New York* (New York: Harper & Row, 1972), pp. 104–5. For wharf proprietors in 1788, see Evert Bancker, Jr., "Names of Owners of Property on the East and North Rivers, 1788, From Battery Place to Desbrosses Street, and from Whitehall Slip to Rutgers Slip," Bancker Papers, NYHS.

13. "Assessment of Real and Personal Property," pp. 320–22. For geographers' analysis of the process of land specialization in central business districts, see Martin J. Bowden, "Growth of Central Business Districts in Large Cities," in *The New Urban History: Quantitative Explorations by American Historians* (Princeton: Princeton University Press, 1975), pp. 75–109; David Ward, *Cities and Immigrants* (New York: Oxford University Press, 1971), pp. 83–103, and "The Industrial Revolution and the Emergence of Boston's Central Business District," *Economic Geography* 42 (1966): 152–71; Alan Pred, *Spatial Dynamics of Urban Industrial Growth, 1800–1860* (Cambridge: MIT Press, 1966), pp. 163–85.

For the geographic distribution of Manhattan's population by occupation in 1789 and 1796, see Wilkenfield, "Social and Economic Structure," pp. 173–74, 196; and for tenure patterns, Willis, "Social Origins and Political Leadership," table II–5, p. 60. The 1807 election census (table 2) shows that the proportion of freeholding households in the lower wards (Wards 1–3) ranged from 30 to 34%, compared to 13 to 24% in the middle wards (Wards 4–7, including Trinity Church farm, Ward 5, and Rutgers' farm, Ward 7), 30% in Ward 8 (north of Grand Street, with roughly

6,000 residents), and 48% in Ward 9 (north of 21st Street, with only 2,680 residents). This pattern suggests that while merchants and wealthier artisans persisted in the lower wharf district, those artisans who migrated to the town's periphery were more likely to be able to purchase land and houses.

14. *CA*, Jan. 1, 1803; Feb. 16, 1803; Feb. 25, 1807. In 1817 Joseph Barber offered for rent the upper part of his three-story house at 29 Wall Street, specifying "persons wishing to occupy it as a dwelling for a small family preferred, if none appears in the course of a few days the rooms will be let for offices"; but he anticipated his own failure by adding, "The parlour floor in the second story would make the most convenient and pleasant counting room in the city" (*CA*, Feb. 9, 1817). See also "History of Wall Street," in *Valentine's Manual* (1866), pp. 533–72. On the formation of new financial institutions, see Robert East, *Business Enterprise in the American Revolutionary Era* (1938; New York: AMS Press, 1969), pp. 285–305, 327–29. For the advent of fire insurance, see Richard Calhoun, "From Community to Metropolis: Fire Protection in New York City, 1790–1875" (Ph.D. diss., Columbia University, 1973), chaps. 1–2.

15. The Bowling Green advertisement is cited in Henry Collins Brown, ed., *Valentine's Manual of Old New York* (New York: Valentine's Manual, Inc., 1948), p. 30. The merchant Archibald Gracie, who had one of the finest houses on lower Broadway, announced in 1785 that he was moving his "counting room from his house 110 Broadway to his new Fire-Proof Store, 52 Pine" (cited in ibid., p. 28). For valuations, see "Private Residences of the City," in *Valentine's Manual* (1855), pp. 561–64, listing 100 prominent houses. See also "New York, 1796–97," in *Iconography*, 2:418–19.

16. Elizabeth Bleecker [McDonald], Diary, 1799–1805, NYPL, passim; and Joseph Scoville [Walter Barrett], *The Old Merchants of New York City* (New York: Thomas Knox, 1885), 5:132–39. In 1804, Janet Roosevelt Inderwick had an illegitimate child by a fellow boarder. After her husband died intestate in 1805, she "went home to his house, and resumed possession as if she had never left it." When she died in 1812, she had made the child her (and implicitly his) heir to an estate that included over 200 acres of Manhattan property, but a nurse had kidnapped the child shortly after Mr. Inderwick's death.

17. *Evening Post*, Dec. 9, 1801, in *Arts & Crafts*, 82:186. William Alexander Duer, in "An Anniversary Address Delivered before the St. Nicholas Society, Dec. 1, 1848," NYHS, p. 11.

18. *CA*, Feb. 3, 1809; Jan. 4, 1803.

19. "Park Row and Chatham," in *Valentine's Manual* (1866), pp. 590–616. On wealthy citizens' continued claim to Broadway, see Edward Pessen, *Riches, Class, and Power before the Civil War* (Lexington, Mass.: D. C. Heath, 1973), pp. 169–79, esp. 172, 177. On examples of successful artisan entrepreneurs and their house and land investments, see Willis, "Social Origins and Political Leadership," pp. 102–4, 122, 124, 170; and Wilentz, *Chants Democratic*, pp. 35–42. For successful entrepreneurs among tanners, see Frank Norcross, *A History of the New York Swamp* (New York, 1901), pp. 51–60.

20. *CA*, Jan. 1, 1800; May 15, 1812.

21. Grant Thorburn, *Forty Years' Residence in America* (Boston: Russell, Odiorne & Metcalf, 1834), pp. 38–39; for an analysis of the politics underlying this incident, see Young, "Mechanics and Jeffersonians," pp. 256–57; and Paul Gilje, *The Road to Mobocracy: Popular Disorder in New York City, 1763–1834* (Chapel Hill: University of North Carolina Press, 1987), pp. 69–84.

22. *CA*, Jan. 1, 1807; the story of the gentleman shoemaker comes from Norcross, *History of the New York Swamp*, p. 221. For examples of furniture makers'

supplying other artisans and engaging in loft manufacturing in lower Manhattan, see *Arts & Crafts*, 81:111, 82:137. For an overview of the economic structure of mercantile cities and the relation of manufacturing to trade, see Alan Pred, "Manufacturing in the American Mercantile City, 1800–1840," in Kenneth Jackson and Stanley Schultz, eds., *Cities in American History* (New York: Knopf, 1972), pp. 111–42; and for a revisionist analysis focusing on Boston and Philadelphia, Diane Lindstrom and John Sharpless, "Urban Growth and Economic Structure in Antebellum America," in Paul Uselding, ed., *Research in Economic History* (New York: JAI Press, 1978), 3:161–316.

23. Bleeker Diary, NYPL, Oct. 30, 1802 (window incident); Feb. 28 and Oct. 28, 1799; May 24, 1803; Dec. 18, 1805 (thefts); Nov. 28, 1804 (woman at the door).

24. John Lambert, *Travels through Canada and the United States of North America in the Years 1806, 1807, and 1808* (London: 1820), 2:213.

25. Bleecker Diary, July 26, 1799; James Ford, *Slums and Housing with Special Reference to New York City* (Cambridge: Harvard University Press, 1936), 1:60–70; John H. Griscom, *A History, Chronological and Circumstantial, of the Visitation of Yellow Fever at New York* (New York, 1858).

26. Bleecker Diary, NYPL, July 30 and Aug. 1, 2, 8, and 9, 1803; Ford, *Slums and Housing*, 1:74.

27. Ford, *Slums and Housing*, 1:74–75; James Hardie, *An Account of the Malignant Fever Which Prevailed in the City of New York during the Autumn of 1805* (New York, 1806). For a history of the city's responses to epidemics, see John Duffy, *A History of Public Health in New York City, 1625–1866* (New York: Russell Sage Foundation, 1968), pp. 73–123.

28. *CA*, Feb. 2, 1803; April 15, 1807, and passim during the spring months, 1795–1815.

29. William Strickland, "Journal of a Tour of the United States of America, 1794–1795," NYHS Collections 82 (1971): 89; see also Timothy Dwight, *Travels in New England and New York* (1822; Cambridge: Harvard University Press, 1969), 3:314–31; "Private Residences of the City," in *Valentine's Manual* (1855), p. 564; and advertisements in *CA*, January–May 1790–1825, passim.

30. Isaac Holmes, *Account of America*, p. 129; for comments on high rents, pp. 151, 268–69; Nielson, *Recollections of Six Years' Residence*, pp. 33–34; Henry Fearon, *Sketches of America: A Narrative of a Journey of 5,000 Miles* (London, 1818), pp. 6–7; "Description of the City of New York by a Resident of Philadelphia, 1806," in *Valentine's Manual* (1868), pp. 828–29; Lambert, *Travels through Canada and the United States*, pp. 102–3. For a comparison of perceptions of opportunity in England and in the United States, see David Montgomery, "The Working Classes of the Pre-industrial American City, 1780–1830," *Labor History* 9 (1968): 11–12.

31. "Description of New York, 1806," p. 828; *CA*, Apr. 4, 1803; Jan. 19 and Feb. 2, 1807. For later travelers' calculations of rent and wages, see, e.g., Fearon, *Sketches of America*, pp. 22, 115; Edmund Blunt, *A Stranger's Guide to the City of New York* (New York, 1818), pp. 290–91; John M. Duncan, *Travels through Part of the United States and Canada, 1818–1819* (Glasgow, 1823) 1:27–29, 2:375–76.

32. Rock, *Artisans of the New Republic*, pp. 249–50; Donald Adams, "Wage Rates in the Early National Period, 1785–1830," *Journal of Economic History* 28 (1968): 404–26. Rock cites sample budgets published by striking carpenters in 1809 which allowed a family of five $55 for rent out of an annual income of $400, or less than 15% of income, with an additional $162 for food and $30 for fuel, for a total boarding budget of $247. What seems remarkable is that, according to the rents listed in housing notices, the journeymen who calculated this budget for five people allotted rent for only one room.

33. *A Season in New York: Letters of Harriet and Maria Trumbull*, ed. Helen M. Morgan (Pittsburgh: University of Pittsburgh Press, 1969), p. 51; Duer, "Anniversary Address," pp. 10–11, 17, describes the terrain at the "upper extremity" of Broadway in the late 1780s and early 1790s.

34. See "Inventory of Church Lots," n.d. (c. 1787), Trinity Church Papers, New York City Miscellaneous Manuscripts, box 29, NYHS; Evert Bancker, "Proprietors, Lessees and Tenants . . . Chambers, Read, Bancker Streets" (1799), Bancker Papers, NYHS; and addresses and occupations from *Longworth's American Almanac, New York Register, and City Directory* (New York, 1800).

35. For a typical Trinity conveyance of property with a restrictive covenant, see RC, 112:14 (Trinity Church to Alexander Hosack, Apr. 17, 1814, for Lot no. 634 Chambers Street).

36. *Elliot's Improved Double Directory* (New York, 1812) has listings by street as well as by name. Clearly this method does not allow for the unrepresentativeness of city directories. Multitenant houses in all likelihood contained more than the listed households, while listings in single-family houses often do not reveal boarding relatives, particularly women.

37. Pessen, *Riches, Class, and Power*, pp. 172–73, notes that in 1828, 10 of the city's 500 wealthiest families lived on Chambers Street; their assessed wealth averaged $48,000.

38. For the early history of what became the Five Points neighborhood, see "Public Acts Relating to Commons, Kings Farm and Fresh Pond," in *Valentine's Manual* (1856), pp. 434–35; and Carol Groneman Pernicone, " 'The Bloody Ould Sixth': A Social Analysis of a New York City Working-Class Community in the Mid–Nineteenth Century" (Ph.D. diss., University of Rochester, 1973), pp. 20–23. For landownership, see *MCC, 1784–1831*, 3:252–53; and for Livingston houses, 2:110, 120; 3:253.

39. *Elliot's Improved Double Directory* (1812); see also the listing of manufacturers in William Bridges, *Map of the City of New York and the Island of Manhattan with Commissioner's Remarks* (New York, 1811), pp. 44–47.

40. For general population figures, see Franklin B. Hough, *Statistics of the Population of the City and County of New York* (New York, 1866), reprinting state and city census figures.

41. "An Act Relative to Improvements Touching on the Laying Out of Streets and Roads in the City of New York," passed Apr. 3, 1807, *Laws of New York, 30th Session*, chap. 115; John Reps, *Town Planning in Frontier America* (Princeton: Princeton University Press, 1965), pp. 196–203; Hendrik Hartog, *Public Property and Private Power: The Corporation of the City of New York in American Law, 1730–1870* (Chapel Hill: University of North Carolina Press, 1983), pp. 158–74.

42. Appleby, *Capitalism and a New Order*, p. 49.

43. Bridges, *Map of the City of New York*. For city precedents of rectilinear street plans, see Peter Marcuse, "The Grid as City Plan: New York City and Laissez-Faire Planning in the Nineteenth Century," *Planning Perspectives* 2 (1987): 287–310.

44. John Brinckerhoff Jackson, "The Order of a Landscape: Reason and Religion in Newtonian America," in D. W. Meinig, ed., *The Interpretation of Ordinary Landscapes* (New York: Oxford University Press, 1979), pp. 153–63, esp. 158–61; John R. Stilgoe, *Common Landscape of America, 1580–1845* (New Haven: Yale University Press, 1982), pp. 99–107.

45. Bridges, *Map of the City of New York*, p. 26.

46. For later critics, see Lewis Mumford, *Sticks and Stones: A Study of American Architecture and Civilization* (1924; New York: Dover, 1955), pp. 68–69, 85–

87; Reps, *Town Planning*, pp. 202–3; Albert Fein, *Landscape into Cityscape: Frederick Law Olmsted's Plans for a Greater New York* (New York: Van Nostrand Reinhold, 1967), pp. 352–54. Hartog answers these critics with a historical reading of the plan which supports my interpretation: *Public Property and Private Power*, pp. 161–66.

47. Bridges, *Map of the City of New York*, p. 24.

48. Ibid., pp. 28, 29.

49. Ibid.

50. The decision to reject the commissioners' proposal for a central market left the Common Council with the task of deciding when neighborhood "convenience" merited the opening of new markets. See, e.g., *MCC, 1784–1831*, 9:718–19, for an 1818 decision to open a Tenth Ward market to remove the "inconvenience" to "mechanics and laboring men" who had to walk from half a mile to one and a half miles to buy food. On butchers, see Rock, *Artisans of the New Republic*, pp. 210–11, 218–19, 222–24. On the demise of market artisans' political influence, see Duffy, *History of Public Health*, pp. 420–39.

51. Webster is cited in Ford, *Slums and Housing*, 1:62.

52. "Public Acts Relating to Commons," *Valentine's Manual* (1856), pp. 435–40; MCC, 1784–1831, 2:2, 8, 478 (Lispenard Meadows); 3:3, 489, 719, 727 (Fresh Pond); and for settling of accounts, 9:9, 37, 94, 120, 178, 218, 263; and land auction, 9:464–65, 509.

53. Citations for ordinances to fill in sunken lots can be found in the index to MCC, *1784–1831* and in the City Clerk Filed Papers, Municipal Archives. For Thompson Street, see City Inspector, "Ordinances," Mar. 8, 1819, City Clerk Filed Papers, box 3080; Ford, *Slums and Housing*, 1:87–88; and Rhoda G. Freeman, "The Free Negro in New York City in the Era before the Civil War" (Ph.D. diss., Columbia University, 1966), pp. 218–19.

54. Charles Lockwood, *Bricks and Brownstones: The New York Row House, 1783–1929* (New York: McGraw-Hill, 1972), pp. 36–40; MCC, *1784–1831*, 3:596; for later city interventions in St. John's Park, see MCC, *1784–1831*, 10:202, 11:282. For the neighborhood in 1812, see *Elliot's Improved Double Directory* (1812). Apparently Trinity leaseholders rejected the 99-year-lease plan and purchased lots outright in the 1820s; see *Iconography*, 5:1629, 1635 (citing *Evening Post*, Dec. 29, 1823), and 1664 (on an 1827 adjustment reserving the right to dispose of the parkland with the consent of two-thirds of the owners). See Asa Greene, *A Glance at New York* (New York, 1837), p. 217.

55. For typical restrictive covenants, see RC, 171:42 (Astor), 495:148 (Lorillard). For elite residential locations, see Pessen, *Riches, Class, and Power*, and Lockwood, *Bricks and Brownstones*, pp. 40–53. Brian Danforth notes that merchants' residential mobility accelerated dramatically after 1825, "The Influence of Socioeconomic Factors upon Political Behavior: A Quantitative Look at New York City Merchants, 1828–1844" (Ph.D. diss., New York University, 1974), pp. 40–45.

56. Pred, *Spatial Dynamics*, pp. 197–213 (for New York, 198–201); Groneman Pernicone, " 'Bloody Ould Sixth,' " pp. 23–31. Tracing masters and journeymen in selected trades (cabinetmakers, coopers, metal trades, shoemakers, stonecutters, and masons) who served as jurors and resided in Wards 3, 5, and 8 in 1816, Wilentz finds that nearly two-fifths of the master craftsmen persisted in Ward 3, below Murray Street, compared to less than 10% of the journeymen; that roughly 50% of the masters and 60% of the journeymen lived in Ward 5 (Murray to Canal); and one-eighth of the masters and one-third of the journeymen lived in Ward 8, north of Canal: *Chants Democratic*, table 4, p. 400. This finding suggests a

shift from the pattern in 1807, when proprietary masters tended to move to the periphery. See n. 13 above.

57. For typical Rutgers ground leases, see RC, 210:66, 67; 212:358.

58. For descriptions of the Seventh Ward, see Henry Taylor, *New York as It Was Sixty Years Ago* (Brooklyn, 1894), pp. 24–25; G. W. Sheldon, "The Old Shipbuilders of New York," *Harper's New Monthly Magazine* 65 (1882): 224–36. For early pockets of poverty in reclaimed marshland of the Seventh Ward, see Ford, *Slums and Housing*, 1:86; and for complaints, MCC, *1784–1831*, 2:440–41, 5:192.

59. Henry B. Yshope, *The Disposition of Loyalist Estates in the Southern District of New York* (New York: Columbia University Press, 1939), pp. 154–56. For construction patterns, see James Hardie, *A Census of New Buildings Erected in the City of New York in the Year 1824* (New York, 1825), pp. 5–14. In 1827 a grocer sold a house at Broome and Sheriff streets to a widow for $3,100, while the cooper Adam Pentz leased a house for four years at Forsyth and Division for $156 a year: RC, 232:292, 210:66–67. See also Rush Hawkins, "Corlear's Hook, 1820," NYHS. Another Hester Street notice in the *Morning Courier and New-York Enquirer*, Dec. 2, 1829, offered "for sale or to let" a two-story brick-front house with nine rooms and two kitchens "for a large or two small families."

60. CA, Mar. 6, 1817.

61. Wilentz, *Chants Democratic*, pp. 107–42, offers the best account of the "metropolitan industrialization" of antebellum New York City. Wilentz's table 11, p. 404, shows that by 1855, 48.6% of manufacturing was done through outwork, 15.5% took place in "garret shops," 5.0% in "neighborhood shops," and 30.9% in factories (predominantly for ironworks, stonecutting, and printing). See also Lindstrom and Sharpless, "Urban Growth and Economic Structure," pp. 170–71, showing that 78.9% of manufacturing was for the local market in 1840.

62. Rock, *Artisans of the New Republic*, pp. 237–63, 266; Pessen, *Riches, Class, and Power*, pp. 33–36.

63. Rock, *Artisans of the New Republic*, pp. 265–68; Wilentz, *Chants Democratic*, p. 402.

64. On ethnicity, see Robert Ernst, *Immigrant Life in New York City, 1825–1860* (New York: New York University Press, 1949), pp. 39–47. The social differentiation of the East Side and West Side below 14th Street can be seen in contrasting density in 1830. On the Lower East Side (Wards 7, 10, and 13) density averaged 11.5 persons per improved lot, while the West Side's Wards 8 and 9 averaged 9.7 persons. The quality of new construction is also reflected in the appreciation of land values. Assessed land values in Ward 7 increased from approximately $4.0 million in 1825 to $5.5 million in 1830 (1,326 improved lots, the majority under Rutgers' covenants). Land values in Wards 10 and 13 rose from $4.3 to $5.9 million in 1830 (2,485 improved lots on the old De Lancey farm). On the West Side between 1825 and 1830, land values in Ward 9 more than doubled, from $4.4 million to $9 million (2,539 improved lots). See BAA Documents 1, no. 37 (Dec. 5, 1831): 130–31, and no. 4 (Dec. 5, 1831), unbound, Appendix. See table 4.

65. On the 1840 journey to work, see Pred, *Spatial Dynamics*, pp. 207–13; Richard B. Stott, *Workers in the Metropolis: Class, Ethnicity, and Youth in Antebellum New York City* (Ithaca: Cornell University Press, 1990), pp. 192–94. See also Peter Knights, "Population Turnover, Persistence, and Residential Mobility in Boston, 1820–1860," in Stephan Thernstrom and Richard Sennett, eds., *Nineteenth-Century Cities: Essays in the New Urban History* (New Haven: Yale University Press, 1969), pp. 258–74.

66. Duer, "Anniversary Address," pp. 18–19; *New York Mirror*, Feb. 2, 1828.

67. Sam Bass Warner coined the phrase "walking city" in *Streetcar Suburbs: The Process of Growth in Boston, 1870–1900* (Cambridge: Harvard University Press,

1973). He suggests the social bonds of proximity in *The Private City: Philadelphia in Three Periods of Its Growth* (Philadelphia: University of Pennsylvania Press, 1968), pp. 10–11, 16, 21, 50.

68. James Fenimore Cooper, *Home as Found* (1838; New York: Capricorn, 1964), pp. 42–43.

4. The Social Meanings of Housing, 1800–1840

1. *Letters of John Pintard to His Daughter Eliza Noel Pintard Davidson, 1816–1833*, ed. Dorothy Barck, NYHS Collections 70–74 (1937–1940), 1:42 (Dec. 18, 1816).

2. For Pintard's biography, see Barck's sketch in her Introduction to ibid., pp. ix–xx; Raymond Mohl, *Poverty in New York* (New York: Oxford University Press, 1971), pp. 242–43; David L. Sterling, "William Duer, John Pintard, and the Panic of 1792," in Joseph Frese and Jacob Judd, eds., *Business Enterprise in Early New York* (Tarrytown: Sleepy Hollow Press, 1979), pp. 99–132; Thomas Bender, *New York Intellect: A History of Intellectual Life from 1750 to the Beginnings of Our Own Times* (New York: Knopf, 1987), pp. 48–50.

3. *Letters of John Pintard*, 1:137 (July 29, 1818), 182 (Apr. 12, 1819).

4. The geographer James Vance offers one of the best theoretical statements of the separation of "work" and "home" in "Housing the Worker: The Employment Linkage as a Force in Urban Structure," *Economic Geography* 42 (1966): 294–325. As Jeanne Boydston argues in "Home and Work: The Industrialization of House-work in the Northeastern United States from the Colonial Period to the Civil War" (Ph.D. diss., Yale University, 1984), pp. 3–25, the picture of domestic households "separated" from the economy and the problem of conceptualizing the ongoing economic value of housework begin with historians' emphasis on the realization of the value of labor through the exchange of cash and commodities. Thus, for example, women's work in manufacturing goods in the household, particularly cloth, is categorized as "productive labor," while the household production of family cloth-ing (which continued well into the nineteenth century) generally is not. The issue then is how to analyze the decline in the household production of commodities for exchange in relation to ongoing housework (including the expansion of some forms of housework, such as, in bourgeois households, the work of entertaining). Boyd-ston and others have tried to demonstrate the economic value of housework through calculations of the savings that derive from "purchase avoidance" as well as from the direct labor of food preparation, the maintenance of houses and clothing, and nursing the sick. When so many of these household "products" are also avail-able through the market, as in the late-twentieth-century service economy, it is perhaps easier to recognize the economic value of the labor that produces them. But analytic language that opposes "work" and "home" continues to impoverish our analysis of nineteenth-century women as historical agents who, though constrained in the exercise of power, fully participated in and contributed to the construction of a new system of social and economic relations. Thus to point to the decline of household commodity production as a removal of "work" from the household is to see but one part of a much larger restructuring of the economy which included an ideological redefinition of what constituted labor, that is, the equating of labor's value with its cash equivalent rather than with its product. See also Jeanne Boyd-ston, "To Earn Her Daily Bread: Antebellum Housework and Working-Class Sub-sistence," *Radical History Review* 35 (1985): 7–25; Christine Stansell, *City of Women: Sex and Class in New York City, 1789–1860* (New York: Knopf, 1986), pp. 11–16; Alice Kessler Harris, *Out to Work: A History of Wage-Earning Women in the United States* (New York: Oxford University Press, 1982), pp. 3–31. Belinda

Bozzoli offers a valuable analysis of another theoretical dimension of this problem, the impact of domestic economic relations on the larger processes of social change, in "Marxism, Feminism, and South African Studies," *Journal of South African Studies* 9 (1983): 139–71.

5. *Letters to John Pintard*, 2:220 (Jan. 27, 1826).

6. In thinking about the question of how people classify social attributes and assign cultural value in relation to housing, I have been influenced by the work of the anthropologist Constance Perin on twentieth-century American housing. See *Everything in Its Place: Social Order and Land Use in America* (Princeton: Princeton University Press, 1977), pp. 20–80.

7. Susan Strasser, *Never Done: A History of Housework* (New York: Pantheon, 1982), pp. 19, 33–37, 51–53, 67–68, 85–96, 104–12; Faye Dudden, *Serving Women: Household Service in Nineteenth-Century America* (Middletown, Conn.: Weslyan University Press, 1983), pp. 127–47; Charles Lockwood, *Bricks and Brownstones: The New York Row House, 1783–1929* (New York: McGraw-Hill, 1972), pp. 17–18 and, for after 1840, 183–89. For heating in New York row houses, see *Letters of John Pintard*, 4:8 (Jan. 28, 1832); and an article in *New-York Mirror*, Jan. 10, 1829, recommending taking a "stove plate and pipe in your rooms which you wish to warm and let[ting] the pipe go round and round until it has distributed the heat." See also Siegfried Gideon, *Mechanization Takes Command* (New York: Norton, 1969), pp. 528–30 (stoves), 659–67 (baths), 684–86, 692 (bathrooms). Boydston, in "Home and Work," pp. 195–96, argues that we should be careful in celebrating "labor-saving" improvements in housing; women at the time often expressed skepticism at inventions that could increase their maintenance responsibilities or introduce new hazards. While such caution is well taken, I am more inclined to accept the claims that plumbing, heating, and cooking utilities made housework less arduous. For respectable women's domestic responsibilities, see Boydston, "Home and Work," chap. 5; Dudden, *Serving Women*, pp. 127–47; Nancy Cott, *Bonds of Womanhood* (New Haven: Yale University Press, 1977), pp. 19–100.

8. Robert Greenhalg Albion, *The Rise of New York Port, 1815–1860* (1939; Boston: Northeastern University Press, 1984), pp. 245–51; Edward Pessen, *Riches, Class, and Power before the Civil War* (Lexington, Mass.: D. C. Heath, 1973), pp. 56, 59, 64, 100–101, 211–14; Frederick Cople Jaher, *The Urban Establishment: Upper Strata in Boston, New York, Charleston, Chicago, and Los Angeles* (Urbana: University of Illinois Press, 1982), pp. 180–81, 205–6. On attitudes toward reciprocity in antebellum marriage, see Carl Degler, *At Odds: Women and the Family in America from the Revolution to the Present* (New York: Oxford University Press, 1980), pp. 26–40.

9. On Mrs. Pintard's efforts to negotiate with her husband's employers, see *Letters of John Pintard*, 2:4–6 (Feb. 17, 1821). The intensity with which Pintard felt his own "shame" was clearly expressed in his response to his son-in-law's financial difficulties following the 1829 recession: 4:39–40, 45–46, 63–64. In 1790 the Pintards had owned two slaves.

10. Dudden, *Serving Women*, pp. 12–43; Carol Lasser, "The World's Dread Laugh: Singlehood and Service in Nineteenth-Century Boston," in Herbert Gutman and Donald Bell, eds., *The New England Working Class and the New Labor History* (Urbana: University of Illinois Press, 1979), pp. 74–75.

11. Jan Lewis, "The Republican Wife: Virtue and Seduction in the Early Republic," *WMQ*, 3d ser., 44 (1987): 689–721; Grant Thorburn, *Forty Years' Residence in America* (Boston: Russell, Odiorne & Metcalf, 1834), p. 211; *CA*, Apr. 20, 1801.

12. For typical travelers' comments, see Bayard Still, *Mirror for Gotham: New York as Seen by Contemporaries from Dutch Days to the Present* (New York: New

York University Press, 1956), pp. 111, 112. Stansell, *City of Women*, pp. 20–30, points to contradictory tendencies in "republican" attitudes toward women and stresses the prevailing mysogyny evident in New York men's attitudes toward women's sexuality at the end of the eighteenth century. See also Lewis, "Republican Wife," pp. 713, 715–16, 720.

13. Linda Kerber, *Women of the Republic: Intellect and Ideology in Revolutionary America* (Chapel Hill: University of North Carolina Press, 1980), pp. 189–231, 269–88; Mary Beth Norton, *Liberty's Daughters: The Revolutionary Experience of American Women, 1750–1800* (Boston: Little, Brown, 1980), pp. 269–88. I have found Hazel Carby, "Uplifting as They Write: The Emergence of the Afro-American Woman Novelist" (Ph.D. diss., University of Birmingham, 1984), pp. 4–77, helpful in thinking about the construction of new gender prescriptions in relation to class hierarchies. Carby analyzes the interdependent figures of planter women's "true womanhood" and female slave "depravity." See Boydston, "Home and Work," pp. 101–24, for attitudes revealed in discourse on "economy" during the early national period.

14. Arson incident in Elizabeth Bleecker Diary, NYPL, Jan. 25, 1805: "Our black girl attempted to set fire to our house by placing a brand of fire in the garret in the eves of the house . . . she claimed that she had done [it] but could give no reason." Cf. Edward Probyn Memorandum Book, NYHS, July 9, 1819: "Black girl expected for setting house on fire." On working conditions, see Dudden, *Serving Women*, pp. 44–103, 193–235; Stansell, *City of Women*, pp. 155–68. See also Richard B. Stott, *Workers in the Metropolis: Class, Ethnicity, and Youth in Antebellum New York City* (Ithaca: Cornell University Press, 1990), pp. 61–63, 106–7.

15. *Letters of John Pintard*, 1:137 (July 29, 1818), 181 (Apr. 8, 1819), 150–51 (Oct. 26, 1818), 148 (Oct. 12, 1818), 169 (Mar. 15, 1819), 184 (Apr. 23, 1819). In Pintard's mind, servants did not relieve a wife of her responsibility for household labor; rather they placed her in a management position. Thus he sympathized with his daughter, who was having "trials and difficulties with bad servants, the most embittering of all domestic evils. . . . A husband can escape from them, but the Wife, if a housekeeper herself, is chained down to the constant scene of reiterated trouble & uneasiness, that keeps her in a continual fret & renders [her] unhappy & unpleasant to all about her": 2:80 (Aug. 29, 1821). For examples of Elizabeth and Louisa Pintard's housework—particularly the annual spring house cleaning—see 1:9, 129, 188, 196, 300, 315–16; 2:43, 46–47, 50–51, 315, 350.

16. Ibid., 1:182 (Apr. 12, 1819). On the recruitment of servants, see Carol Lasser, "Domestic Service in New England" (Ph.D. diss., Harvard University, 1981), pp. 123–67.

17. Dudden, *Serving Women*, pp. 34, 63–65; Robert Ernst, *Immigrant Life in New York City, 1825–1863* (New York: King's Crown Press, 1949), p. 67. For a powerful example of a black servant's ability to maintain personal autonomy in a New York City white household, see the Harriet Jacobs [Linda Brent] letters in Dorothy Sterling, ed., *We Are Your Sisters: Black Women in the Nineteenth Century* (New York: Norton, 1984), pp. 73–79.

18. *Letters of John Pintard*, 1:182 (Apr. [12], 1819), 215 (Aug. 28, 1819), 125 (June 1, 1818). Hannah cared for her one-year-old child at the Pintard house and then returned to New Brunswick, N.J., according to Pintard, "to exchange her brawling brat for as troublesome a boy about 3 years old." Two months later she left with her husband, who was to be emancipated; her replacement, Jane, had "left her husband in the country who came to town in quest of her, & found her out by means of her sister." These women or their parents may have been former slaves of the Bayard family in New Jersey. Pintard refused to pay Hannah wages,

"as Mr. Bayard desired me to stop them to discharge some debts wh she had left unpaid in Princeton. I discharged her for her conduct and her ingratitude": 1:184, 188, 204, 298.

19. Ernst, *Immigrant Life*, pp. 65–68; and for the 1855 ethnic distribution of domestic workers (92% of whom were foreign-born), 215; Dudden, *Serving Women*, pp. 63–64; see also the observations of Karl Bernhart in Still, *Mirror for Gotham*, p. 111. Dudden suggests that when it became increasingly difficult for New York employers to maintain a mixed staff in the mid–nineteenth century, white women, particularly Irish women, displaced blacks from domestic service. Although Afro-Americans had dropped to 5% of the city's population in 1840 and to less than 2% by 1855, the fears and pressures of job competition exacerbated the hostility of the Irish toward them. For Pintard's view of servants as "insect vexations," see *Letters of John Pintard*, 3:271.

20. Society for the Encouragement of Faithful Domestic Servants, annual reports, 1826–1830, NYHS. Pintard was vice-president of the society; see *Letters of John Pintard*, 2:240, 254, 259–60, 271; 3:23–24, 27.

21. *New-York Mirror*, March 25, 1826.

22. On the classificatory language of moral reform, see chap. 5 below.

23. Stott, *Workers in the Metropolis*, p. 61; *New York State Census* (New York, 1855).

24. For travelers' comments on boarding couples, see, e.g., John M. Duncan, *Travels through Part of the United States and Canada, 1818–1819* (Glasgow, 1923), 2:375–6; Francis Grund, *The Americans in Their Moral, Social, and Political Relations* (London, 1837), 1:238; and Still, *Mirror for Gotham*, pp. 90–91. Frances Trollope describes young Philadelphia boarding couples in *Domestic Manners in America* (1832; New York: Vintage, 1960), pp. 282–85. The Pintards made an exception for the summer boarding of Mrs. Pintard and Louisa, but Pintard complained to Eliza of the "general promiscuous boarding houses with confined apartments & crowded inmates, who might or might not be agreeable to your very particular Mother": *Letters of John Pintard*, 1:80 (Sept. 28, 1817). For Pintard's dismay that his mother-in-law would have to board rather than live with family members, see ibid., pp. 136, 182–83. For Thorburn's calculus, see *Forty Years' Residence*, p. 211.

25. John Griscom, "Annual Report of the City Inspector," BAA Documents 9, no. 59 (1842): 190. For changes in household utilities after 1840, see Lockwood, *Bricks and Brownstones*, pp. 183–89; Elizabeth Cromley, *Alone Together: A History of New York's Early Apartments* (Ithaca: Cornell University Press, 1990), pp. 27, 117. Utilities—gas, water, and sewerage—became increasingly important in the organization of new respectable neighborhoods. On the geography of water, gas, and sewer lines in relation to elite residential districts before 1860, see Eugene P. Moehring, *Public Works and the Pattern of Urban Real Estate Growth, 1835–1894* (New York: Arno Press, 1981), pp. 94, 98, 100–104.

26. Isaac Holmes, *An Account of America Derived from Actual Observations during a Residence of Four Years in That Republic* (London, 1823), p. 128. The Italian visitor Salvatore Abbate e Migliore found in 1845 that "second rank society" had "two or three servant girls, boarding houses three to six," at $4 to $6 a month: Still, *Mirror for Gotham*, p. 91. On artisan housekeeping, see Sean Wilentz, *Chants Democratic: New York City and the Rise of the American Working Class* (New York: Oxford University Press, 1984), pp. 51–52; Howard Rock, *Artisans of the New Republic* (New York: New York University Press, 1979), pp. 306–8.

27. *Letters of John Pintard*, 3:63, 4:8 (Jan. 28, 1832), noting that "were it not for the Pennsylvania anthracite coal mines, this city wd be in a most awful condition.

The consumption of Fuel with every economy is immense. . . ." Stott, *Workers in the Metropolis*, pp. 168–74, points out that working-class housing conditions were far better in New York City than in most immigrants' native lands; my own emphasis is on the decline of domestic working conditions in relation to those of an earlier generation and of other households in the city.

28. Boydston, "To Earn Her Daily Bread," pp. 19–22.

29. John commons et al., *Documentary History of American Industrial Society* (Cleveland: Arthur H. Clark, 1910), p. 315; Rock, *Artisans of the New Republic*, pp. 253–54.

30. National Trades Union, "Report of the Committee on Female Labor," in Commons, *Documentary History*, 6:281, 282; cf. Stansell, *City of Women*, pp. 137–41. It is noteworthy that the committee called upon "benevolent women" to support striking needleworkers without reflecting on the extent to which those benevolent women, as the employers of domestics, had a vested interest in reduced female wage rates.

31. Stansell, *City of Women*, pp. 106–20.

32. For the shifting literary construction of ideal places, see Raymond Williams, *The Country and the City* (New York: Oxford University Press, 1973). I find Nina Baym, *Woman's Fiction: A Guide to Novels by and about Women in America, 1820–1870* (Ithaca: Cornell University Press, 1978), a particularly useful reading of the literature of domesticity. See also Ann Douglas, *The Feminization of American Culture* (New York: Knopf, 1977), and Karen Halttunen, *Confidence Men and Painted Ladies: A Study of Middle-Class Culture in America, 1830–1870* (New Haven: Yale University Press, 1982).

33. See chap. 2 above. Pintard recalled New York City's "boisterous" New Year's visiting in the 1760s, with a "dram at every house." To "keep up acquaintance with kindred branches," children "were universally sent to visit the family relations": *Letters of John Pintard*, 2:382 (Dec. 27, 1827). Paul Gilje describes colonial New Yorkers' tolerance of plebeian "frolics" on New Year's: *The Road to Mobocracy: Popular Disorder in New York City, 1763–1834* (Chapel Hill: University of North Carolina Press, 1987), pp. 21, 22, 252. For regulation of sexual mores, see John D'Emilio and Estelle Freeman, *Intimate Matters: A History of Sexuality in America* (New York: Harper & Row, 1988), pp. 30–32, 34–38.

34. Esther Singleton, *Social New York under the Georges, 1714–1776* (New York: Ira Friedman, 1902). Although historians have generally dismissed Joseph A. Scoville [Walter Barrett], *The Old Merchants of New York City*, 5 vols. (New York, 1885), its anecdotes offer glimpses into bourgeois manners in the late eighteenth and early nineteenth centuries.

35. "Tea Party," *New-York Mirror*, Apr. 17, 1824. On front and back parlors, see Lockwood, *Bricks and Brownstones*, pp. 14–25, and "The Bond Street Area," *NYHSQ* 16 (1972): 378–87. For parlor rituals, see Halttunen, *Confidence Men and Painted Ladies*, pp. 92–123. Trollope, *Domestic Manners*, pp. 336–38, was delighted by the gentility of prominent New York houses after "sojourning among an 'I'm-as-good-as-you population' " in the provinces.

36. James Fenimore Cooper, *Home as Found* (1838; New York: Capricorn, 1964), p. 78. Trollope particularly disliked the custom of men's and women's separate entertainment; see *Domestic Manners*, pp. 298–99, 339.

37. *Letters of John Pintard*, 1:143–44 (Sept. 14, 1818). Bender analyzes Clinton's and Pintard's activities as examples of "patrician culture": *New York Intellect*, pp. 50–58.

38. Charles Lockwood, *Manhattan Moves Uptown* (Boston: Houghton Mifflin, 1976), pp. 31, 96, 215–25; Rev. Ward Stafford, *New Missionary Field: A Report to the Female Missionary Society* (New York, 1817), pp. 6–7.

39. Carroll Smith Rosenberg, *Religion and the Rise of the American City: The New York City Mission Movement, 1812–1870* (Ithaca: Cornell University Press, 1971), pp. 120–24; Mary Ryan, *Cradle of the Middle Class: The Family in Oneida County, New York, 1790–1865* (New York: Cambridge University Press, 1981), pp. 60–98; Cott, *Bonds of Womanhood*, pp. 126–59; Nancy A. Hewitt, *Women's Activism and Social Change: Rochester, New York, 1822–1872* (Ithaca: Cornell University Press, 1985), pp. 24–37. On evangelicalism and work discipline, see Paul Johnson, *A Shopkeeper's Millennium: Society and Revivals in Rochester, New York, 1815–1837* (New York: Hill & Wang, 1978), pp. 79–115. Trollope, *Domestic Manners*, pp. 343–45, reported on a Sunday excursion to a Hoboken park:

> Many thousands of people were scattered through the grounds; of these we ascertained, by repeatedly counting, that nineteen-twentieths were men. The ladies were at church. . . . It is impossible not to feel, after passing one Sunday in the churches and chapels of New York, and the next in the gardens of Hoboken, that the thousands of well-dressed men you see enjoying themselves at the latter, have made over the thousands of well-dressed women you saw exhibited at the former, into the hands of the priests, at least, for the day. The American people arrogate to themselves a character of superior morality and religion, but this division of their hours of leisure does not give a favourable idea of either.

40. Edward Probyn Memorandum Book, NYHS, e.g., Feb. 4 and Feb. 5, 1812 (church visits); Jan. 4 (Fourth Ward committee for visiting the poor) and Feb. 3, 1814; Jan. 5 and Feb. 2, 1815 (twenty people to tea); *The Diary of Michael Floy, Jr.: Bowery Village, 1833–1837*, ed. Richard A. E. Brooks (New Haven: Yale University Press, 1941), passim. Perceptions of legitimate continuities between church and home were demonstrated in a different way in 1811 when a "Mrs. Touchstone" vigorously answered a letter in the *Independent Mechanic* denouncing women who nursed their babies in church. See Howard Rock, ed., "A Woman's Place in Jeffersonian New York: The View from the *Independent Mechanic*," *New York History* 83 (1982): 437–44.

41. *Letters of John Pintard*, 3:51 (Dec. 16, 1828). To help spread the temperance word, the *New-York Mirror*, Jan. 1, 1830, reported on New Year's open houses: "The ladies were holding their annual levee, receiving and exchanging the compliments of the season with their male visitors and treating them to coffee instead of wine and punch."

42. Stansell, *City of Women*, pp. 41–62, gives a vivid portrait of antebellum tenant neighborhood life. See also Boydston, "To Earn Her Daily Bread"; and Carol Groneman, " 'She Earns as a Child; She Pays as a Man': Women Workers in a Mid-Nineteenth-Century New York Community," in Milton Cantor and Bruce Laurie, eds., *Class, Sex, and the Woman Worker* (Westport, Conn.: Greenwood, 1977), pp. 83–100.

43. *Diary of Michael Floy*, p. 81 (Apr. 28, 1834).

44. Thomas Chamberlain Diary, May 26, 1835, NYPL. Cf. James Boardman's description, quoted in Still, *Mirror for Gotham*, p. 112:

> The boarding houses of those numerous classes, the smaller shopkeepers and merchants' clerks, are in general miserably furnished. . . . It is by no means uncommon to see four, or even five or six beds in the same room, and these are of the meanest description without furniture even in the depth of winter: a chest of drawers is, indeed, a rara avis; each boarder making a general de-

pository of his trunk or portmanteau, as poor Jack does of his chest in the forecastle of a ship.

45. Holmes, *Account of America*, p. 128.

46. See, e.g., *MCC, 1784–1831*, 3:101 (Aug. 5, 1802), 4:71 (Aug. 26, 1805). On the male youth in the city, see Diane Lindstrom, "The Economy of Antebellum New York City" (paper presented to the Social Science Research Council, New York, November 1983, table 7, p. 24). On journeymen's popular culture, see Wilentz, *Chants Democratic*, pp. 52–56; on hours, Rock, *Artisans of the New Republic*, pp. 250–52.

47. *MCC, 1784–1831*, 4:389 (Mar. 30, 1807); 7:729 (Apr. 14, 1814); see also 4:327, 396; 7:669; and for non-Sunday complaints, 4:371; 7:415, 677. Gilje, *Road to Mobocracy*, pp. 207–20, identifies Sunday harassment of evangelical churchgoers as "a clash between middle class and plebeian cultures" or between "evangelicals and traditionalists."

48. "Report of the Committee for Suppressing Immorality," *MCC, 1784–1831*, 7:71–76 (Mar. 18, 1812); proposal to the Legislature, 7:82–84. For identification of the Presbyterian lawyer Joseph Hedden (Ward 6), the Dutch Reformed sailmaker Peter Wendover (Ward 8), and the tanner Richard Cunningham (Ward 4) and their property holdings in 1808 and 1815, see Edmund Willis, "Social Origins and Political Leadership in New York City from the Revolution to 1815" (Ph.D. diss., University of California, Berkeley, 1968), pp. 338, 342, 356. Gilje, *Road to Mobocracy*, discusses "street and tavern riots," pp. 239–46.

49. On licensing, see "Report of the Joint Select Committee on the Subject of the Reorganization of the Police Department," BA Documents 3:564–65; and on licenses by ward, 592–93. See also *New-York Mirror*, Jan. 10, 1829.

50. Historians have richly documented the rituals of male working-class sociability in the nineteenth century, but we still have a very limited understanding of how the institutions of popular culture intersected with home life. See, e.g., Bruce Laurie, "Nothing on Compulsion: Life Styles of Philadelphia Artisans, 1820–1850," *Labor History* 15 (1974): 366–77, and *Working People of Philadelphia, 1800–1850* (Philadelphia: Temple University Press, 1980); Roy Rosenzweig, *Eight Hours for What We Will* (New York: Cambridge University Press, 1984), chap. 2; Wilentz, *Chants Democratic*, pp. 53–59, 257–66; and Elliott J. Gorn, *The Manly Art: Bare-Knuckle Prize Fighting in America* (Ithaca: Cornell University Press, 1986). Paul Groth, "Forbidden Housing: The Evolution and Exclusion of Hotels, Boarding Houses, Rooming Houses, and Lodging Houses in American Cities, 1880–1930" (Ph.D. diss., University of California, Berkeley, 1983), does explore the housing side of casual laborers' experience of the city.

51. See Stansell, *City of Women*, pp. 63–75, 170–92; and Timothy J. Gilfoyle, "City of Eros: New York City, Prostitution, and the Commercialization of Sex, 1790–1920" (Ph.D. diss., Columbia University, 1987), chap. 3, on the emergence of "parlor houses"; Carroll Smith Rosenberg, "Beauty, the Beast, and the Militant Woman: A Case Study in Sex Roles and Social Stress in Jacksonian America," in *Disorderly Conduct: Visions of Gender in Victorian America* (New York: Oxford University Press, 1985), pp. 109–28.

52. Stott, *Workers in the Metropolis*, pp. 205–7, discusses the social geography of boardinghouses in the 1850s, and notes their concentration below Canal Street (table 7.1).

53. *New-York Mirror*, Jan. 15, 1832. See also, Peter Buckley, "To The Opera House: Culture and Society in New York City, 1820–1860" (Ph.D. diss., State University of New York, Stony Brook, 1984), chap. 3. Also expressive of the declining social respectability of boardinghouses in the period 1830–1860 is Thomas Gunn's

satire, *Physiology of New York Boarding Houses* (New York, 1857).

54. *New-York Mirror,* Jan. 15, 1832; June 11, 1836. Hotels, of course, have a much longer history of accommodating transients; see, e.g., Henry Fearon's descriptions in *Sketches of America: A Narrative of a Journey of 5,000 Miles* (London, 1818), pp. 22, 115. For residential hotels, see also Cromley, *Alone Together,* chap. 1. Another response to the problematic position of boarding or hotel-residing gentlemen in the structures of respectable socializing was the formation of men's clubs. See *Diary of Philip Hone,* ed. Allan Nevins (New York: Dodd, Mead, 1927), p. 263 (May 27, 1837), on the formation of the Union Club as an alternative for "bachelors" who dined "en garçon."

55. Thornstein Veblen, *Theory of the Leisure Class* (1899), in *The Portable Veblen,* ed. Max Lerner (New York: Viking, 1948), p. 110.

56. Joseph Kett, "The Stages of Life, 1790–1840," in Michael Gordan, *The American Family in Socio-Historical Perspective,* 3d ed. (New York: St. Martin's, 1983), pp. 229–54, esp. 244–45; Degler, *At Odds,* pp. 66–85.

57. Halttunen, *Confidence Men and Painted Ladies,* pp. 9–20, 92–123.

58. *New-York Mirror,* Dec. 27, 1823.

59. Ibid., Dec. 29, 1832. See also, Edward Pessen, "Philip Hone's Set: The Social World of the New York City Elite in the Age of Egalitarianism," *NYHSQ* 56 (1972): 285–300; Jaher, *Urban Establishment,* pp. 246–50.

60. *Diary of Philip Hone,* p. 235. For New Year's rowdiness in the late 1820s, see Gilje, *Road to Mobocracy,* pp. 254–60.

61. On the decline in parental control, see Degler, *At Odds,* pp. 9–14; and Daniel Scott Smith, "Parental Powers and Marriage: An Analysis of Historical Trends in Hingham, Massachusetts," *Journal of Marriage and the Family* 35 (1973): 419–28. In stressing the antebellum decline in parental control of courtship and the rise of an ideology of companionate marriage, historians have tended to overlook the construction of circles of socializing that indirectly regulated the marriage market. For an exploration of the relation of feminism to the changing ideology of marriage in the mid–nineteenth century, see William Leach, *True Love and Perfect Union* (New York: Basic Books, 1980), pp. 38–129.

62. *Diary of Michael Floy;* see, e.g., pp. 126, 203, 205, 206, 226, 228, 230, 234, 236, 238–40, 242–43; and p. 3 (Oct. 10, 1833) for "women's business."

63. Jane Mount v. James Bogert, *New-York City Hall Recorder* 3, no. 12 (December 1818): 193–202.

64. *Letters of John Pintard,* 1:164–66 (Jan. 21, 1819), 288 (Apr. 14, 1820), 178 (Mar. 27, 1819), 173–74 (Mar. 15, 1819).

65. For Louisa's marriage and arrangements for the house, see ibid., 2:147, 195–96, 219, 221–25, 227, 231–32; 4:32. For Elizabeth Brasher Pintard's dissatisfactions, see 3:37 (Oct. 13, 1828), 65 (Feb. 27, 1829), and 134. For another prominent New Yorker's anxieties over housekeeping expenses with a $2,500 annual income, see *Diary of George Templeton Strong,* ed. Allan Nevins and Milton Halsey Thomas (New York: Macmillan, 1952), 1:324–25.

66. *New-York Mirror,* Jan. 3, 1824.

67. Ibid., Aug. 6, 1826.

68. The tradesman's letter is reprinted in Rock, ed., "A Woman's Place," pp. 456–58. Cf. "Women's ostentation is the ruin of half the tradesmen," *Weekly Messenger,* Nov. 8, 1817; see also Jan. 17, 1818; Dec. 12, 1817. The *Messenger's* publisher, Alexander Ming, had been a leader of Painite free-thinking circles in the early nineteenth-century, and went on to become a Working Men's candidate for the state legislature in 1829: Wilentz, *Chants Democratic,* pp. 184, 196, 198, 200, 201. Although the *Messenger* (1817–1820) was oriented to a slightly less self-

conscious middling audience than the later *Mirror*, it still disseminated a new vocabulary of domesticity, in part through the frequent reprinting of English articles.
In keeping with Ming's political sympathies, the *Messenger*, like the *Mirror*, advocated female education (e.g., Jan. 10, 1818), even as its stories expressed concern
over whether "an expensive education" would "unfit [daughters] for life" (Nov. 8,
1817). Joining the debate over "unnecessary ceremonies in our republican institutions," Ming reprinted on Jan. 3, 1816, a controversy in the *National Register* over
whether Mrs. Monroe would follow the precedent of other presidents' wives and
return visits; cf. Apr. 25, 1818, on Mrs. Monroe's "levee."

69. For New York women's defense of their virtue, see *New-York Mirror*, July
16, 1825, and Feb. 4, 1826; on choosing a good husband, Aug. 27, 1825; and on
saving the fruit of the husband's labor, Jan. 1, 1824. See also May 1, 1824, and July
2, 1825. A *Mirror* article of Aug. 14, 1824, typically recommended "order in the
arrangement of our employments and industry in their performance," with an "ex-
actness in distribution of [the wife's] time" to allow for a program of self-
improvement. These same recommendations form the core of two of the most
widely consulted manuals on housekeeping, Lydia Child's *American Frugal Housewife* (1836) and Catharine Beecher's *Treatise on Domestic Economy* (1841). My
reading of the *Mirror*'s articles and stories supports Nina Baym's argument that
woman's fiction in this period "represented a protest against long-entrenched triv-
ializing and contemptuous views of women": *Woman's Fiction*, pp. 22–50.

70. *New-York Mirror*, Dec. 12, 1819.

71. Stansell, *City of Women*, pp. 77–83.

72. James Fenimore Cooper, *Notions of the Americans* (Philadelphia, 1833), pp.
129–30; cf. James Hardie's observation in his *Census of New York Housing in 1824*
(New York, 1825), p. 3, that readers could calculate two households per house. For
Floy's principled rejection of luxury, see *Diary*, p. 5 (Oct. 16, 1833). For a discus-
sion of "consumption" in relation to new class formations, see Stuart M. Blumin,
"The Hypothesis of Middle-Class Formation in Nineteenth-Century America: A
Critique and Some Proposals," *American Historical Review* 90 (1985): 318–37.

73. *New-York Mirror*, Jan. 22 and June 4, 1825; Nov. 3, 1832. The *Mirror* campaigned especially hard for the improvement of the Battery, including the addition
of park benches, which the Common Council resisted for fear of attracting vagrants; see, e.g., articles on Mar. 5, May 23, June 18 and 15, July 2 and 23, 1825;
and victory declared, Apr. 8, 1826. On keeping to the right, particularly on Broadway, June 25, 1825. See also Daniel Bluestone, "From Promenade to Park: The
Gregarious Origins of Brooklyn's Park Movement," *American Quarterly* 39 (1987):
529–50.

74. Stansell, *City of Women*, pp. 34–36, 68–75; Carroll Smith-Rosenberg,
"Beauty, the Beast, and the Militant Woman"; Hewitt, *Women's Activism and Social Change*, pp. 38–68. The "ritual" of home visiting by members of committees
and benevolent societies was followed by meetings that heard and decided on the
merits of individual cases. The *Weekly Messenger*, Dec. 5 and 27, 1817, reprinted
the Fourth Annual Report of the Association for the Relief of Respectable Aged
Indigent Females.

75. Floy (*Diary*, e.g., pp. 205, 206, 212–13, 215–16, 219–20) organized a benevolent society at Bowery Street Church to make visits to the "deserving" poor in the
neighborhood and then negotiated with almshouse commissioners on behalf of particular recipients, especially for fuel. On Feb. 9, 1836, Floy visited

the Police office to see that all my widows were supplied with wood. . . . A
poor black man who had his ticket for potatoes was constantly shoved off and

the most degraded Irishman supplied. I spoke rather sharp and asked the man that supplied him if he was not ashamed of himself to serve a poor aged man thus, altho black. He looked somewhat sheepish, saying, "well let him wait until his betters are served." The black man after many fruitless efforts went away with nothing. I found out he was a member of the Methodist Church; that his wife and daughter were sick. I promised to visit him.

One wonders what the man's fate would have been had he not been a Methodist.

76. Veblen, *Theory of the Leisure Class*, p. 144.

77. Asa Green, *A Glance at New York* (New York, 1837), p. 93; *Morning Courier*, Jan. 30, 1847.

5. Public, Private, and Common: The Regulation of Streets and Neighborhoods

1. *New-York Mirror*, Apr. 29, 1826.

2. Montgomerie's charter is in *A Compilation of Laws of the State of New York Relating to the City of New York*, comp. Henry E. Davies (New York, 1855), p. 163. Hendrik Hartog, *Public Property and Private Power: The Corporation of the City of New York in American Law, 1730–1870* (Chapel Hill: University of North Carolina Press, 1983), pp. 13–43, stresses that the business of the corporation was managing its own properties.

3. George Ashton Black, *History of Municipal Ownership of Manhattan Island . . . to 1844* (New York: Columbia University Press, 1897); Hartog, *Public Property and Private Power*, pp. 44–68.

4. Black, *Municipal Ownership*, pp. 18–19, 26; Raymond Mohl, *Poverty in New York, 1783–1825* (New York: Oxford University Press, 1971), pp. 41–51; and David M. Schneider, *The History of Public Welfare in New York State, 1609–1866* (Chicago: University of Chicago Press, 1938), pp. 45–51; *MCC*, *1675–1776*, 5:77–81, 196–97; *Iconography*, 4:664–65.

5. Hartog, *Public Property and Private Power*, pp. 84–100, quote on p. 99; Gary Nash, *The Urban Crucible: Social Change, Political Consciousness, and the Origins of the American Revolution* (Cambridge: Harvard University Press, 1979), pp. 362–74; Edward Countryman, *A People in Revolution: The American Revolution and Political Society in New York, 1760–1790* (Baltimore: Johns Hopkins University Press, 1981), pp. 161–90.

6. *MCC*, *1784–1831*, passim. On the city's licensed trades, see Howard Rock, *Artisans of the New Republic* (New York: New York University Press, 1979), pp. 205–29, and Graham Hodges, *New York City Cartmen* (New York: New York University Press, 1986), pp. 108–28. See Hartog, *Public Property and Private Power*, pp. 133–39, on the issue of sovereignty in relation to the municipal corporation's shift to "governmental" identity.

7. For eighteenth-century political patronage and factions, see Hodges, *New York City Cartmen*, pp. 31–40, 42–46; Nash, *Urban Crucible*, pp. 140–48, 366–68. For New York politics in the 1790s, see Alfred F. Young, *The Democratic Republicans of New York: The Origins, 1763–1797* (Chapel Hill: University of North Carolina Press, 1967), pp. 84–86, 521–23, 538 (noting that suffrage became a lively issue starting in 1797), 568–72. For a discussion of Federalists' and Jeffersonians' rhetorical and ideological differences in the 1790s, see Joyce Appleby, *Capitalism and a New Social Order: The Republican Vision of the 1790s* (New York: New York University Press, 1984), pp. 55–73. For an overview of New York political parties, leaders, and factions, see Jabez Hammond, *The History of Political Parties of the*

State of New York from the Ratification of the Federal Constitution to December 1840, 2 vols. (Albany, Van Benthuysen, 1842), vol. 1. For a valuable interpretation of the powers of government and particularly of the Legislature's sovereignty in this period, see L. Ray Gunn, *The Decline of Authority: Public Economic Policy and Political Development in New York State, 1800–1860* (Ithaca: Cornell University Press, 1988), pp. 64–74.

8. Hodges, *New York City Cartmen,* pp. 82–83, 107, 112–13; Hartog, *Public Property and Private Power,* pp. 135–36.

9. *MCC, 1776–1831,* 3:61–62, 73–85 (Ward 4), 60–61, 72 (Ward 5).

10. *MCC, 1776–1831,* 3:65–70.

11. Merrill D. Peterson, *Democracy, Liberty, and Property: The State Constitutional Conventions of the 1820s* (Indianapolis: Bobbs-Merrill, 1966), p. 194. Dixon Ryan Fox, *The Decline of Aristocracy in the Politics of New York, 1801–1840* (New York: Columbia University Press, 1919), remains a classic, if flawed, account of New York politics in this period.

12. Peterson, *Democracy, Liberty, and Property,* pp. 205–6.

13. The 1821 constitution is reprinted in *Revised Statutes of New York* (Albany, 1836), 2:39.

14. Peterson, *Democracy, Liberty, and Property,* pp. 230, 226. For context see Dixon Ryan Fox, "The Negro Vote in Old New York," *Political Science Quarterly* 37 (1917), 252–75; Leon F. Litwack, *North of Slavery: The Negro in the Free States, 1790–1860* (Chicago: University of Chicago Press, 1961), pp. 77–78, 82–83 on New York, and 64–112 for a discussion of the disenfranchisement of Afro-Americans in other northern states. Leonard Curry, *The Free Black in Urban America, 1800–1850* (Chicago: University of Chicago Press, 1981), pp. 217–18, corrects Fox's interpretation of Federalist and Whig patronage of black voters and finds that only 16 Afro-Americans were qualified to vote in New York City in 1825, 68 in 1835. For the defeat of New York's 1846 constitutional amendment abolishing the property qualification for Afro-Americans, see Curry, pp. 222–23.

15. Amendment 2, ratified Nov. 6–8, 1826, in *Revised Statutes* (1836), 2:50; new city charter in Davies, *Compilation of Laws,* p. 50.

16. Edward D. Durand, *The Finances of New York* (New York: Macmillan, 1899), pp. 16–17.

17. Peterson, *Democracy, Liberty, and Property,* p. 211.

18. On the Workingmen's movement, see Sean Wilentz, *Chants Democratic: New York City and the Rise of the American Working Class* (New York: Oxford University Press, 1984), pp. 172–216. On the evolution of New York City politics and patronage, see Amy Bridges, *City in the Republic: Antebellum New York and the Origins of Machine Politics* (New York: Cambridge University Press, 1987), pp. 20–27, 70–78.

19. Hartog, *Public Property and Private Power,* pp. 33–43.

20. *MCC, 1784–1831,* 4:25–26 (July 1, 1805). For examples of unelaborated approval of street improvements, see ibid., 3:35, 50, 118 (1801); 4:47 (1805), 201 (1806); 7:528 (1813), 730, 740 (1814); 8:785 (1818). Cf. Sam Bass Warner, *The Urban Wilderness* (New York: Harper & Row, 1971), pp. 55–84.

21. *Laws of New York, 36th Session* (Albany, 1813), chap. 136, secs. 177–92. After the aldermen mandated the opening or widening of a street, street commissioners were appointed by district supreme courts to award damages for the taking of land and to apportion the costs among adjoining proprietors, including those within a prescribed "vicinity" of the improvement, who, unlike abutting proprietors, could not offset the assessments with awards for land taken for streets. See

Stephen Diamond, "The Death and Transfiguration of Benefit Taxation: Special Assessments in Nineteenth-Century America," *Journal of Legal Studies* 2 (1983): 201–40 (on New York City in this period, 206–14); and Hartog, *Public Property and Private Power*, pp. 167–75, who notes (pp. 171–73) that the courts thwarted landowners' efforts to cash in on the 1807 plan by retaining the fee on land that was intended for streets and for which the city would award damages.

22. Petitions and remonstrances were referred to a street committee, which then made a recommendation. Although the aldermen rejected the argument that improvements could be undertaken only upon proprietors' petition as early as 1807, the absence of such petitions in some instances sufficed to block action. See *MCC, 1784–1831*, 4:667 (Dec. 14, 1807) and 18:11–12 (Apr. 20, 1829), in which a committee argued that there was no precedent for exercising the power of eminent domain or imposing assessments for "improving" a block in Five Points without adjoining proprietors' support. Proprietors who opposed the regulation of 17th Street in 1831 invoked the principle of "no taxation without representation" and complained that "a number of those whose names are attached to the objectionable petition are not responsible for the payment of a single cent of the expenses which they seem willing to impose on others": petition, Sept. 30, 1831, Common Council Documents, "Streets," box 2761, Municipal Archives, City of New York. By the 1830s, aldermen had introduced a distinction between improvements that were "local" in character, and therefore required the support of adjoining proprietors, and those that served "the public at large." See, e.g., the Street Committee's rejection of a proposal to close Art Street: BA Documents 2, no. 5 (Aug. 22, 1835): 24–26. Street committees, however, were far from consistent in recognizing this distinction. See also Eugene P. Moehring, *Public Works and the Pattern of Urban Real Estate Growth* (New York: Arno Press, 1981), pp. 53–76.

23. Astor v. Hoyt, 10 New York Common Law Reports 965 (1830).

24. Thomas Gannett, "A History of Pleasure Gardens in New York City, 1700–1865" (Ph.D. diss., New York University, 1978), pp. 336–39; on Lafayette Place, *New-York Mirror*, Nov. 3, 1832; Charles Lockwood, *Bricks and Brownstones: The New York Row House, 1783–1929* (New York: McGraw-Hill, 1972), pp. 78–81.

25. *MCC, 1784–1831*, 11:24 (Mar. 13, 1820).

26. BA Documents 2, no. 128 (Apr. 26, 1836): 667; cf. BAA Documents 2, no. 23 (Dec. 30, 1833): 149–53, esp. 151.

27. The comptroller was proposing to purchase land adjoining Government House: *MCC, 1784–1831*, 7:556 (Sept. 6, 1813).

28. Durand, *Finances of New York*, pp. 16–17. In supporting the city's $20,000 investment in filling and landscaping Tompkins Square, aldermen noted that "considering the depressed state of property in this part of the city, your committee deem it a matter of policy to afford it every opportunity of improvement." The city would be "reimbursed by rising taxes" from the anticipated construction of houses costing from $6,000 to $10,000 on lots that two years earlier "would not sell for $200": BA Documents 2, no. 7 (June 9, 1834): 54–55. Aldermen also continued to view improvements in the light of the municipal corporation's own interests as a proprietor. Thus in endorsing a proposal to open a public square from 23d to 28th streets at Fifth Avenue, on the site of the House of Refuge, the Committee on Public Lands and Places had "no hesitation in saying that a material benefit will result to the city treasury" from the "large appreciation of value" of thirty-four acres of common land "but a short distance above": BA Documents 3, no. 98 (Feb. 29, 1836): 517. See a similar statement of the municipal corporation's "interests" in embellishing Union Square in order to "increase taxes paid into the city treasury"

and promote "the pecuniary interest of the public by encouraging the extension of the city toward the great body of common land": BA Proceedings 7:317–19.

29. For merchants' support of commercial upgrading of lower Manhattan streets, see, e.g., proposals to widen Mill, Stone, and John streets, BA Documents 2, no. 41 (Nov. 11, 1835): 179–82; and no. 42 (Nov. 23, 1835): 183–86. For the aldermen's consciousness of the "great variety of persons many of whom are anxious to erect buildings" between 14th and 42d streets (which, they noted, had been "entirely laid out into town lots"), see a report in favor of opening streets to 42d Street in ibid., no. 36 (Nov. 4, 1835): 155–62. For a table listing all street improvements from 1830 to 1839, see ibid., 5, no. 45 (Mar. 25, 1839): 462–97.

30. [Clement Moore], A Plain Statement Addressed to the Proprietors of Real Estate in the City and County of New York (New York, 1818), in NYPL.

31. New-York Mirror, Jan. 15 and June 11, 1825. In its issue of May 20, 1826, the Mirror introduced a "City Improvement" column that regularly reported and advocated street improvements; see, e.g., July 29, 1826; Feb. 2, 1828; Mar. 27, 1830; July 16, 1836. The concern with city embellishment is noticeably absent from earlier New York "parlor publications," such as Alexander Ming's Weekly Visitor, published in the late teens. For the Evening Post's advocacy of improvements, see, e.g., Nov. 17, 1835.

32. New York County Clerk, Register of Conveyances, 234:514; BA Proceedings 6:410; Lockwood, Bricks and Brownstones, p. 42.

33. Lockwood, Bricks and Brownstones, pp. 78–79, and for Irving Place, BAA Documents 2, no. 47 (Jan. 28, 1833): 289–91. For Washington Place and Waverly Place, see BA Proceedings 4: 148, 238, 283. For University Place, BA Documents 5, no. 77 (Mar. 26, 1838): 579–81.

34. BA Proceedings 6 (May 23, 1835): 321–22. Although from 1831 street committees repeatedly objected to renaming blocks within continuous streets, they were less consistent in deciding what constituted spatial continuity. For examples of other rejections, see ibid., 6:323; 7:14, 65, 80, 141. Cf. Street Committee's endorsement of proprietors' petition to change the name of Augustus Street to City Hall Place "with a view to neutralize unpleasant associations connected with the present name of the street . . . the more so in as much as a great number of very elegant houses are now in the course of being erected": ibid., 6:260 (Mar. 7, 1834).

35. D. G. Thompson, Ruggles of New York: A Life of Samuel B. Ruggles (New York: Columbia University Press, 1946), pp. 56–60; Board of Aldermen and Assistant Aldermen Documents (1831–1832) 1, no. 3 (Dec. 5, 1831): 2, 6–7; BAA Documents 1, no. 37 (Dec. 5, 1831): 125–33.

36. BAA Documents 1, no. 43 (Dec. 19, 1831): 153–61.

37. For other examples of the Common Council's policy on public squares, see BA Proceedings 4:157–59 (Jan. 21, 1833; 31st to 34th streets at Fourth Avenue); and BA Documents 2, no. 10:39–41 (June 22, 1835; Mount Morris Park), no. 17: 67–68 (July 20, 1835; Murray Hill), no. 47:203–5 (Nov. 23, 1835; Abingdon Square), no. 85: 439–46 (Feb. 15, 1836; Madison Square). For the embellishment of Washington Square (and indeed its successive transformation from a burial ground to a parade ground to a "park"), see BA Proceedings 3:31–32, 52, 64. For a debate over policy with respect to taxing such "private squares" as St. John's Park and Gramercy Park, see BA Proceedings 2:43, 131–33. For the Art Street blacksmith, see BA Documents 2, no. 69 (Sept. 14, 1835): 335–37.

38. BAA Documents 2, no. 45 (Feb. 25, 1833): 329–31.

39. BA Documents 2, no. 36: 160.

40. Moehring, Public Works, pp. 94, 98, 100–104.

41. BA Documents 3, no. 28 (Apr. 26, 1836): 152.

42. *MCC, 1784–1831*, 4:577 (Sept. 28, 1807); cf. p. 1 (May 20, 1805).

43. Christine Stansell, *City of Women: Sex and Class in New York City, 1789–1860* (New York: Knopf, 1986), pp. 11–23. Vivienne L. Kruger, "Born to Run: The Slave Family in Early New York, 1626–1827" (Ph.D. diss., Columbia University, 1985), pp. 926–27, 943, shows that concern over the economic position of free blacks, who were largely excluded from skilled jobs, was not misplaced. In 1814–15, 70% of New York City's black families received outdoor public relief.

44. *MCC, 1784–1831*, 8:360–62 (Nov. 17, 1817); cf. *Weekly Visitor*, June 27, 1818.

45. Mohl, *Poverty in New York*, pp. 87–88, 90, 134–36, 243–58; Stansell, *City of Women*, pp. 34–36, 64–75; Carroll Smith Rosenberg, *Religion and the Rise of the American City* (Ithaca: Cornell University Press, 1971), chaps. 3–5, 7.

46. Stansell, *City of Women*, pp. 13–14, 50–51, 184, 193, 204–5; Jeanne Boydston, "To Earn Her Daily Bread: Antebellum Housework and Working-Class Subsistence," *Radical History Review* 35 (1985): 13–14, 18.

47. "Memorial of the Mayor and Aldermen for Passage of a Law on the Subject of Hawking and Peddling," County Clerk Filed Papers, box 3080, Municipal Archives, City of New York.

48. *MCC, 1784–1831*, 17:587, 643, 652, 760; 18:632; *New York Mirror*, Apr. 18 and May 9, 1829.

49. *MCC, 1784–1831*, 18:19–20 (Apr. 20, 1829).

50. Ibid., pp. 11–12 (Apr. 20, 1829).

51. On the residential locations of Afro-Americans, see the maps in Curry, *Free Black in Urban America*, pp. 35 (1835) and 69 (1852); Rhonda Freeman, "The Free Negro in New York City in the Era before the Civil War" (Ph.D. diss., Columbia University, 1966), pp. 218–19. See also Timothy J. Gilfoyle, "City of Eros: New York City, Prostitution, and the Commercialization of Sex, 1790–1920" (Ph.D. diss., Columbia University, 1987), pp. 52–59 on Five Points, esp. 58–59 on black brothel proprietors and 63 on Church Street's "African Grove," on Trinity Church land. Gilfoyle has done a remarkable job of mapping New York City's brothels throughout the nineteenth century. For the racial, ethnic, and occupational structure of the Sixth Ward, including Five Points, from 1810 to 1835, see Carol Groneman Pernicone, "The 'Bloody Ould Sixth': A Social Analysis of a New York City Working-Class Community in the Mid-Nineteenth Century" (Ph.D. diss., University of Rochester, 1973), pp. 22–31.

52. For racial and ethnic conflicts in Five Points and Lispenard Meadows, including the 1834 anti-abolition riot, see Paul Gilje, *The Road to Mobocracy: Popular Disorder in New York City, 1763–1834* (Chapel Hill: University of North Carolina Press, 1988), pp. 145–70.

53. BAA Documents 1, no. 44 (Dec. 19, 1831): 163–67. For the *Evening Post's* advocacy of the clearance of Five Points in the early 1830s, see James Ford, *Slums and Housing, with Special Reference to New York City* (Cambridge: Harvard University Press, 1936), 1:92–93.

54. BAA *Documents* 1, no. 68 (Jan. 13, 1832): 281.

55. Ibid., 3, no. 106 (Mar. 13, 1837): 689–90. Identifications from *Longworth's American Almanac and New York City Directory* (New York, 1836–1837). The aldermen had rejected an earlier petition because owners on the street opposed the project 3 to 1: BA Proceedings 6:52–53 (Dec. 23, 1833).

56. BA Documents 3, no. 106: 685–89, 691–92.

57. Ibid., pp. 700–704, 707–9.

58. Ibid. Gilfoyle, "City of Eros," describes the economics of leaseholding

brothel proprietors, pp. 143–49, and lists leaseholding proprietors of brothels on Anthony Street, pp. 132–33.

59. BA Documents 3, no. 106: 693, 696. For John L. Livingston's properties in the area (and his extensive investment in brothels) see Gilfoyle, "City of Eros," pp. 128–36.

60. BA Documents 3, no. 106: 694–96, 698–99. Another group of proprietors in the vicinity, including other East Broadway householders, who would be assessed for the widening of Anthony, also protested the cost: pp. 704–6.

61. Ibid., p. 696.

62. For the discontinuance of the Anthony Street improvement see ibid., 4, no. 6 (June 17, 1839): 91–98; cf. 4, no. 28 (Aug. 2, 1837): 183–86 (William Street merchants).

63. The panic of 1837 and the subsequent depression prompted a larger re-evaluation of city policy and particularly of rising taxes and assessments. Thus in a reversal of policy, a committee charged with evaluating the city budget over the 1830s concluded that the nearly $46,000 spent on "embellishing" public spaces, and particularly Union Place, had been an "extravagant expenditure" and "improper charge on the city treasury, inasmuch as it increases the taxes of individuals not interested in the improvement": ibid., 6, no. 5 (June 3, 1839): 69–70, 90. The committee urged that in the future such assessments be charged to the "owners of property adjacent to, and benefitted" by, the improvements. In the 1840s, landowners organized to protest the entire benefits assessment system, particularly as it affected the opening of uptown streets. Their newspaper, The Municipal Gazette, offered a running commentary on the abuses of the assessment system, including aldermen's "corruption in promoting particular public improvements," which became a recurring theme in city politics in the 1840s and 1850s. For these struggles of "property against property" in uptown development and the building of Central Park, see Elizabeth Blackmar and Roy Rosenzweig, "The Park and the People: A History of Central Park" (manuscript), chaps. 1 and 2.

64. Charles Dickens, American Notes and Reprinted Pieces (1846; London: 1871), pp. 52–55.

65. "Report of the Commissioners of the Almshouse, Bridewell and House of Detention," BA Documents 4, no. 32 (Sept. 11, 1837): 210, 212; italics in the original.

66. James F. Richardson, "To Control the City: The New York Police in Historical Perspective," in Kenneth Jackson and Stanley Schultz, eds., Cities in American History (New York: Knopf, 1972), pp. 272–89; and New York Police: Colonial Times to 1901 (New York: Oxford University Press, 1970), pp. 44–50.

67. "Police Report," BA Documents 12, no. 33 (Feb. 9, 1846): 537–43.

68. Letters of John Pintard to His Daughter Eliza Noel Pintard Davidson, 1816–1833, ed. Dorothy Barck, NYHS Collections 70–74 (1937–1940), 1:174.

6. Building a Housing Crisis

1. Niles Weekly Register, Aug. 27, 1825; New York Mirror, July 11, 1835; Morning Courier and New-York Enquirer, Jan. 13, 1847.

2. Howard Rock, Artisans of the New Republic: The Tradesmen of New York in the Age of Jefferson (New York: New York University Press, 1979), p. 240.

3. New-York Mirror, July 11, 1835.

4. New York Association for Improving the Conditions of the Poor, First Report

of a Committee on the Sanitary Conditions of the Laboring Classes (New York, 1853), p. 8; NYHS.

5. Evarts B. Greene and Virginia Harrington, *American Population before the Federal Census of 1790* (New York: Columbia University Press, 1932), pp. 88–91, 94, 101, 102, 104; *Longworth's American Almanac and New York City Directory* (New York, 1800), pp. 386–87; Sidney Pomeranz, *New York: An American City, 1783–1803* (New York: Columbia University Press, 1938), pp. 226–37. On colonial building trades, see Carl Bridenbaugh, *Colonial Craftsmen* (New York, 1950), p. 95; Samuel McKee, *Labor in Early America, 1664–1776* (New York: Columbia University Press, 1935), pp. 42, 89–90; George Edwards, *New York as an Eighteenth-Century Municipality* (New York: Longman, 1917), pp. 89–90. For examples of eighteenth-century building contracts, see Matthew Norris, contract, Apr. 15, 1738, in New York City Miscellaneous Manuscripts, NYHS; building agreement, May 7, 1763, no. 39, in De Lancey Papers, NYHS.

6. *CA*, Feb. 7, 1800, and May to June, 1800–1820, passim; for Clinton, see RC, 91:248, 254, 256. Astor's project is noted in an entry of May 26, 1813, in Richmond Hill Debit Accounts, House and Land Books, 1833–1847, Astor Papers, NYHS; Astor's only other speculative housing venture, five houses on Grand Street, was noted in 1831: Schedule 21, Astor Papers.

7. Late-eighteenth-century rentiers' building covenants in ground leases are discussed in chap. 1 above.

8. *CA*, Oct. 9, 1800; Jan. 4, 1803; Feb. 6, 1800; Mar. 10, 1803. There appears to have been a fair amount of variation within the short term for mortgages, e.g., 10% on day of sale, 25% on execution of deed, remainder by mortgage for five years (*CA*, Jan. 19, 1807); one-half May 1, rest in six months (*CA*, Mar. 7, 1807); one-fourth in cash, remainder in one, two, or three years (*CA*, Jan. 15, 1812).

9. See, e.g., mortgage, Apr. 19, 1800, box 3, no. 5, Leake Papers, NYHS; RC, 40:460 (1773), 91:263 (1811), 112:18 (1815). Henry Bayard's projects are cited in n. 30 below. Kearney v. Post, 1 Sandford 105, follows the ground lease, assignments, and mortgages of 1½ acres on the Bowery from 1799 to 1836.

10. On Astor's Manhattan real estate investment strategies, see Kenneth Wiggins Porter, *John Jacob Astor: Businessman* (Cambridge: Harvard University Press, 1931), 2:910–52.

11. On charter restrictions, see, e.g., "Act to Incorporate the North River Insurance Company," *Laws of New York, 1822*, p. 16, and a court case contesting the company's discounting of notes: North River Insurance Company v. Lawrence, 3 Wendell 482. The Union Insurance Company advertised in the 1819 *Longworth's American Almanac and New York City Directory* that "their funds being secured by mortgages on real estate within this state of the value of 50% more than the sums loaned thereon give a sure pledge of their entire ability to meet their engagements." James Hardie, *A Census of the New Buildings Erected in This City in the Year 1824* (New York, 1825), pp. 37–40, lists insurance companies. For the persistence of personal mortgages, see John Disturnell, *New York as It Is in 1833* (New York, 1833), p. 171.

12. Contracts with George Gossman, mason (May 30, 1804), and Joseph Newton, builder (June 30, 1804), box 3, Leake Papers, NYHS; "To Amount deductions for contract deficiencies and overcharge on day work account," Jan. 10, 1812, in Rhinelander Day Book, NYHS.

13. Robert Christie, *Empire in Wood* (Ithaca: Cornell University Press, 1956), pp. 7–9, 19–21; John Commons et al., *History of Labor in the United States* (New York: Macmillan, 1918), 1:69–71; *History of Architecture and the Building Trades*

of Greater New York (New York: Union History Co., 1899), 1:387–89. In his *Sketches of America* (London, 1818), p. 22, Henry Fearon described New York's building system for a European audience:

> Building appears to be brisk in the City. It is generally performed by contract. A person intending to have a house erected contracts with a professed builder, the builder with a brick layer, and he with all others necessary to the completion of the design. In some cases the builder is a sort of head workman, for the purpose of overseeing the others; receives for his agency seven pence per day from the wages of each man. . . . There are occasional instances where there is no contract, everything being paid for according to measure and value.

14. In his contract of Jan. 1, 1794, with George Gossman, mason, and Robert Gossman, house carpenter, John Leake added, "No advantage to be taken of anything omitted to be noted": Leake Papers, NYHS. On labor see Rock, *Artisans of the New Republic,* pp. 249–53.

15. Commons et al., *History of Labor,* 1:70; for price setting, see, e.g., *Daily Advertiser,* Mar. 30, 1795, cited in *History of Architecture and the Building Trades,* pp. 389–90; and Rock, *Artisans of the New Republic* pp. 249–50.

16. *Independent Journal or the General Advertiser,* Sept. 12, 1785, *Arts & Crafts,* 81: 207–8; see also "To the Journeymen Carpenters and Mechanics," broadside, Mar. 11, 1805, NYPL. Journeymen proposed a similar step in 1809; see Rock, *Artisans of the New Republic,* pp. 275–76. For building unions, see also Commons et al., *History of Labor,* 1:365–66. For the further development of subcontracting in the building trades, see Sean Wilentz, *Chants Democratic: New York City and the Rise of the American Working Class, 1788–1850* (New York: Oxford University Press, 1984), pp. 132–34.

17. *Niles Weekly Register,* Sept. 24 and Oct. 22, 1825; see also *New-York Mirror,* Sept. 24, 1825, and Nov. 30, 1833; *Diary of Philip Hone,* ed. Allan Nevins (New York: Dodd, Mead, 1927), 2:900. For owners' dissatisfactions with contractors' supervision, see the entries of Apr. 20, 27, and 29, 1819, in the memorandum book of the architect Edward Probyn, NYHS. Owners who made installment payments did not succeed in removing themselves entirely from the building process. See, e.g., George Furst (contractor) to Samuel Ruggles (developer), July 6, 1832 (and July 7, 1832), in Ruggles Papers, NYPL, citing the application of two builders for a $1,000 installment.

18. For a good review of New York cases on building contracts, see Smith v. Brady, 17 New York Reports 172 (N.Y. Ct. of Appeals, 1858). In *Transformation of American Law* (Cambridge: Harvard University Press, 1977), pp. 187–88, Morton Horwitz suggests that antebellum judges were inclined to make exceptions in contract law to assist such "infant industries" as speculative building. In the Smith case, the judge distinguished New York from other states that allowed *quantum meruit* for partial performance, insisting that the "settled law of this state" required builders, "like other men . . . , to perform their contracts in order to entitle themselves to payment." He then threw the question of compliance with future contracts back to juries, acknowledging that "it is true that such [building] contracts embrace a variety of particulars and that slight omissions and inadvertences may sometimes innocently occur. These should be indulgently regarded, and they will be so regarded by courts and juries." It was rare for antebellum New York judges to welcome juries into arbitrations affecting property. See also Lutz v. Ely, 3 Smith 621 (1853), and Smith v. Briggs, 3 Denio 73 (1846).

19. Commons et al., *History of Labor*, pp. 279–81, 329; see also "Report of Committee of Fifty in Favor of a Lien Law on Buildings, Education and the District System for Presidential Elections," 1829, NYHS. The precedent for lien legislation appears to come from admiralty law, according to which a ship could be impounded to meet mariners' claims for wages. See Richard B. Morris, *Government and Labor in Early America* (New York: Columbia University Press, 1946), pp. 242–46; and for the political context that made the campaign for lien legislation successful, Wilentz, *Chants Democratic*, pp. 201–8.

20. *Morning Courier and New York Enquirer*, Dec. 2, 1829.

21. Doughty v. Devlin, 1 E. D. Smith (1851) at 638–39; *Laws of New York* for the following years: *1830*, chap. 330, p. 412; *1832*, chap. 120, p. 181; *1844*, chap. 220, pp. 339, 451; *1851*, chap. 513, p. 953; *1855*, chap. 404, p. 760. In the case reports of the New York Court of Common Pleas, 1850–1858, the reporter E. Delafield Smith usefully organized the legal issues in an annotated index; under "Cases under the Lien Law." The clearest summary of the courts' interpretation of lien legislation can be found in Doughty v. Devlin; in Sullivan v. Decker, 1 Smith 699 (1851); and in Haswell v. Goodchild, 12 Wendell 163 (1834). These cases also offer useful examples of the variety of building contracts.

22. Studies of nineteenth-century building cycles do not examine the period before 1850, but they do suggest the systematic connections between building activity and the larger economy. See John R. Riggleman, "Variation in Building Activity in United States Cities" (Ph.D. diss., Johns Hopkins University, 1934); Walter Isard, "A Neglected Cycle: Transport Building Cycles," *Review of Statistics and Economics* 24 (1942): 149–58. I have also found Clarence Long, *Building Cycles and the Theory of Investment* (Princeton: Princeton University Press, 1940), and Roger Starr, *Housing and the Money Market* (New York: Basic Books, 1975), helpful in thinking about variables that affect the rate of new construction. For the Midwest, see Donald Adams, "The Residential Construction Industry in the Early Nineteenth Century," *Journal of Economic History* 35 (1975): 794–816.

23. *Niles Weekly Register*, June 27, 1818; *Letters from John Pintard to His Daughter Eliza Noel Pintard Davidson, 1816–1833*, ed. Dorothy Barck, NYHS Collections 70–74 (1937–1940), 1:154 (Nov. 16, 1818), 187 (Apr. 28, 1819).

24. *Longworth's Almanac* (1820), p. 492. New construction again dropped off during the 1829 recession. For land values from 1817 to 1850, see table 3.

25. Hardie, *Census of New Buildings*, pp. 5–12, with tables showing number of stories and material of new houses by street. *Niles Weekly Register*, June 27, 1818, estimated an average building cost of $2,000. John Jacob Astor's five houses on Grand Street cost $3,023 each in 1831: Schedule 21, House and Land Books, 1833–1848, Astor Papers, NYHS. House prices are also taken from RC, e.g., 213:390 (1827; Ward 8, $3,225), 230:177 (1827; Ward 6, $2,600), 234:517 (1828; Ward 7, $3,300), 232:232 (1828; Ward 10, $3,100). See also nn. 30 and 31 below.

26. Articles of agreement between Richard B. Morris and Samuel Martin, builder, June 20, 1831, Morris Papers, NYHS.

27. Contract specifications in ibid. See also Charles Lockwood, *Bricks and Brownstones: The New York Row House, 1783–1929* (New York: McGraw-Hill, 1972), pp. 13–21, 70–78; and house advertisements in CA, January–May 1825–1840.

28. Miscellaneous accounts and receipts in Morris Papers, NYHS.

29. *Letters of John Pintard*, 2:219. In *Census of Housing*, pp. 3–4, Hardie estimated that "in each house there would be an average of, at least, two families," and in each family "between children, servants, relations, apprentices, and boarders, six persons (and the supposition is not extravagant)." Daily notices in the *Morning*

Courier and New York Enquirer in the 1820s usually note numbers of parlors, bedrooms, and kitchens.

30. My observations on building patterns are based on a reading of deeds in the Register of Conveyances. I used three methods: (1) I looked up the names of particular builders and landholders in the Index of Grantors and Grantees in the County Clerk's Office; (2) I traced the development of particular blocks, which inevitably entailed adjacent blocks, in three areas of the city: block 245, bounded by Montgomery, Clinton, Cherry, and Water streets, in Ward 7; block 592, bounded by West Fourth Street, Washington Place, Sixth Avenue, and Waverly Place, in Ward 9; and block 161, at Five Points in Ward 6, bounded by Orange (Baxter), Anthony, Mulberry, and Chatham streets. (3) As I searched particular deeds in the microfiche libers, I also collected other examples to extend my data. Some deeds record the transfer of more than one lot, and frequently conveyances record mortgage transactions and long-term leases. My inferences on construction are based on fluctuations in the recorded prices for particular lots.

Henry Bayard's transactions can be found in 91:211 (1824) and 323, 325, 327, 330, 520 (1825); 212:267 (1815), 213, 229 (1824), and 212, 214, 220, 221, 225, 234, 235 (1826); 271:336 (1831); 313:361 (1829). Some of these transactions involved Trinity Church's consent for assignment of leases, either for mortgages or to new leaseholders who paid for the new houses. Thirteen recorded conveyances name Bayard as grantor, including four to the hardware merchant James Jenkins for mortgages: 212:226, 234, 236; 271:336. Bayard made his last conveyance in 1834: 313:363.

Lockwood, *Bricks and Brownstones*, pp. 26–34, describes builders' guides in use in this period.

31. Working in partnership with the carpenter Robert Hanford, Underhill developed lots 42–51 on block 245. For some of these transactions, see RC, libers 198:256; 210:54, 212:258, 264; 213:404; 217:205, 210; 237:100, 196, 511.

The Deklyns' project illustrates some of the problems of reconstructing the history of particular lots. Barant Deklyn and the carpenter George Weeks acquired "lot 87" of block 592 (a triangle bounded by Grove and Christopher streets) for $2,750 in May 1828 (RC, 236:394). In September 1828, Deklyn and Weeks conveyed lot 87 to Samuel and Henry Quirepel, painters, for $6,400 (241:171). From the difference in price I infer the addition of new buildings. Apparently Deklyn retained partial interest in the lot, which he assigned to his brother Charles. Following a fire in 1834, residents in the area petitioned the Common Council to widen Grove Street to prevent reconstruction on lot 87, which had been "occupied by 41 families, being covered with buildings, without yard in front or rear, or intervening space of any kind": BA Documents 2, no. 35: 144–54 (Nov. 4, 1835). Charles Deklyn appears to have then invested in better construction, and in January 1837 he conveyed five two-story brick buildings on four lots, noted as lot 87 in the Block Index, to Joseph M. Faulkner for $35,000; this figure included three mortgages totaling $13,500 (RC, 371:39). The price, $7,000 a house, appears to reflect the speculative bubble that broke in May 1837. It is not clear what happened to the Quirepel interest in the land, if indeed the five houses were erected on the same lot 87.

Wells acquired lots 49–56 on Waverly Place from Alfred Pell and Samuel Ruggles in 1827 and 1828 at $1,025 a lot (e.g., RC, 220:178; 229:29; 230:173, 290, 451). He erected houses and conveyed them to a broker; e.g., 332:179, conveying two houses at $10,000 with mortgages for $6,000. For the architecture of elite neighborhoods from the 1820s to the 1840s, see Lockwood, *Bricks and Brownstones*, pp. 40–89.

32. For Gramercy Park, see D. G. Thompson, *Ruggles of New York: A Life of Samuel B. Ruggles* (New York: Columbia University Press, 1946), pp. 60–62.

33. See, e.g., the conveyance from George Lorillard to Lewis Carpenter, RC, 213:397 (1827), and building transactions reported in Holsman v. Abrams, 2 Duer 438; RC, 212:135 (Eckford, 1826); RC, 220:178 (Pell); RC, 495:148 (Schermerhorn, 1847); RC, 499:150 (Stuyvesant, 1847). Although Clement Moore resisted street openings on his Chelsea farm in 1819, by the 1830s he and his trustees were distributing lots with building covenants; see chap. 5 above and RC, 339:504, 368:56, 373:11 (1835). See also Morgan Lewis account in George L. Osborn Account Book, 1842–1848, and the following letters: Margaret Livingston to Charles Osborn, July 8, 1842, and Morgan Lewis to Charles Osborn, Aug. 12, 1842, all in Osborn Papers, NYPL. For an example of Astor's restrictive covenants, see RC, 171:42; see also Astor House and Land Book, 1833–1848, NYHS.

34. Thompson, *Ruggles of New York*, pp. 56–74; "Title of Samuel B. Ruggles to Lands between 15th Street on the South, 28th Street on the North, Bloomingdale Road on the West and First Avenue on the East," 1834, NYHS; and accounts in Ruggles Papers, NYPL.

35. Real Estate Record and Guide, *History of Real Estate, Building and Architecture in New York City during the Last Quarter of the Century* (New York, 1898), p. 135; for other examples, see RC, 499:499; 504:253. For examples of Ruggles' transactions with Nichols and Cummings, see RC, 285:75, 78; 286:275, 278, 280, 283; 287:388, 391; 304:135, 137; 363:356; and accounts in Ruggles Papers, NYPL. Furst and Ruggles also took contracts from the City of New York to open and pave streets north of 14th.

36. A classic statement of this theory appears in the "Report of the Select Committee to Examine into the Conditions of Tenant Houses in New York City and Brooklyn," New York State Legislature, Assembly, A.D. 205, 80th sess. (1857), p. 10. See also James Ford, *Slums and Housing, with Special Reference to New York City* (Cambridge: Harvard University Press, 1936), 1:135–38.

37. For density and land values by ward, see BAA Documents, no. 4 (Dec. 5, 1831), unbound, Appendix, tables 1–4 (Columbia University); and BAA Documents 1, no. 37 (Dec. 5, 1831): 130–31. See table 4.

38. Hardie, *Census of New Buildings*, pp. 5–12. Cf. summaries of 1834 and 1835 construction in John Disturnell, *New York as It Is in 1835* (New York, 1835), pp. 22–23, and *New York as It Is in 1837* (New York, 1837), p. 20, both reprinting the census of new buildings by size and type from the City Inspector's annual report. In 1824, only two-fifths of new buildings (720 out of 1,624)—the majority commercial structures—were constructed entirely of brick or stone. For inflationary tendencies after 1825, see Dorothy S. Brady, "Relative Prices in the Nineteenth Century," *Journal of Economic History* 25 (1964):145–203; Peter Temin, *The Jacksonian Economy* (New York: Norton, 1969), pp. 68–91. On rising labor costs, see Commons et al., *History of Labor*, 1:365.

39. Disturnell, *New York as It Is in 1833*, p. 168; and see table 3.

40. See building reports and new construction by street listed in Report of the City Inspector on New Buildings for 1835, BA Documents 3, no. 119 (Mar. 31, 1836): 627–34; and for 1839, ibid., 6, no. 63 (Mar. 23, 1840): 621–28.

41. Ford, *Slums and Housing*, 1:95, 2:868–69.

42. Alan Pred, *Spatial Dynamics of United States Industrial Growth, 1800–1840* (Cambridge: MIT Press, 1966), pp. 153–55; Ruggles to Talmadge, Jan. 23, 1832, Ruggles Papers, NYPL. See also John Jacob Astor's bond books (1826–1833), Astor Papers, NYHS.

43. On mortgages, see BAA Documents, no. 4, Appendix, table 5, rpt. in Disturnell, *New York as It Is in 1833*, p. 171; and *Niles Weekly Register*, May 14, 1831. On the opening of new streets, see, e.g., *Evening Post*, Oct. 3, 1835; and BA Documents 3, no. 36 (Nov. 4, 1835): 145–54. For the costs and constraints of public transportation in the 1830s and 1840s, see Pred, *Spatial Dynamics*, pp. 211–12.

44. Ruggles to Talmadge, Jan. 23, 1832, Ruggles Papers, NYPL.

45. Peter G. Stuyvesant to Ruggles, Feb. 6, 1838, Ruggles Papers, NYPL.

46. For the multiple causes of the panic, see Temin, *Jacksonian Economy*, chap. 4. For the impact of the panic and the depression that followed, see ibid., p. 120; Samuel Rezneck, "Social History of an American Depression, 1837–1843," *American Historical Review* 40 (1935): 562–87; Wilentz, *Chants Democratic*, pp. 299–359; Edward K. Spann, *The New Metropolis: New York City, 1840–1857* (New York: Columbia University Press, 1981), pp. 67–91.

47. For land values, see table 3; on the 1835 fire, *History of Architecture and the Building Trades*, 2:241, and Ford, *Slums and Housing*, p. 92; on postfire construction, see John Disturnell, *New York as It Is in 1837* (New York, 1837), p. 20.

48. Table 3. For a typical deed carrying multiple mortgages, see the conveyance from Deklyn to Faulkner, RC, 371:39, with a mortgage of $4,500 to Deklyn and assignment of two mortgages for $4,000 to the North River Insurance Company. *Diary of George Templeton Strong*, ed. Allan Nevins and Milton H. Thomas (New York: Macmillan, 1952), 1:130–31.

49. For building mechanics working as landlords' agents, see the accounts of William Gibbons, Morgan Lewis, and Uriah Levy in George Osborn Account Books, NYPL. For Astor see, e.g., transactions with Christopher Keyes, 1837–1839, discussed in Porter, *John Jacob Astor*, 2:932–33, 935. For other land investments, see, e.g., William S. Johnson to Charles Johnson, Jan. 11, 1840, Johnson Papers, NYHS.

50. Samuel Ruggles to Charles Ruggles, Dec. 31, 1840. See also lease to Henry Batts with covenant to purchase five houses on Third Avenue, Dec. 23, 1837; account of house sale, Dec. 12, 1839; 1840 and 1841 tax accounts; memo, Dec. 1, 1841; and accounts in "Lands Held by Philo T. Ruggles under Deed from Samuel Ruggles, Dec. 28, 1842," all in Ruggles Papers, NYPL. See also Thompson, *Ruggles of New York*, pp. 50–56, 65–72; and G. T. Strong on his father-in-law in *Diary*, 2:43–54.

51. Ruggles to Talmadge, Dec. 23, 1832. In the boom year of 1836, New Yorkers had raised 1,620 new buildings, more than 600 of which replaced commercial buildings destroyed by the December 1835 fire. In 1837, new construction dropped by half, to 840. Total construction in the years 1838–1841 continued below 1,000 buildings a year, reaching a low of 674 buildings in 1839. See tables 5 and 6.

52. John Griscom, "Annual Report on the Interments in the City and County of New York for the Year 1842, with Remarks Thereon and a Brief View of the Sanitary Condition of the City" BAA Documents 9, no. 59:163. See also Griscom, *The Sanitary Condition of the Laboring Population of New York* (New York, 1845). For "homeless" (listed as "indigent lodgers"), see the quarterly reports of the Chief of Police (1846), BA Documents 12, nos. 33 and 47. See also Edward Lubitz, "The Tenement Problem in New York City and the Movement for Its Reform, 1856–1867" (Ph.D. diss., New York University, 1970), chap. 1.

53. *Evening Post*, Apr. 3, 1846; "Annual Report of the City Inspector on New Building for the Year 1844," BA Documents 11, no. 59:625–631. For the mortality rate, see Thomas K. Downing, "Report of the City Inspector for the Year 1852," BA Documents 20, no. 5:109–110; and Lubitz, "Tenement Problem," p. 152.

54. E.g., in January 1843 Daniel Green began to fall behind in his quarterly rent of $71.25 on the house at 81 Clinton Street, on the Lower East Side. In June his landlord, Morgan Lewis, secured a second tenant at $7.50 monthly, and Green paid $35 quarterly for his share of the house. In November 1843 Lewis added a third tenant at $5 a month. The three households paid an annual rent of $290, compared with the $285 that Green paid originally. See Morgan Lewis account in Charles and George Osborn Account Books, NYPL.

55. For a summary of new construction in the 1840s, see *History of Architecture and the Building Trades*, p. 119; and on tenements, 32, 144. For Bergh's investment, see G. W. Sheldon, "The Old Shipbuilders of New York," *Harper's New Monthly Magazine* 54 (1882): 236. See also Ford, *Slums and Housing*, 1:111–13, 2:Plate 1; *Evening Post*, Mar. 19, 1847, and Aug. 20, 1850. On layout and dimensions, see Lubitz, "Tenement Problem," pp. 75–80.

56. "Annual Report of the City Inspector on New Building for the Year 1845," BA Documents 12, no. 45: 744–70; for 1846, ibid., 13, no. 22:463–93. *CA*, Apr. 2, 1846, announced that the city "has completely recovered from the effects of the terrible revulsion" and took as its evidence the "magnificent buildings" being erected "in all quarters of the city."

57. *Morning Courier and New-York Enquirer*, Jan. 13, 1847, and follow-up articles Jan. 28 and 30, 1847. The *Albion*, Feb. 6, 1847, and the *Mirror*, Feb. 13, 1847, took up and redirected the *Courier*'s suggestions to address the housing problems of the city's "small and genteel families" or "second class of society, small-incomes," and proposed the building of middle-class "flats" like those found in Edinburgh and Paris. The apartments in four-story buildings would have two parlors, three chambers, and a kitchen, rent for $300–350 a year, and return 10–12% to the builder.

58. Griscom, "Annual Report on Interments" (1843), p. 176.

59. Ibid.

60. AICP, "Tenth Annual Report" (1853), pp. 26–27, NYHS; Ford, *Slums and Housing*, 1:136–37.

61. Astor project, *Evening Post*, Mar. 19, 1847.

62. For building costs, see Loonie v. Hogan, 2 Smith 681 ($3,000 to build a four-story, 25-by-50-foot building on 12th Street in 1849); and Lutz v. Ely, 3 Smith 621 ($4,310 building, dimensions not given). The *Evening Post*, Mar. 18, 1847, joining the newspaper discussion of the housing crisis, complained that a recently erected 25-by-25-foot building "finished in a common manner . . . could not have cost more than $2,000." The *Mirror*, Feb. 13, 1847, estimated that lots cost from $2,500 to $3,500 and that a four-story middle-class apartment building could be erected for $6,500 "at the outside."

For a comparison with British housing problems, see Anthony Whol, "The Housing of the Artisans and Laborers in Nineteenth-Century London, 1815–1914" (Ph.D. diss., Brown University, 1966), pp. 1–84; W. Beresford, "The Back-to-Back Houses in Leeds, 1787–1927," and John Blatt, "Working-Class Housing in Glasgow, 1851–1914," both in Stanley D. Chapman, ed., *History of Working-Class Housing* (Totowa, N.J.: Rowman & Littlefield, 1971).

63. Real Estate Record, *History of Real Estate*, provides capsule summaries of New York's major building firms, roughly twenty of which predate the Civil War; see also Richard Nevius, *History of Horace Ely and Company* (New York, 1955); on savings banks, see Alan Olmstead, *New York City Mutual Savings Banks, 1819–1861* (Chapel Hill: University of North Carolina Press, 1975), pp. 75, 91–94, 113. On incorporation of building companies, see *Laws of New York, 1853*, p. 179; and for the context of general incorporation laws, L. Ray Gunn, *Decline of Authority:*

Public Economic Policy and Political Development in New York State, 1800–1860 (Ithaca: Cornell University Press, 1988), chap. 8. Robert Ernst, *Immigrant Life in New York City, 1825–1863* (New York: Columbia University Press, 1949), p. 248, no. 150, notes that 300 of 849 "building contractors" in the 1855 census were immigrants.

64. For blaming the Irish, see AICP, "Sixth Annual Report" (1849), pp. 15–16, 22–23; and Amy Bridges, *A City in the Republic* (New York: Cambridge University Press, 1984), pp. 91–98 (on nativism in the 1844 election), 68, 93, 95–96 (on nativism among builders); Wilentz, *Chants Democratic*, pp. 315–24; Spann, *New Metropolis*, pp. 34–37; Ernst, *Immigrant Life*, pp. 99–111.

65. Lubitz, "Tenement Problem," summarizes and reprints much of the discussion of the 1850s in chaps. 2–5. See also Ford, *Slums and Housing*, 1:123–48; and Spann, *New Metropolis*, pp. 142–53.

66. *New-York Tribune*, Jan. 14 and 19, 1847; *Morning Courier*, Jan. 18, 28, and 30, 1847.

7. "The Quality of Pay": Landlord–Tenant Relations

1. *New-York Mirror*, May 7, 1825; *Evening Post* (biweekly), May 2, 1845; *CA*, May 1, 1846. References to May Day moving can be found annually on Apr. 30, May 1, and May 2 in virtually every New York newspaper in the antebellum period.

2. *Letters of John Pintard to His Daughter Eliza Noel Pintard Davidson, 1816–1833*, ed. Dorothy Barck, NYHS Collections 70–74 (1937–1940), 4:44 (May 1, 1832).

3. For moving day disorders, see Paul Gilje, *The Road to Mobocracy: Popular Disorder in New York City, 1763–1834* (Chapel Hill: University of North Carolina Press, 1987), pp. 161–62; Graham Hodges, *New York City Cartmen* (New York: New York University Press, 1987), pp. 160–64; and a novel by Seba Smith, *May-Day in New York, or House-Hunting and Moving* (New York, 1843).

4. Margaret Livingston to Charles Osborn, Aug. 21, 1843 (drafts from Paris); Robert Turnbull to Osborn, Feb. 2, 1847; C. W. Wilkes to Osborn, Jan. 3, 1848, all in Charles Osborn Letters, NYPL; Morgan Lewis account in George L. Osborn Accounts, and Livingston to Osborn, July 8 and Aug. 12, 1842 (De Lancey Street houses), in ibid.; Richard McCormick to Sarah D. Johnson, June 29, 1849, and Accounts, 1850–1851, in Johnson Papers, NYHS; John Jacob Astor House and Land Books, Astor Papers, NYHS.

5. John N. Taylor, *A Treatise on the American Law of Landlord and Tenant in a Series of Letters Addressed to a Citizen of New York* (New York, 1840), pp. 3–4.

6. Frederick Pollock and Frederick Maitland, *The History of English Law*, 2d ed. (1898; Cambridge: Cambridge University Press, 1968), pp. 10–22, 80–106. See also Alan McFarland, *Origins of English Individualism: The Family, Property, and Social Transition* (New York: Cambridge University Press, 1978), pp. 80–130.

7. James Kent, *Commentaries on American Law*, 5th ed. (1828; Boston, 1844), 3:460–61.

8. Ibid., pp. 9, 484–85; Taylor, *Treatise*, 2d ed. (1852), pp. 35–38, 348–49; I. R. Butts, *The Law Cabinet*, bk. 3, *Landlord's and Tenant's Assistant* (Boston, 1852). Representative New York cases include Mumford v. Brown, 6 Cowen 475 (1826); Rowan v. Lyttle, 11 Wendell 616 (1834); Hall v. Ballantine, 7 Johnson 536 (1811).

9. F. A. Enever, *History of the Law of Distress for Rent and Damage Feasant*

(London, 1931), pp. 1, 3; and William Blackstone, *Commentaries on the Laws of England* (1788), ed. William Casey Jones (1915; Baton Rouge, 1976), p. 1498.

10. Kent, *Commentaries*, 3:9, 684–85.

11. For colonial landlord–tenant struggles, see Sung Bok Kim, *Landlord and Tenant in Colonial New York: Manorial Society, 1664–1775* (Chapel Hill: University of North Carolina Press, 1978), pp. 281–415. For the issue in the revolutionary period, see Edward Countryman, *A People in Revolution: The American Revolution and Political Society in New York, 1760–1790* (Baltimore: Johns Hopkins University Press, 1981), pp. 221–51. For rentiers and tenants during the constitutional period, see Alfred Young, *The Democratic Republicans of New York: The Origins* (Chapel Hill: University of North Carolina Press, 1967), pp. 69–75, 262–67.

12. Young, *Democratic Republicans*, pp. 206–7, 536; and on Van Rensselaer's political influence, 437–38, 440–41; David Ellis, *Landlords and Farmers in the Hudson-Mohawk Region. 1790–1850* (Ithaca: Cornell University Press, 1946), pp. 34–35, 151–55.

13. "Report of John Woodworth, William Van Ness and Spencer Ambrose to the Assembly, February 17, 1812," cited in A. G. Johnson, *A Chapter in History, or the Progress of Judicial Usurpation* (Troy, N.Y., 1863), p. 4. For leaseholders' ideology, see Allan David Heskin, *Tenants and the American Dream: Ideology and the Tenant Movement* (New York: Praeger, 1983), pp. 9–10.

14. Taylor, *Treatise* (1840), pp. 84–85; *Revised Statutes of the State of New York* (Albany, 1836), 3:761.

15. *The Colonial Laws of New York* (Albany, 1894), 5:624–36.

16. Enever, *Law of Distress*, pp. 262–63.

17. "An Act Concerning Distress, Rents and the Renewal of Leases," passed Apr. 5, 1813, in *Laws of New York Revised at the 36th Session* (Albany, 1813), pp. 434–44; "reasonable" distress, 434. See also 2 Greenleaf 64 (1788).

18. "An Act to Exempt Certain Articles of Property from Liability to Execution, and from Being Distrained for Rent," passed Apr. 15, 1814, in *Revised Statutes of the State of New York* (Albany, 1836), 3:260. See also law passed Apr. 17, 1815, in *Laws of New York, 38th Session*, p. 231.

19. Christine Stansell, "The Origins of the Sweatshop: Women and Early Industrialization in New York City," in Michael Frisch and Daniel Walkowitz, eds., *Working-Class America*, (Urbana: University of Illinois Press, 1983), pp. 78–104.

20. *Revised Statutes* (1836) 3:413.

21. "Landlords and Tenants," *Hunt's Merchant Magazine*, December 1839, pp. 484, 485.

22. Ibid., pp. 489–90.

23. *New-York Mirror*, Feb. 26, 1831.

24. *Revised Statutes* (1836), 2:290, consolidating exemptions of household goods in a law passed Apr. 18, 1815.

25. *Revised Statutes* (1836), 2:412–13, consolidating earlier acts.

26. New York State Legislature, Senate, *Report of the Committee of the Judiciary on several petitions for a law to extend the exemptions of personal property from sale on execution or distress for rent*, S.D. 81, Apr. 22, 1841, 63d sess., pp. 3–4. Norma Basch, *In the Eyes of the Law: Women, Marriage, and Property in Nineteenth-Century New York* (Ithaca: Cornell University Press, 1982), pp. 113–35, esp. 121–24.

27. S.D. 81, pp. 1–2; "An Act to Amend the Act to Extend the Exemption of Household Furniture and Working Tools for Distress for Rent and Sale under Execution," passed Apr. 11, 1842, *Laws of New York, 65th Session*, p. 193.

28. Kent, *Commentaries*, 3:635–36.

29. S.D. 81, p. 5. See also New York State Legislature, Assembly, *Report of the Committee on the Judiciary on the Subject of Exempting Household Furniture and Implements of Industry or Art from Levy or Sale on Execution*, A.D. 145, Mar. 28, 1842, 64th sess., and S.D. 43, Feb. 21, 1843, 66th sess.

30. Ellis, *Landlords and Farmers*, pp. 265–67, 272–75; "An Act to Abolish Distress for Rent and Other Purposes," passed May 13, 1846, *Laws of New York, 69th Session*, p. 369. See also Anthony Dyett, *A Law and Practice Relative to Summary Proceedings to Recover Possession of Lands* (New York, 1848). The Court of Appeals upheld the abolition of distress in Van Rensselaer v. Snyder, 13 N.Y. 299 (1855). Some city tenants—such as John J. White, who met his landlord and the constable at the door with a carving knife—also violently resisted distress: *Evening Post* Nov. 12, 1845. For distress on a store on Broadway, see Burr v. Buskirk, 3 Cowen 263 (1824).

31. *Revised Statutes* (1836), 3:599.

32. Meeks v. Bowerman, 1 Daly 99 (Ct. of Common Pleas, 1859); Taylor, *Treatise* (1852), pp. 194–95.

33. Dyett v. Pendleton, 4 Cowen 581 (1825).

34. 8 Cowen 727 (Ct. of Errors, 1826).

35. Ibid., at 733, 738.

36. Ibid., at 745.

37. Ibid., at 739–40.

38. Kent, *Commentaries*, 3:464; Kent also noted the British case of Marrable v. Smith, 1 Carr and Marsh 479, distinguished in Cleves v. Willoughby, 7 Hill 83 (1845), because it applied to the leasing of furnished rooms.

39. Ogilvie v. Hull and Hull, 5 Hill 52 (1843). New Yorkers particularly resented landlords' insistence on showing apartments or posting "to let" notices, which indicated that tenants faced eviction or higher rents at the end of the rental year: *New-York Herald*, Feb. 1, 1848.

40. Vanderbilt v. Persse, 3 Smith 428 (Ct. of Common Pleas, 1854), at 430; cf. Westlake v. De Graw, 25 Wendell 669 (1841).

41. Morton Horwitz, *The Transformation of American Law* (Cambridge: Harvard University Press, 1977), pp. 160–210.

42. Cleves v. Willoughby, 7 Hill 83 (1845); see also McCarty v. Ely and Ely, 4 Smith 375 (Ct. of Common Pleas, 1855); Academy of Music v. Hackett, 2 Hilton 217 (Ct. of Common Pleas, 1856).

43. New York v. Cushman, 10 Johnson 96 (1812).

44. *Revised Statutes* (1828), 2:165; Taggart v. Roosevelt, 2 Smith 100 (Ct. of Common Pleas, 1853).

45. Speckels v. Sax, 1 Smith 253 (Ct. of Common Pleas, 1851); *New-York Tribune*, Mar. 3, 1843. See also *CA*, Apr. 2, 1845: another tenant who sued his landlord for knocking him down was awarded $50. In Post v. Vetter, 2 Smith 248, the Court of Common Pleas upheld a parole agreement subsequent to the lease if there had been an exchange of "new consideration to support it."

46. Cohen v. Dupon, 1 Sandford at 264 (Superior Ct., 1848). In this case a tenant had leased a second-story apartment with the express provision that it was to "be occupied as a dwelling privileged for a dentist." The landlord's family, sharing the house, harassed their tenant and his clients by pranks, including stopping up the doorbell so the patients couldn't notify the dentist of their arrival, littering the stairs with nutshells and dirt, and placing "snow balls in the window sills to drip upon the carpet."

47. McCarty v. Ely and Ely, 4 Smith 375 (Ct. of Common Pleas, 1855); reports of cases in the Marine Court and Court of Common Pleas in the 1840s also note tenants' continued use of "constructive eviction" as a defense. See, e.g., CA, Jan. 4 and 13, 1845. See also Hegeman v. McArthur, 1 E. D. Smith 147.

48. See, e.g., Mumford v. Brown, 6 Cowen 475 (1826); Lemetti v. Anderson, 6 Cowen 302 (1826); Eaken v. Brown, 1 Smith 36; Lageman v. Kloppenburg, 2 Smith 126 (1853); Kastor v. Newhouse, 4 Smith 21 (1855); and Taylor, *Treatise*, pp. 155–57.

49. Livingston to Osborn, July 12, 1842, Osborn Letters, NYPL.

50. William Gibbons to Hannah Wheelwright, June 13, 1842; Dr. Binsse to Charles Osborn, Feb. 1, 1848, Osborn Letters, NYPL.

51. Livingston to Osborn, Aug. 31, 1843, and July 13, 1842 (italics in original); George Abbe to Osborn, Sept. 21, 1842; for other letters about maintenance and the problem of tenants' resistance to repairs that benefited the landlord but disrupted their own use of the property, see Livingston to Osborn, Aug. 31 and Sept. 18, 1843; and Gibbons to Osborn, June 10 and June 25, 1848. For a tenant complaining about the condition of the privy, see S. K. Wrightman to Osborn, June 23, 1848; all in Osborn Letters, NYPL.

52. Annual expenditures on maintenance from 1842 to 1849 for the multifamily dwellings at 109 and 111 Mulberry Street (Charles and George Osborn accounts) and 184 Hester Street, rear (Jacob Handley account), ranged from 2% to 5% of gross rents, as compared to 8% to 15% of gross rents on 19, 21, 23, and 25 Herbert Street and on 34 and 36 Spruce Street (William Gibbons accounts); 202, 204, 206, and 208 Houston Street (George Abbe accounts); all in George L. Osborn account books, NYPL. Landlords, of course, had to put less into the painting, reroofing, and masonry work of new middle-class dwellings, e.g., 3% for 227 Tenth Street (Francis Lathrop account).

53. For a statement of the logic, see Graves v. Berdan, 26 N.Y. (1863), at 500.

54. Howard v. Doolittle, 3 Duer 464 (Sup. Ct., 1854), at 474, 473. The case that gave rise to this confrontation involved the Irving House, a hotel on Chambers Street. An adjacent property owner removed the building next door to the hotel in order to rebuild, thereby exposing "the western part of the Irving House to the imminent danger of falling down unless shored up and protected." The issue was whether the tenant or the landlord should pay to keep the building from falling down. In a similar case four years earlier the court had concluded that although the "chief landlord," Philip Hone, had consented to building activity that destroyed a building on his leased lot on Cortlandt Street, the subtenants remained liable to the leaseholder for the full rent. In other words, rentiers risked little in condoning building activity that affected their leaseholders. Tenants stood in double jeopardy: they risked both the cost of protecting their interest in a building and the cost of rent even should the building be lost. See Lucky v. Frantzkee, 1 Smith 47 (Ct. of Common Pleas, 1850). See also Hardrop v. Gallagher, 2 Smith 523 (1854) (a sublandlord lost rent from subtenants when his building was damaged by blasting).

55. Horwitz, *Transformation of American Law*, pp. 63–139. For New York politics in the 1840s, see Jabez D. Hammond, *Political History of the State of New York* (New York, 1848), vol. 2; and De Alva S. Alexander, *A Political History of the State of New York* (New York, 1906), pp. 56–144. For the New York codification movement, see Lawrence Friedman, *A History of American Law*, 2d ed. (New York: Simon & Schuster, 1986), pp. 240–41; and for the "crisis of distributive politics" which contributed to the move to a "neutral" law, see L. Raymond Gunn, *The Decline of Authority: Public Economic Policy and Political Development in New York State, 1800–1860* (Ithaca: Cornell University Press, 1988), chap. 5.

56. *New-York Tribune*, Jan. 19, 1847. *Hunt's Merchant Magazine*, December 1839, pp. 487–88, had objected to the doctrine of absolute liability alongside its attack on distress. For commercial cases, see n. 54 above.

57. "An Act in Relation to the Rights and Liabilities of Owners and Lessors, Lessees, and Occupants of Buildings," passed Apr. 13, 1860, *Laws of New York, 83rd Session*, p. 592. In Graves v. Berdan, 26 New York 498 (1863), the Court of Appeals used Dyett v. Pendleton as a precedent in deciding a case that had arisen before the passage of the law to relieve the tenant of obligation for rent.

58. Ronald Lawson with Mark Naison, eds., *The Tenant Movement in New York City, 1904–1984* (New Brunswick: Rutgers University Press, 1986), pp. 219, 229.

59. "Rents," *New-York Mirror*, Feb. 26, 1831; italics in original.

60. See, e.g., *Hunt's Merchant Magazine*, December 1839, pp. 484–90; September 1855, p. 378; *Niles Weekly Register*, Nov. 12, 1836, and Feb. 11, 1837.

61. John Commons et al., eds., *Documentary History of American Industrial Society* (Cleveland: Arthur H. Clark, 1910), p. 315; Sean Wilentz, *Chants Democratic: New York City and the Rise of the American Working Class* (New York: Oxford University Press, 1984), pp. 230–31.

62. William Gibbons to Charles Osborn, Feb. 2, 1842, Osborn Letters, NYPL; see also *Diary of Philip Hone*, ed. Allan Nevins (New York: Dodd, Mead, 1927), 1:656 (May 13, 1843): "taxes are doubled the rents reduced by one-half."

63. Gibbons to Osborn, Sept. 16, 1842, Osborn Letters, NYPL.

64. Julian Gwyn, *The Enterprising Admiral: The Personal Fortune of Sir Peter Warren* (Montreal: McGill/Queens University Press, 1974); Morris Papers, NYHS; Johnson Papers, NYHS.

65. Gibbons to Wheelwright, June 6, 1842, Osborn Letters, NYPL; Charles Osborn accounts (1814–1828), George L. Osborn accounts (1842–1851), Charles F. Osborn accounts (1847–1851), and Charles F. and George L. Osborn accounts (1851–1854), together with letters of Charles Osborn (1832–1852); all in NYPL. In addition to leasing out property and collecting rents, arranging repairs, and paying taxes, assessments, insurance premiums, and interest on bonds and mortgages, agents such as the Osborns acted as informal bankers for their clients, extending credit to cover expenses, arranging mortgages, and maintaining the elaborate flow of rent revenues into other financial transactions. See also Richard Nevius, *History of Horace Ely and Company* (New York: private printing, 1955).

66. Gibbons to Osborn, Sept. 16, 1842.

67. For Church Street tenants, see Livingston to Osborn, Aug. 31, 1843. Between 1842 and 1849, the George L. Osborn accounts show separate running credit and debit accounts for the multiple properties of twenty-five clients. Holdings ranged from the one house on Eldridge Street owned by Isaiah Townsend to the more than fifty rental properties held by Morgan Lewis. For selected accounts, I have broken down the tenancy and expenses by house to arrive at the conclusions in this chapter. Unless I have noted otherwise, data from the accounts are from May 1842 to May 1849. For examples of "reliable" tenants paying quarterly rents, see 202, 204, and 133 Houston Street (George Abbe account); 19, 21, 23, and 25 Hubert Street and 34 and 36 Spruce Street (Gibbons account); sailmaker at 67 Eldridge (1844–1845, Isaiah Townsend account). Tenants' occupations are from *Doggett's New York City Directory* (New York, 1842–1848); in general I was able to identify approximately two-fifths of the tenants listed in the Osborn account books, which often give only last names. The problem of identification is complicated by leaseholders or agents who did not reside at the address.

It was not always the case that middle-class tenants were more reliable than wage earners. See Frederick De Peyster to Land Commissioners, Mar. 9, 1832 (memo), complaining that the tenant "had absconded" from 33 Park Row, which rented for $800 a year: John Leake Papers, box 3, NYHS. One common solution was for landlords to require that tenants find a cosigner to serve as surety for the rent, another practice that came under attack from the *New-York Mirror*, Feb. 26, 1831. For an example of surety, see Rosenbaum v. Gunter, 3 Smith 203 (1854).

68. Buildings at 73, 75, 81, and 83 Clinton Street and 94, 46, 98, 110, and 112 Allen Street (Morgan Lewis account); multifamily houses at 136½ Mulberry (Richard M. Blatchford account); 66 Mott and 109½ Mulberry, front (Charles F. and George L. Osborn account); 184 Hester, rear (Jacob Handley account); 78 and 82 Sullivan (Uriah Levy account); and unidentified and unenumerated tenants in rear houses at 105 Thompson (Uriah Levy account) and on Allen Street (Morgan Lewis account); all in George L. Osborn account books, NYPL. Livingston to Osborn, Aug. 31, 1843, Osborn letters, NYPL.

69. Gibbons to Osborn, Apr. 3, 1843, Osborn Letters, NYPL.

70. House at 202 Houston Street, 1842–1845 (George Abbe account), George L. Osborn account books, NYPL. Abbe was a lawyer.

71. Gibbons to Osborn, Nov. 29, 1842, Osborn Letters, NYPL.

72. Gibbons to Osborn, May 4, 1843, Osborn Letters, NYPL; 52 Beekman, 1842–1843 (Gibbons accounts), George L. Osborn account books, NYPL.

73. Debits, 1842–1843 (Gibbons account), in George L. Osborn account books. One of the tenants at 16 Washington Street had apparently absconded without making the last quarterly payment, as had Meyer Isaacs at 506½ Greenwich Street. In October, Gibbons evicted from 506 Greenwich Street a Mrs. Freyer, who had not paid her $16 monthly rent since August. See also 235 Centre Street (Estate of James Brown account, 1845–1849), Dec. 15, 1847; Jan. 20 and Feb. 18, 1848; in ibid.: the Osborns collected $97 from the surety of a butcher who absconded, and sold fixtures "taken from" him to the new tenant, an awning maker.

74. House at 111 Mulberry Street, 1845–46 (George L. Osborn in account with Charles F. Osborn), George L. Osborn account books, NYPL. The Osborn brothers appear to have managed 109½ and 111 Mulberry (on long-term lease from Charles Van Rensselaer) as their own investment. See also rear houses at 184 Hester Street (Jacob Handley account), with one stable tenant and 19 other tenants moving through two other units between April 1845 and May 1849.

75. The 109½ and 111 Mulberry accounts were merged May 9, 1846; for the price, see Debits, Nov. 10, 1846, in ibid.

76. Accounts for 109½ and 111 Mulberry Street, 1847–1849, in ibid. One source of gain for landlords of older buildings was underassessment and reduced tax expenses. See Elizabeth Blackmar, "Housing and Property Relations in New York City, 1785–1850" (Ph.D. diss., Harvard University, 1982), pp. 584–97.

77. For an earlier example of a carpenter acting as an agent, see Joseph Newton's lease agreement with Thomas Wilson, Feb. 22, 1808, in box 2, Leake Papers, NYHS. The Osborns paid their tenant Benjamin Powell, a blacksmith/wheelwright, a 10% commission to collect rents from Morgan Lewis's rear houses on Allen Street, and the carpenter D. Hoyt worked as a subagent for Lewis's De Lancey Street properties; it is also possible that the two carpenters and a mason who leased Lewis's Allen Street houses were sublandlords (Morgan Lewis accounts, 1842–1844), George L. Osborn account books, NYPL.

78. Houses at 502, 504, 506, and 506½ Greenwich Street (Gibbons account), George L. Osborn account books.

79. John Griscom, *The Sanitary Condition of the Laboring Population of New York* (New York, 1845), pp. 8–9; italics in original.

80. *CA*, Feb. 15, 1845; "Annual Report of City Inspector" (1842), p. 170.

81. See Iver Bernstein, *The New York City Draft Riots: Their Significance for American Society and Politics in the Age of the Civil War* (New York: Oxford University Press, 1990), pp. 83–85, 107–8, 247–48 (on subcontracting). Also on working-class neighborhoods, see Robert Ernst, *Immigrant Life in New York City* (New York: Columbia University Press, 1949), chaps. 11–14; Richard B. Stott, *Workers in the Metropolis: Class, Ethnicity, and Youth in Antebellum New York City* (Ithaca: Cornell University Press, 1990), chap. 8. Kenneth Scherzer, "The Unbounded Community: Neighborhood Life and Social Structure in New York City, 1830–1875" (Ph.D. diss., Harvard University, 1982), finds greater neighborhood stability after 1850.

82. *New-York Tribune*, Feb. 24, 1848.

83. On workingmen and land reform, see Helene S. Zahler, *Eastern Workingmen and National Land Policy, 1829–1862* (New York: Columbia University Press, 1941), pp. 19–23, 48–50, 75–76, 82, 87–88, 91–92; Wilentz, *Chants Democratic*, pp. 186–90, 194–95, 335–43, 356–57.

84. *New-York Herald*, Feb. 1, 1848.

85. Ibid., Feb. 24, 1848; *New York Tribune*, Feb. 24, 1848.

86. On the Industrial Congress, see Wilentz, *Chants Democratic*, pp. 369, 371, 383; Bernstein, *Draft Riots*, chap. 3. On land reform and demonstrations by the unemployed, see Zahler, *Eastern Workingmen*, p. 183; Carl Degler, "Labor in the Economy and Politics of New York City, 1850–1860" (Ph.D. diss., Columbia University, 1952), pp. 159–60, 165–66, 194. On New York land reformers' movement into the Republican party, see Degler, pp. 305–6, 312. The movements for tenant-house and land reform were most directly linked through A. J. H. Duganne, a land reformer who chaired the 1856 Assembly tenant-house investigations (A.D. 205, Mar. 9, 1857).

87. See, e.g., Wilentz, *Chants Democratic*; Alan Dawley, *Class and Community: The Industrial Revolution in Lynn, Massachusetts* (Cambridge: Harvard University Press, 1976); David Montgomery, "The Working Classes of the Pre-industrial American City, 1780–1830," *Labor History* 9 (1981): 1–22; Bruce Laurie, *Working People of Philadelphia*, 1800–1850 (Philadelphia: Temple University Press, 1980); Jonathan Prude, *The Coming of Industrial Order: Town and Factory Life in Rural Massachusetts, 1810–1860* (New York: Cambridge University Press, 1983); and essays in Frisch and Walkowitz, *Working-Class America*.

Conclusion: The Housing Question

1. For uptown landholding patterns in the 1850s, see Elizabeth Blackmar and Roy Rosenzweig, "The Park and the People: A History of Central Park" (manuscript), chap. 3. On the real estate investors' political relation with Tammany Hall, see Iver Bernstein, *The New York City Draft Riots: Their Significance for American Society and Politics in the Age of the Civil War* (New York: Oxford University Press, 1990), chap. 6. On further negotiations over the plan of streets, see Peter Marcuse, "The Grid as City Plan: New York City and Laissez-Faire Planning in the Nineteenth Century," *Planning Perspectives* 2 (1987): 295–310.

2. The controversy over Trinity's property centered on whether the vestry could exercise exclusive control of property granted in the eighteenth century to the church "and all those in communion with the Church of England." See New York State Legislature, S.D. 86 (1846) and A.D. 130 (1854); Morgan Dix, ed., *A History of the Parish of Trinity* (New York: Putnam, 1906), chap. 4.

3. For trade journals, see *Real Estate Record and Builders Guide* (1868) and *American Architect and Building News* (1874); for real estate consolidation, see *A*

History of Architecture and the Building Trades of Greater New York (New York, 1899) and *A History of Real Estate, Building and Architecture in New York during the Last Quarter Century* (New York, 1898). On the formation of uptown real estate associations, see Bernstein, *Draft Riots*, pp. 205–9.

4. On Central Park, see Blackmar and Rosenzweig, "The Park and the People," chaps. 1–3; on transportation and competing suburbs, Edward Spann, *The New Metropolis: New York City, 1840–1857* (New York: Columbia University Press, 1981), pp. 289–95; and Kenneth Jackson, *Crabgrass Frontier: The Suburbanization of the United States* (New York: Oxford University Press, 1985), chap. 4.

5. On the construction of row houses in the 1850s, see Charles Lockwood, *Bricks and Brownstones: The New York Row House, 1783–1929* (New York: McGraw-Hill, 1972), pp. 139–211. Elizabeth Cromley, *Alone Together: A History of New York's Early Apartments* (Ithaca: Cornell University Press, 1990), traces the architectural and cultural history of middle-class apartments. See also Christine Boyer, *Manhattan Manners: Architecture and Style, 1850–1900* (New York: Rizzoli, 1985).

6. For the history of Harlem, see Gilbert Osofsky, *Harlem: The Making of a Ghetto, New York, 1890–1930* (New York: Oxford University Press, 1968).

7. On the social geography of New York City in the 1850s, see Richard B. Stott, *Workers in the Metropolis: Class, Ethnicity, and Youth in Antebellum New York City* (Ithaca: Cornell University Press, 1990), chap. 7; and Robert Ernst, *Immigrant Life in New York City* (New York: Columbia University Press, 1949), pp. 39–47. The best survey of neighborhoods in the 1860s is the Citizens' Association's *Report of the Council of Hygiene and Public Health* (New York, 1865). Edward Lubitz, "The Tenement Problem in New York City and the Movement for Its Reform" (Ph.D. diss., New York University, 1970), pp. 351–98, draws on that report and newspaper accounts in his ward-by-ward survey of tenement housing in the early 1860s. See also James Ford, *Slums and Housing, with Special Reference to New York City* (Cambridge: Harvard University Press, 1936), 1:122–204.

8. See chap. 7, n.81.

9. Examples of guides include George G. Foster, *New York in Slices, by an Experienced Carver, Being the Original Slices Published in the New-York Tribune* (New York, 1849); James Dabney McCabe, *The Secrets of the Great City* (New York, 1868); Matthew Hale Smith, *Sunshine and Shadow in New York* (New York, 1869); and Charles Loring Brace, *The Dangerous Classes of New York: Twenty Years' Work among Them* (New York, 1872). On the development of this literary genre, see Peter Buckley, "To the Opera House: Culture and Society in New York City, 1820–1860" (Ph.D. diss, State University of New York at Stony Brook, 1984), pp. 353–66.

10. C. R. James, *The Black Jacobins: Toussaint L'Ouverture and the Santo Domingo Revolution* (New York: Vintage, 1963); and C. B. Macpherson, *Property: Mainstream and Critical Positions* (Toronto: University of Toronto Press, 1978).

11. Eric Foner, *Nothing but Freedom: Emancipation and Its Legacy* (Baton Rouge: Louisiana State University Press, 1983), pp. 54–58, 82–86.

12. L. Ray Gunn, *The Decline of Authority: Public Policy and Political Development in New York, 1800–1860* (Ithaca: Cornell University Press, 1988), chap. 6; E. P. Cheyney, "The Anti-Rent Movement and the Constitution of 1846," in Alexander Flick, ed., *History of New York*, 10 vols. (Port Washington, N.Y.: I. J. Friedman, 1972), 6:283–321.

13. The classic works on the shift from commonwealth to laissez-faire ideology are Louis Hartz, *The Liberal Tradition in America* (New York: Harcourt Brace,

1955); Oscar Handlin and Mary Handlin, *Commonwealth: A Study of the Role of the Government in the American Economy, Massachusetts, 1774–1861*, rev. ed. (Cambridge: Harvard University Press, 1969); and Willard Hurst, *Law and the Conditions of Freedom in the Nineteenth-Century United States* (Madison: University of Wisconsin Press, 1956). Morton Horwitz traces the development of new concepts of property in *The Transformation of American Law, 1780–1860* (Cambridge: Harvard University Press, 1977), pp. 160–210.

14. *Constitution of the State of New York* (Albany, 1846), art. I, sec. 14. See also *Report of the Debates and Proceedings of the Convention for the Revision of the Constitution of 1846* (Albany, 1846), pp. 802–5, 899–902.

15. *Debates and Proceedings*, p. 804.

16. In Bedford v. Terhune (1864), for example, the Court of Appeals overlooked the constitutional status of a covenant against subletting in adjudicating a dispute between a chief landlord and a leaseholder.

17. Norma Basch, *In the Eyes of the Law: Women, Marriage, and Property in Nineteenth-Century New York* (Ithaca: Cornell University Press, 1982), esp. pp. 133–35; Linda E. Speth, "The Married Women's Property Acts, 1839–1865: Reform, Reaction, or Revolution," in D. Kelly Weisberg, ed., *Women and the Law: A Social Historical Perspective* (Cambridge, Mass.: Schenkman, 1982), 2:69–91; Lawrence Friedman, *A History of American Law* (New York: Simon & Schuster, 1971), pp. 184–86. For further discussion of the contradiction between the feminist and protective contents of the married women's property acts, see William Leach, *True Love and Perfect Union: The Feminist Reform of Sex and Society* (New York: Basic Books, 1980), pp. 174–89.

18. Macpherson, *Property*, pp. 75–99.

19. *Workingman's Advocate*, Dec. 5, 1829. For a full discussion of Skidmore and his relation to the Working Men's Party, see Sean Wilentz, *Chants Democratic: The Rise of the American Working Class* (New York: Oxford University Press, 1984), pp. 182–90, 193–96.

20. Wilentz, *Chants Democratic*, pp. 335–43; Helene S. Zahler, *Eastern Workingmen and National Land Policy, 1829–1862* (New York: Columbia University Press, 1941); Eric Foner, *Free Soil, Free Labor, Free Men* (New York: Oxford University Press, 1970), pp. 27–29, 275.

21. See Blackmar and Rosenzweig, "The Park and the People," chaps. 2 and 6. It is worth noting that prominent housing reformers opposed the creation of Central Park, and urged that smaller parks be located in working-class neighborhoods.

22. Combinations of moral, public health, safety, and economic interpretations of the consequences of tenement conditions can be found in the annual reports of the AICP, 1846–1860, and in John Griscom, *The Sanitary Condition of the Laboring Population of New York* (New York, 1845). On the formation of the AICP and the shift from moralism to environmentalism, see Roy Lubove, "The New York Association for Improving the Condition of the Poor: The Formative Years," *NYHSQ* 43 (1959): 307–327. On industrialists' involvement in the AICP and interest in housing, see Bernstein, *Draft Riots*, ms. pp. 381–400 and app. J. On the medical profession's interest in moral reform, see Charles E. Rosenberg and Carroll Smith Rosenberg, "Pietism and the Origins of the American Public Health Movement," *Journal of the History of Medicine* 23 (1968): 16–35; John Duffy, *A History of Public Health in New York City, 1625–1968* (New York: Russell Sage Foundation, 1968), pp. 515–70.

23. For a survey of newspaper coverage of the housing crisis and delineation of editors' differing positions on housing reform, see Lubitz, "Tenement Problem," pp. 238–51.

24. John H. Griscom, "Annual Report of the Interments of the City and County of New York for the Year 1842, with Remarks thereon and a Brief View of the Sanitary Condition of the City," BAA Documents 9, no. 59:191–92, 204. See also Griscom, *Sanitary Condition*, pp. 42–48.

25. John Comer, *New York City Building Control, 1800–1941* (New York: Columbia University Press, 1942), pp. 6–8; Ford, *Slums and Housing*, 1:75–76. On the failure of efforts to apply nuisance and fire laws to housing, see Lubitz, "Tenement Problem," pp. 208–10, 274–76.

26. Griscom, "Annual Report, 1842," pp. 175–76.

27. John Griscom, "Annual Report of the City Inspector for the Year 1845" (1846), p. 163, Municipal Archives.

28. For tenants' resistance to repairs, see chap. 7, n. 51; Lubitz, "Tenement Problem," pp. 519–20.

29. New York State Legislature, Assembly,"Report of the Special Committee on Tenement Houses in New York and Brooklyn," A.D. 199 (1856), and "Report of the Select Committee Appointed to Examine into the Condition of Tenant Houses in New York and Brooklyn," A.D. 205 (1857); Senate, "Report of the Select Committee Relative to the Improvement of Public Health, and a Sanitary Law in the City of New York," S.D. 115 (1857); Lubitz, "Tenement Problem," pp. 219–37.

30. Fire reform legislation that included building codes began in 1856 with "An Act to Provide against Unsafe Buildings in the City of New York," passed Apr. 14, 1856, *Laws of New York, 79th Session*, p. 314. This law was amended in 1859 and 1860. The 1860 act, creating a superintendent of buildings with enforcement powers, was declared unconstitutional. Its provisions were successfully incorporated in 1862 in "An Act to Amend an Act, entitled 'An Act to Provide for the Regulation and Inspection of Buildings, the more effectual Prevention of Fires, and the better Preservation of Life and Property in the City of New York,'" passed Apr. 19, 1862; *Laws of New York, 85th Session*, p. 574. In 1860 a series of tenement fires mobilized the press behind building codes. See Lubitz, "Tenement Problem," pp. 159–67, 211–18, and on sanitary police, 209–11. For the involvement of fire insurance companies in lobbying for reform legislation, see James C. Mohr, *The Radical Republicans and Reform in New York during Reconstruction* (Ithaca: Cornell University Press, 1973), pp. 30, 32–34, 47, and on the creation of the Metropolitan Fire District in 1865, 52–53.

31. Mohr, *Radical Republicans*, pp. 15–20; Bernstein, *Draft Riots*, pp. 187–88; Lubitz, "Tenement Problem," pp. 409–21. For links between the draft riots and housing, see Citizens' Association, *Report of the Council of Hygiene*, pp. xv–xviii. On the cholera threat, see Duffy, *History of Public Health*, pp. 540–68.

32. On Metropolitan Board of Health legislation, see Mohr, *Radical Republicans*, pp. 69–106; Lubitz, "Tenement Problem," pp. 483–87.

33. "An Act for the Regulation of Tenement and Lodging Houses in the Cities of New York and Brooklyn," passed May 14, 1867, *Laws of New York, 90th Session*, chap. 908, sec. 17. On the passage of the Tenement Bill, see Mohr, *Radical Republicans*, pp. 139–52; Lubitz, "Tenement Problem," pp. 497, 500, 511–18.

34. On the problems of enforcing building codes, see Superintendent of Buildings, annual reports, 1867–1870, NYHS; Lubitz, "Tenement Problem," pp. 494–95. On enforcement of the 1867 bill and subsequent housing reform legislation in the second half of the nineteenth century, see Roy Lubove, *The Progressives and the Slums: Tenement House Reforms in New York City, 1890–1917* (Pittsburgh, 1962), pp. 28–32; Lawrence Veiller, "Tenement House Reform in New York City, 1834–1900," in Robert W. De Forest and Lawrence Veiller, *The Tenement House Problem* (New York, 1903), pp. 71–92; Ford, *Slums and Housing*, pp. 163–64.

35. Henry George, *Progress and Poverty: An Inquiry into the Cause of Industrial Depressions and of Increase of Want with Increase of Wealth* (1879; New York: Random House [1949]), pp. 295, 413.

36. Ibid., p. 323.

37. Ibid., pp. 438–39.

38. David Scobey, "Boycotting the Politics Factory: Labor Radicalism and the New York Mayoral Election of 1886," *Radical History Review* 28–30 (1984): 280–325; Thomas J. Condon, "Politics, Reform, and the New York City Election of 1886," *NYHSQ* 44 (1960): 363–93.

39. Scobey, "Boycotting the Politics Factory," p. 311. The George campaign won 68,000 votes, 22,000 less than the combined total Democratic vote for two candidates: Scobey, p. 286. On housing reform after 1886, see Ford, *Slums and Housing*, pp. 170–85; and Lubove, *Progressives and the Slums*.

40. Frederick Engels, *The Housing Question* (Moscow: Progress, 1975), offers a classic critique of reformers' tendency to isolate housing relations from the larger dynamics of capitalist class relations. On landownership as "fictitious capital" and circulating revenues, see David Harvey, *The Urbanization of Capital: Studies in the History and Theory of Capitalist Urbanization* (Baltimore: Johns Hopkins University Press, 1985), pp. 90–108.

41. For a discussion of weighing of rights sympathetic to private property rights, see Peter Wolf, *Land in America: Its Value, Use, and Control* (New York: Pantheon, 1981), pp. 79–100, 139–334. For a theoretical model for examining housing conditions with reference to larger social, economic, and political forces, see Peter Marcuse, "The Determinants of Housing," manuscript. On the cultural dimension of contemporary housing debates, see Constance Perin, *Everything in Its Place: Social Order and Land Use in America* (Princeton: Princeton University Press, 1977). For twentieth-century tenant organizing, see Ronald Lawson and Mark Naison, eds., *The Tenant Movement in New York City, 1904–1984* (New Brunswick: Rutgers University Press, 1986). For a thoughtful statement of how property rights might be reconceptualized as common rights, see C. B. Macpherson, *Property*, pp. 199–207.

Index

Absconding, 219, 241, 246
Afro-Americans. *See* Blacks; Slaves
Agents, 233–34, 238–39, 243–44
Allaire, James, 201
Allen, Senator Ethan B., 229
Allen Street, 240
Anthony Street, 176–79
Apprentices, 50, 55, 57–59
Architecture, 47–48, 193–94; building height, 200–201. *See also* Brick houses; Wooden houses
Artisan entrepreneurs, 81, 94, 137; vs. artisan wage earners, 103–5; as landowners and landlords, 26, 40, 76, 106
Artisans, 19, 50, 83, 88, 93–94, 101, 137; in building trades, 33, 183, 188; in colonial period, 21, 26, 28; decline of freeholding by, 40; displacement of, 28, 78–79, 101, 167; as employers, 27, 61, 63; households of, 57–59, 62, 64–66, 135; and independent proprietorship, 36, 40, 105–6; as leaseholders, 32, 36, 37; and moral reform, 135–36
Art Street, 166
Astor, John Jacob, 160, 186–87, 196, 201, 239, 244; land accumulation by, 33, 204, 216
Astor, William, 208, 239

Bancker Street, 84
Banks, 188, 209
Bayard family, 18–19, 24–26, 30, 195, 216
Beekman family, 18, 24–25
Beekman Street, 240
Bennett, James Gordon, 246
Bergh, Christian, 206
Blacks, 45; as domestic servants, 57, 61–62, 118–19; housing patterns of, 17, 99, 173, 252–53; legal discrimination against, 20–21, 56–57, 156, 173–74; vs. white wage earners, 56–67, 119. *See also* Race; Slaves
Blackstone, Sir William, 52, 57

Bleecker [McDonald], Elizabeth, 80, 83–84, 118
Bleecker, Leonard, 186–87
Bleecker Street, 164
Bloomingdale Road, 25
Boarding, 57, 63–64, 69, 113, 121–22, 129
Boardinghouses, 60, 63, 88, 134–35
Bogert, James, 141
Bond Street, 193
Boston Post Road, 25, 34–35
Bowery, 49
Bowery Road, 25
Bowery Village, 101, 133
Bowling Green, 48, 79–80, 84, 99
Boydston, Jeanne, 112
Brick houses, 41, 93, 102, 193, 247
British colonial rule, 3–4, 14, 18–21, 27, 53–54; land grants under, 14, 18–19
Broad Street, 47, 77
Broadway, 25, 200; lower, 48, 79, 89
Buel, David, Jr., 155–57, 181
Builders, 187–88, 192–97, 205–6, 208–9; labor practices of, 188–92, 197
Business cycles, 23–25, 75, 192–93. *See also* Depression of 1837–1843; Panic of 1837

Carver, William, 64–65, 116
Caveat emptor (buyer beware), 10, 231, 234–35, 260
Central Park, 252, 258
Chambers Street, 89–94
Chapel Street, 92, 161, 176
Chatham Street, 206
Chelsea, 162–63, 206
Cherry Street, 82, 206
Children, 55, 138–39
Churches, 131–32, 141. *See also* Trinity Church
Church Street, 92
City government, 153–54, 157, 172; and propertied classes, 157–60, 164–67; and wealthy neighborhoods, 150–51, 164–66; and working-class street life, 151, 171–72,

City gov't. (*cont.*)
    180–81. *See also* Municipal corporation
City Hall common, 81–82, 84, 92, 99
Class distinctions, role of housing in
    creating: through attitudes toward
    servants, 116–19, 126; through
    deterioration of working-class housing,
    122–23, 146–48, 168, 197–99, 208–9,
    232–34; through embrace of modern
    dwellings, 113, 128–38; through
    homogeneous neighborhoods, 11–12,
    82–86, 89–92, 100–104, 106–8, 250;
    through ideology of domestic
    respectability, 146–48; through
    intersection with wage labor market, 5–6,
    65, 68, 71, 76, 112, 250–51; through
    policies on public improvements, 150–51,
    157–60, 163–68; through profitability of
    real estate ownership, 173, 192, 194,
    197–99, 201–2, 209, 242–43; through rise
    of rentiers, 14–15, 18–19, 23–26, 28–38, 40
Clinton Street, 240
Colden, Senator Cadwallader, 229–30
Collect Pond, 98–99
Colonial rule: British, 3–4, 14, 18–21, 27,
    53–54; Dutch, 14–18, 20
Columbia College, 81–82, 87, 92
Commerford, John, 247
"Commonalty," 152–55
Common law, 222–25, 227; and landlords,
    10, 217, 219–20, 232, 234–35; on women's
    status, 52–53. *See also* Blackstone,
    Sir William
Constructive eviction, 228–32
Contract law, 10, 231–32, 234–35
Contractors, 188–90. *See also* Builders
Contract system, 188–90
Conveyances, 196–97
Cooper, James Fenimore, 107–8, 130, 145
Corlear's Hook, 101, 166–67
Country houses, 25–26
*Courier (Morning Courier and New York
    Enquirer)*, 183, 191, 207, 211–12, 259
Coverture, 2, 52–53, 225
Crary, Senator John, 229, 231

De Lancey, James 30, 33–35, 37–39
De Lancey family, 24, 33–34, 238
Democratic party, 235, 262–63
Depression of 1837–1843, 7, 106, 179, 185,
    202–6, 225, 238–41
Developers, 196–97
De Witt, Simeon, 95
Dinner parties, 130
Displacement, 2, 76, 104, 168–69. *See also*
    Slum clearance
"Distress," 10, 217, 220, 222–27
Dock Ward, 27, 45, 79

Domestic respectability, 114–17, 121–22,
    146–48. *See also* Dwellings, modern
Dover Street, 84
Duer, Judge John, 234–35
Duer, William, 91, 106, 109
Dutch colonial rule, 14–18, 20
Dutch West Indies Company, 16–18
Dwellings, modern, 76, 105, 145–46; and
    class culture, 113, 128–38; as displays of
    wealth, 72, 80–81; separation of, from
    workplace, 11, 109; social meanings of,
    109–12, 128–33, 140, 142–46, 184
Dyett v. Pendleton, 228–32

East Broadway, 102
East Ward, 27, 45, 79
England, property relations in, 2–3, 9, 217.
    See also Common law
Epidemics, 45, 84–86, 98–99, 166
Erie Canal, 7, 149, 197
Evans, George, 246
Evening Post, 163–64, 213
Eviction, 226–27; constructive, 228–32

Fifth Avenue, 200
Fires, 45, 203
Five Points, 93, 172–80
Floy, Michael, 132–33, 141, 145
Food markets, 97–98
"Found labor," 5, 57–59, 62
Fourth Avenue, 197
Franchise (suffrage), 19, 40, 154–58
Freeholders, 9, 23; decline of, 28, 36, 40
Fresh Pond, 17, 49, 99
Fronting parks, 100–101
Front Street, 34–35, 78, 84

Geer, Seth, 137
George, Henry, 8, 265–67
Gibbons, William, 233, 238–41, 243
Gramercy Park, 166
Greeley, Horace, 211–12, 235, 259
Greene, Asa, 100, 147–48
Greenwich Street, 78–79, 89, 240
Greenwich Village, 25, 30, 97, 101, 104,
    162, 166, 197
Grid street system, 77, 94–99, 104–6;
    modification of, 164–66; and republican
    ideology, 6, 77, 95–97
Griscom, John B., 122, 205, 207–8, 243–44,
    247, 260–62
Ground leases, 9–10, 26, 30–38, 41–42;
    length of, 30, 32–33; restrictive covenants
    in, 38, 41–42, 89, 92, 100–101
Ground rents, 31–32, 35, 39, 89, 201, 251
Growth: economic, 38, 45, 75, 78, 105, 149;
    population, 20, 27, 38, 44–45, 75, 94,
    185–86, 204, 273

Hague Street, 84
Hanover Square, 80
Hardman, Aaron, 242–43
Harlem, 24, 252–53
Hartog, Hendrik, 153
Hester Street, 240
Holmes, Isaac, 72, 87, 122, 134
"Home," the, 11, 110, 120; as both private
    and public, 126–27, 138; social meanings
    of, 126–28, 134. See also Domestic
    respectability; Dwellings, modern
Home as Found (Cooper), 107–8, 130
Homelessness, 12, 183. See also "Vagrants"
Hone, Philip, 140
Horwitz, Morton, 235
Hotels, 137–38
Households: artisan, 57–59, 62, 64–66, 135;
    composition of, 52, 55–57; hierarchy in,
    51–60; servants in, 50, 57–59, 61–62,
    116–22, 126; slaves in, 27, 55, 62, 116;
    unpaid labor in, 11, 53, 58, 112–13,
    122–25, 133, 138. See also Dwellings,
    modern; Integrated households; Tenant
    housing
Housing: chronic shortage of, 183–85,
    197–99, 205, 211; cost of building, 193;
    pace of construction of, 185–86, 192–93,
    204–6, 275–76; and wage labor market,
    5–6, 65, 68, 71, 76, 112, 250–51; as work
    site, 10–11. See also Class distinctions,
    role of housing in creating; Dwellings,
    modern; Real estate
Housing construction, 33, 122, 184–89;
    capital for, 186–88, 195, 201–2, 209; labor
    practices in, 188–92, 197
Housing market and class divisions, 5–6, 65,
    68, 71, 112, 250–51
Housing reformers, 210, 234–35, 243,
    259–65. See also Griscom, John B.
Houston Street, 240
Howard Street, 206
Hubert Street, 240
Hudson Square (St. John's Park), 100, 131,
    193
Hudson Valley, landholding in, 17–18, 21,
    72, 220–22, 226; vs. Manhattan, 15, 21,
    24, 36

Immigrants, 27, 44–45; as domestic
    servants, 119; housing of, 175, 205, 209,
    253; Irish, 119, 175, 209, 246–47
Indians, 16–17, 21
Integrated households, 2, 11, 47–51, 78,
    82, 88–89, 116, 127; decline of, 59–65,
    87; of merchants, 78, 82. See also "Found
    labor"
Irish immigrants, 119, 175, 209, 246–47
Irving Place, 164

James Street, 87–88
Journeymen, 61, 120, 122, 124, 189–92;
    wages of, 88, 103, 134–35. See also Labor
    movement

Kent, Chancellor James, 155, 219–20,
    226–27, 230, 254

Laborers, 50, 60, 88, 162–63
Labor movement, 76, 123–24, 158, 189–90,
    237–38, 257–58, 266; and lien laws,
    190–91
Lafayette Place, 160, 164
Land, use of, as collateral, 25, 187
Landfill, 78, 99
Land grants, colonial, 14, 17–19
Landlords, 10; and common law, 10, 217,
    219–20, 232, 234–35; and tenant housing,
    168, 173, 197–99, 209, 232–44. See also
    Rentiers; Tenants
Landowners. See Freeholders; Rentiers
Land prices, 23, 27, 39–40, 200, 202–3
Land reformers, 212, 246–48, 257–59
La Rochefoucault-Liancourt, 47–48
Leaseholders, 9–10, 15, 31–37, 219, 228; as
    investors, 32–33, 35–36, 38
Leases, 9–10, 213–14, 218; legal
    interpretations of, 10, 231–32, 227–35.
    See also Ground leases
Leroy Place, 164, 193
Levy, Uriah, 239–40
Lewis, Morgan, 39, 41–42, 95, 196, 216,
    239, 244
Lien laws, 190–91, 197
Lispenard Meadows, 99, 173
Livingston, John R., 39, 102
Livingston, Margaret, 232–33, 240
Livingston family, 18, 24–25, 93, 178,
    195–96, 232–33, 239
Locke, John, 3
Lorillard family, 81, 178, 195–96
Lower East Side, 41, 97, 102, 200–201;
    wage earners living in, 101, 131, 197,
    206, 253
Loyalists' estates, 38–39, 72–73. See also
    De Lancey, James

McDonald, Elizabeth Bleecker, 80, 83–84,
    118
Macpherson, C. B., 3
Maintenance, 232–34, 236
Marriage, 52–55, 59, 142–45. See also
    Women
Marriage market, 140–42
Married Women's Property Act, 257
Martin, Samuel, 193–94
May Day (moving day), 213–16
Mechanic neighborhoods, 104, 134–36

Mechanics, 61, 82–83, 103, 105, 122–23, 203–4, 257. *See also* Journeymen
Merchants, 48, 50, 76, 82–86, 94, 223–24; households of, 77–84; as landowners, 25, 28. *See also* Rentiers, emergence of, as a class
Monroe Street, 102
Montgomery Ward, 37
Moore, Clement, 169, 206
Moore family, 195–96
Moral reform, 135–36, 146. *See also* Slum clearance
Morning Courier and New York Enquirer, 183, 191, 207, 211–12, 259
Morris, George, 139–40, 224, 236–37
Morris, Gouverneur, 95–96
Morris, Richard B., 193–94
Morris family, 18, 239
Mortgages, 25, 190, 201–3
Mott Street, 206, 240
Mount, Jane, 141
Moving day, 213–16
Mulberry Street, 92–93, 206, 240, 242
Municipal corporation, 19, 26, 152–53, 157
Municipal government. *See* City government

National Reform movement, 246
Native Americans, 16–17, 21
Neighborhoods, 76; homogeneous, 11–12, 82–86, 89–92, 94, 100–104, 106–8, 250; respectable, 11, 99–102, 106–8, 133, 150–51, 164–67; trade, 11, 88, 101–4, 133–35. *See also* Tenant neighborhoods
New-York Mirror, 143–46, 164, 184, 213
New-York Tribune, 211, 259
Niles Weekly Register, 183, 192–93
North Ward, 37
Notions of the Americans (Cooper), 145

Oak Street, 87–88
O'Connor, M. T., 246–47
Oliver Street, 206
Orange (Baxter) Street, 92–93
Orchard, John, 26, 39
Osborn, Charles and George, 232, 238–39, 242–43
Out Ward, 37
Outwork system, 113, 124–26, 223

Paine, Tom, 64–65, 73, 116
Panic of 1837, 179, 193, 202–4, 225, 238
Party politics, 154–55, 158, 235, 262–64
Pearl Street, 23, 82–84
Pearson, Isaac, 164
Peddlers, 171
Phyfe, Duncan, 81–82
Pintard, Elizabeth Brasher, 115, 142

Pintard, John, 109–10, 112, 114–15, 118–22, 130, 141–42; observations by, 9, 181, 193, 213–14
Police force, 181
Political parties, 154–55, 158, 235, 262–64
Poor relief, 170
Promenades, 145–46
Proprietorship, independent, 2, 15, 210–11; and control over others' labor, 2, 11, 21, 67–68, 73, 125; decline of, 94, 105–6, 125, 168; as republican ideal, 2, 106, 168, 210
Public improvements, 150–51, 201; assessments for, 159–63; disputes over, 160, 162–64, 167, 172–73, 177–80; and real estate values, 161–62, 167; working-class responses to, 162–63. *See also* Slum clearance

Race: divisiveness of, 56–57, 119; and housing patterns, 17, 99, 173–75, 252–53. *See also* Blacks; Slaves
Real estate: vs. alternative investments, 23–24, 210, 251; beginnings of investment in, 26–28, 35–36; profitability of, 173, 192, 194, 197–99, 201–2, 209, 242–43. *See also* Housing
Rentiers, 201, 251, 266–67; defined, 9; development of housing by, 37–38, 187, 210–11; emergence of, as a class, 14–15, 18–19, 23–26, 28–38, 40; in Hudson Valley, 15, 17–18, 21, 24, 36, 220–22; and long-term ground leases, 30–33, 41–42; and slum clearance, 177–78
Rents: collection of, 68, 219, 238–41; level of, 32, 87–88, 194, 201, 251. *See also* Ground rents
Repairs, 232–34, 236
Republican party, 235–36, 262–64
Republican simplicity, 72, 95, 109, 117, 139
Republican thought, 72–75, 120, 149–50, 153, 218; vs. landlords' privileges, 218, 220; vs. white supremacy, 156; on women's household role, 116. *See also* Proprietorship, independent
Respectable neighborhoods, 99–102, 106–8, 133; defined, 11; and public policy, 150–51, 164–67
Restrictive covenants, 38, 164, 170, 220, 256; in ground leases, 38, 41–42, 89, 92, 100–101, 256
Rock, Howard, 103
Roosevelt family, 39–40, 77, 80
Roosevelt Street, 206
Row houses, 193, 208
Ruggles, Samuel, 166, 196–97, 200–202, 204, 210
Rutgers, Henry, 30, 37, 41, 101–2, 210
Rutgers family, 24, 26

Rutgers farm, 99–102, 176
Rutgers Street, 82, 102
Rutherford, John, 95

Scobey, David, 266
Selden, Dudley, 166, 233
Servants, 50, 57–59, 61–62, 112–13, 116–22;
  attitudes toward, 116–19, 126; expanded
  hiring of, 112–13, 117, 121; turnover
  among, 118
Skidmore, Thomas, 258
Slave codes, 20, 52
Slaves, 18, 27, 55–57, 62; emancipation of,
  54, 170; proportion of, in city population,
  20, 45, 50, 56; resistance by, 20–21, 27,
  59; under Dutch rule, 16–17; work done
  by, 20, 24, 27
Slum clearance, 151, 172–79
South Street, 78
South Ward, 79
Speculative building. See Housing
  construction
Spencer, Senator John C., 228
Spruce Street, 240
Stansell, Christine, 145
State Street, 49, 77, 79
Streets: class differences over use of, 82–84,
  151, 170–72, 180–81. See also Grid street
  system; Public improvements; Slum
  clearance
Stuyvesant family, 18–19, 30, 195–96, 202
Sublandlords, 10, 243–45, 262
Subtenancy system, 243–45
Suffolk Street, 193–94
Suffrage, 19, 40, 154–57, 158
Sullivan Street, 240

Taxes, property, 157, 161–62
Temperance, 132, 136
Tenant housing, 11, 129, 205–9; adaptation
  of houses for, 69–70; condition of, 122–23,
  146–48, 168, 183, 208–9; crowding of,
  197–99; emergence of, 68–71; landlords'
  reluctance to repair, 232–36; new
  (tenements), 9, 185, 201, 206, 208–9;
  profitability of, 173, 197–99, 209, 242–43;
  shortage of, 183–85, 197–99, 211
Tenant League, 246–47
Tenant neighborhoods, 101–3, 131, 133,
  253; defined, 11–12; street life of, 171–73,
  180–81
Tenants, 51; absolute liability of, 227–36;
  attempts to organize, 246–48; collection of
  rents from, 68, 219, 238, 240–41; leverage
  of, vs. landlords, 238–45, 248–49; seizure
  of possessions of, 217, 222–27
Tenement House Act, 264–65
Tenements, 9, 185, 201, 206, 208–9

Third Avenue, 197
Thompson Street, 99
Thorburn, Grant, 44–45, 65–68, 82, 122
Three-story houses, 200–201
Tiered system of tenures, 10, 28–38, 69. See
  also Leaseholders; Sublandlords
Tompkins Park, 166
Topography, natural, 19, 24, 96, 98–99
Trade neighborhoods, 11, 88, 101–3,
  133–35; eclipse of, 104, 135
Trinity Church, 30–33, 39, 68, 89, 93, 100,
  210
Turnover of housing, 103–4
Two-story houses, 200

Unions. See Labor movement
Union Square, 166–67, 200, 204
University Place, 164
Utilities, 115, 193–94; lack of, in tenant
  housing, 122–23, 168, 208–9

Vacancies, 193, 242
"Vagrants," 169–70, 183
Van Buren, Martin, 157
Van Cortlandt family, 18, 24
Vanderbilt v. Persse, 230
Van Rensselaer family, 17–18, 221, 239
Vauxhall Gardens, 160
Veblen, Thorstein, 138, 147
Visiting, social, 80, 107–8, 129, 131–32; New
  Year's, 127, 139–40
Visiting cards, 139
Visiting the poor, 145–46

Wage labor market, 103–4, 189; and housing
  market, 5–6, 65, 68, 71, 76, 112
Wages, 27, 59, 88, 181
Wall Street, 47, 49, 77, 79–80
Wards, post-1791: 5, 99–100, 135, 197, 206,
  253; 6, 99, 101, 135–36, 197; 7, 41,
  101–2, 135, 197; 8, 135–36, 197, 253; 9,
  104, 197; 10, 102, 135–36, 197; 11, 197,
  207; 13, 102, 197; 14, 101, 135, 197; 15,
  206; 16, 206; 17, 206–7
Wards, pre-1791: Dock, 27, 45, 79; East,
  27, 45, 79; Montgomery, 37; North, 37;
  Out, 37; South, 79; West, 32, 37
Warren family, 24–25, 30, 33
Washington Square, 100, 166–67, 200
Washington Street, 78
Water Street, 23, 77, 80, 83–84, 201
Watts family, 24, 39, 196
Waverly Place, 164, 195
West Street, 78
West Ward, 32, 37
Whitehall Street, 77
William Street, 84
Willis, Edwin, 39–40

Women: black, 27, 57, 62; in churches, 131; as enforcers of behavioral standards, 131–32, 146; keeping of boarders by, 63, 67; meaning of modern dwellings to, 115–16, 130, 142–45; power of, in marriage, 52–55, 59, 115–16, 130–32; in propertied families, 80, 115–16, 123, 130–31, 133; property ownership by, 2, 9, 24–25, 52–54, 257; unpaid household work of, 53, 58–59, 112, 122–25, 133, 138; wage labor by, 54, 59, 61–62, 124–26, 136–37; in working-class families, 122–25, 133, 144–45, 212. *See also* Coverture; Servants

Wooden houses, 41–42, 93, 102, 199

Woodworth, John, 221

Woodworth, Samuel, 129–30, 143, 164

Yards, 48, 80–81, 123

Yellow fever, 45, 84–85, 98–99

Library of Congress Cataloging-in-Publication Data

Blackmar, Elizabeth, 1950–
  Manhattan for rent, 1785–1850.

  Bibliography: p.
  Includes index.
  1. Rental Housing—New York (N.Y.)—History. 2. Real estate development—New York
(N.Y.)—History. 3. Land tenure—New York (N.Y.)—History. 4. Landlords—New York
(N.Y.)—History. 5. Manhattan (New York, N.Y.)—Economic conditions. 6. Manhattan
(New York, N.Y.)—Social conditions. I. Title.
HD7288.85.U62N53 1989   333.33'7   88–47926
ISBN 0–8014–2024–5 (alk. paper)

DATE DUE

FEB 1 5 2010			
SEP 3 0 2010			
FEB 1 5 2012			
JUN 0 1 2012			
JUN 0 1 2015			
JUN 0 6 2016			
2 2 JUL 2019			
GAYLORD			PRINTED IN U.S.A.